From Slavery to Poverty

From Slavery to Poverty

The Racial Origins of Welfare in New York, 1840–1918

Gunja SenGupta

NEW YORK UNIVERSITY PRESS
New York and London

NEW YORK UNIVERSITY PRESS
New York and London
www.nyupress.org

© 2009 by New York University
All rights reserved

Library of Congress Cataloging-in-Publication Data

SenGupta, Gunja.
From slavery to poverty : the racial origins of welfare
in New York, 1840–1918 / Gunja SenGupta.
p. cm.
Includes bibliographical references and index.
ISBN-13: 978-0-8147-4061-3 (cl : alk. paper)
ISBN-10: 0-8147-4061-8 (cl : alk. paper)
1. Public welfare—New York (State)—New York—History.
2. African Americans—New York (State)—New York—History.
I. Title.
HV99.N59 S43   2009
362.5'570890097471—dc22   2008045882

New York University Press books are printed on acid-free paper,
and their binding materials are chosen for strength and durability.
We strive to use environmentally responsible suppliers and materials
to the greatest extent possible in publishing our books.

Manufactured in the United States of America
10 9 8 7 6 5 4 3 2 1

For my parents,
Dibyendranath and Rukmabai SenGupta

Contents

Acknowledgments		ix
List of Illustrations		xi
Introduction		1

PART I

1	Subaltern Worlds in Antebellum New York	29
2	The White Republic and "Workfare": Blackwell's Island	69
3	Not White, but Worthy: Maternalists and the "Pious Poor" of the Colored Home	107

PART II

| 4 | The Color of Juvenile Justice: The New York House of Refuge | 131 |
| 5 | Celtic Sisters, Saxon Keepers: Class, Whiteness, and the Women of the Hopper Home | 170 |

PART III

6	Black Voluntarism and American Identities: The Howard Orphanage and Industrial School	207
	Epilogue	243
	Appendix: Tables	249
	Notes	275
	Index	325
	About the Author	335

Acknowledgments

In the long years that I took to complete this book, I moved from Texas to New York, incurring all sorts of debts along the way. Texas A&M University-Commerce provided not only the seed money for researching this project, but also the camaraderie of some very special people, of whom I name only a few: Pat Browning, Janice Connell, Linda Frazier, Keith McFarland, Donald and Martha Reynolds, Judy and the late Robin Rudoff, Nicholas Sarantakes, and Harry Wade and Dora Wade (who taught me to parallel park, among other things). I will always cherish my memories of Frank Barchard.

At Brooklyn College, I profited from valuable comments on the earliest incarnation of this book from Adina Back, David Berger, Renate Bridenthal, Donald Gerardi, and Leonard Gordon. Bonnie Anderson, who fits perfectly the definition of a word that she herself taught me—mensch—has inspired a generation of feminist scholars and activists. Jocelyn Wills's Canadian perspectives on American dreams and American poverty, shared with me over many years (and many more martinis), have entered this book in ways that she will recognize. Edwin Burrows is a talented fount of knowledge about New York history, of which I have been a grateful beneficiary. Philip and Mary Gallagher added new perspectives to my understanding of race relations in New York by telling me all about their campaign against redlining in East Flatbush. David Troyansky qualifies as a dream chair: at once a scholar, manager, diplomat, and friend, who has provided a framework within which all manner of historians can flourish.

I have profited from the interdisciplinary feedback and emotional support of many friends: Teesta Ghosh, Salim Darbar, Sabita Manian, Sunita Manian, Nandini Mookherjee, Nita Roy, Christopher Vaz, Craig Hoek, Cheryl Hicks, David Herrmann, Shahana Sen, Mitul Foster, Gina Guerriero, Nandita Ghosh, Patricia Antoniello, Barbara Winslow, and Anjna Kirpalani. I have appreciated Manthia Diawara's intellectual catholicism as much as his friendship. Barun De has offered a model of scholarship within my own family. Clarence Mohr remains an invaluable teacher and mentor.

The generosity of the Mrs. Giles Whiting Foundation, the Claire and Leonard Tow Trust, and the Ethyl R. Wolfe Institute for the Humanities gave me much needed time to complete this book even as I got other projects off the ground. A PSC-CUNY grant funded travel to Albany for a summer's worth of research, where several staff members of the New York State Archives offered critical help. Back in New York City, archivists at the Municipal Archives and the New York Public Library, especially the Schomburg Center for Research in Black Culture, helped me to navigate their rich holdings in race and welfare. I thank the Schomburg Center for allowing me to reproduce a pledge card belonging to the Brooklyn Howard Colored Orphan Asylum; I thank the New York City Department of Records and Information Services for permission to publish facsimiles of two alms-house department tables.

I am indebted to the American Historical Association for permission to reprint in chapter 6 portions of my article "Elites, Subalterns, and American Identities: A Case Study of African American Benevolence," which appeared in the October 2004 issue of the *American Historical Review*. I also thank the Association for the Study of African American Life and History for allowing me to publish in chapter 4 portions of my article "Black and 'Dangerous'? African American Working Poor Perspectives on Juvenile Reform and Welfare in Victorian New York, 1840–1890," featured in the Spring 2001 issue of the *Journal of Negro History*. I thank Deborah Gershenowitz and the staff at New York University Press, especially Gabrielle Begue and Despina Papazoglou Gimbel, for their enthusiasm for this project.

My parents, Dibyendra Nath and Rukmabai SenGupta, and my sister, Monji Shivaram, supplied the welcome interruptions that sustained my scholarship. The memories of my grandparents Parul and Sourin SenGupta inform every page of this book. Finally, of all the wonderful things that have happened to me since I moved to New York City, by far the best is Awam Amkpa. He has opened up vistas and vocabularies that have made both my life and my work make sense.

Illustrations

Figures

1. A pledge card from the Brooklyn Howard Colored Orphan Asylum. Courtesy of the New York Public Library, 217.

Tables (in Appendix, 249–273)

1. Frequency Distribution by Sex of Individuals Living in Different African American and Irish/Irish American Household Types in NYC, 1855
2. Close-up of African American Nuclear Families without Boarders: Frequency Distribution of Individuals Living in Such Families by Age, Sex, and Length of Residency in NYC, 1855
3. Close-up of African American Nuclear Families with Boarders: Frequency Distribution of Individuals Living in Such Families by Age, Sex, and Length of Residency in NYC, 1855
4. Close-up of African American Extended/Communal Families: Frequency Distribution of Individuals Living in Such Families by Age, Sex, and Length of Residency in NYC, 1855
5. Close-up of African American Families Headed by Single Women with Children and/or Boarders: Frequency Distribution of Individuals Living in Such Families by Age, Sex, and Length of Residency in NYC, 1855
6. Close-up of African American Single Women Householders without Children: Frequency Distribution by Age and Length of Residency in NYC, 1855
7. Close-up of African American Boarders: Frequency Distribution by Age, Sex, and Length of Residency in NYC, 1855
8. Close-up of Irish/Irish American Nuclear Families without Boarders: Frequency Distribution of Individuals Living in Them by Age, Sex, and Length of Residency in NYC, 1855

9. Close-up of Irish/Irish American Nuclear Families with Boarders: Frequency Distribution of Individuals Living in Them by Age, Sex, and Length of Residency in NYC, 1855
10. Close-up of Irish/Irish American Extended/Communal Families: Frequency Distribution of Individuals Living in Them by Age, Sex, and Length of Residency in NYC, 1855
11. Close-up of Irish/Irish American Boarders: Frequency Distribution by Age, Sex, and Length of Residency in NYC, 1855
12. Close-up of Irish/Irish American Servants: Frequency Distribution by Age, Sex, and Length of Residency in NYC, 1855
13. Close-up of Irish/Irish American Single Women–headed Households: Frequency Distribution of Individuals Living in Them by Age, Sex, and Length of Residency in NYC, 1855
14. Frequency Distribution of Married/Widowed African Americans by Age and Sex in NYC, 1855
15. Frequency Distribution of Married/Widowed Irish/Irish Americans by Age and Sex in NYC, 1855
16. Birthplaces of Migrant Members of African American Households by Sex in NYC, 1855
17. Occupational Distribution by Sex of Individuals in One Hundred African American Households in NYC, 1855
18. Occupational Distribution by Sex of Individuals in One Hundred Irish/Irish American Households in NYC, 1855
19A. African American and Irish/Irish American Population of NYC, 1855
19B. Frequency Distribution of Adults Receiving Outdoor Assistance by Color/National Origin in NYC, 1855
20. Statistics and White Identity Creation I: Facsimile of Penitentiary Hospital Table E, 1855
21. Statistics and White Identity Creation II: Facsimile of Penitentiary Hospital Table K, 1855
22. Frequency Distribution of New Yorkers Admitted to Major Municipal Relief Institutions by Color/National Origin in 1855
23. Age Distribution of One Hundred African American and One Hundred Irish Applicants for Institutional Relief, Alms House Department, 1848
24. Occupation/Marital Status of One Hundred African American and One Hundred Irish Applicants for Institutional Relief, Alms House Department, 1848

25. Admission Causes of One Hundred African American and One Hundred Irish Applicants for Institutional Relief, Alms House Department, 1848
26. Birth Places of One Hundred African American Applicants for Institutional Relief, Alms House Department, 1848
27. Statistics and White Identity Creation III: Facsimiles of NYHR Tables I and III, 1860
28. Statistics and White Identity Creation IV: NYHR Tables II (1890) and III (1900)
29. Parentage of New Admissions to NYHR by National Origin/Color and Sex, 1850–1890
30. Proportion of African American Population in NYC and NYHR, 1850–1890
31. Distribution of Inmate Population by Color and Sex, NYHR, 1850–1890
32. Parties Committing African American Children to NYHR, 1840–1890
33. Reasons for Commitment of African American Children to NYHR by Kin and Non-Kin, 1840–1890
34. Parties Committing White Children to NYHR, 1850–1890
35. Reasons for Commitment of White Children to NYHR, 1850–1890
36. Number and Relationship of Parents of African American Children Received by NYHR, 1840–1890
37. Proportion of African American Children Living with Non-parent or Surrogate Kin
38. Birthplaces of African American Children Received by NYHR, 1840–1890
39. Occupations of Female Guardians of African American Children at NYHR, 1840–1890
40. Occupations of Female Guardians of White Children at NYHR, 1850–1890
41. Occupations of Male Guardians of African American Children at NYHR, 1840–1890
42. Occupations of Male Guardians of White Children at NYHR, 1850–1890
43. Occupations of African American Female Inmates of NYHR, 1840–1890
44. Occupations of White Female Inmates of NYHR, 1850–1890

45. Occupations of African American Male Inmates of NYHR, 1840–1890
46. Occupations of White Male Inmates of NYHR, 1850–1890
47A. Disposition of African American Children by NYHR, 1840–1890
47B. Success Rate of Indentures of African American Children by Sex

Introduction

In August 1996, a bipartisan coalition of politicians in Congress voted to "end welfare as we know it." Their handiwork, the Personal Responsibility and Work Opportunity Reconciliation Act (PRWORA), replaced income support to needy families—guaranteed since the New Deal by some version of Aid to Families with Dependent Children (AFDC)— with "transitional" public assistance in exchange for work. Two years later, the antiwelfare commentator Heather MacDonald invoked a familiar trope to raise the alarm against "the future downfall of welfare reform." In a piece published online in *City Journal*, the organ of the Manhattan Institute (a conservative public policy think tank), she introduced readers to an eighteen-year-old unwed mother named "Tamiesha," who had apparently deposited her two-year-old child in a "lavish high school day-care center on Manhattan's Upper West Side." MacDonald reported that as the toddler flung his bowl of cereal "over his head," his mother played with her gold chain and "impassively" watched day care workers clean up her child. According to the article, Tamiesha was habitually unpunctual and "emphatically" opposed to marriage: "My aunts 'n' stuff tell me what's going on, and it's, like, a hassle." So how were New Yorkers to solve a problem like Tamiesha? How to guard the "front door, where the next two generations of dependents are forming right now"? MacDonald proposed, among other measures, an end to state-funded day care and parenting classes, in order to prevent the likes of Tamiesha from having "illegitimate" children. To underscore the futility of public reform enterprises aimed at unfit mothers, she conjured an encounter with a persistently abusive parent of five—a "large-boned broad woman with few teeth and wild dreadlocks . . . on her second tour through the parenting curriculum," at a Bedford-Stuyvesant social services agency.[1]

Welfare "as we know it" may be dead, but the racially charged "welfare queen" of conservative imagination is alive and well. MacDonald's Tamiesha represents a latter-day incarnation of the infamous Chicago cheat whose parable the late President Ronald Reagan mustered in order to advance his campaign to dismantle America's modest welfare state in the 1980s. Reagan's welfare queen took on a life of her own. Before long, she evoked for many the enduring specter of a dissolute urban single mother who adopted numerous aliases to bilk hard-working taxpayers. Many indignant voters assumed that she was black and judged her conduct un-American. The radical overhaul of AFDC in 1996 was guided in part by the widespread belief that welfare—and the behavior it apparently encouraged—breached fundamental American values of individual autonomy, hard work, and the heterosexual nuclear family.

The language of what we understand as "welfare" has long served as a way of both policing and contesting the meaning and boundaries of American identity. The Tamiesha trope tapped into a particular meta-narrative of race and nation, freedom and dependence, and republicanism and relief, all of which anointed the American Union at birth. Constituting the ideological bedrock of structures of power and constructs of identity, this storyline establishes a vital historical context for understanding why, in popular parlance, the notion of welfare—with all its derogatory connotations in the U.S. context—is associated not with middle-class entitlements like Social Security and Medicare, but rather with programs targeted at the poor like AFDC, which were wrongly assumed to primarily benefit urban African Americans. The welfare queen epitomizes a tapestry of remarkably resilient themes that in the nineteenth-century governed policy discussions about destitute European immigrants, especially the Irish: the alliance of the city with wickedness; the association of (frequently female) sexual promiscuity with "pauperism"; the transmission of ostensibly aberrant matriarchal "cultures of poverty" across generations; and the conviction that poor people owed their condition to inherent character failings such as indiscipline, idleness, and profligacy, all of which public relief served to promote rather than cure. An overarching conception of American nationalism that linked citizenship with race constructs, however, interacted with and subsumed all these themes. It endowed "free white" males—however impoverished—with the right to vote and dictated that they be assimilated into a white republican imaginary buttressed by Victorian gender norms. In that queen of all cities—New York—this version of American nationalism spawned quasi-public relief and reform regimes that aimed to acculturate peoples of European descent to American society; at the same time, these programs sought to colonize, segregate, or exclude black New Yorkers altogether. In the process, these regimes complemented other structures in American society that cemented the transition of African Americans from slavery to poverty. Welfare—a term that historians of the nineteenth century have interpreted to encompass private benevolence as well as public relief (for reasons I explain later in this chapter)—developed its color-conscious character over a century before the New Deal formally inaugurated America's welfare state in the 1930s.[2]

The story of black people, whiteness, and welfare recounts more, however, than simply the dynamics of this process from the perspective of politicians, reformers, and social workers. It also weaves together the everyday survival tales of working poor New Yorkers—predominantly black, but also white. These women and men—whether native-born or immigrant, in their multiple roles as patients and clients, workers and consumers, parents and children, Protestants and Catholics, and, above all, as aspiring *citizens*—drew on the language and institutions of benevolence (rhetorically, symbolically, and especially materially) to challenge stereotypes and offer alternative visions of community. Out of the dialectic that they helped generate within the politics of poverty in Victorian and Progressive New York, there emerged a raucous, pluralistic interpretation of national identity that vastly complicated the linear narrative of America as a ruggedly individualistic "white republic."

This is a book that explores connections among race, reform, and narratives of the nation by studying welfare discourse as a site for the creation and negotiation of individual, communal, and national identities by Victorian Americans from all walks of life. It offers intimate portraits of a range of charitable and reform institutions that constituted New York's interlocking network of private benevolence and municipal relief from the 1840s through about 1918. They included the Alms House Department, the city's main agency of municipal relief; the Colored Home (CH), run by conservative, elite, white female reformers and commissioned by the city to receive all public charges of color; the New York House of Refuge (NYHR), the first juvenile reformatory in the country, established by wealthy New York merchants and philanthropists; the Hopper Home, a halfway house for female ex-convicts, operated privately by the more progressive Women's Prison Association of New York (WPA); and the Howard Orphanage and Industrial School (HOIS), which evolved from a black-run haven for the children of freed women in postbellum New York into a Tuskegee-style, Northern industrial school under predominantly white management after 1913.

The brick walls of these institutions harbored multilayered human stories that raise salient questions about the dynamics of relief in a contentious era of national self-definition: in what ways did constructions of race and nation, and relations of class and gender, shape public discourse on "pauperism," crime, and reform in New York from the antebellum through the Progressive eras? How did different groups of historical actors use the forum of benevolent reform to invent or subvert identities? Under what conditions and in what ways did working poor African Americans enter into relationships with Victorian and Progressive New York's benevolent institutions? How did the experiences and self-representations of these African Americans compare with those of white immigrant and native-born relief-seekers? To what extent were the varieties of plebeian agency contingent on the theory and practice of benevolence constructed by elite or middle-class reformers. In what ways did the dynamic that ensued—at the intersection of race and religion, class and gender—complicate or even fracture the abstract symbolism of a unified white civic identity?

The racialization of dependence—long in use as a way of regulating national belonging—was forged in experiences that predated the emergence of the American republic. African slavery imprinted on blackness its particular meaning and fateful visibility in early New York no less than in the plantation realms farther south. It also helped shape white identity as a pivotal relation of difference from blackness. According to historian Thelma Foote, after English warships coasted into Nyack Bay to wrest the fledgling port town of New Amsterdam from Dutch control in 1664, imperial authorities in the colony (renamed New York) used black slavery and antiblack racism as a "disciplinary mechanism" to win the allegiance of a volatile settler population divided by nationality, religion, language, and economic status but bound by its shared sense of entitlement to the "English rights" of freedom. Liberty was now cast as the prerogative of "white" men.[3]

It was on the foundation of this paradox of black bondage and white freedom that there arose out of the Revolutionary ferment of the eighteenth century a "white republic" in which the capacity for self-government was thought to rest on economic self-sufficiency, which guaranteed freedom from the political will of others. "Republican citizenship" not only excluded enslaved African Americans from its purview but also fused American nationality with the ostensibly immutable attribute of race.[4] A 1790 law restricted the right of naturalization to "free white persons"—presumably male, judging by the statute's prescription that *"he* shall have resided for the term of one year at least." The institution of what historians have described as "herrenvolk democracy" (democracy for a dominant "race") in the aftermath of the American Revolution drew on the premise of a unified "white manhood" that, in the words of Dana Nelson, "worked symbolically and legally to bring men together in an abstract but increasingly functional community." This imagined white fraternity was designed to override gathering conflicts rooted in ethnic, religious, and political differences, in sectional and state affiliations, and, most importantly, in the competitive individualism of an emerging market economy. With the inauguration of universal white male suffrage in the nineteenth century, the idealization of democracy as an American norm unfolded in tandem with the construct of the color white as normative—all the more powerful for its "structured invisibility," defined against the aberration of slavery and its all-too-visible, equally aberrational, marker, blackness. The ostensibly race-neutral label "American" came to be loaded with the meaning of whiteness in the politics and culture of the new republic.[5]

Herrenvolk democracy also racialized the operation of public relief in New York—both the largest slave state north of the so-called Mason-Dixon Line *and* a magnet for impoverished European immigrants. How it did so—in other words, the ways in which race making, relief, and the right to citizenship intersected in antebellum New York—becomes clear when we compare the fate of a nineteenth-century immigrant slave-turned-pauper named Peter Bense with that of the bulk of Irish newcomers to Victorian New York.

Bense was no ordinary member of what the reformer Charles Loring Brace called the "dangerous classes." He reportedly regaled the custodians of the Colored Home, a refuge for needy black New Yorkers, where he spent his last days, with astonishing tales of cosmopolitan adventures in distant lands. A collection of inmate biographies published by the CH recorded that Bense, nicknamed "Peter Polite" on account of his refined manner, was born in bondage in the Anglophone West Indies sometime in the last quarter of the eighteenth century. He was taken to England while still a boy. At the age of twenty he accompanied his master, a British "public functionary" of uncertain identity, to the Court of St. Petersburg as his valet. The members of the Russian royal court saw Bense as "a curiosity" because of his complexion but treated him "with marked kindness and favor." He was said to speak of "the Empress Catharine with strong expressions of respect and esteem, and even of affection, on account of her great kindness and attention to him." The former bondsman recalled that on one occasion, during his master's absence from St. Petersburg, he served the palace royal as valet and coiffeur. During his days in Russia, he married a Russian woman and had two sons. Soon thereafter (about 1810), his master was recalled to England. Bense sailed back with his owner, heartbroken at having to leave his family behind but determined to reunite with them in the future. On the way back to England, master and slave were waylaid by a French cruiser off the coast of France, carried to Brest, and imprisoned in Paris. During his Parisian days, Bense claimed to have waited on distinguished European personages, including Napoleon himself. He returned to England only after France's vanquished emperor had been dispatched to Elba, at which point he plunged into a whirlwind of service in aristocratic circles: "He was in London at the visit of the Emperor of Russia and the King of Prussia to the Prince Regent, and appeared familiar with all the gay scenes of that period. He saw the Prince Regent on horseback ride around Hyde Park."[6] We are told that through all his adventures among Europe's rich and powerful, Bense never forgot his wife and children. When his persistent investigations into his family's whereabouts revealed that they had moved to New York, he obtained his master's permission to join them there. He proceeded to America, presumably in the 1830s, "full of hope and anticipated happiness of clasping to his bosom the wife of his youth, and his children."

It is difficult to verify the authenticity of Peter Polite's account of his life in Europe. The women who published his story for fund-raising purposes no doubt recognized that its themes of black respectability, familial spirit, and service to a white peerage would carry an intrinsic appeal for wealthy Whig patrons. What can be verified is that Peter Bense—whatever the details of his early history—ended up in New York. As such, he was one of over three and a half million immigrants who helped transform the city into the Western Hemisphere's most populous and dynamic metropolis between 1820 and 1860.[7] Yet Bense must have discovered quickly upon his arrival that his complexion, which had rendered him a "curiosity" in Russia, marked him out for New World experiences rather different from those that awaited white newcomers. Unfortunately, this Afro-Caribbean wayfarer, who apparently came of age in aristocratic Europe, left no record of his first impressions of the great American city that would be his last home. We can only imagine that upon disembarking from an emigrant ship, as he wended his way past the "forest of masts" silhouetting the harbor and into the teeming island beyond, he must have noted New York's significant black presence. Amid the city's "hum and buzz, the clinking of capstans, the ringing of bells, the barking of dogs, [and] the clattering of wheels," African American men of a myriad hues and diverse origins handled freight along the waterfront, hauled mortar and bricks at construction sites, tended to curbside oyster stands in the Bowery, armed with horse and cart collected street garbage, and drove coaches down the graceful promenade that was Broadway. Black women peddled buttermilk, fruit, and corn on the cob along narrow alleys and throbbing thoroughfares. Youthful chimney sweeps paraded the streets laden with blanket and scraper, uttering plaintive cries of "Sweep-ho!" Black children mingled with their white peers as they played on the docks, scavenging for rags, sugar, iron, wood, blackened boots, and huckstered food and knickknacks in public spaces. Long after the sun went down, the strains of "Negro" fiddles and the beat of tap dances filled the infamous, enticing haunts of Five Points dance halls, salons, and brothels (the reputation of these establishments for wanton self-indulgence and interracial sex filling the city's nascent bourgeoisie with dread).[8]

It was this working poor world of blackness and indeterminate whiteness that Peter Bense entered as he began his quest for his lost, biracial family. In many ways it was a standard plebeian world of the Victorian era where middle-class distinctions between private and public spheres were hard to maintain, where home and marketplace merged, and where women and children worked alongside men in order to keep body and soul together. Yet it was also a vibrant, resilient, but nonetheless troubling testament to New York's foundation on racial slavery, its complicity in the invention and sustenance of America's "white republic" where constructs of race determined the distribution of social and political power.[9] The decline in Bense's fortunes illustrated this sad fact. He found no trace of his family in the New World. Disappointed, he secured a position as a waiter with the hope of saving enough money to return to St. Petersburg. But alas, that was not to be either: he drifted into destitution instead. Quite likely a tenant in an insanitary cellar, separated from friends and family and excluded from most trades by his blackness, Bense suffered from periodic bouts of unemployment. But even if he had—against all odds—achieved the economic self-sufficiency that American political philosophers and practical reformers associated with republican citizenship, he would have been ineligible for naturalized national belonging. As noted above, a 1790 law restricted that privilege to "free white persons" unencumbered by the burden of chattel bondage. In any case, Bense's health broke down. In 1841 he entered the Colored Home, run by a group of patrician New York women—many of them daughters of former slaveholding families—for the relief of spent servants judged worthy of assistance. The Colored Home received a commission from the city Alms House Department to house all black supplicants for relief after 1844. This arrangement illustrated the hybrid nature of nineteenth-century welfare, which frequently rested on collaboration between private benefactors and state authorities.[10]

Bense's days in the segregated poorhouse began against the backdrop of urgent public debates about the meaning of whiteness, generated by the advent of waves of destitute Europeans to metropolises scattered across North America's Atlantic shore and the Gulf Coast. In this context, public relief became a hydra-headed signifier: simultaneously the resort of those feared to be unsuitable for self-government by virtue of their impoverishment, *and* an instrument for turning white paupers into independent citizens. Steeped in the imagery of blackness, the alleged pathology of "pauperism" became the target of New York's quasi-public "benevolent empire."

Benevolent reformers and poor-relief officials sought not simply to save tax dollars, but also to assimilate (through work and moral training) European relief-seekers—entitled to naturalization and armed with the power to vote—into a racialized construction of American nationalism. Contrast this "naturalization through relief" approach with the ambiguous counterpoint posed by Bense's Quaker and evangelical custodians at the Colored Home. On the one hand, they embraced a democratic discourse of Christian benevolence that challenged the authority of a unified white civic fraternity by upholding the *spiritual* equality of men and women, black and white. Yet their egalitarian religious discourse did not translate into a vision of multiracial republicanism founded on civic equality. Rather, pessimistic about the African diaspora's prospects for incorporation into a color-blind national community, the benevolent women of the Colored Home proposed to proselytize and colonize their "pensioners" outside the United States. Blacks, they wrote, shared with women the "inherent" trait of piety, fitting them best for missionary work in "Other" parts of the world, such as Africa. That Bense personally proved too frail to emigrate does not alter the fact of his caregivers' complicity in the exclusionary rhetoric and practices of the white republic even as they defied some of its gendered premises.[11]

Slavery in the Empire State ended in 1827, but as Peter Bense's experience suggests, African American independence in post-emancipation

New York was tenuous at best and could yield suddenly and quickly to "pauperism" and long terms in the Alms House. It is true that antebellum America's market revolution subjected all manner of Euro-American workers to whimsical business cycles and new modes of production, driving many to the brink of dependence. Yet various circumstances flowing from the legacy of racial slavery rendered black New Yorkers even more vulnerable than their white counterparts to the ravages of riots, disease, unemployment, and the loss of not only family, but of freedom itself, leaving them in urgent need of relief.[12]

Nineteenth-century observers often noted African Americans' reluctance to seek public assistance. For instance, the *New York World*, a Democratic newspaper not renowned for its affection for blacks, suggested (in a surprisingly astute survey of African American life in New York City during Reconstruction) that the black tradition of mutual aid rendered "Negroes" less prone than their white immigrant counterparts to live off public charity. Historians in our own time have confirmed the prevalence of a venerable heritage of self-help that, embodied in a plethora of voluntary associations, saw African Americans through difficult times. The historian Robert Cray has drawn on censuses, compiled by the New York City Alms House preacher John Stanford from 1816 to 1826, to argue that the ratio of black inmates to whites declined during the era of slavery's demise, equaling "but two-thirds the proportion of blacks to whites in the city." Cray concluded that emancipation left blacks faced with the threat of economic dependence with the freedom to choose modes of relief that did not interfere with their newfound sense of autonomy. The Alms House—with its racially segregated quarters and suggestion of closely monitored regimen—smacked of the restraints of slavery. Thus poor blacks rejected the institutionalization it offered in favor of more sanguinary alternatives such as outdoor relief (assistance in the form of money or fuel in their own homes). Between April 1813 and April 1814, 887 black families and 1,975 white families received home relief in the shape of coal or cash. In other words, blacks made up nearly 31 percent of the population receiving outdoor assistance—a share considerably in excess of the black proportion of New York's population.[13]

The present work finds that this pattern of African American relationship with public welfare underwent an important shift by the middle of the nineteenth century, about the same time that the arrival of multitudes of destitute Europeans spawned a critical new language of race, relief, and their implications for the future of the republic. The black fraction of outdoor relief declined precipitously in relation to that of whites—whether native-born or immigrant. At the same time, the number of New Yorkers of African descent institutionalized in the Alms House and juvenile reformatories grew exponentially in proportion to their ratio in the general population. For instance, while African Americans made up only 4 percent of the city Alms House population in 1824, in 1855 they accounted for close to 22 percent of all inmates, white and black, admitted to the Alms House and its quasi-public contractor, the Colored Home, even as their numbers dwindled to less than 2 percent of the city's population. It seems clear that the most vulnerable sections of the urban black population supplemented the relief work of their benevolent, often middle class, "race" brethren by incorporating public (or semipublic) resources like alms houses, orphanages, prisons, and juvenile reformatories into their subsistence strategies. They sought public assistance not simply to shore up family wage economies and seek medical care and education, but also to secure refuge against slavery and mediate a range of family conflicts and personal crises. In the process, they forged an oppositional subaltern identity that intersected in many places with the self-representations of poor whites who used reform institutions in similar ways. Subaltern identity centered around the working poor's adoption of symbolic, rhetorical, and material devices of empowerment shaped by, and embedded partly in, discourses of relief and reform mounted by their benevolent patrons. Subaltern devices aimed to make Gotham's quasi-public benevolent empire serve goals that the working poor themselves helped define, but always in dialogical interaction with reformers. It also rested on what I call the relief-seekers' "proto-structural" conceptualization of pauperism and its relationship with crime—a formulation that challenged bourgeois diagnoses of the problem of the "dangerous classes" and undermined the distinctions embraced by Victorian reformers between the "worthy" and "unworthy" poor. I argue that interracial "client" identity embedded in subaltern agency—defined as the working poor's will to use the idiom of reform in their negotiations with those more powerful—at once belied and complicated the racialized character of welfare discourse in the demographic kaleidoscope that was Victorian New York.[14]

For then, as now, welfare discourse served as a shorthand for definitions of race and nation. U.S. national narratives celebrated the country's unique commitment to the ideals of "liberty, egalitarianism, individualism, populism and laissez-faire" as hallmarks of its identity.[15] Yet those conjoined twins, American slavery and American freedom, made for a nation not unlike empires conceived in relations of group difference. Accordingly, white (masculine) civic identity—whether vested in the icons of the "common man," "citizen-soldier," or "partyman"[16]—assumed the qualities of self-control, independence, and manly honor and virtue defined in opposition to white imaginings of the sometimes-noble savagery of the American Indian, the childlike dependence of the African American, and the irrationality of women. In the age of capitalist transformation, the racialized and masculinized political models of self-determination came to be associated with a bourgeois ethic of competitive individualism. Rugged and self-made, the idealized Euro-American male was a free agent who made rational decisions guided by enlightened self-interest. He strode through the pages of Victorian dime novels and, later, Horatio Alger fiction, overcoming an adverse environment no matter what form it assumed—whether the Indian-infested wilderness of the West or the grimy sweatshop of the metropolitan East—to ascend from rags to riches in America's dynamic, fluid, expansive society. Incidentally, this construction of rugged individualism was fully compatible with the projects of entrepreneurial reformers to fashion a disciplined working class imbued with enough virtue and industry to believe in America's success ethic. The black male was the ideal American's reverse mirror image—the contented, infantile "Sambo" of the slaveholders' imagination; the prancing, singing, undisciplined Jim Crow conceived in minstrelsy; the pretentious but bumbling "coon" of media construction.

The white republic accorded married white women—whose civic identity was subsumed within that of their husbands under the doctrine of *femme covert* inherited from English common law—an indirect (and subordinate) role in the body politic as mothers and nurturers of potential male citizens. "Republican motherhood" accorded well with the ideal of a middle-class world divided into two gendered spheres, forged in the infancy of Victorian America's market revolution. As market society evolved, the home took on a new importance as an organic refuge of affection from the competitive world of commerce beyond, under the moral guardianship of the "true woman," the mother of worthy republican citizens. Defined by the virtues of piety, domesticity, purity, and deference to white men, this feminine ideal did have its detractors. Nevertheless, it paved the way for benevolent women to enter the public domain of reform and guided the efforts of many to mold immigrant women into good mothers and diligent workers. The domestic ideal was at variance, however, with stereotypes of black "Jezebels" held in bondage. Moreover, mothers of the white republic were expected to safeguard the racial purity of their political family—an expectation that translated into severe social (and in some states, legal) sanctions against interracial unions. Thus the female icons of the "republican mother" and "true woman" were as racialized as their male counterpart of the economically independent "rugged individual." Fixed notions of the white "self" and the black "Other" became firmly ensconced in the evolving perspective of racial nationalism.[17]

In his work on white identity creation, Matthew Frye Jacobson has shown that the 1790 naturalization law, which reserved the right of naturalized citizenship to "free white persons," assumed the "republican convergence" of a unified "white" race and "fitness for self-government." This conception of unvariegated whiteness broke down in the 1840s as legions of destitute Europeans flooded American shores, muddying the bipolar construction of American society into "whiteness and its Others." In New York's poorest quarters, most notably the notorious Five Points, the Irish in particular lived, worked, traded, drank, fought, danced, and made love with African Americans in a world that quite literally assumed the darkened hue of amalgamation. It was small wonder, then, that nativist lore lumped African Americans and the Irish together, essentializing them in similar ways: as savage, simian creatures who shared the "inherent" traits of intemperance, idleness, and, above all, lasciviousness. Impoverished European Catholic newcomers of uncertain "whiteness" appeared to threaten the venerable national institutions of individualism, economic independence, and "true" womanhood—and hence the republic itself. White elites engaged in furious debates over the capacity of different groups of European newcomers for self-government.[18]

The present work maintains that New York's quasi-public benevolent empire entered this controversy over race and nation in complex ways, prompted in part by the dynamics of partisan politics; the political/cultural identities of different groups of reformers; and the workings of subaltern agency from the interlocking locations of race, class, gender, and religious affiliation. Thus, for example, the Commissioners of the Alms House, persuaded in part by the entreaties of benevolent women concerned about the plight of aged African Americans confined in Alms House cellars, contracted to segregate black paupers in the Colored Home. As we have already noted, the historical context of slavery molded the CH's racialized philosophy of almsgiving. It sought to cater to a constituency constructed, ironically enough, as the ultimate "worthy poor"—pious, elderly ex-slaves who had dedicated their productive lives to the service of their former masters. For such people, dependence was assumed to be a natural condition and public relief a well-deserved but *temporary* expedient until they and their descendants could be colonized outside the United States.

The politics of whiteness, however, vested the dependence of immigrant groups such as the Irish with an entirely different meaning. Entitled under the immigration law of 1790 to the privileges of citizenship (eventually), they had to be prepared to exercise those privileges—whether by achieving economic self-sufficiency or by cultivating the virtues of "true womanhood." Thus New York's public relief officials—whether Democrats or Whigs—aimed to put white paupers to work, prompted in no small part by the exhortations of evangelical industrialists (belonging to groups like the Whig-Republican Association for Improving the Condition of the Poor) concerned about creating a disciplined and individualistic working class.[19] As wage labor became a permanent condition for working class men and women, this faction of the bourgeoisie adopted a new political language of reform, fashioned by the ideology of free labor. Associated with the pre–Civil War Republican Party, the free labor ideology celebrated the dignity of, and free market for, labor; its harmonious relationship with capital; and the prospect of social mobility that it supposedly offered. The idea of upward mobility was associated with the ascription of personal success or failure to individual abilities—the Protestant ethic of "honesty, frugality, diligence, punctuality and sobriety." Thus, free labor Republicanism complemented the premise of individual redemption that lay at the heart of Christian benevolence; furthermore, it could be applied to train virtuous domestic servants as well as disciplined factory workers imbued with aspirations to realize the "American dream" of independent property ownership.[20]

Free labor capitalism, which animated a great deal of antebellum relief and reform, was interwoven with white identity creation in complex ways. On the most explicit level, Republican cries of "free soil," "free labor," and "free men" tied a free West to white laboring men's chances for independent land ownership through hard work. In practice, for many white Americans both in the Midwest and along the Atlantic seaboard, a free West meant the absence not only of slavery, but of free blacks as well. Moreover, it entailed the expropriation of Indian land through war and treaty in ways that, according to the legal scholar Cheryl Harris, made whiteness a "prerequisite to the exercise of enforceable property rights." For those with *aspirations* to own property—whether they realized those aspirations or not—whiteness itself became "a property interest" capable of being "deployed as a resource" in the pursuit of wealth and happiness.[21] In this nexus between whiteness and property ownership, free labor Republicanism intersected with the populist white identity politics of the national Democracy. The Democrats sought to weld slave-owning Southerners, slaveless yeomen, and penniless Irish immigrants into a national coalition by invoking their common white lineage. In this context, white identity as *property*—to which all European immigrants, no matter how poor, were ultimately given access—became a ticket to citizenship.

New York's interlocking network of municipal relief and private benevolence—for both males and females—drove home these lessons in white privilege by *treating* and *naming* European newcomers differently from African Americans. Even as black New Yorkers, disfranchised by property qualifications, faced exclusion or segregation in the city's relief institutions, the rising political clout of European immigrants within the Democratic Party expanded the white share of outdoor relief. Moreover, the racialization of welfare discourse was manifested in the epistemology of relief promoted by charity and reform organizations. For instance, institutions participated in the symbolic process by which the Irish became "white" by compiling statistical tables of inmate populations that elevated color over national origin as the chief signifier of difference among the needy, even as black Americans were sometimes labeled "African." As the historian Joan Scott has pointed out, statistical reports constitute "ways of establishing the authority of certain visions of social order, of organizing perceptions of 'experience.'" Thus, numerical data on dependent populations embodied particular ideas about race that "became naturalized" in the process of the tabulation and dissemination of the data in question. Relief and reform organizations assumed the power to define "reality" by *representing* that reality in a certain way, so that the Irish—however ambiguous their "racial" identity in the eyes of their detractors–"became white" by being *depicted* as white in poverty policy documents, at least for the purposes of apportioning the resources of welfare.[22]

Ironically enough, from the location of privilege that whiteness offered, European immigrants often responded to the more coercive initiatives of acculturative reform by asserting their local identities as white *workers* entitled to unemployment insurance in the form of public works or even Work House wages; as white *Catholics* entitled to the constitutional right of religious freedom; and, above all, as white *citizens* entitled to the civil liberty of habeas corpus in matters of discharge from reform institutions.

Thus, they used the "property" of whiteness to open yawning schisms in the racialized imaginary of a unified republican masculinity.

The Civil War, when it came, conferred citizenship on African Americans, eclipsing colonization as a goal of public relief for black New Yorkers. It did little, however, to check the hegemony of whiteness in defining the American nation after Reconstruction. Indeed white racial nationalism gained momentum toward the close of the nineteenth century with the advent of a deluge of "new immigrants" from southern and eastern Europe at home, the inauguration of America's imperial adventures abroad, and the rise of de jure Jim Crow in the New South. Yet the salience of whiteness as a mark of American identity did not go unquestioned. As the United States entered an era of unprecedented prosperity amid intense social conflict, the architects and "clients" of many African American voluntary associations used the language of reform to contest the racial assumptions of American exceptionalism. This book concludes with the story of one such organization—the Howard Orphanage and Industrial School—which mounted micro-level challenges to the power of whiteness and offered in its stead a pluralistic reading of the American nation in the early twentieth century.

The issues that concern this book straddle several fields of scholarship—those of African American history, welfare history, "whiteness" studies, and theories of "subaltern" agency. First and foremost, the work incorporates a "bottom-up" approach to the story of black benevolence; it examines African American working poor relationships with not only black voluntarism but with the apparatus of white-run *public* and semipublic welfare as well. The history of benevolence and social welfare in nineteenth-century America has been written overwhelmingly from the perspective of middle-class reformers who ensured their visibility in the historical record by leaving an impressive trail of documentation in their wake. There are, to be sure, notable exceptions to the "top-down" approach to welfare history. Some scholars have analyzed the case histories of reform institutions to offer invaluable portraits of historically marginalized populations—collective profiles defined by a degree of sophistication impossible to generate through census data alone. Their accounts, however, focus more on whites than on African Americans, especially for the period before the 1890s. This scholarly emphasis understandably mirrors the concern of Victorian charitable institutions with the waves of European immigrants who statistically engulfed the relatively small numbers of African Americans among the destitute populations of North America's greatest metropolises.[23]

Historians of the black experience, on the other hand, have invoked with subtlety and insight the evolution of "inner-city" communities vibrantly sustained amid formidable constraints by a host of black-built institutions—family and church, mutual aid societies and benevolent associations, and civil rights organizations and trade unions.[24] Their work has prompted adjustments in the definition and periodization of social welfare history so as to collapse the neat chronological and intellectual boundaries between benevolence (conceived as private/evangelical/nineteenth century) on the one hand, and social welfare (thought to be statist/professionalized/post-1890s) on the other. Historians have noted that dating back to colonial times, black women bereft of government influence established privately funded voluntary associations. These institutions not only provided African Americans with services denied them by whites (such as homes for the aged, the infirm, and unwed mothers; and kindergartens, libraries, and settlement homes), but in the late nineteenth century they also addressed problems such as lynching, rape, and the convict lease system in the South. Moreover, the historian Linda Gordon maintains that because the black vision of welfare differed from that of whites, the inclusion of black perspectives has produced a far more nuanced portrait of American reform than existed before. Much of the scholarship on black benevolence, however, has been written from the standpoint of African American operators of voluntary associations, whose relationship with the black working poor was, after all, mediated by their positions of relative privilege within their own communities. Moreover this impressive body of work tells more about black voluntarism than about the experiences of those African Americans of the "dangerous classes" who were forced to seek public assistance.[25]

Yet the statistics of Victorian American alms houses and prisons suggest that, driven both by structural upheavals in the economy and virulent racism, African Americans constituted a disproportionate share of the poor and the imprisoned in the nineteenth-century urban North. Moreover, the racialization of welfare discourse—which has, in our own time, planted an impoverished black face on the quintessential beneficiary of public largesse—invites reflection on the nineteenth-century origins of what in popular parlance is labeled the black "underclass" and its relationship with the shifting values and structure of a "white" welfare establishment. My study seeks to address gaps in welfare history not only by incorporating the most marginalized of African American voices into the story of nineteenth-century American reform, but also by examining how those voices interacted with agencies of public and semi-public relief as much as with those of black voluntarism. Most important, the work assumes that the paradoxical legacy of black slavery and white freedom makes any study of black encounters with Victorian New York's benevolent empire more meaningful when placed in a comparative context with the experiences of the white poor.

The book's "subaltern perspective" demands that it engage some of the theoretical issues in debates over the conceptualization of "underclass" agency and its relationship with dominant discourses, raised most penetratingly by two groups of scholars—those of feminism and reform on the one hand, and of the subaltern school of Latin American, South Asian, and African studies on the other. Was such agency "a discursive effect," as Joan Scott has argued—contingent on the language and institutions constructed by middle-class benevolent men and women—rather than "an attribute or trait inhering in the will of autonomous individual subjects"? Or was it the product of "conflict among the 'constructions' of various parties, the subordinate no less than the superordinate," as the welfare historian Linda Gordon has observed? In her immensely important work on the history of family violence, Gordon argued that client narratives of domestic abuse encouraged social workers to identify new problems, like wife beating. Although the social workers interpreted such problems in light of their own values and mission, "this contested definition and redefinition of problems" paved the way for social change. Some scholars have shown that it is possible to reconcile the insights of Scott and Gordon. In an essay on prospective unwed mothers' responses to fictional representations of single pregnancy in a mass-circulation confession magazine sponsored by the Children's Bureau, Regina Kunzel argued persuasively that the "fallen" could function as "both discursive figures and authors." She found that single pregnant women who wrote to the Bureau drew on the narrative plots and vocabulary of the moralistic "pulp fiction," approved by social workers, to recount their own experiences. In the process, however, they occasionally transformed the narrative of single pregnancy from one in which "shame was the driving force to one in which their own economic hardship took center stage."[26]

In this context, I find some of the insights of the subaltern studies school of South Asian and Latin American history about the workings of hegemony and marginal agency particularly helpful in understanding relations of class, race, and gender in North American welfare history. The Latin Americanist William Roseberry has proposed that "we use the concept [of hegemony] *not* to understand consent but to understand struggle; the ways in which the words, images, symbols, forms, organizations, institutions, and movements used by subordinate populations to talk about, understand, confront, accommodate themselves to, or resist their domination are shaped by the process of domination itself. What hegemony constructs, then, is not a shared ideology but a common material and meaningful framework for living through, talking about, and acting upon social orders characterized by domination." Like Latin American peasants or Kunzel's "problem girls," black and white clients of welfare frequently fashioned out of the reform idiom employed by their socially superior custodians—idioms that varied from Christian benevolence, gender solidarity, and whiteness discourse, to American exceptionalism— a set of rhetorical, symbolic, and material strategies of empowerment that not simply served their material needs, but also defied their received subaltern identities. It is also important to keep in mind that subordinate persons are, in Florencia Mallon's words, simultaneously "dominated and dominating" based on the circumstances in which we encounter them. For instance, a working-class pensioner might abuse his wife. Or a middle-class black orphanage superintendent might adopt a supercilious attitude toward the working poor parents of her charges. An Irish inmate of the New York House of Refuge might use his prerogative of whiteness to assert his citizenship right to Catholic worship, thus simultaneously challenging his Protestant superintendent *and* setting himself apart from his black peers. Thus, in this study, I use the term "subaltern" to mean individuals or groups whose subordination in terms race, ethnicity, class, gender, and religion was *relational* rather than absolute, and who practiced a brand of subversion that operated at least partially from *within* the systems that sought to reform them.[27]

Any historian with the temerity to claim insight into subaltern perspectives comes up squarely against the problem of sources. It is easy enough to document the values and objectives of relief officials and benevolent reformers, who left tomes of government records, census data, promotional literature, press clippings, and the annual reports, minutes of meetings, and correspondence of the organizations they ran. It is far harder to reach the mentalité of their often-illiterate clients, visible only fleetingly through the prism of their custodians in a census record here, a journal entry there. Fortunately, a few of the working poor inmates of reform institutions who appear in the following pages left letters, which offer as direct an access to their worldview as one can hope to find. In addition, the records of the African American Howard Orphanage and Industrial School include cultural "texts," such as a series of pantomimes produced by its staff. These pantomimes represent a rich resource for understanding a black bourgeois world of acculturative reform engaged in a dialectic of accommodation and resistance with its Progressive white counterpart.

For the most part, however, I, like other historians, have relied mostly on far more mediated sources in my quest to unearth underclass self-portraits and experiences. These include inmate case histories, census data, and, in one case, a collection of ex-slave "client" biographies published as a pamphlet. As students of benevolence and social welfare know, many nineteenth-century institutions recorded fragments of the life stories and rehabilitation trajectories of their clients—including those of color if they had any—in case histories designed to both identify the sources of vice and reform its victims. These documents, supplemented by statistical records, constitute an invaluable tool in reconstructing the social profile and survival strategies of the interracial "dangerous classes" who drew on public resources in their hour of need. Crafted through the lens and represented in the language of their middle-class, often-Protestant, white recorders, these case histories, not surprisingly, tell more about the values and agenda of their authors than about their ostensible subjects.

Yet case records—like other symbols and forms of dominant reform discourses—could *also* serve as subaltern instruments to contest established narratives about the working poor condition: these documents had to rely, at least partly, on the word of the inmates whose lives and reform trajectories they purported to document. Thus, when read in conjunction with the official pronouncements of the institution concerned, they frequently reveal the presence of a panoply of racial, class, and gender identities, with inmate perspectives meshing in dynamic interaction with those of their "benefactors," muffled but not mute. By providing intriguing insights into the self-image, aspirations, and survival tactics of working poor men, women, and children across a wide spectrum of race and ethnicity, these case histories afford an *entré* into the elusive consciousness and lives of working poor New Yorkers. In the context of Roseberry's formulation of hegemony as an arena of struggle, case records became subaltern vehicles to defy establishment constructs of "underclass" degradation—vehicles shaped by "the process of domination," to be sure, but subaltern vehicles nonetheless.[28]

Finally, this book draws on the work of whiteness studies scholars to place the story of welfare in the context of the nation's preoccupation with race making in the nineteenth century. Historians of public policy have understandably traced the racialization of welfare to the advent of a national welfare state in the twentieth century. Jill Quadagno, for instance, has argued that the United States enacted national welfare policies later than European countries did, not primarily because of its tradition of liberal individualism, the weakness of its working class, or because it democratized before it industrialized, as other scholars have suggested; rather, the politics of racism impeded the war on poverty. The New Deal's unemployment, old age, housing, and labor policies that discriminated against blacks set the stage for racial conflict over the New Deal legacy, which in turn spurred the war on poverty in the 1960s.[29] I combine the insights of scholarship on black benevolence and whiteness studies to argue that the "colors of welfare"—to modify Quadagno's words—developed historically at a time when African Americans constituted a fraction of relief-seekers, well before the emergence of the twentieth-century welfare state. In a republic founded on the association of freedom with whiteness, and dependence with blackness, the condition of pauperism marked a person as not quite white and, thus, incapable of exercising the responsibilities of citizenship. New York's relief and reform agencies sought to Americanize poor and imprisoned newcomers by "whitening" them through lessons in self-sufficiency, industry, and virtue, as well as by discriminating between them and their black neighbors. Thus while other scholars have described the conflict over whiteness and the invention of Caucasians within the paradigms of labor movements and law courts, domestic politics and imperial aspirations, the sciences and the arts, consumer culture and popular culture, and European "diasporic imaginations" and nativist tracts, this work focuses on the role of welfare in training Europeans to define their racial identities in relation to that of African Americans.

The themes of the book unfold in the course of case studies of five institutions that spanned New York's turbulent age of reform, from the 1840s through about 1918. The overarching topic of public welfare's relationship with ideas about race in antebellum New York frames the three chapters in part 1. Chapter 1 weaves the story of racial formation in the United States with a survey of New York's poor relief policy toward African Americans from colonial times through the end of black bondage in 1827. Slavery's demise both coincided with a crucial moment in Jacksonian America's redefinition of the poverty problem and galvanized movements for institutional relief and reform. The chapter draws on census materials on black and Irish families inhabiting the city's sixth and eighth wards in 1855 to offer intimate social portraits of the lives that animated the renewed discourse of pauperism. As black New Yorkers in particular adapted their household structures to their migration patterns, age and sex ratios, marriage rates, child care needs, and, most importantly, the political economy of race, they infused new meaning into familiar concepts like the "nuclear family" and "boarding," which distinguished them in some respects from their white counterparts. Comparative demographic profiles of "underclass" Gotham portrayed in this opening chapter help establish a context for understanding the patterns of welfare use by Victorian New York's most marginalized groups.

Chapter 2 examines the evolution of poor-relief thought amid an emerging racial typology of pauperism that amalgamated various metaphors of nonwhiteness and savagery into sensational specters of sin. The interest of Whig-Republican evangelical entrepreneurs in nurturing a virtuous and industrious working class came to be articulated in growing concerns about the future of the republic. These anxieties added urgency to calls for a shift from indiscriminate almsgiving to what twenty-first-century Americans call "workfare" as a tool for turning paupers into citizens. At the same time, the Democrats' romance with a burgeoning Irish electorate accentuated the very different treatment that white voters and black nonvoters received at the hands of the municipal authorities in New York, most clearly evident in the reallocation of "outdoor relief." The chapter examines the ways in which the evolving political meaning of whiteness was manifested in the reorganization of the city's Alms House Department—the principal vehicle of municipal benevolence—in the 1840s and the 1850s. It also probes the dynamic of white identity creation in the epistemology of public relief. It traces the uses of the labels "white" and "colored" in tabular representations of inmate populations that, by subsuming distinctions of nationality, conveyed a sense of whiteness as homogenous and color as the chief marker of difference among relief-seekers.

The chapter goes on to argue that if the goal of public relief was to integrate European newcomers seamlessly into a unified civic community of self-sufficient white voters, it floundered in the face of inmate agency. The apparently unintended uses to which the predominantly white working poor put the department's facilities on Blackwell's Island—the Alms House, the Lunatic Asylum, the Penitentiary Hospital, and, above all, the

Work House—prompted official laments that the island had become a new "land of promise" for the idle and unworthy poor. Yet from their vantage point as politically empowered *whites*, inmates defined their recourse to relief and employment under municipal auspices as a *right of citizenship* rather than charity—a logic that culminated in mass rallies, initially supported by Democratic mayor Fernando Wood, by jobless workers during the financial panic of 1857.

Chapter 3 offers a detailed social portrait of the Colored Home of New York City, run by wealthy white female reformers and commissioned by the city to receive all public charges of color after 1844. It explores the worldviews of the institution's benevolent architects and their impoverished black charges by analyzing a collective biography of freed people-turned-"clients" that CH published in 1851 as part a fund-raising drive. Entitled *Broken Gloom: Sketches of the History, Character, and Dying Testimony of the Beneficiaries of the Colored Home in the City of New York*, this pamphlet suggests that constructs of the shared piety of reformers and their charges could potentially serve as a code for subverting hierarchies of race and gender. *Broken Gloom* described a logic and experience of benevolence that began by implicitly challenging proslavery allegations about the harshness of free labor society toward the weak, and ended by questioning conventional male, materialistic standards for assessing human worth. Yet the ideology of the Colored Home also exposed the ultimate conservatism of antebellum "maternalist" reformers, as it advocated the colonization of African Americans beyond the shores of the land of their birth. Nevertheless, the reformers' democratic language of Christian benevolence provided the inmates a framework, not available elsewhere in the world of white benevolence, within which to raise their own voices against slavery and race prejudice, in however mediated a fashion. Just as enslaved Southerners used black Christianity to transcend the worst psychological havoc wrought by bondage, elderly black inmates of the Colored Home found in evangelical religion strategies to defy the legitimacy of antiblack racism. Chapter 3 goes on to chart demographic and cultural shifts in the Colored Home's inmate population after 1844 and compares black relief experiences with those of their white counterparts. It closes by noting the ways in which Civil War landmarks—from the New York City draft riots to the Fourteenth Amendment—highlighted the obsolescence of the Colored Home's maternalist brand of racial comity, powered by an appeal to religious sameness but constrained by its embrace of colonization.

Part 2 consists of two chapters that deal with the benevolent empire's mission to secure the future of the white republic by reforming "fallen" women and children across the span of the nineteenth century. Chapter 4 focuses on the variegated tapestry of interracial subaltern engagement with the nation's first juvenile reformatory, the New York House of Refuge, established by local merchants and philanthropists in 1824. Such engagement contradicted the premise of absolute racial difference inherent in the institution's practices of segregating and labeling African American children as belonging to a race apart from their immigrant and native-born white peers. On the other hand, the institution's policies of indefinite commitments and contract labor, applied equally to all inmates, clouded the boundary between freedom and coercion, which distinguished white privilege from black subordination. As the city entered a Gilded Age defined by deepening class antagonisms, Irish inmates reacted to the NYHR's mixed signals about race by erupting in violent acts of confrontation with their custodians. The public investigations that followed offered white inmates an occasion to assert the racialized prerogatives of citizenship that they had learned not only from the larger society, but also from the NYHR's own segregationist attitudes. Insurgent Irish inmates affirmed their rights to fair wages, habeas corpus, and the freedom of religious worship. By contrast, African Americans, deprived of political capital, mounted more private, local, and informal modes of negotiation with authority figures within the structure of the NYHR, which questioned dominant conceptions of subaltern identity. In the process, they underscored, no less than the Irish rebels, the nature of hegemony as a ground of struggle rather than consensus.

Chapter 5 illustrates the themes of class relations and race making embedded in women's benevolent work. It profiles the history of the Hopper Home, a halfway house overwhelmingly for Irish female prisoners, operated by the Women's Prison Association of New York (WPA). The racialized underpinnings of the WPA's agenda were manifested in the association's tacit exclusion of African American women from its project of salvation on the one hand, and its emphasis on the assimilability of "fallen" Irish sisters to Protestant middle-class norms of womanhood on the other. The ideology and language of gender solidarity, then, mediated female prison reformers' collusion with the larger benevolent project to make European immigrants into white Americans. At the same time, the rhetoric of sisterhood provided the objects of reform a sympathetic framework within which they could author their own autobiographies of plebeian hardships. Celtic sisters in dialogic interaction with their Saxon keepers crafted the icon of the "fallen woman." That icon, as represented by reformers, was a white woman, her race both normative and invisible, even though subaltern Irish perspectives on crime, pauperism, and sexual politics closely paralleled the outlook of their black sisters in institutions like the NYHR. As the century progressed, the inmates' growing rebellion against acculturation assumed a heightened significance in the strife-torn world of Gilded Age New York. As battalions of culturally alien "new immigrants" arrived to complicate the WPA's mission, a new generation of prison reformers, imbued with eugenic thinking, launched a movement to establish a state reformatory with indeterminate sentences and a more structured environment for reform. This initiative, designed among other things to staunch the reproduction rates of undesirable aliens, anticipates in interesting ways modern-day concerns about the alleged propensity of (black and immigrant Latina) unwed mothers to take advantage of welfare to propagate disagreeable species of dependent cultures. The WPA's campaign culminated in the creation of a reformatory at Bedford Hills at the turn of the twentieth century. Unlike the more informal Hopper Home, Bedford Hills incarcerated black women as well as Catholics and Jews from southern and eastern Europe.

Part 3 of this work shifts its gaze to the internal dynamics and external relations of African American voluntarism. Chapter 6 probes black benevolent strategies to pluralize, on the most local and palpable of levels, American identity at the turn of the twentieth century. It explores the ways in which New Yorkers of African descent, in their multiple roles as reformers and "clients," workers and consumers, surrogate children and guardians, men and women, and as black and American, negotiated the tension between Progressive America's nationalisms of race and civic equality on a micro plane. The struggles it describes occurred within the institutional framework of the Brooklyn Howard Colored Orphan Asylum, originally established in 1866 as a haven for the children of Southern freedwomen (later reincarnated as the Howard Orphanage and Industrial School [HOIS] of Long Island, New York). The story of Howard's evolution, from a black-run civic organization into a Northern industrial school under predominantly white management after 1913, is rich with clues to the parallels and differences between elite black and Protestant white interpretations of national identity implicit in their respective views of benevolence management and the goals of welfare. On the one hand, Howard's black staff joined its mostly white Progressive-era Managers in turning hallowed American ideals like individualism and equal opportunity into arguments against racial nationalism. On the other hand, the peculiar experiences of race—manifested in a combination of black-client needs, scarce resources, and African American historical experiences–prompted them to craft an alternative community identity within the framework of their benevolent work. Such an identity, grounded in an informal, extended familial, black Christian, participatory democratic style of management, sometimes clashed with the white trustees' campaign to introduce a spirit of individualism and "efficiency" to Howard's operation. The chapter goes on to argue that the perspectives of Howard's interracial custodians provided a complex filter through which the institution's orphans and students articulated their own senses of self. It draws on the invaluable letters that Howard alumni wrote their former guardians in order to illustrate the myriad ways in which they strove to inject colors other than white into a national narrative premised on whiteness.

Taken together, the snapshots of New York relief and reform institutions captured in this study show that long before the advent of the twentieth-century welfare state, the discourse of welfare functioned as a crucible for negotiating individual and group identities. It provided a language and forum to talk about community, race, nation, what it meant to be "American," who belonged, and who did not. Moreover, it was a conversation in which working people of all race constructs participated by adapting benevolent institutions to their own material, familial, or political needs, and by offering reformers their own versions of the sources of, and solutions for, dependence. Aged pensioners at the Colored Home found in their patrons' ideology of Christian benevolence the rhetorical strategies to question antiblack racism. Interracial inmates at the New York House of Refuge turned the institution's commitment to saving children from criminal lives into a welfare resource in ways that defied the fabrication of poverty as a personal, moral failure. Celtic "sisters" at the Hopper Home used Saxon reformers' discourse of gender solidarity to help devise a more sympathetic and complex portrait of the "fallen woman" than allowed by bourgeois constructions of "underclass" debasement. Work House inmates on Blackwell's Island, and Irish insurgents at the juvenile reformatory, tapped implicitly into the dominant discourse of whiteness to assert their prerogatives as workers, citizens, and Catholics. And African American operators and clients at the Howard Orphanage and Industrial School turned to the national narrative of American exceptionalism to challenge their own status as the ultimate Other of whiteness.

Thus, hegemonic institutions of public relief and private benevolence became what William Roseberry called "common material and meaningful" frameworks for negotiation and struggle.[30] They became contested spaces within which all manner of historical actors—situated at the intersection of multiple discourses of power structured around the relations of race, class, gender, age, and religion—inscribed complex, cosmopolitan identities, confounding and straining the national imaginary of a monolithic white fraternity.

PART I

1

Subaltern Worlds in Antebellum New York

> We live in . . . a land of opportunity. If black leaders would spend as much time encouraging people to be self-reliant as they spend encouraging the free handouts from the government, then the people left in New Orleans would have had the means . . . to have bought that $50 bus ticket and have gotten out ahead of the storm.
> —Retired railroad operator from Georgia commenting in *USA Today* after hurricane Katrina hit New Orleans

The language of welfare has long functioned as a code of race and nation. In order to understand why, we must plumb the earliest recesses of cross-cultural encounters in what Europeans called the New World. The association of whiteness with freedom and self-sufficiency on the one hand, and blackness with dependence and degradation on the other, may ultimately be traced to the coerced migration of hundreds of thousands of African workers to help build the colonies of British North America in the seventeenth century. From this history emerged a meta-language of color that gave meaning to almost everything in our society, tangible and intangible—from aesthetic attitudes and popular culture, to political economy and social structures. It supplied a vocabulary to describe the worlds of the poor in Victorian New York, and it influenced policies designed to deal with those poor. The evolution story of this meta-language of color therefore serves as a useful preface to the history of race and reform in the United States.

The Background:
Race and Dependence in New York from Slavery to Emancipation

The very idea of "race" connoting categories of natural attributes identified by bodily traits and amenable to arrangement in hierarchical social orders evolved as European explorers, taking their cue from natural history, sought to classify and represent the varied populations they conquered and colonized in far-flung parts of the world. From the dawn of European settlement in North America, confrontations with American Indians prompted white colonists to define their political identity in terms that conflated religious difference with the physical features of "race." The earliest colonial charters enjoined the community to bring "savage" or "barbarous" Indians into the civil and humane fold of Christianity.[1] Arguably, however, what cemented the equation of black African descent with dependence was the marriage of American slavery with American freedom in seventeenth-century Virginia, at once the first home of representative government in what would become the United States and the trendsetter of racial slavery. The historian Edmund Morgan has suggested that before 1660, although most (if not all) Virginia blacks arrived as slaves, several of them became free and enjoyed many of the same privileges as other Virginians, including the right to sue (and be sued) and to own property. As the tobacco revolution in the Chesapeake region gained momentum, white indentured servitude declined with the disappearance of the conditions necessary for its operation. These conditions, including a high mortality rate and economic expansion, held out for white servants the promise of independent land ownership upon the completion of their terms of labor. By the mid-seventeenth century, however, a depression in the tobacco trade, combined with a fall in the settler death rate, created a class of raucous and frustrated former servants who, in alliance with small holders and slaves, threatened to disrupt the existing order of power. That threat, materializing in the famous Bacon's Rebellion of 1676, contributed to the transition to African slavery. Virginia slaveholders tapped into the century-old Atlantic slave trade to forge a self-reproducing labor force of Africans. At the same time that an increasingly stringent slave code institutionalized the new order of racial slavery, free white males in the colony (and all whites, including those held in indentured servitude, eventually became free) won many of the "rights of Englishmen." Black slavery and white freedom went hand in hand—the grant of political concessions won the allegiance of non-slaveholding whites to a society that could no longer realize their economic ambitions.[2]

The advent of racial slavery was accompanied by a shift in the terminology used to describe the statuses of freedom and unfreedom. The earlier equation of the term "Christian" with freedom gave way to the less changeable attribute of color as a mark of status. By the dawn of the eighteenth century, blackness, the inalienable physical feature of the "Negro," had become synonymous with slavery; whiteness, the natural complexion of the European, had become synonymous with freedom. In actual practice (as David Roediger has pointed out), various degrees of bondage among white laborers throughout the eighteenth century—indentured servitude, apprenticeship, impressment, and convict labor, to name a few—made it hard to establish "fast lines between any idealized free white worker and a pitied or scorned servile Black worker."[3] Nevertheless, not only was the bondage of African Africans perpetual and hereditary, but its advent was accompanied by the institution of race-based legal and political disabilities that survived the demise of slavery as a labor system.

The Chesapeake set the tone for the trajectory of racial slavery in the rest of British North America. Colony after colony followed Virginia's lead in enacting statutes that restricted the rights of the enslaved to earn wages, move freely, assemble in groups, carry arms, marry whites, resist punishment, or testify in court. Free blacks not only represented an anomaly in societies where Negro identity signified eternal unfreedom (at least here on earth), but they were also viewed as potential instigators of servile insurrection. Thus in the first fifty years after the institutionalization of slavery, most colonies excluded free African Americans from the right to vote or hold office, muster in the militia, bear arms, and employ indentured servants. The imposition of legal disabilities on free blacks, which conflated their status with that of their brethren in bondage, underscored the distinctions between white privilege and black subordination. The emergence of a system of race privileges secured European American investment in a sense of "white identity." Thus, as modern historians have almost universally pointed out, race was neither natural nor transhistorical; rather, it was a social construction, based on physical differences, that emerged in a specific historical context and represented relations of power between different social groups.[4]

African slavery racialized New York, the largest slave society outside the plantation South. Inaugurated by the Dutch West India Company to meet the labor demands of white merchants, farmers and artisans, black bondage expanded in the century after the conquest of the colony by the English. The enslaved—drawn variously and in successive waves from the British and Dutch Caribbean islands of Jamaica, Barbados, Antigua, and Curacao; the west African nations of the Akan-Asante, Popo, Moko, Ibo, Yoruba, Adra, and Jon; and the east African coast—made up over one-third of the newcomers to New York between 1732 and 1754. Colonial Manhattan's racial formation paralleled that of its Chesapeake sister in important respects, resting on the twin prongs of the European settler population's Anglicization and the Africans' civil marginalization. London sought to weld a motley crew of European colonists—fractured into English and Dutch, Anglican and Calvinist, merchant and artisan, rich and poor—into an English national community by stressing their common Germanic ancestry, teaching them the English language, and proselytizing them in Anglican doctrines. In 1706 Parliament passed the Naturalization Act, which conferred English liberties on all foreign-born Protestants who had lived in English-reigned dominions for at least seven years, passed a sacramental test to prove their Protestant affiliations, and pledged loyalty to the English Crown. The glue that cemented Anglo-Saxon Protestant ties to *white* English nationalism, however, was the *exclusion* of nonwhites from this colonial national imaginary. Colonial statutes clearly distinguished between white servants and black slaves; in 1706, the equation between slavery and race constructs was naturalized by making slave status contingent on descent from a "Negro, Indian, Mulatto, or Mestee" mother, rather than on the changeable condition of "heathenism." Moreover, a black code adopted in the wake of the slave revolt of 1712 prohibited free blacks from inheriting or willing land to their heirs, thus depriving them of a key path to the economic independence with which republican identity was to be bound.[5]

On the eve of the American Revolution, Africans and African Americans accounted for 14 percent of New York's population. Slaves, originally predominantly urban, toiled as domestic servants in the homes of the wealthy; as workers in artisan shops manufacturing boats, making sails, and spinning rope; and in printing establishments, tanneries, and breweries. In the mid-eighteenth century, slavery transformed portions of the city's hinterland. In the grain-producing regions of the Hudson River valley, Long Island, and northern New Jersey, farmers increasingly relied on enslaved men for agriculture and cattle raising, and on women for farm and domestic labor. Indeed, slaves and servants outnumbered free white workers in New Jersey's Monmouth, Middlesex, and Bergen counties, while one in every three Kings County residents was held in bondage. With one in five households in New York City owning slaves as late as

1790, the widespread mastery over black bodies and black labor nurtured racism in defense of social power.[6]

The legacies of hereditary bondage (and, later, herrenvolk republicanism) were to shape a racialized policy of relief and reform that treated destitute African Americans differently from their European immigrant counterparts. The public relief of a class of people long constructed in the New World as private property was discouraged since colonial times. New York's slave code conferred on slaveholders nearly absolute control over their human chattel, including the right both to punish them short of death and to sell them. In exchange, masters were required, by law and custom, to provide their bondspeople, however old, sick, or decrepit, with subsistence. That slaveholders often reneged on their part of the bargain is evident from the periodic passage of laws to prevent masters from passing their responsibilities for the care of the aged enslaved on to the public purse. In colonial America, as in England, local communities—whether the town, county, or parish—were far more likely to provide outdoor relief to the dependents in their homes than to institutionalize them in poorhouses. Children with no means of support were apprenticed; freedmen and -women, bereft of independent households, and most likely to be manumitted after they had exhausted their productive years, posed a particular problem to local taxpayers unsympathetic to African Americans.[7]

After the slave revolt of 1712, a strict new manumission law required masters to post a bond, worth two hundred pounds, that pledged support for any ex-slave who became a public charge. The law no doubt aimed to impose strict social and racial control on slaves and stymie the growth of what many whites saw as a subversive free black community, quick to instigate slave insurrections. Yet tightened manumission procedures also served to insulate taxpayers from the potential burden of supporting freed slaves. In 1773 the colony of New York passed a law to "Prevent Aged and Decrepit Slaves from becoming Burthensome." The measure targeted masters who forced their black dependents into beggary, thus rendering them "burthensome on the humanity and charity of others." The law punished any slaveholder guilty of this practice with fine of ten pounds, of which 50 percent would be donated to the poor of the community victimized by the offense.[8]

The American Revolution triggered a chain of events that put slavery on the course of gradual extinction in what became the state of New York. The exigencies of war disrupted the stability of chattel bondage: patriots and loyalists confiscated each others' human property, driving slaveholders to "refugee" their bondspeople into safe havens in the interior, far away from their homes and farms. Enslaved men and women seized the opportunity to run away, fight whichever side promised them freedom, or else subvert their work routines and the etiquettes of social relations between themselves and their masters. War and the erosion of slavery progressively absolved masters of responsibility toward their former slaves and brought many black New Yorkers without means into a new relationship with the state. In 1784 the legislature authorized the sale of confiscated Tory estates and the manumission of slaves belonging to those estates. Until they became self-sufficient, "forfeited" freedmen and women were to be supported with a portion of the proceeds of such sales. The aged and infirm among them were consigned to public assistance. A statute passed in 1785 eased the path to manumission by allowing masters to free self-sufficient slaves under the age of fifty without posting security, on the condition that they first obtain written permission from the local overseers of the poor and two justices of the peace in their town.[9]

Meanwhile, African Americans petitioned courts and legislatures against slavery in language that invoked the revolutionary ideals of liberty and equality. In addition, the New York Manumission Society, established in 1785 by Quaker and Anglican merchants and lawyers, launched a campaign to legislate slavery into gradual extinction. Despite their efforts, however, the new republic's largest slave state north of the Mason-Dixon Line embraced emancipation with decided reluctance. Indeed, black bondage spread its tentacles through even the lower orders of New York society in the aftermath of American independence from British rule. The slaveholders of 1790 included those who owned little real estate, such as tailors, grocers, and female boardinghouse keepers. Slaveholding was also widespread in the state's agricultural hinterland, especially in Kings County, where nearly 60 percent of white households owned slaves, over 40 percent of them in units quite large by Northern standards (over five slaves). Between 1790 and 1800, the number of slaves in New York increased by 22 percent, and those of slaveholders by 33 percent, the ranks of the latter fortified not only by domestic migrations but also by the arrival of French-speaking refugees from the Haitian Revolution.[10]

At the turn of the nineteenth century, the social profile of slaveholders underwent some change. As former artisan slaveholders turned increasingly to European immigrant wage labor, the new mercantile and financial elites (forged in New York's "business revolution") purchased ever more liveried black "servants" to maintain their opulent mansions along graceful Broadway. By this time, however, a gradual-emancipation law had assured slavery's eventual death and created a new class of "state poor." New York's Gradual Manumission Act, passed on March 29, 1799, freed all children born into slavery after July 4, 1799, with the proviso that such children serve their mothers' masters until they reached the age of twenty-eight (for men) and twenty-five (for women). A slaveholder reserved the right to give up his claim to the services of such a child within one year after its birth. The overseers of the poor would then assume the care of the child until it was bound out for a sum not exceeding $3.50 a month (reduced to $2.00 in 1802), payable by the state. Former masters could apply to look after the children of their slaves at the expense of the state, thus earning "a sizeable return for their acts of conscience," as Graham Russell Hodges has observed. This "abandonment law" proved so expensive that it was repealed in 1812. Five years later, on July 4, 1827, New York sealed slavery's fate by enacting a law that freed all slaves born before July 4, 1799.[11]

Emancipation did not confer equal citizenship on African Americans. Indeed, on the national stage, the American Revolution failed to stem the resilience of racialism, which became manifest in the emergence of a white republic on the ashes of Britain's imperial domain. Revolutionary republicanism meshed the notions of public good, civic virtue, independence, and citizenship into an implicitly racialized discourse that called into question African Americans' fitness to participate in American democracy; at the same time, this ideology opened the way for unlimited white immigration. Republican ideology held that the success of any political order resting on the "consent of the governed" depended on the capacity of its citizenry to safeguard the "public good," or *commonwealth*. In order to preserve the "public good," republican citizens had to exercise civic virtue; this attribute was a function of self-sacrifice, discipline, and, most importantly, economic independence, which guaranteed sovereignty from the political domination of others. The notion of the commonwealth called for a homogeneous group of members with shared interests. Furthermore, the attributes of civic virtue were, as Matthew Frye Jacobson has suggested, "racially inscribed in eighteenth-century Euro-American thought," so that "the republican ideal of 'the consent of the governed' became inextricably linked to its unfortunate shadow, the gendered, almost always racial question of 'fitness for self-government.'" The white republic's assumption of the Europeans' fitness for republican citizenship was institutionalized in the naturalization law of 1790, which extended the privilege of naturalized citizenship exclusively to Europeans defined as free whites.[12]

As chattel, African Americans had represented the very negation of republican citizens. As free people, they were portrayed as witless outcasts incapable of stepping out of the shadow of bondage to exercise civic virtue. Although New York State's earliest constitution (1777) did not limit voting rights on racial grounds, the prospect of emancipation changed not a few legislators' minds during a subsequent constitutional convention that convened in Albany in 1821. A member of that august body, Samuel Young of Saratoga County, publicly adjudged blacks likely to "sell their votes to the highest bidder." That his was not a cry in the wilderness became clear when the legislature voted to impose a $250 property qualification for suffrage on black men. A provision that exempted white men from property requirements as long as they served in the militia or paid taxes was later rescinded: by 1826, New York had capitulated to the forces of herrenvolk democracy.[13]

Even as the state became less hospitable to black aspirations for equality, New York City emerged as an attractive destination for free people of color. It drew refugees from the Haitian Revolution and liberated African Americans from the metropolis's agricultural hinterlands (in which slavery survived well into the nineteenth century). Pushed out by the dearth of affordable land in their native localities, black migrants from Kings County, Staten Island, and New Jersey may have been lured to the city by the promise it offered of a new beginning untainted by the stigma of their slave pasts; they may also have been drawn by employment opportunities as domestics, launderers, sweeps, barbers, wood sawyers, whitewashers, sailors, and day laborers. In the early nineteenth century, about one-third of free black New Yorkers lived in white households as domestic servants. Others managed to maintain independent households—however precariously—by pooling the earnings of family members working as casual day laborers, mariners, peddlers, chimney sweeps, oystermen, washerwomen, porters, hackney coach drivers, street musicians, and even petty criminals and prostitutes.

Yet what made early national New York singular (compared with, say, Philadelphia) was the presence of a significant coterie of skilled black workers—a legacy, in part, of the predominance of artisans over merchants and shopkeepers among New York's eighteenth-century slaveholders. While Philadelphia craftsmen preferred white indentured labor,

Gotham artisans employed slaves through much of the eighteenth century, so that city directories and census records in the first two decades of the nineteenth century listed an impressive number of African American carpenters, coopers, cabinetmakers, upholsterers, sailmakers, butchers, bakers, printers, papermakers, shoemakers, goldsmiths, and tallow chandlers, all living on their own or in white households. Together with journalists, clergymen, and teachers, they constituted the kernel of an emerging black middle class, which both championed freedom and civil rights and nurtured a vibrant community life through newspapers (like the *Colored American*) and churches and benevolent societies. Class was, of course, a fluid entity in nineteenth-century America, especially so in black America. No artisan, no matter how skilled, was entirely safe from catapulting into the swirling "underclass" of transients who inhabited the putrid basements and disease-ridden cellars of the Old Brewery in Lower Manhattan or tramped through the country in search of work.[14]

What is striking about the history of black New Yorkers and poor relief in the age of emancipation, however, is that no matter how vulnerable to the ravages of destitution and sickness, African Americans apparently proved reluctant to seek institutional relief. As the historian Robert Cray has shown on the basis of censuses compiled by the New York City Alms House preacher John Stanford from 1816 to 1826, the ratio of black relief-seekers to whites declined during the era of slavery's demise, equaling two-thirds the ratio of blacks to whites in the city. In 1824, for example, African Americans made up only 4 percent of the Alms House population. Cray concluded that destitute freedmen preferred the autonomy offered by outdoor relief over institutionalization in a segregated alms house. Between April 1813 and April 1814, black families made up nearly 31 percent of the population receiving fuel or cash in their own homes—a proportion that greatly exceeded the ratio of African Americans to whites in New York's population.[15]

Other historians have drawn attention to the rich tradition of mutual aid that sustained African Americans in need. The New York African Society for Mutual Relief—incorporated in 1810 and located after 1820 in a Five Points tenement on Orange (now Baxter) Street—inspired similar cooperative associations on both sides of the East River. The Brooklyn African Woolman Benevolent Society, the Wilberforce Philanthropic Association, the African Marine Fund, and the New York African Clarkson Association—and later the Garrison Literary and Benevolent Association, the Abyssinian Benevolent Daughters of Esther Association, and the Brooklyn

African Tomkins Association, among others—not only promoted moral uplift, education, abolition, and civil rights, but also provided a range of benefits to their members, such as sick aid, burial assistance, educatiôn, and the relief of widows and orphans.[16]

Undoubtedly, it was due in no small part to the efforts of these associations that African Americans registered a disproportionately low presence among Alms House inmates in the 1820s. Thirty years later, however, the relationship of black New Yorkers to municipal relief mechanisms had changed markedly. Their share of outdoor relief, although higher than the black percentage in the general population, fell substantially, while that of whites—native-born even more than immigrant—climbed from early nineteenth-century levels. On the other hand, even as the black proportion of the total population in the city declined (reaching nearly 3 percent at mid-century), African Americans accounted for more than one out of every five clients obtaining relief at the alms house and its privately operated arm, the Colored Home. On the eve of the Civil War, African Americans figured prominently among the inmates of quasi-public relief and reform institutions, championed by New York's burgeoning bourgeoisie as a solution to the increasingly urgent and *visible* problem of "pauperism," with all its implications for the future of the white republic.[17]

Progress and Poverty in Antebellum New York

The demise and aftermath of slavery in New York coincided with a confluence of circumstances that trained a glaring new light on the problem of poverty. The paradoxes flowing from capitalist transformation appeared in their most exaggerated as Gotham emerged as North America's mercantile, and later manufacturing, capital, as well as its greatest population center. Jacksonian America's market revolution generated optimistic visions of unending progress—of technological marvels, rising incomes, a growing middle class, burgeoning cities, booming trade, and continental expansion. During the first sixty years or so following American independence, nature contrived with human enterprise to turn New York into the first city of the Western Hemisphere. In the first quarter of the nineteenth century, the city's fine harbor—accessible to larger deep-draft vessels—and its waterways to the interior established it as the major entrepôt of trade with Britain. The introduction of regular transatlantic postal packet service cemented this commercial alliance. Westward expansion up the Mohawk Valley and into the Adirondacks gave New York merchants control of grain and other food stuffs. The demand for Southern cotton (stimulated by Eli Whitney's cotton gin), gave them command over the country's single most important export. The inauguration of the Erie Canal in the 1820s connected New York with the Great Lakes and redirected the Ohio River traffic in timber and farm produce from the South to the East. Aided by court decisions supporting unfettered enterprise, by 1836 a dense network of steamboats, packet lines, and canals concentrated 62 percent of the nation's import trade in the hands of the city's mercantile class. An excellent financial infrastructure—consisting of a stock exchange, banks, and insurance companies—kept the gears of this business behemoth well-oiled.[18]

In the 1840s and 1850s, the advent of transatlantic steamers and majestic clippers, which circled the globe from Liverpool to Southeast Asia, established New York's supremacy in the international carrying trade and turned the city's riverfronts into humongous hives of chaotic activity. Meanwhile, with the California gold rush of 1849, New York shipbuilders reaped fabulous riches outfitting westbound merchants. Shipping offices, warehouses, eateries, and junk shops did thriving business along the harbor in Lower Manhattan, while an assortment of vehicles—horse-drawn omnibuses and stagecoaches, carts and express wagons—noisily crisscrossed cobblestone pathways, plying goods and people from shore to shore. The introduction of the Erie and Hudson rail lines solidified New York's control over commerce in Western commodities. The infusion of Western gold fueled a boom in banking, making New York America's leading creditor city and galvanizing the stock market into a hub of trade in railroad, canal, and coal mine securities for investors from Europe and elsewhere. Mercantile wealth and finance capitalism fed a roaring manufacturing sector. Iron foundries, sugar refineries, drug companies, and consumer manufactories spilled into the surrounding areas of Brooklyn, the Bronx, Staten Island, and New Jersey. Early in the century, the presence of a vibrant pool of consumers drawn from migrants, immigrants, and tourists, as well as the explosion of wealth and availability of credit and raw materials, drew many artisans into production for the market; a few became wealthy entrepreneurs. In the second quarter of the nineteenth century, New York became the most productive manufacturing city in the United States—in the words of Sean Wilentz, "a metropolitan labyrinth of factories and tiny artisan establishments, central workrooms and outworkers' cellars, luxury firms and sweatwork strapping shops."[19]

This immensely diverse world of "metropolitan industrialization" spawned an army of casualties—a growing population of low-wage workers in a series of "bastardized" crafts, especially the consumer finishing trades. Taking advantage of a plentiful supply of labor sustained by immigration, many manufacturers subdivided their work into numerous parts and delegated semiskilled assembly tasks to contractors or directly to outworkers, who labored at piece rates in their own homes. Only the most skilled tasks were reserved for in-shop workers. In the clothing industry, for instance, after New York merchants gained control over the profitable business in slave clothing in the 1820s, outdoor manufactories and master tailors hired women to sew the rough "Negro cottons" for their Southern customers, as well as cheap ready-made attire for the urban masses and, later, dungarees for Western farmers and miners. "Outwork" was fraught with abuses of the most exploitative variety. A chain of middlemen—manufacturers and subcontractors—cut piece rates continuously in order to increase their own profit margins and to outbid other contractors competing for manufacturers' orders. Moreover, because retailers and country dealers bought the finished goods on credit, employers often postponed the payment of wages to all workers; in fact, they occasionally withheld wages on the pretext of shoddy work by an outworker. Whimsical business cycles and the seasonal nature of work in very many trades–needlework included—compounded the woes of New York's ballooning industrial proletariat. The antebellum seamstress scraping together between $0.75 and $1.50 a week to support a family of dependents epitomized the "worthy" poor in the reform literature of the day.[20]

Economic expansion sharpened lifestyle distinctions and helped shape the cultural identities of social groups congealing into distinguishable classes in antebellum New York. Moreover, it reconfigured the social geography of the burgeoning city. In the early republic, transplanted New Englanders and Anglo-Dutch and Huguenot knickerbockers made up a cosmopolitan mercantile and business elite united as much by their aggressive pursuit of business opportunities as by their shared taste in the high culture and haute couture. They patronized the arts, dispensed charity, and dominated the municipal government. In the late 1820s, the encroachment of lesser folks on their residential neighborhoods on the Lower West Side of Manhattan along Broadway prompted New York patricians to move farther uptown. The graceful tree-lined environs of Hudson Square, Bond Street, and Bleecker Street became residential refuges from the seaminess of downtown business districts, to which the wealthy now traveled in horse-drawn omnibuses. By the 1850s, New York's rich, their ranks swollen by a tide of successful newcomers in banking and brokerage, trade and manufacturing, and real estate and railroads, had moved even farther uptown—north of Bleecker to Union Square Park, Gramercy Park, and, above all, Fifth Avenue. There, elegant Italian Renaissance-style homes sheltered well-proportioned rooms lavishly furnished with imported furniture, tapestries, and porcelain; and equipped with Croton water, indoor plumbing, and central heating. Members of the upper crust socialized among themselves at balls and dinner parties, attended Episcopalian and Presbyterian churches, patronized the theater on Broadway and the Astor Place Opera House, went horse riding on macadamized Third Avenue, and immersed themselves in a host of benevolent causes.[21]

The market revolution produced a diffuse and segmented middle class of professionals, lesser merchants, manufacturers, businessmen, master artisans, and clerks dispersed in living quarters—whether brick homes, brownstones, or even boardinghouses—in emerging neighborhoods throughout the city, as far uptown as Forty-second Street in Manhattan and as far east as Brooklyn. Unstable as the material foundations and markers of this class were, its identity was defined in large part by the manners and morals to which its members aspired. At the heart of bourgeois mentalité lay a new conception of the family. As many historians have noted, market society engendered the ideal of a genteel world separated into a "public" sphere of politics and commerce run by men, and a private domain of housework and child care supervised by women. The moral guardian of this private sphere was the "true woman"—pious, virtuous, and domesticated, the epitome of the good wife and mother. The cultural invention of childhood proceeded as a logical corollary to this "cult of domesticity." Children were conceived as entitled to the right to be nurtured and educated by loving mothers who stayed home while fathers went into the public realms of business, law, and politics to earn a livelihood for their families.

Bourgeois ideals of the family bore little resemblance to the realities of life in the plebeian quarters of Manhattan. As New Yorkers of substance retreated into genteel uptown neighborhoods, an omnibus's commute away from the unwholesome commercial districts farther south, the city's growing proletariat swarmed into boisterous enclaves that recognized few boundaries between private and public. A burst of immigration, primarily from European shores, lent these neighborhoods an increasingly polyglot, multiethnic character and made them seem more alien than ever to respectable sons and daughters of the soil. Germany, England, and the Italian peninsula sent forth peasants, artisans, and political refugees fleeing agricultural depressions, proletarianization wreaked by mass production, and official repression (following the failure of English Chartism, Europe's liberal revolutions of 1848, and the Italian war of independence from Austria). But the group that provoked the greatest consternation of all, by appearing to defy the premises of the white republic, was the Irish.[22]

A speaker at an Irish meeting in 1844 predicted the wave of the future when he claimed that New York was "the most Irish city" in America. Myriad circumstances fueled the Irish exodus to Victorian America. In the first quarter of the nineteenth century, as the British wartime demand for Irish textiles plummeted, English landlords drove their tenants off the land. With the advent of cheap transport on packet ships from Liverpool to New York, the prospect of work on the canals, railroads, and factories of the New World lured thousands of artisans, peasants, laborers, and single women to the promised land across the Atlantic. Many of these newcomers were Presbyterian and Anglican Scotch-Irish émigrés from Ulster. Those who remained in the old country, especially the vast majority of Irish Catholic peasants, faced an ever harder lot. Widespread unemployment, low wages, a dearth of arable land, overpopulation, and stratospheric rents forced cash-hungry farmers to grow their own food on modest plots of rented land. Potato became the staple of choice because it could be grown on the tiniest of plots and offered the largest returns. An acre of potatoes both fed more mouths than any other vegetable and burnt cheaply for fuel. Ireland's potato culture encouraged farmers to apportion their holdings among all their children, fueling early marriages and intensifying population pressure on the land.[23]

No wonder then, that when a fungus devastated the potato crop beginning in the summer of 1845, it shook the very foundations of peasant life in Ireland. Starving beggars and emaciated children dotted the countryside, contributing to a death toll that reached 1.5 million in five years. Some landlords launched schemes of assisted emigration as a way of reducing work-house costs and other famine-relief expenditures. Between 1845 and 1855, 1.5 million Irish made their way to North America, tightly packed into "coffin ships," sometimes racked by typhus or "ship fever." This new wave of immigrants was far more impoverished than its Celtic predecessors in America and tended to be overwhelmingly Catholic. The newcomers were also likely to migrate in family units rather than singly.[24]

Meanwhile, the famine transformed landholding patterns and marriage practices in Ireland. A system of non-partible inheritance evolved in which one child inherited the lease or ownership of the family holding, making it possible for him to raise a family. Economic hardship discouraged people from marrying young (and sometimes from marrying at all). Material considerations prevailed over romantic love in governing decisions about wedlock. Dowry enhanced a woman's prospects in the marriage market because it served to fund her sister-in-law's path to wedded bliss. Under these circumstances only one daughter in a family of modest means could hope to marry, just as one son could hope to inherit land. Their siblings usually joined the ranks of nubile men and women without prospects for employment or marriage at home. Of those that turned their gaze overseas, the majority were women, so that Irish emigration to New York in the aftermath of the famine took on an increasingly feminized cast. Job opportunities on railroads and canal construction projects drew many Irishmen away from New York to the West, increasing the ratio of women to men among the New York Irish.[25]

According to the 1855 census, there were 175,735 Irish-born New Yorkers—28 percent of the city's total population. Although they were dispersed throughout the city and its hinterland, the densest Irish enclaves sprang up in Manhattan's first, fourth, sixth, and fourteenth wards, where nearly one of every two residents was Hibernian. Lured by the availability of unskilled work and relatively cheap housing, the poorest among them flocked to Lower Manhattan. By mid-century, Five Points in the sixth ward—named after the five-cornered intersection of Anthony, Orange, Mulberry, Little Water, and Cross streets—had emerged as a predominantly Irish slum. This most infamous of the city's underclass haunts occupied the damp, marshy ground in and around the filled-in Fresh Water (Collect) Pond in the vicinity of which blacks had originally settled on half-freedom plots granted by the Dutch in the seventeenth century. By the 1850s, racial violence had fueled an exodus of African Americans from Five Points, which now became the closest thing the city had to an Irish "ghetto." There, swarms of newcomers from the Emerald Isle, both recent and long-term, rubbed shoulders with immigrant Germans, Poles, Italians, and Chinese. It was also there that they interacted in what reformers and sections of the media viewed as promiscuous proximity with the remaining African Americans. Another conspicuous immigrant neighborhood emerged in Kleindeutschland (Little Germany), radiating north and east from its original site between Canal and Rivington streets. Farther uptown, homeless immigrants erected shantytowns on the rocky periphery of urban settlements. At Dutch Hill, a Fortieth Street bluff overlooking Turtle Bay, a colony of newcomers raised cows, pigs, goats, and fowl, and worked in the area's quarries and manure heaps. The Hudson River waterfront between Fortieth and Eightieth streets housed Irish and German ragpickers, cinder gatherers, and casual laborers who worked on construction projects and in the stables of the city railroads and stages companies.[26]

For the most part, working poor black New Yorkers lived among their European immigrant and native-born white counterparts. In 1825 the African Methodist Episcopal Zion Church laid out a farm community (later Seneca Village) between Eighty-third and Eighty-eighth streets and Seventh and Eighth avenues (now covered by Central Park). The bulk of impoverished African Americans, however, crowded into rented outbuildings and cellars farther south, in portions of plebeian neighborhoods that cut a swath across Manhattan from Trinity Church's farm along the Hudson River through the swampy terrain of the filled-in Fresh Water (Collect) Pond to Corlear's Hook on the East River. From Five Points in the sixth ward, they moved north and west to the fifth and eighth wards, which by mid-century had become the centers of New York's black population. While all-black neighborhoods were rare, racial segregation prevailed *within* working poor enclaves. For instance, the African Americans who remained in Five Points in 1855 occupied all-black tenements on Park Street between Baxter and Mott, as well as in Cow Bay, Baxter, Mulberry, and Pell streets. The blocks of Bancker Street between Pearl and Catherine, on the other hand, remained the site of the city's most identifiably black ghetto.[27] Private and public appeared to merge seamlessly in these raucous, communal regions of plebeian life. Working-class women did not lead their lives out of public sight, in the inner sanctum of their hearths. It wasn't just that many earned their bread on the streets and in the marketplace—in garment manufactories; behind ice-cream stalls, fruit carts, and "grocery" counters; or as sex traders, plying their wares on busy thoroughfares at night. They also socialized, fought with and helped each other, protested against exploitative landlords and unruly bawds, and disciplined their children and sent them scavenging—all in the public spaces of working-class neighborhoods.[28]

The physical and spatial moorings of what a prison reformer called "that best of all moral schools, the humane and religious private family"[29] seemed conspicuous by their absence in the cramped living quarters of impoverished New Yorkers. Indeed, by the 1850s, Lower Manhattan's tenement housing had become the most sordid public symbol of working-class and underclass "Otherness." As the economic boom of the 1830s sent rents soaring, profit-minded landlords and speculators jammed working people who needed to live near their workplaces in the city's lower wards into minutely subdivided two-room apartments in existing single-family homes or two-to-five story buildings constructed especially for the poor. Partitioned without regard to light, ventilation, or sanitary concerns, these ill-maintained brick-and-frame hovels barely sheltered from wind and water the multitudes who packed into them from cellar to garret. Often enough, a landlord or speculative builder squeezed two buildings on a street-fronted lot capable of accommodating only one structure. A wall separated the two buildings, "the rear only accessible through the first floor entry of the first house, or by an alley-way at its side." Deprived of light and cross ventilation, rear buildings usually overlooked backyards mired in the stench of outhouse effluvia. Cramped working-class quarters lacked the physical icons of middle-class homes by the early 1840s, such as running water, indoor plumbing, and piped gas. Family members dragged pails filled with water from rain barrels and street-corner pumps up dilapidated stairs, lighted their homes with candles and kerosene lamps, and relieved themselves in backyard privies.[30]

In public discourse, tenement houses evoked a physical and social world almost surreal—certainly un-American—in its concentration of human misery. The report of a legislative committee to investigate these slums in 1857 led its readers on a "virtual" tour of the squalid realms in the "wells of the city." It conjured vivid images of narrow alleys with garbage-choked gutters and broken sidewalks, "rum-holes" shaded by discolored curtains, and pawn shops that displayed damaged wares in their windows. Swarms of "half-naked, dirty and leering children" lurked in street corners and at the doorless entrances of rickety buildings. Inside a standard tenement house, "creaking, moldy stairs" stained with the germs of cutaneous disorders ascended into narrow and noisome passageways infested with vermin and opening into dimly lighted rooms. Tiny, with windowless bedrooms, these apartments were unfurnished, save perhaps for a three-legged stool, a broken pine table, and a bed of rags or straw, which might be dismantled during the day. In flagrant violation of genteel decorum, the scantily clothed residents of such places—parents and children, boarders and extended kin—were likely to "perform all their personal and domestic duties in view of each other's presence," a course calculated to subdue "the nice moral distinctions so necessary to a life of virtue."[31]

Ridden with alcoholism, crime, disease, and—horror of horrors—the specter of racial "amalgamation," the most notorious of these lower-class haunts exacerbated bourgeois anxieties about rising pauperism, increasing rowdyism, the spread of vice, and, above all, the implications of a degraded electorate for the future of the evolving republic. At the heart of these anxieties about the health of the social fabric and the fate of the body politic lay the swelling tide of impecunious Emerald Isle immigrants, who threatened to turn New York into a hotbed of interracial debauchery. They jostled against African Americans not only at work and play in some of downtown New York's most squalid quarters, but also within the walls of a growing complex of refuges and reformatories designed to regulate and redeem the character of the poor.

A complete story of race and relief in Victorian New York must therefore accommodate the sprawling worlds of the city's two most marginalized communities.

Plebeian Lives: Inside Black and Irish Household Economies

The menacing stereotypes of "New York by gaslight" retreat before the plebeian profiles—at once humdrum and resourceful—that come to life in between the handwritten words and figures scrawled across New York County's census records for 1855. The records themselves lent the authority of the state to the vision of a social order in which the household was the basic unit of sociopolitical organization, where men worked for wages, and married women and children were expected to stay out of the public sphere. They did, however, list (usually single) women's occupations for the first time, spelled out the relationship of family members to the heads of each household, identified boarders and lodgers, and recorded the length of time that each respondent had spent in the city. At the same time, the census conformed to the paradigm of the white republic by institutionalizing the division of society into white and hues of black. The premise of whiteness as normative was embedded in the structure of the census. The category "color" was demarcated by the signifiers "black or mulatto," defined implicitly against the unnamed, ostensibly "race"-less, "color"-less grouping "white." However indeterminate the color of the Irish "race" may have appeared in the nativist discourses of the day, the census implicitly bestowed a white identity on Hibernians by leaving them out of the category labeled "color (whether black or mulatto)." The political privilege attached to whiteness emerged in the column designating "naturalized" individuals—a qualification that, in the case of males, conveyed the right to vote.[32]

I compare a random sample from the 1855 census of one hundred predominantly eighth ward African American households with one hundred sixth ward households having at least one Irish member. (Single Irishmen and -women frequently lived in non-Irish households as boarders and servants; moreover, some Irishwomen married outside their communities; hence the formulation "households having at least one Irish member.") The sixth and eighth wards were generally well represented in the relief rolls of the Alms House and the Colored Home, and both contributed a significant number of inmates to reform institutions like the New York House of Refuge and the Hopper Home. Census data from these wards afford intimate glimpses into the variety of family arrangements and household structures that plebeians sported both within and outside the middle-class nuclear norm. The variegated familial cosmos they inhabited was adapted to their demographic profiles, the circumstances of their migration to the city and the length of their residence there, the presence or absence of existing networks of kin and friends, the limitations of the job market for the working poor, and their child care needs. Familiar concepts like the "nuclear" family and "boarding" assumed new meaning in the context of these variables. (See tables 1–18, in appendix.) The correlation between household and work in subaltern neighborhoods offer keys to understanding the assorted nature and patterns of welfare use by Victorian New York's most disadvantaged communities.

The one hundred black households turned out to consist of 347 individuals, of which over 58 percent were women and over 61 percent were under the age of thirty. Children below the age of fifteen accounted for nearly 29 percent of the population, and relatively older African Americans (over forty-six years of age) nearly 17 percent of the total. The sex ratio of the group as a whole, balanced in the younger cohorts, showed a sharp increase in favor of women with the progress of age. Thus, while females made up 48 percent of children below the age of fifteen, their proportion jumped to nearly 58 percent in the sixteen-to-thirty age group, climbed to approximately 64 percent in the thirty-one-to-forty-five cohort, and remained at that level among still older people. Although poverty, overcrowding in cellars, and the resulting scourge of epidemics like cholera and yellow fever (as well as omnipresent diseases like consumption, pneumonia, and bronchitis) spelled soaring mortality rates for all black New Yorkers, the additional hazards of racial violence and industrial accidents at construction sites and on the docks took a particularly heavy toll on black men.

A little over 36 percent of the individuals living in the black households surveyed had been born outside New York City (see table 16, in appendix). More than two-thirds of this group (69 percent) had arrived from the city's hinterlands in Kings County and New Jersey, or from urban centers in upstate New York and Pennsylvania. The next largest contingent (14 percent) came from the Upper South slave states of Virginia, Maryland, and Delaware. Another 8 percent had emigrated from islands in the Caribbean—Bermuda, Cuba, and Santo Domingo. In general, the migrant population was older and more female than the black population sampled as a whole. Persons below the age of thirty-one constituted less than 36 percent, blacks over forty-six years of age nearly 31 percent, and women, in excess of 60 percent of the group. A majority—57 percent of the men and 64 percent of the women—had lived in New York at least eleven years. Several had arrived in the age of emancipation and its immediate aftermath. By the 1850s, racial violence and the lack of economic opportunities had tarnished New York's reputation as a land of promise for African Americans.

Regional variations in demographic profiles did, however, complicate the picture. Those born in the West Indies had the highest ratio of women to men (80 percent) but were younger than the migrant population as a whole, with only a fifth of the group older than forty-six years. Among the Northeasterners, women predominated numerically but men were younger on average. Nearly 53 percent of the males but only 31 percent of the females were under thirty years of age. The largest proportion of women migrants from the Northeast (39 percent) were between the ages of thirty-one and forty-five—older on average than their Irish sisters.

The social profile of migrants from the Upper South diverged from that of their Northeastern counterparts in interesting ways. For one thing, men from Virginia, Maryland, and Delaware outnumbered women by more than three to two. Upper Southerners were also older than the black population as a whole, with 63 percent of the men and 71 percent of the women over the age of forty-six. Most of these individuals had migrated to New York shortly before, or within a decade after, slavery's demise in the state, and before the rising tide of Southern nationalism in the 1830s and 1840s impeded the movement of African Americans out of rapidly closing slave societies. Not surprisingly, the few slave-state blacks in the sample who migrated fewer than ten years before the 1855 census were overwhelmingly male. As many historians have shown, it was far more difficult for black women, especially those enslaved, to migrate to free territory. They often had children, were hired out less often, performed tasks tied to the plantations where they lived, and were thus less mobile than enslaved men. The census does not, of course, reveal whether recent Southern black migrants had been born slave or free. Whatever the case, it is reasonable to assume that men drawn by the urban North's promise of freedom, jobs, and anonymity had greater opportunity to flee the lands of their birth than did their sisters, mothers, and wives.

The demographic features and migration circumstances of working poor African Americans shaped a variety of family arrangements and household structures, ranging from nuclear, extended or "communal," and single parent–headed households, on the one hand, to independent living and boarding/domestic service in private families and institutions, on the other. Of the hundred black households surveyed, forty consisted of nuclear families, defined here as married couples living either on their own or with their unmarried children (see tables 2 and 3, in appendix). In the context of the black community confronted with restricted economic opportunity, however, the concept of the nuclear family took on a distinctive meaning. It was characterized by a relatively high incidence of grown children who postponed marriage and exchanged the autonomy of independent living for the economic security of boarding with their parents. For instance, twenty-one-year-old Henry Sparrows, a sailor, belonged to the household of his parents, a forty-three-year-old waiter named George Sparrows and his thirty-seven-year-old wife, Sarah.[33] By contrast, a large proportion of white immigrant groups, like the Irish, arrived as young singles and established families of their own in America. Thus, the average age of "children" living in nuclear families was higher for African Americans than for their white counterparts.

Given the high ratio of black women to men, especially in the upper age brackets, black men were more likely than women and children to live in nuclear families. Nearly 47 percent of all men over the age of sixteen, but only approximately 26 percent of their female counterparts, lived in nuclear families. Only 35 percent of all children below the age of fifteen years lived in nuclear families. These figures for nuclear families do not, however, signify a correspondingly low marriage rate for black adults. More black men and women married than the frequency distribution of individuals in nuclear family arrangements would suggest (see table 14, in appendix). Indeed, nearly 72 percent of all men over the age of sixteen in the sample reported that they were married, as did 44 percent of the women. Nearly 24 percent of all women above the age of sixteen were widowed, leaving 32 percent who had never been married. Approximately 80 percent of all married women were in their twenties and thirties. Imbalanced sex ratios in the higher age groups, shaped in large part by high mortality rates among black men, produced more widows and single women over the age of forty. Men in their twenties and thirties, on the other hand, accounted for less than 60 percent of all married men. Many older men married young women, and occasionally some married white women.

One reason why nuclear families accounted for a lower proportion of black individuals than marriage rates among black adults would imply was that a small proportion of married people, primarily women (7 percent of the married women in the sample), did not live with their spouses. Presumably, this occurred because of marital disputes or because the circumstances of certain kinds of work—domestic service and sailing, to name just two—separated married couples regularly. Men were also more likely than women to travel outside the city in search of work during lean seasons, leaving their wives and children periodically to fend for themselves. Judging by the census data, however, by far the most important reason that marriage rates among New York blacks did not translate into a correspondingly high proportion of adults living in nuclear families was that married couples often formed what I call "communal" households with their extended kin. The Day-Bush family was a case in point. An interracial couple, thirty-six-year-old laborer Daniel Day and his white wife, Ann, shared a home with Daniel's uncle Joseph Bush and his wife, June.[34]

"Communal" households might consist of extended families of grandparents and parents, siblings and cousins, and aunts and uncles living in the same tiny "apartment." Or they might involve "roommates"—*not* identified as boarders or lodgers, sharing the same living space, and listed as belonging to the same family unit—whose kin relationship to the head of household, if any, was undocumented. Under the roommate arrangement, two widows with their respective children, or several unmarried adults, might rent a space together. It is difficult to tell from the census whether they were kin, friends, acquaintances, or simply strangers brought together by the housing shortage and lofty rents.

Communal households—primarily those based on kinship—dominated the family arrangements of African Americans (see table 4, in appendix). The largest proportion of black women, children, and older African Americans belonged to intergenerational extended families. Forty-six percent of all blacks younger than fifteen, nearly 43 percent of all women over that age, and half of all individuals over the age of forty-six lived in twenty-five extended families of many varieties. Young widows accompanied by children moved in with their siblings; younger migrants, whether from the city's hinterlands or across the seas, entered the households of relatives and friends who had preceded them to the city; older parents, especially mothers, found refuge with the families of their grown children, usually daughters. Thus, the household of Robert Bruce, a twenty-six-year-old sailor, included his thirty-three-year-old widowed sister Delia and her four children, one of whom worked as a waiter. Seventy-five-year-old Charlotte Blake, who had migrated sixty years before from Bermuda, shared a home with a thirty-eight-year-old daughter, two nephews in their twenties, and one nine-year-old niece. Porter Chas J. Williams, who had arrived in the city from New Jersey seven years before, lived with the family of his brother, a forty-year-old peddler. Even more typical was sixty-year-old Diannah Kinney, originally of Connecticut, who belonged to the household of her married daughter Margaret Bryan. Like many black families, the Bryan-Kinney family included at least two wage earners: Kinney's son-in-law John Bryan was a porter, and her seventeen-year-old granddaughter, Sarah, a dressmaker. Networks of female kin—often widowed or orphaned—became the basis of other extended families. The twenty-year-old widowed Serina Smith headed a household consisting of her forty-year-old mother as well as three sisters with ages varying from two to fourteen years.[35]

The numerical preponderance of women over men within both the African American and the Irish populations gave rise to other overwhelmingly female household types. One consisted of households headed by single parents, with or without a boarder or two (see table 5, in appendix). The second involved single individuals without children or other kin—usually women over the age of thirty-five—who emerged in the census as *independent* householders living on their own (see table 6, in appendix). By contrast, single Irishmen and -women were far more likely to live with private families or institutions as kin members, boarders, or domestic servants—or even with roommates whom the census taker described as part of the same household—than to live by themselves. Although members of their community surrounded independent black householders, they emerged in the census as freestanding, single-member households—a category that does not appear among the Irish.

The presence of these arrangements raises the question of whether "female-oriented" households—defined as those either headed by women or consisting of lone women—represented the norm among African Americans. The data suggests that thirty-eight of the one hundred households surveyed were "female-oriented." Eight of these consisted of extended families headed by women but with wage-earning males—both married and unmarried—often present; fifteen consisted of women living on their own; and another fifteen were headed by single women with unmarried, usually young, children and/or boarders. The size of female-headed households (not including those consisting of lone women) was generally larger than that of other household types. Thus, although they represented 23 percent of all households surveyed, they accounted for 46 percent of households consisting of more than five members. Overall, the data lead to the conclusion that while "female-oriented" households did not constitute the "norm," they did occur more frequently among the African Americans in the sample than among comparable "white" groups, like the Irish (as shall be presently explained). It is important to keep in mind, however, that "female-headed" households did not denote the absence of adult males. Rather, extended families headed by women often included wage-earning adult male "children"—both married and unmarried—living with their widowed mothers, who were designated the family "head." This meant that a majority of children belonging to female-headed extended families shared a home with at least one male relative. Only in households headed by single mothers with unmarried, usually younger, dependents were children were likely to grow up without adult male influence—these accounted for about a tenth of all children under the age of sixteen. The importance of this discussion lies not so much in its relevance to the enduring debate over the alleged pathology of female-headed households; rather, the relatively widespread presence of adult males in the lives of working poor black children did not necessarily secure these children from the effects of poverty.

A minority of individuals in the sample (5 percent) "boarded" or "lodged" with private families (see table 7, in appendix). Boarders paid for food as well as accommodations, while lodgers paid for a place to sleep. Despite their small number, they are significant in terms of what they reveal about the distinctive nature of boarding in New York's black community. The subculture of boarding generally represented a housing option for adults of limited means. According to historian Kenneth A. Scherzer, it may also have served as a transitional stage of semiautonomy between adolescence and marriage for young men and women in the early stages of their work lives, with boarding establishments—whether institutions or private families—often discouraging the presence of children.[36] Such, however, was clearly not the case with the eighth ward's Gardney household, with whom little Alice Mulberry boarded. Alice stood out among the boarders listed in the 1855 census by virtue of her age—she was only ten months old. Her host family consisted of a thirty-four-year-old New Jersey–born chimney sweep, his wife, daughter, and mother-in-law.[37] Alice was not unique among "boarders" in the homes of black New Yorkers. Children figured prominently in this group, making up 42 percent of all boarders in the sample, suggesting that the "culture of boarding" carried a different—or at any rate additional—meaning in the context of African American households. For blacks, it may have represented not so much a transitional life-cycle phase associated with young adulthood, as an aspect of the mutualist tradition of fosterage. While they were at work, single parents, especially women who engaged in domestic service and lived with their employers, frequently left their children in the custody of "race" kin.[38]

Other women boarded with private families *together* with their children, thus defying the conception of boarding as a form of carefree youth culture inimical to the presence of children. Approximately 73 percent of boarders above the age of sixteen consisted of women, most of whom were in their twenties or thirties. Several had migrated to the city relatively recently in search of work, occasionally accompanied by their children. The role of acquaintances and kin in shaping the boarding subculture among these migrants may have been substantial. A case in point was twenty-one-year-old Mary Whittington, who together with her five-month-old baby boy boarded with the Lee-Peterson family in the eighth ward. Whittington hailed from Orange, New Jersey, which was also the birthplace of her landlady's father, Henry Peterson. It is thus quite likely that Whittington's connection with her host family stretched back to her hometown.[39] Such connections also operated in the case of boarders and lodgers from overseas. They resulted in a degree of both regional and occupational clustering in the cultures of boarding and lodging, as host families may have helped the newcomers to their households find jobs. For example, John Lumpnep, a twenty-year-old lodger in the Simons-

Reed household, had, like his host family, migrated from Bermuda. Moreover, he was a waiter, like Nelson Reed, the son-in-law of the household head, Margaret Simons. It is reasonable to speculate that Reed, a long-term resident of New York, helped the recently arrived Lumnep to land a position as waiter. Thus boarding served multiple functions in the African American context: it catered to the child care needs of working mothers who boarded with their employers; it afforded low-cost accommodations to working adults usually without family in the city; and it cushioned migrants and immigrants from the traumas of moving to a foreign metropolis. Boarding families may have operated like micro-level immigrant enclaves that preserved familiar cultural mores, helped the newcomers find jobs, and introduced them to the ways of the city.

A higher proportion of migrants (7 percent) than New York–born blacks boarded with private families. Two-thirds of these boarders were women who had arrived alone fewer than ten years before. Other black migrants, especially those in the upper age cohorts, established families of their own. Unlike many famine-era Irish, who arrived with their families intact, a majority of African American migrants came singly in the first three decades of the nineteenth century. They established families in New York on the ashes of the domestic disarray wrought by slavery—families with which they frequently found refuge in their old age. Catherine Anthony serves as a typical example. Seventy years old in 1855, she had migrated from Richmond forty years earlier and was found by the census taker to be living with an adult daughter born in New York, a son-in-law who worked as a porter and had migrated from Westchester, and two grandchildren aged four and five.[40] The largest proportion of African Americans born outside New York (41 percent) lived in extended families, like Anthony, with those from the Northeast most likely to find a home with relatives who had preceded them to the city. Yet a higher proportion of migrants (19 percent) than the black population in general lived in households headed by women living on their own or with children.

Migrants who married usually forged alliances with native New Yorkers or newcomers from elsewhere; interregional marriages, therefore, were quite common among African Americans. For instance, twenty-five-year-old Cuban-born Richard Alexander married a New Jersey woman and established a household that included a young son and his forty-year-old mother-in-law. Interestingly enough, in the households surveyed, interracial marriages were also more common among black migrants than among native-born New Yorkers. Irish women in particular entered black families not just as boarders but also as wives. To cite just one example, Rosanna Thompson, who had left Ireland at the age of twelve in 1843, was found in 1855 to be married to a thirty-year-old New Jersey laborer named William Thompson, who had lived in the city for the past five years.[41] Upper Southern men, outnumbering women from their region by three to two, were especially likely to marry local women or other migrants, with whom they generally formed nuclear families. Virginia-born Patrick Brown was typical. A sixty-six-year-old upholsterer who had arrived in New York thirty years before, Brown was recorded in 1855 as having established a household with fifty-year-old New York native Ann Brown.[42]

Thus, the resilience of family and communal impulses among African Americans appears to have survived the ravages of slavery. Overall, the 1855 census yields a collective portrait of black family support structures robust and flexible enough to adapt to the vicissitudes of working poor fortunes. The vulnerability of the community to poverty lay not in the disorganization of its family life, but rather in the progressive constriction of its economic, political, and civic freedoms. The occupational profile of the same one hundred households surveyed provides only one measure of the limited range of work options available to black New Yorkers, both male and female. Squeezed out of the skilled trades by hostile whites in the decades after emancipation, mid-century African Americans fought a losing battle with the newly arrived Irish on the menial rungs of the occupational ladder. The census listed the occupations of 86 of the 96 men and 35 of the 152 women above the age of sixteen in the sample of black households. African American workers, like all others of their day, were segregated by sex. Men labored as waiters, casual day laborers, seamen, peddlers, porters, cartmen, chimney sweeps, whitewashers, wood sawyers, upholsterers, butchers, barbers, and preachers. Women found work as seamstresses, laundresses, cooks, servants, and teachers.[43]

The occupational profiles of the sexes differed not only in terms of the kind of work they did, but also because far fewer women than men were recorded as being engaged in wage work at all (see table 17, in appendix). Indeed, over three-quarters of the women above the age of sixteen in the sample were listed without any occupation. Moreover, while three-quarters of the men whose occupations were recorded lived in nuclear or extended families, 68 percent of women who *were* listed as wage workers were single women—whether unmarried, widowed, or separated from their spouses—who lived with their children, took in boarders, or themselves boarded with private families. Married women in nuclear and even extended families emerged in the census as homemakers (whether by their own design or that of the census taker is hard to say). Historians have long noted that wage work carried a different meaning for black women, less than a generation away from slavery, than it did for middle-class white women. For freedwomen, independence consisted of working for their own families rather than performing wage work for whites. Domestic service, the chief professional option open to African American women, was hardly calculated to appeal to married women, because it required that they live with and serve their employers around the clock, leaving little time for their own families. Married women were more likely to contribute to the family wage economy by keeping boarders, selling corn on the streets, or taking an occasional washing assignment; they may not have thought fit to define any one particular kind of wage work for themselves. On the other hand, the underrepresentation of married women in the female occupations recorded in the census may have had something to do with the census taker's inclination to focus on male occupations in nuclear and extended families where men were present, rendering invisible the paid employment of their wives and mothers.

Of the women whose occupations were listed, the largest group—fifteen in number—consisted of laundresses. Washing was less subject to seasonal and business fluctuations than many other occupations. Nonetheless, it took a heavy toll on the health of its practitioners, especially at the height of winter. No wonder then that laundresses figured prominently in the sick rolls of relief organizations like the Colored Home. The next most numerous group consisted of ten women engaged in the needle trades. As has already been seen, seamstresses in the age of "metropolitan industrialization" faced poor and uncertain pay. It is safe to assume that, in the cutthroat world of outwork tailoring, African American women made even less than the average weekly wage of seventy-five cents to a dollar earned by white seamstresses. Moreover, they were the first to face unemployment or underemployment outside the peak seasons of October and April, when employers prepared to fill their winter and summer stock. Long-term health problems compounded the hazards endemic to the antebellum garment industry. The drudgery of crouching over needlework with necks craned in dimly lighted tenement rooms left many an impoverished tailor with bad eyes and a stooped posture. It was no wonder that Irish women spurned tailoring in favor of domestic service, if they could help it.[44]

Although domestic service employed more black women than any other occupation in the city, it ranked third among the eighth ward householders surveyed, in part because most servants lived with their employers in more prosperous wards. Moreover, the advent of Irish domestics had reduced the proportion of their black counterparts to only 3 percent of the city's servants. Black domestic servants in the eighth ward were frequently attached to brothels as cooks, laundresses, and maids. The relief needs of domestic servants clearly varied from, those of say, seamstresses. Poorly paid as many domestics were, they enjoyed the advantage of free board and lodging as well as relatively steady employment; their most pressing need related to child care. Black mothers in domestic service adopted a variety of strategies to care for children who could not live with them. Fosterage or boarding their young dependents with friends and family was one method. Moreover, as shall presently be seen, juvenile reformatories like the New York House of Refuge also served as temporary havens for black children who could not live with their mothers' employers.[45]

The 1855 census is significant not only for it what it reveals about the types of work open to black women, but also for the gaps that it leaves in their occupational profile. Unlisted occupations were not a feature of married women alone. Although single women dominated the ranks of female wage earners whose work was recorded in the census, they made up only 54 percent of *all single women* above the age of fifteen in the sample. In other words, 46 percent of women who lived on their own or with their dependents specified no wage work at all, suggesting the possibility of widespread unemployment among these black women. Such women would, of course, have been particularly susceptible to destitution and spells in relief institutions. It is also possible that a few of the women who claimed no wage work earned their keep as occasional prostitutes. According Marilyn Wood Hill, between 1850 and 1865 prostitution expanded greatly in the area west of Broadway, its theater shifting north toward Washington Square, from ward five to ward eight. The black householders surveyed lived in this geographical heart of the city's sex trade.

A variety of economic and personal crises may have driven black women to prostitution. Irish competition pushed them out of their traditional preserve—domestic service. Whitewashing, tailoring, and peddling offered abysmally low earnings and little stability or security. In addition to economic imperatives, however, a quest for autonomy from harsh parental discipline, or respite from marital problems, may have spurred younger women, especially teenagers, to exchange sex for money (at least once in a while). As shall be seen, the case histories of the New York House of Refuge suggest high levels of anxiety among some working poor black parents about their daughters' alleged penchant for "bad company." Prostitutes mingled freely with other elements of the working poor, sometimes sharing the same tenements and socializing with their friends and neighbors. The better-off worked out of parlor-house brothels and boardinghouses, which provided food and lodging to their inmates. Others were streetwalkers, leading their customers to assignation houses, which rented rooms for illicit sex by the hour. Theaters and dance halls also served as venues for recruiting suitors, both white and black. Mixed-blood Creoles—ostensibly Southern-born–were especially popular among gentlemen callers. Often better paid than women wage workers in the needle trades and domestic service, prostitutes had relief needs of a different kind: they drew on public resources for medical treatment of venereal diseases.[46]

The census provided a much fuller picture of black men's work worlds, recording the professions of nearly 90 percent of males above the age of fifteen in the sample. Over one-fifth of the men in the sample identified as having an occupation were employed as waiters—a breed that later astonished journalist James McCabe by the dispatch with which it served and disposed of wave upon wave of hungry customers thronging downtown restaurants during the lunch-hour rush. Waiters moved about swiftly, shouting out the orders of guests above the deafening din of clattering cutlery and slamming doors. It is likely that black waiters found work in the many catering establishments run by black entrepreneurs, such as Thomas Downing's Oyster Bar on Broad Street, as well as in the many hotels that flourished in the city. Indeed, it was a black man, William Hamilton of the Union Palace Hotel, who presided over the creation of the interracial Waiter's Protective Union Society in 1853.[47] Well over four-fifths of the waiters in the sample were in either nuclear or communal family arrangements. While those in nuclear family situations were generally older, and the primary breadwinners for their dependents, those who lived communally were more often than not younger men pooling their wages with a mother-in-law who washed for a living, a sister who worked in the needle trades, or an uncle who spent months at sea. A collective family economy provided some insurance against the seasonal and cyclical unemployment and underemployment in the limited number of low-wage jobs open to blacks.

After waiters, the two largest occupational groups among the black male householders surveyed consisted of laborers and seamen, each of which numbered sixteen. Casual laborers built foundations, dug wells, laid sewer lines, and hauled freight on the docks. On average, these workers made one dollar a day, whereas a family of four in 1853 needed to earn an annual income of six hundred dollars in order to survive. The market for menial labor was vulnerable not only to business and seasonal cycles, but also to bad weather. Unemployed laborers without savings to see them through the bleak months of winter had little recourse other than to seek public assistance. Their work, moreover, exacted a heavy toll in life and limb. As Tyler Anbinder had written, newspapers were filled with "reports of hod carriers falling from ladders, longshoremen crushed by falling cargo, and laborers buried by the collapsing walls of unfinished buildings." Such accidents left grievous injuries and destitute families in their wake—circumstances that drove their victims over the brink of self-sufficiency and into the ranks of pauperism. Of course, families that relied primarily on the wages of a casual laborer were especially vulnerable to destitution. Only 37 percent of the black laborers surveyed lived in extended families, sharing their expenses with a father who worked as a porter or a brother who sawed wood or swept chimneys. The rest—as heads of nuclear households, single fathers, or the barely adult sons of widowed mothers—shouldered the lion's share of the responsibility for their dependents' care—a responsibility that workplace accidents and the uncertainties of the casual labor market often made difficult to discharge.[48]

Seafaring, like construction and dock work, carried dangers of its own. To be sure, it was one of the few professions open to African Americans after the postwar shipping boom that lasted into the early nineteenth century. It had historically served as a channel to freedom and a vehicle for pan-African communications and identity formation. By making similar demands on black and white sailors, it had fostered an egalitarian maritime culture unknown on the shore. Over the course of the nineteenth century, however, seafaring became an increasingly precarious vocation for black men. As the rising tide of racism gradually restricted the opportunity to become career seamen, many African Americans turned to sporadic casual labor aloft whaling ships, infamous for their low wages, "faulty gear, frenzied whales, hurricanes, and endemic violence." The gathering storm of sectional crisis in the 1840s and 1850s injected fresh dangers into the black mariner's world. Southern states enacted laws that subjected allegedly subversive Northern sailors not only to quarantines in slave-state prisons, but to outright kidnapping as well. Periodic financial panics further eroded the livelihood of blackjacks, forcing an increasingly transient population of surplus maritime labor to seek other work in construction, blacking boots, and peddling.[49]

Thus, by the 1850s seafaring no longer offered black men the financial security that it had before. The historian William Bolster has written that the superintendent of the much-respected Colored Sailor's Home in New York described 13 percent of his boarders in 1843 as "true objects of charity." Besides poverty, seamen increasingly faced another circumstance that undermined the integrity of their family structures. Boardinghouse residency frequently became a prerequisite for securing a job at sea. Shipmasters relied on boardinghouse keepers to supply them with labor, giving such middlemen enormous leverage to force aspiring sailors—even those that were married—to forsake their homes for boardinghouses. Fifty percent of the seamen in my sample headed nuclear families. The prolonged absence from home of these primary wage earners would have spelled special hardships for their wives and children, who sometimes took in boarders to make ends meet. Sailors with motherless dependents or aged parents had to leave them in the care of public or private relief institutions. Even when sailors lived in extended families, a high degree of occupational clustering meant that a single family might send all its male breadwinners off to sea. Indeed, four of the five seamen who lived in communal family arrangements in my sample belonged to two families. Such clustering may have undercut the benefits of pooling wages by subjecting the families to the structural vicissitudes of the same occupation, presumably at the same time.[50]

Occupational diversity within a family offered some degree of security against the whimsies of working poor job markets. Among the eighth ward men sampled, peddling and marketing constituted the most common adjuncts to casual labor and seafaring, especially in extended families. Black peddlers represented an integral part of the urban scene. George Foster noted that no sooner did daylight break than urban vendors and rural hucksters arrived by cart and boat at the city's many marketplaces. There they skillfully rearranged "yesterday's withered remainder" with "the freshness of the morning's store." Before long, the air rang out with loud cries advertising an assortment of wares from curbside stands and market stalls. Ravenous morning commuters wolfed down pies and oysters, fruits and yam. Black women specialized in preparing and selling corn on the cob. For less-hungry passersby and their working-class neighbors, African American peddlers offered firewood, animal skins, and straw for bedding.[51]

Like peddlers, a majority of the porters, coachmen, cartmen, and chimney sweeps in the sample lived in communal family situations. Excluded by political patronage from carting for decades, African Americans were only just beginning to reenter this Irish-dominated trade in the 1850s with Mayor Fernando Wood's willingness to grant them carting licenses. Chimney sweeping, on the other hand, had long been a preserve of black males, especially the very young, who were small enough to climb through the large chimneys of their day. By the 1850s, German and Irish immigrants had displaced African Americans in a majority of the artisanal and building trades. Eight of the men in the sample who described themselves as upholsterers, wood sawyers, and whitewashers came closest to this occupational category. It is revealing that women outnumbered men among black "craft workers" and consisted entirely of underpaid seamstresses. While a majority of males in the "craft worker" category (63 percent) lived in nuclear families, an overwhelming proportion of their female counterparts (90 percent) lived *outside* that norm.[52]

Although black entrepreneurs made their mark in many food trades, they were not well represented among the impoverished households surveyed. Only two of the male householders claimed an affiliation with that remaining bastion of the artisan system—butchering.[53] Tammany controlled the Market Committee at City Hall, which regulated butcher's licenses, ensuring that Irish and German immigrants would prevail over blacks in this trade. The lone barber in the sample no doubt served an African American clientele; like the butchers, he headed a nuclear family.

A sample of 417 Irish men, women, and children living in one hundred sixth ward households suggests some interesting parallels as well as differences with working poor African Americans. The Irish population was generally younger, slightly less female, and more immigrant than its black counterpart (see tables 8–13, in appendix). Of all the householders sampled, 54 percent consisted of women and girls, nearly 74 percent were under thirty-one years of age, with only 10 percent over forty-six years old; 60 percent of those above the age of fifteen had arrived in New York in the ten years following the potato famine (hitherto referred to as "famine-era" immigrants). As Hasia Diner has noted, the lack of opportunity to marry or inherit land, especially in the rural regions of Munster and Connaught, fueled an exodus of young people to the New World after 1850. Two-thirds of Irish newcomers were between the ages of fifteen and thirty-five. My sample bears out these observations. In the young adult cohort, between ages of sixteen and thirty, 74 percent of the men and nearly

71 percent of the women had spent fewer than ten years in New York. By contrast, famine-era migrants were in the minority in the age groups below fifteen and over thirty years. Most children younger than fifteen years old had been born in America of Irish or Irish American parents, suggesting that a significant proportion of recent migrants—especially those who left Ireland after 1850—arrived as single people and established families in America.[54]

The workings of female kin networks, coupled with job opportunities for men in the West, feminized New York's Irish immigrant community. Yet, although females made up 54 percent of all householders in my sample, their proportion in different constituent groups within the population varied according to age and period of emigration to the city. In striking contrast with the African American population, which grew progressively female with age, Irish women predominated most heavily among famine-era immigrants in their late teens. Fully three-quarters of post-1845 arrivals from the Emerald Isle were women. Among Irish persons between the ages of twenty-one and twenty-five, on the other hand, men outnumbered women, constituting 55 percent of the cohort as a whole and 54 percent of famine-era emigrants. The sex ratio reversed itself again among those in their late twenties, with women making up 53 percent of the general population in the twenty-six-to-thirty age group and 50 percent of its famine-era component. The sex ratio remained more or less balanced among Irish New Yorkers over the age of thirty, with women accounting for just under 52 percent of this group.

The sex ratio, age profile, and immigrant experiences of the Irish contributed to family structures and living arrangements that diverged from their black counterparts in some respects. One difference concerned the relative proportions of women and children who lived in female-oriented households on the one hand, and in nuclear families on the other. Compared to the case with African Americans, female-headed extended families and households headed by single women with children and/or boarders claimed a lower proportion of all Irish households surveyed (14 percent); furthermore, only 7 percent of children under fifteen years of age lived in such situations. On the other hand, a greater proportion of Irish women and children lived in nuclear families. Forty-seven percent of all Irishwomen above the age of fifteen and 45 percent of those who arrived after 1845 lived in sixty-four nuclear families. A majority of all children below the age of fifteen—nearly 68 percent—also lived in these nuclear families. The experiences of Irishmen in this regard, on the other hand, diverged based on whether they had emigrated before or after the 1845 famine. Thus, while 53 percent of all Irishmen over fifteen years old belonged to nuclear households, only 42 percent of famine-era males did—a smaller proportion than that for comparable black men.

The marriage rate among the Irish corresponded more closely to the percentage of all Irish individuals living in nuclear families than was the case with African Americans (see table 15, in appendix). In this context, it is interesting to note that although a greater proportion of Irish women than black women were married, the proportion of Irishwomen who had *never* married was also slightly greater. Nearly 52 percent of all Irishwomen above the age of fifteen were married. They had greater opportunities to marry than their black sisters did, however, in part because the sex ratio of the Irish population was more balanced than that of African Americans. Moreover, Irishwomen married outside their community, forging alliances with native-born Americans, usually white, but occasionally black as well (in addition to men from other immigrant groups). Black women, by contrast, rarely married men outside the "race" community. In light of the options for marriage available to Irishwomen, what is striking about those sampled is the large number who apparently chose either to marry late in life or *not* to marry at all. Irishmen were even more likely than the women to stay single. That both sexes married late is suggested by that fact that in the sixteen-to-thirty age group, less than a third of the women, and under a quarter of the men, were married. About 14 percent of all women over fifteen years of age were widowed, leaving nearly 35 percent who had never been married. Among Irishmen, the rate of bachelorhood was even higher—38 percent of men over fifteen were unmarried. The lessons of the famine encouraged the Irish to adopt a cautious approach to marriage. Economic security weighed more heavily than romantic considerations in governing the decision to marry.

Another difference between black and Irish household structures emerged in the relative importance of "communal households" to each group. Communal families grounded in family ties claimed a far smaller proportion of the Irish individuals sampled than their black brethren: only 23 percent of all Irishmen and 26 percent of all Irishwomen over fifteen years of age in the sample sported these arrangements. These proportions were even lower among famine-era migrants—approximately 19 percent for women and 22 percent for men. A little over a fifth of all children below the age of fifteen lived in communal households. It is necessary to add the caveat that the Irish entered into "roommate" arrangements with other tenants more frequently than blacks did, yet they were undoubtedly more detached from extended kin networks than African Americans. The circumstances of Irish immigration to the United States, and the experiences of the newcomers upon arrival, may help explain this phenomenon. Many nubile women and men, pushed out by the dearth of marriage and employment opportunities in Ireland's agricultural districts, arrived in New York on their own. Many failed to establish contact with their relatives in the city—if they had any—because the poor moved from one residence to another so frequently. Accustomed to the localism and easy familiarity of much smaller, rural spaces, newcomers in search of their kin or friends sometimes floundered in the vast, impersonal confusion of urban America. The historian Hasia Diner has cited the instance of a young Irish woman who thought she could find her aunt who lived "somewhere near Boston" by making enquiries at "the chemists."[55]

For whatever reason, recent immigrants frequently lived autonomously, outside nuclear or extended family arrangements. The high proportion of boarders and lodgers among post-1845 emigrants reflected this trend (see table 11, in appendix). Nearly a third of all famine-era males over fifteen years of age in the sample, and a fifth of the women, boarded or lodged with private families or in boardinghouses, making up over 86 percent of all Irish boarders in the sample. The nature and meaning of boarding among the Irish constituted yet another difference with African Americans. The absence of infants among Irish boarders, and the fact that close to half of all Irish boarders in the sample (all of them post-1845 immigrants) were between the ages of twenty and twenty-five, suggests that the Irish may have conformed more closely than African Americans to Scherzer's notion of the subculture of boarding. For young immigrants bereft of family support, boarding offered not simply inexpensive accommodation and meals, but also the camaraderie of fellow immigrants and the warmth of "quasi-familial" ties without obliging the boarders to shoulder marital responsibilities. Institutional boarding provided its residents with a greater degree of freedom than private homes did: they were large and more impersonal, with mealtimes less closely tied to the routine of the host family. For Irish singles of lean means, loosened from the restraints of parental authority and wary of marriage, boarding may indeed have appeared attractive not simply as a low-cost housing option, but also for the personal independence it afforded.[56]

Unlike African American boarders, among whom women predominated, 60 percent of famine-era Irish boarders were men. The lower representation of Irishwomen among the boarders in the sample may have had something to do with the fact that they had the option to live with their employers in domestic service. Servants boarding with their employers made up only a small proportion of the Irish sixth ward householders surveyed (approximately 4 percent), no doubt because a majority of such women were likely to live in middle-class households in the city's better-off wards. Live-in servants in the sixth ward frequently worked in boardinghouses or in the homes of native-born or German artisans.

Not surprisingly, the Irish population surveyed presented a more diverse occupational profile than its black counterpart (see table 18, in appendix). The census listed the occupations of 88 percent of all men over the age of fifteen years in the sample—115 in all. These men held a variety of jobs as laborers and "bastardized" artisans, sailors and stewards, peddlers and porters, cartmen and coachmen, waiters and butlers, grocers and butchers, plumbers and policemen, lenders and speculators, clerks and even a doctor. A minority of these positions held out prospects for social mobility. The police force, like the fire department, paved many an Irishman's path to a career in politics. The growth of mercantile firms spawned a profusion of clerks, bookkeepers, copiers, and errand boys, a few of whom might rise to become merchants in their own right. Notwithstanding the presence of a few of these "white-collar" workers, the largest number of working men in my plebeian sample filled poorly paid jobs in the lowest echelons of the industrial and service sectors. The census defined the greatest proportion—over one-third of the total—as generic "laborers." As noted before, the unskilled laborer faced a hard lot in surplus labor market—low wages, industrial accidents, seasonal and cyclical unemployment and underemployment, and competition from his neighbors displaced from other lines of work, like seafaring and artisanship. Over half the laborers lived in nuclear families of which they were the primary breadwinners, so that any loss of work, limb, or life on their part was likely to subject their families to great hardship.[57]

The next most numerous group of male wage earners consisted of thirty-five workers in what Sean Wilentz describes as the "debased crafts." Tailors, shoemakers, and cabinetmakers led this group. A smaller proportion held jobs in the printing and building trades. All these consumer finishing and construction trades suffered the ravages of outwork and "sweating" to a lesser or greater extent. For instance, in shoemaking (as in tailoring), a few skilled cutting jobs were concentrated in custom shops and ladies' shoe shops, while the more menial, monotonous, and repetitive chores were subcontracted out to an army of ill-paid crimpers, fitters, and bottomers. In printing, too, the new technology of steam presses facilitated the division of labor and transformed some print shops into sweatshops for unskilled chores. The building trades, on the other hand, paid better: the bull market in construction in the 1840s created openings for Irish building contractors. The lumberyards, stone yards, and coal yards they established hired carpenters, masons, plasterers, bricklayers, stonecutters, and glaziers who built not only public edifices and private mansions, but also the Croton Aqueduct High Bridge and the Hudson River Railroad, reaching deep into the Bronx; transformed Brooklyn's Red Hook marshlands into docks; and laid down the arteries of turnpikes in Queens. Yet even in the building trades, subdivided tasks on construction projects could be farmed out to contractors and were subject to all the abuses that stemmed from such arrangements. On the whole, the plebeian sixth ward men in the sample filled the least skilled positions in the artisan and building trades. Predominantly nuclear family heads or boarders, they shouldered the major responsibility for their own or their families' upkeep. Cost cutting, bred by bidding wars among contractors, and seasonal and cyclical downswings in the demand for their labor, could plunge them into the depths of destitution more readily than some critics of "able-bodied" paupers were willing to acknowledge.

Women straddled an even finer line between self-sufficiency and dependence; they presented an occupational portrait closer to their black sisters than Irishmen did. As in the case of African Americans, the census listed the occupations of a minority of Irish women in the sample. Forty-two women representing 27 percent of 153 female householders over the age of fifteen were recorded as having wage work of some kind. Nearly three-quarters of them were single, living either in their own households with children or as boarders with private families or institutions. As was the case with African Americans, married women living in nuclear families were underrepresented among wage earners documented by the census taker, who no doubt saw such women as homemakers. It may be that Irishwomen tended to forsake wage work after marriage. Yet given that over one-quarter of all Irish-headed nuclear families in the sample took in boarders, it is clear that the wives and mothers who ran these households made a substantial economic contribution to their family wage economies.

Not surprisingly, domestic servants made up the largest wage-earning occupational group (57 percent). Domestic service conferred certain advantages that made it a more attractive profession to single Irish women than the needle trades. As has been noted before, it was relatively immune to reverses in business cycles and provided board and lodging so that the women could save most of their wages and even send some back to their families in Ireland. Yet, however favorable these living circumstances, domestic service was hard work. The paraphernalia of genteel Victorian homes called for endless rounds of cleaning, polishing, cooking, and serving. Moreover, the summer months, when wealthy New Yorkers retreated to the country, left many servants without jobs. It is revealing that 92 percent of Irish domestic servants in the sample were described as "boarders" not living with their employers in June 1855 when the census was taken. It is quite possible that the advent of summer had deprived these women of their jobs, and with it their free board and lodging.[58]

While single Irishwomen without children preferred domestic service, those who lived in nuclear and extended families, or headed households with children, preferred craft work. They constituted the second largest occupational category in the sample—38 percent of the total. A majority of these dressmakers, hatmakers, and umbrella makers (56 percent) lived with families and dependents rather than on their own as boarders. As outworkers who labored at piece rates at home either on their own or as adjuncts to their husbands, they were able to combine their domestic and child care chores with wage work. Yet the precarious nature of their work posed an ever-present threat to the integrity of their livelihoods. A minority of women with dependents took in laundry. Thus the working worlds of poor Irishwomen shared more parallels with their African American counterparts than did those of Irishmen. In contrast with the diversity of occupations evident among Irishmen, Irishwomen faced the same limited options as their black sisters. Yet despite the relative variety of their occupational profile, the largest proportion of impoverished Irishmen engaged in casual labor, just as many black men did. In the end, *because* the kinds of work African Americans and the Irish did were so similar, the Irish progressively displaced African Americans from traditionally black preserves like domestic service, exacerbating the economic challenges faced by the black community.

The census was generally silent on a significant aspect of working poor family economies—children's uses of the streets. It mentioned an occasional newsboy but failed to record a phenomenon that distressed many reformers—the ubiquity of street "urchins" rummaging through garbage, scavenging for coal, scrap iron, wood, and rags to sell to junk shops. Boys blacked boots and sold newspapers. Girls peddled an assortment of goodies, from cakes and fruit to hot corn at street corners, and swept street crossings in exchange for a few pennies from passersby. Occasionally these children of the "dangerous classes," as the reformer Charles Loring Brace called them, crossed the limits of acceptable huckstering to pick pockets, pilfer articles from storefronts or the hallways of private residences, and exchange sex for money in the city's red-light districts. The high visibility of the juvenile street trades they plied, in flagrant defiance of the proper role of children as prescribed by genteel sorts, dramatized the problem of "pauperism" and its implications for the future of the white republic.[59] No wonder then, that these allegedly miserable specimens of future voters, together with the parents who "spawned" them, were to occupy center stage in energetic debates over the direction of relief and reform in antebellum New York.

2

The White Republic and "Workfare"
Blackwell's Island

> These men [the poor of Europe], embittered not only by their own sufferings, but by the traditions of the past, when they come to this country are easily roused to commit acts of violence by anything that reminds them of their old oppressions. They have tasted the wormwood and the gall, and refuse to have it pressed to their lips in a country where liberty is the birthright of all. This is what has made, and still makes, the foreign population among us so dangerous.
> —Joel Tyler Headley, *Great Riots of New York*

Like many of his Whig-Republican contemporaries, Joel Tyler Headley, sometime–associate editor of the abolitionist *New York Tribune*, doubted that the most dreadful flour riot of his early adult years would have happened at all had it not been for the demagoguery of vote-grubbing politicians and their allies in the Democratic media. The year was 1837, a trying time for New Yorkers of all stripes, but particularly so for laboring men and women. In the course of the past three years, their city had weathered a cholera epidemic that took a few thousand lives, plus a great fire that ravaged downtown Manhattan's commercial district, grinding business—and with it, the livelihoods of hundreds of workers—to a halt. Then in 1836, even as a speculative frenzy—fueled largely by the influx of European capital in American lands, canals, and railroads—peaked, sending commodity prices soaring and building projects humming, wheat crops failed thanks to the depredations of the Hessian fly. The bitter winter that year brought with it an alarming rise in flour prices—twelve dollars a bushel, up from seven in the early fall. From the wheat granaries of

Virginia came word that further price increases—up to fifteen or twenty dollars a barrel—were in the offing. Amid rumors that the city had in stock no more than three or four weeks' supply, the penny papers of the day pointed fingers at the Washington Street commission merchants Hart and Co. These businessmen were said to be hoarding vast amounts of grain and flour, keeping them out of the market in order to compel even higher price increases. In an account of the flour riot published in 1873, Headley wrote that through the early winter weeks of 1837, faced with inflationary pressures on the prices of other necessities like meat and coal, working men gathered in knots outside Hart and Co., "muttering threats and curses."[1]

Then in the afternoon of February 10 came a clarion call for mass action, inscribed on placards posted throughout the city. "bread, meat, rent, fuel! *The voice of the people shall he heard and will prevail,*" proclaimed the signs. They invited "all friends of humanity, determined to resist monopolists and extortioners," to attend a meeting three days later at City Hall Park. The architects of the protest belonged to the Equal Rights or Locofoco Party, a radical antimonopoly wing of the Democratic Party. According to Headley, the Sunday before the meeting, idle crowds gathered before the placards, "some spelling out slowly, and with great difficulty, the words for themselves—others reading the call to those unable to read it." Excited men interspersed "their oaths with copious drought of liquor, . . . threatening openly to teach these rich oppressors a lesson they would not soon forget." On the appointed day, five thousand people assembled in front of City Hall and shivered through speeches by Locofoco leaders, including Alexander Ming Jr. He "forgot all about the object of the meeting," however, and launched instead into a harangue against soft money, urging his listeners to take only specie. To Headley, Ming's speech was "the more comical, as not one out of ten of the poor wretches he addressed had the chance to refuse either. Half starving, they would have been glad to receive anything in the shape of money that would help them through the hard winter." Yet when Ming offered a resolution demanding hard money, "The deluded people, who had been listening with gaping mouths, rent the air with acclamations. It was a curious exhibition of the wisdom of the sovereign people—this verdict of a ragged mob on the currency question. They were so delighted with this lucid exposition of the cause of the scarcity of flour, that they seized the orator bodily, and elevating him on their shoulders, bore him across the street to Tammany Hall, where something beside specie was received from behind the bar to reward their devotion." From Ming's perspective, it was perfectly logical to make a connection between the inflation of food prices and the issue of bank notes. To Headley, however, the whole exercise at the park that cold February afternoon epitomized the problem of political demagoguery nourished by the enfranchisement of witless foreign dupes.[2]

We are told that other speakers at the February 10 event castigated landlords for charging high rents and monopolists for keeping flour from hungry families, all to the accompaniment of "loud oaths and deep muttered curses." The final speaker closed with an incendiary summons to action: "Fellow-citizens, Mr. Eli Hart has now 53,000 barrels of flour in his store; let us go and offer him eight dollars a barrel for it." Upon hearing this, his listeners streamed down Broadway and passed through Courtland into Washington Street. They stormed the brick edifice of the Hart flour warehouse just as the clerks inside had finished bolting two of the three iron doors opening on the sidewalk. Before the melee ended, the rioters had trashed the counting room and seized numerous barrels of flour all over the store, pitching them out into the street, yelling in one instance, "*Here goes flour at eight dollars a barrel!*" The mayor, who arrived to plead with the crowd to desist, was showered with brickbats, sticks, and pieces of ice. Hours later, under a clear moonlit sky, the rioters—some in rags, others with their aprons hitched up "like sacks"—roamed the street, which looked as though it had been blanketed in white by a sudden snowstorm. They "knelt amid the flour, and scooped it up" eagerly as barrels continued to hit the sidewalk with loud thuds. Order was finally restored by a heavy force of police reinforced by detachments of the National Guard brandishing muskets, but not before the crowd had assaulted other flour stores in the city. Headley concluded, "It was certainly a very original way to bring down the price, by attempting to destroy all there was in the city . . . With little to eat, [the rioters] attempted to make it impossible to eat at all. A better illustration of the insensate character of a mob could not be given." Other critics concurred, shaking their heads over the perverse populists who had thus misled the "pillaging canaille, the colored people, thieves and Irish."[3]

The Problem of Poverty in Republican Society

Both the flour riot and Headley's representation of it offer insights into bourgeois anxieties over the problems of poverty, immigration, and republican government in Victorian New York. The rendition of the flour riot of 1837 by Headley and other critics evoked the disturbing spectacle of an irrational, interracial coalition of paupers and criminals, ignorant of the workings of the marketplace, unleashing class warfare against hapless landlords and merchants. In Headley's narrative, the political instigation of the "mob" by the manipulative Locofocos underscored the readiness with which democracy was liable to sink into anarchy when unsuitable alien-turned-citizens held the power of the ballot. These concerns would seep into a discourse of "pauperism" and reform that approached a crescendo as social tensions, evident at the dawn of 1837, mounted in the months that followed. Although critics of the flour riot paired "the colored people" and the "Irish" as fellow plunderers and class warriors against their betters, a majority of reformers would come to make distinctions that embodied very different public visions of the destinies of the two groups in New York society.

The year 1837 took a turn for the worse as the financial panic settled in to a prolonged depression. European bankers—whose heavy investments in American land, businesses, and infrastructure had triggered the speculative mania of recent years—helped turn the boom into a bust by recalling their loans. This precipitated the collapse of interlocking financial and mercantile interests in America that reached from New Orleans cotton factors and country retailers up to Wall Street financiers, commission houses, and dry goods jobbers. Between 1837 and 1843, sector after sector of New York's economy succumbed to the panic—the stock market, the building trades, the construction of railroads and canals, and manufacturing—decimating the livelihoods of thousands of working people. Even as the unemployed rallied to demand a public works program, and as private soup kitchens proliferated to serve the destitute, an assemblage of the city's elites (consisting of wealthy industrialists, bankers, and merchants) launched a campaign to "rationalize" the dispensation of relief. The institution that they founded—the Association for Improving the Condition of the Poor (AICP)—brought together important threads of poor-relief thought going back to early republican New York. Rooted in Enlightenment rationalism, evangelical revivalism, and American exceptionalism, such thought had redefined the poverty problem in the years between the American Revolution and the depression of 1837.[4]

As we have seen, the spectacular creation and display of wealth and high culture in early nineteenth-century New York threw into sharp relief the increasingly populous "underground" world of poverty, portrayed with sensationalist flair by a succession of reporters, reformers, and government officials throughout the antebellum era. The seemingly fearful realms of New York's "dangerous classes," defined by "the festivities of prostitution, the orgies of pauperism, the haunts of theft and murder, the scenes of drunkenness and beastly debauch" within sight of magnificent Broadway, became more visible than ever during an earlier financial panic—that of 1819. The municipal Alms House—removed as recently as 1816 to a magnificent new twenty-six-acre site at Bellevue by the bank of the East River on the northern periphery of the city—quickly filled to capacity. Expenditures for outdoor relief—the grant of food, fuel, and money to the needy at home—soared, as New York City earned the dubious distinction of ranking first "in the scale of pauperism" of all counties in the state by 1822. Recurrent economic crises and rising relief expenditures exacerbated social tensions generated by a new plebeian "culture of conflict" on the streets and in the workplace. Historian Paul A. Gilje has argued that changes in labor relations under the impact of commercialization renewed workingmen's commitment to a "form of plebian [sic] street life which emphasized drinking, carousing, and general rowdyism." Although this culture of "disorderly conduct" apparently represented an extension of traditional notions of time, work and play, the rising entrepreneurial bourgeoisie—attached to the values of order, sobriety, and industry—regarded it as deviant behavior that needed to be regulated or outlawed.[5]

It was in this context of economic change and cultural strife that respectable New Yorkers revised premodern conceptions of poverty. In an emerging free market society obsessed with, yet troubled by, material progress, indigence was no longer regarded as divinely ordained; rather, it was a product of individual character failings and therefore eradicable. The Enlightenment faith in human reason, coupled with the advent of a wave of religious revivalism associated with the Second Great Awakening, buttressed this confidence in the possibility of redeeming the poor. The evangelical revivals moved away from Calvinist ideas of original sin and emphasized instead the notion of free will and the perfectibility of every individual in preparation for the millennial coming of Christ. The domestic missions they inspired developed into a multipronged "benevolent empire" that sought to bring religion to the profane; reform prostitutes; end drinking, gambling, and dancing; and minister to the material needs of the poor. The formation of the Society for the Prevention of Pauperism (SPP) in 1817 by business and religious elites reflected this connection between Christian benevolence and public policy. Led by such respected public figures as the Quaker chemist John Griscom and Thomas Eddy, a former warden of Newgate Prison well connected with British reformers, the SPP blamed the paradox of poverty amid plenty on the vices of the urban poor: "Imprudent and hasty marriages, ignorance, idleness, intemperance, thriftlessness, gambling and promiscuous sex." The prevention of poverty had important implications for the health of the republic. In a polity where the people—no matter how poor—were politically sovereign, the social conflict and public disorder stemming from vast inequalities in material conditions were apt to foster the ascendancy of radical demagogues bent on redistributing wealth.[6]

The redefinition of poverty as a moral problem was accompanied by the vigorous resurgence of moral categories among the poor. Helpless victims of misfortune, such as widows, children, the elderly, and the handicapped, were deemed worthy of relief. Able-bodied recipients of public assistance, on the other hand, were thought to have brought their condition of pauperism on themselves through idle and dissolute behavior. Reformers argued that to provide outdoor relief to these unworthy social parasites would both perpetuate the pathology of dependence and erode the work ethic necessary to succeed in an increasingly individualistic and competitive capitalist society. One analysis of the problem addressed to the New York State Assembly in 1820 attributed the alarming increase in pauperism not to any rise in living costs, but rather to "idleness and dissipation." New York Secretary of State John V. N. Yates underscored this point further in a statewide report on the condition of poor relief that he submitted to the legislature in 1824. Indeed, some free market advocates argued that any kind of "home relief"—whether disbursed by the government or private agencies—would stifle both the incentive of employers to maintain subsistence wages and the will of workers to leave surplus labor markets.[7]

The solution to the "moral" crisis of pauperism lay, instead, in institutionalizing the destitute in specialized institutions like alms houses and poorhouses, orphanages and insane asylums, juvenile reformatories and women's halfway houses. In these institutions they would be "saved from mendacity," as SPP member James W. Gerard put it, through training in thrift, hard work, orderliness, cleanliness, and temperance—and, for women, chastity and domesticity as well. For instance, the Yates report recommended that each county in the state of New York establish at least one house of employment attached to a farm in order to engage paupers "in some beautiful labor" and subject their children to "careful" instruction. At the same time, Yates wanted "sturdy beggars" and vagrants to be dispatched to a work house where a regimen of "rigid diet" and "hard labor would restrain their "vicious appetites and pursuits."[8] Thus, reformers argued, poverty could be alleviated through a combination of reform and punishment aimed at transforming the character and lives of the poor as both individuals and families by inculcating in them the cultural attributes necessary to succeed in a free market economy. In a maturing industrial order where wage labor was becoming the norm and radicals from Fanny Wright adherents to the burgeoning trade unions demanded economic justice, the reform agenda envisioned by evangelical industrialists sought to create individualistic, disciplined workers who believed in market-driven social mobility. In turn, working people's capacity to earn their own bread—linked closely with their adherence to Christian piety—was essential to the successful exercise of republican citizenship. It would both confer on men the self-sufficiency they needed in order to vote responsibly and equip their wives with the feminine virtue and skills required to rear worthy sons to secure the future of the republic.

The view that pauperism, as it afflicted the able-bodied, was a "great social disease" rooted not so much in the lack of employment opportunities but a "natural repugnance" to hard work gained a new lease of life amid the hard times brought by the economic downturn of 1837–43. The AICP, established in 1843 as a secular offshoot of the New York City Tract Society by mostly Whig philanthropists drawn from the business community, attributed the explosion in pauperism to society's encouragement of improvidence and idleness through the lavish "dispensation of relief." The Association based this judgment on the proliferation of soup kitchens for the needy, as well as better-off citizens' allegedly indiscriminate almsgiving during the recent depression. It created a centralized system of private "scientific" charity in which a volunteer visitor was dispatched to each ward to investigate applications for aid, weed out the worthy poor from the unworthy, and send them to appropriate public agencies governed by the Alms House Department and the Emigration Commissioners. Visitors would not only help deserving parties with just enough food, clothing, and fuel for subsistence, but would also counsel them in the habits of economy (such as lessons in making four gallons of soup for twenty-two cents) so as to transform them into "self-reliant, responsible citizens." Moral regeneration remained central to the AICP's reform agenda. The group's ideological debt to the early-republican SPP was underscored by the presence among its leaders of the sanitary reformer Dr. John H.

Griscom, the son of SPP founder John Griscom. The leading light of the Association was its executive secretary, Robert H. Hartley, a Presbyterian merchant and public health advocate. Hartley hoped to harness the power of government in his project of rehabilitating habitual paupers through work; he submitted to municipal authorities a plan to confine "vagrant and disorderly persons" in a house of employment and reform on Blackwell's Island in the East River. Leaders of both parties—Democratic and Whig—proved receptive to Hartley's vision. By the mid-1840s, pauperism had not only assumed an intransigent cast, but also had come to be associated with an alien invasion that threatened to subvert the very foundations of the nation's political institutions.[9]

The Racial Typology of "Pauperism": Immigration and Citizenship in the White Republic

The republican assumption that the rehabilitation of "paupers" would qualify them for responsible self-government was inherently racialized, because it assumed the undifferentiated "whiteness" of its candidates for reform. *Implicitly*, if not explicitly, it excluded from its purview the masses of African Americans; already disfranchised and shut out of several professions, they had little hope for either economic mobility or republican citizenship. The surge of Irish immigration in the 1840s and the 1850s severely tested the tacit racial assumptions of poor-relief thought. As Matthew Frye Jacobson has shown, before the 1840s whiteness was characterized by "its powerful and cultural contrast to nonwhiteness," especially in the context of national debates over slavery and Indian removal. The advent of the famine-ravaged Irish, however, challenged the notion of a monolithic white "race." A variety of discourses—from science through literature, journalism, and the arts to politics—established a hierarchy of distinct, indeed separate, white "races," with the Anglo-Saxons at the top and the Celtic Irish at the very bottom. Not surprisingly, this development went hand in hand with the overt racialization of pauperism, because New York's pauper population drew so overwhelmingly from the Irish newcomers. Nativist commentators and some Whig reformers assigned to the Irish a set of allegedly inherent physical and behavioral traits that defined prevailing cultural constructs of the larger problem of dependency.[10]

The imagery of blackness permeated descriptions of "Irishness," nowhere more graphically than in the context of sensationalist contemporary exposés of pauperism. The supposedly *natural* propensity of the Irish for public dependency was linked to a physiognomy that the white American mind commonly associated with the black African, signifying unfitness for freedom. The foolish, drunken Pat shared the "simian" features of the happy-go-lucky, simpleton Jim Crow—the same "brutish," "low-browed" facial type and the "black tint of the skin." The Whig diarist George Templeton Strong was struck by the "prehensile paws" of Irish workers laboring on a cellar for his home. Above all, the Celts were thought to possess an attribute that had defined English constructions of the "Negro" since the sixteenth century—namely, lasciviousness.[11]

Lust—sexual excess—violated the most fundamental values of the bourgeoisie. When practiced by women, it ran counter to the notion of feminine virtue that constituted the bedrock of the middle-class family in the nineteenth century. When indulged by men, it signified a lack of internalized self-discipline, which was so important to successful wage work in the industrial economy, and hence fundamental to the exercise of responsible republican citizenship. A New York State Senate document on statewide poor relief in 1855 included a letter from one "Franklin" to the New York secretary of state citing "licentiousness" as a major source of pauperism. The correspondent claimed that itinerant vendors who frequented steamboats and railroad cars had approached him. "When I refused to purchase," he went on, "the seller has, in five different instances, turned up the corner of a leaf and exhibited an obscene picture as an inducement to buy, with an assurance that there was more of the same sort in the volume." Such vulgarity was bound to exercise "a most pernicious influence on the community." Underclass lust was most conspicuously dramatized by the open display of interracial promiscuity between blacks and the Irish in the dance halls, taverns, and theaters of the city's most notorious slum, defying the white republic's bipolar organization into "whiteness and its Others." Pauperism seemed to breed a culture of racial "amalgamation" fed by a lasciviousness that quite literally lent the subalterns' world a dark hue.[12]

Five Points, that most infamous habitat of all kinds of vice, and the closest thing the city had to an Irish "ghetto," epitomized sexual depravity. As early as the 1820s and 1830s, the neighborhood received frequent notice in some business publications like the *Journal of Commerce*, Whig party organs like the conservative *Courier and Enquirer*, and widely read penny papers like the *New York Sun*. Perhaps the most interesting aspect of these lurid reports of tenement lives and loves was that they juxtaposed their discussions of appalling material deprivation, disease, lack of hygiene, and crime with their suggestion of the widespread practice of interracial sex in the slum. To be sure, these reports devoted much space to documenting the Five Pointers' violation of bourgeois configurations of space and the sanctity of the private family. Yet it was their vivid sketches of the promiscuous mixing of black bodies and white bodies that gave these exposés more than an ordinary flavor of sensationalism; these descriptions metaphorically pitted the evils of pauperism and vice against both the conventions of civilized society and the racial logic of the white republic. A piece that appeared in the *Sun*, for instance, described "white women and black and yellow men, and black and yellow women, with white men, all in a state of gross intoxication, and exhibiting indecencies revolting to virtue and humanity," intermingling in the interior of a Five Points apartment, "with scarcely anything to hide their nakedness."[13] The imagery of sexual depravity conveyed by the frequent use of words like "nakedness"—even when employed in the context of the slum dwellers' inability to afford decent clothing—established a clear link between turpitude and material want.

Prostitution offered the clearest symbol of the allegedly noxious nexus among blackness, sex, pauperism, and vice. The reporter from the *Sun* described Cowbay, a notorious neighborhood on Little Water Street, north of Anthony, as "the resort and residence of white, black, and mulatto prostitutes, and the bullies and blackguards who keep and visit them," and as the seat of "vice, hotbeds of debauchery, wretchedness, and poverty, such as few eyes have witnessed."[14] The neighborhood's dimly lighted, smoke-filled dance halls served as the stomping grounds of these sex traders and presented the most public spectacle of interracial mating to visitors who watched with fascinated revulsion. In his impressionistic sketch of New York City published in the mid-nineteenth century, the reporter George Foster depicted one such Cowbay dance floor in language shot through with the imagery of bestial lust and racial transgression. It featured black and white dancers gyrating in frenzied motions to music played by a "negro fiddler, mounted on a barrel in one corner." The two black women were partnered by a pair of "shiny buck negroes," and the white women by "a couple of drunken sailors." The women were scantily clothed, "one of the negresses being merely in her chemise, and one of the white women absolutely stark naked." Foster attributed their state of undress to the fact that they had been "aroused in a drunken hurry" from the bunks that lined the room "to partake of this mid-night orgy"; they had "evidently found the process of dressing altogether too slow for the occasion." As for the men, their racial identities merged in the frantic frolic in which they were locked: "They are furious with the excitement of the dance, and whirl intertwined about in such swift evolutions that it is almost impossible to distinguish one from the other." The dancers grew "more animated" by the moment until "one of the negroes trips, either accidentally or by design, and falling, the whole party tumble over him in a heap, and roll indiscriminately upon the floor, amid such yells, screams and laughter as would mock the saturnalia of hell."[15] Foster's allusion to noise and nakedness, to indecorum and profligacy, and his use of words like "orgy" and "saturnalia," described the standard vices that characterized underclass Otherness in the bourgeois mind. What made his portrait especially unsettling, however, was its suggestion of the indeterminacy of whiteness in the city's most impoverished haunts. In what was perhaps a metaphor for the awfulness of "amalgamation," the dance Foster described climaxed with the coalescence of black bodies and white bodies into an indistinguishable heap of vice-ridden humans.

Animal metaphors underscored the Otherness of the mostly Irish "dangerous classes" in the same way that they were used by some to signify the Otherness of African Americans or American Indians. Tenements were frequently likened to pigsties. A senate report on the poor described the scene inside a hovel that followed when a youthful pauper came in with a bag slung over his shoulder, which he immediately emptied onto a filthy floor: "The bag contained bones with a little meat adhering to them, yet the children seized upon them as though they were the most delicious morsels, and gnawed them as ravenously as though they had been a pack of wolves." The narrator of this portrait concluded that these children, "tainted with scrofula ... and brutal ignorance," were likely to grow up to be unfit for labor.[16]

Likewise, Foster compared the lifestyle of white prostitutes who indiscriminately embraced a medley of undesirable customers—"sailors, loafers, green-horns, negroes"—to the "habits ... of swine"; their "licentious wills and loves" had "made them beasts in this life."[17] The reporter's representation of interracial merrymaking at the Orange Street dance hall of black saloon keeper Pete Williams—made famous by the attention it attracted from Charles Dickens—evoked the same sense of subhuman transgression. Foster wrote that three-quarters of the women who frequented that establishment were "negresses, of various shades and colors." He went on to add that they were "less horribly disgusting" than their white "companions"—a set of "bleary-eyed, idiotic, beastly wretches." As the orchestra struck its first note, each such "gentleman" at the bar "now 'drawrs' his 'chawr' of tobacco, and depositing it carefully in his trowsers pocket, flings his arms about his buxom inamorata and salutes her whiskey-breathing lips with a chaste kiss, which extracts a scream of delight from the delicate creature, *something between the whoop of an Indian and the neighing of a horse*."[18] This passage is notable for the association it makes between the various Others of incontrovertible "whiteness": Irishmen cavorting with Negro women, who in response emit sounds that represent an amalgam of domesticated beast and "savage" man.

The racialized imagery of Irish debauchery and dependence, fortified by reports of the high proportion of immigrants among the city's Alms House and prison populations, provoked a great deal of anxiety in some quarters not only about rising pressures on the public treasury, but also over the hazards of the foreign vote. Down the ages, the poor-relief statute of 1788 and its successors had proved remarkably ineffective: shipmasters were required to report the names and occupations of all passengers aboard vessels under their command, and to post a bond for each foreign passenger to indemnify the government in case such a person should become a public charge. In 1819 the Society for the Prevention of Pauperism cited the immigration of Europe's "surplus population" as a leading source of social malaise. It was, however, the depression era of 1837–43—followed by an immigration boom—that resuscitated a formal politics of nativism. The nativist movement culminated in calls for immigration restriction and sought to extend the length of time required for naturalization and officeholding, based on the assumption that many immigrants—especially the Irish—were unwilling to undertake "that ceaseless unrequited toil of liberty."[19]

Partisan politics inevitably fueled the dynamics of this discourse. The city's Democratic Tammany machine had wooed foreign-born voters since the enactment of white manhood suffrage in the 1820s by disbursing food, fuel, patronage, money, jobs, and influence through ward bosses, saloon keepers, policemen, and fire companies drawn from the immigrant communities themselves. The Whigs, with their emphasis on cultural uniformity, suspicion of "popery," support of temperance and public schools, and elitist image, attracted few Irish Catholics; in 1837 the party supported the nativist Aaron Clark for mayor. In the first half of the 1840s, Whigs and nativists, under the banner of the American Republic Party, exercised intermittent control over the mayoralty and the Common Council, which appointed the five Alms House Commissioners, and thus helped shape an impassioned debate over the fitness of destitute newcomers for the racialized rights and responsibilities of citizenship.[20]

By the early 1840s, the Alms House Department played multiple roles, which muddied the boundary between charity and punishment. Besides the Bellevue complex, which included the Alms House, Bellevue Hospital, a penitentiary, a school, a morgue, and some workshops, it ran a nursery for homeless children on Long Island, provided outdoor relief, and operated the Tombs—an imposing city prison built in 1838 on the site of the old Fresh Water Pond on Center Street.[21] The administration of these institutions, and the uses to which the poor put them, served to confound their functions. The Prison Association of New York observed:

> Very many are confined at the Penitentiary, not because they have committed any crime or offence, but avowedly because they are destitute, or diseased. This includes a class of persons who go to the police office and "give themselves up," as they term it, because they want a place of refuge; a large number of diseased prostitutes, who go there as to a hospital; and many strangers and foreigners, who, in the ignorance of our institutions, apply for relief to the Police Officer, and are (relieved) by being sent to the Penitentiary. . . . The result is, that instead of being a terror to evildoers, our prisons are fled to as a desirable refuge.[22]

In nativist poor-relief discourse, the overlapping populations of prisons and the Alms House underscored allegedly organic links among pauperism, crime, and immigration, with treacherous implications for the destiny of the commonwealth. In 1844 an Alms House committee charged with examining existing public relief arrangements recommended federal action to regulate immigration in order to prevent the "refuse population" of Europe—"the lawless and depraved, as well as destitute . . . vagabonds and thieves as well as paupers"—from burdening taxpayers and contaminating the "seeds of American Commonwealth." Noting the high ratio of "foreign" to "American" births at the Alms House, it reported that "an unusual number of [destitute] young women far advanced in gestation" gave birth at public expense and left without their children as soon as they recovered their strength, returning pregnant a year later "so that at the termination of the bondsman's liabilities, the city has a family of three to support, in the place of one originally bonded."[23] The Committee on Charity and the Alms House complained that "sturdy paupers" had been maintained winter after winter "in idleness" at the expense of the "tax-paying citizen" for no other reason "than that of securing suffrage for the dominant party. The state election in the fall is no sooner over than crowds of able-bodied paupers throng our alms house. They are clothed, fed and lodged well during the inclement season of the year; and in the spring without having contributed a penny in money and labor for their winter's entertainment, they are marched up to the polls to vote away the rights and property of the self-supporting laborers and independent citizens." In the Committee's thinking, the reform of public relief was inextricably connected with the immigration issue. It called for the adoption of "such regulations as may . . . secure the city against the danger and disgrace of being governed by an administration elected by tenants of an Alms House administration."[24]

The mass invasion of the famine-stricken Irish further fueled Whig and nativist fears about the impact that immigrant dependence would have on the future of the white republic. In 1849 nativists formed a secret fraternal society known as the Order of the Star Spangled Banner, which grew into a formidable national political movement. The American Party, labeled the "The Know Nothings" after its members' customary response to outsiders' queries about their activities, generally supported temperance, campaigned against public funding for parochial schools, campaigned for Protestant Bible reading in public schools, favored a twenty-one-year residency requirement for naturalization, and advocated the deportation of foreign paupers and criminals. Although they attracted largely white-collar and skilled blue-collar men, their sentiments resonated with more genteel sorts as well.[25]

A New York State Senate report on pauperism issued in 1855 contained a dire warning about the exponential growth of the immigrant pauper class and its impact on republican institutions, whether political or cultural. One letter included in this document remarked that "in 1831 there was one pauper to every *one hundred and twenty-three* inhabitants, while in 1851 there was one pauper to every *twenty-four* inhabitants." If pauperism increased at this rate during the next two decades, "There will be in 1871 one to every *five* inhabitants. . . . If one person in every five is a pauper, will universal suffrage be safe!" According to the author, the answer to this rhetorical question lay in the fate of Rome, where rising inequalities in wealth created "an order of *Nobility*" followed by the institution of an "*Emperor King*." Roman history suggested to this observer that "the spirit of liberty declined as pauperism increased. Wealth, there, was more unequally divided. . . . The poor Roman was too happy to enroll himself among the retinue of the wealthy patrician, for then bread would be given him, and his water would be sure. But then the maintenance of the Republic became impossible, and the establishment of the Empire was an inevitable necessity." Not only would a permanent class of dependents spell a death knell for republican government, it would devastate public education, religion, and internal improvements: "Will not many a graceful spire which now rises heavenward crumble into decay? . . . Can a nation of lazaroni construct railroads and dig canals? What will become of our commerce? Do paupers build ships or fill them? Let Spain and Portugal and Naples answer." Interestingly enough, the notion of a hierarchy of "white races" was inherent in the writer's reference to Europe's Mediterranean South as an example of decline and failure.[26]

In antebellum New York, however, the nativist case against immigrants lost out to voices that called for the *acculturation* through benevolent reform, rather than exclusion, of allegedly undesirable European aliens. Such reform would imbue the newcomers with the economic self-sufficiency and morality necessary for the exercise of self-government through the promotion of work, thrift, temperance, and moral virtue. The political touchstones of the era—black slavery, Manifest Destiny, and the Mexican War—sustained the central idea enshrined in the naturalization law of 1790: that the most important difference was that which lay between white and nonwhite peoples. What emerged was a notion of political whiteness characterized by fluid racial identities. According to one commentator, Irishmen and Germans who crossed the Atlantic settled down and became American citizens, and "their offspring born and raised on American soil differ in no appreciable or perceptible manner from other Americans" (here, of course, "American" meant Anglo-Saxon Protestant). Even the physical features of such groups, "the course skin, big hands and feet, the broad teeth, pug nose etc., of the Irish and German laborer pass away in a generation or two." The "Negro," on the other hand, was "as absolutely and specifically unlike the American as when the race first touched the soil and first breathed the air of the New World."[27]

The implication of this observation was that environment played a major role in shaping the destinies of European immigrants; reform institutions could make good "Americans" out of them, but the inherent differences of black people rendered them immune to such influences. The national Democratic Party, which in the course of the 1840s and 1850s came increasingly to be associated with continental expansion (at the expense of nonwhite Mexico), black slavery, and the South, frequently appealed for

Irish votes in the urban North not simply by embracing cultural pluralism and economic populism, and by opposing temperance and nativism, but also by invoking a common heritage of whiteness. Participation in Democratic Party politics constituted one of the primary ways in which the Irish "became white" in America. In the slave South, Democrats sought to obliterate class tensions among whites by upholding the idea that black slavery guaranteed the honor and independence of all whites regardless of their wealth, and that it made possible an aristocracy of color in which white men, no matter badly situated in the material order of things, could claim membership. David Roediger has argued that the appeal to white supremacy worked in similar ways to alleviate divisions within the ranks of the Democratic Party in Northern cities like New York. Despised by nativists, and too poor to move West, the Irish remained unimpressed by Free-Soil opposition to slavery expansion, welcoming instead the Democratic argument that they belonged in America because they were white. Thus, in "areas with virtually no Black voters, the Democrats created a 'white vote.'" Their vision of Irish assimilation was manifested in the contrast that James Buchanan drew between Mexican mongrels, unsuited for freedom, and the "mixed" "American" population of English, Scotch-Irish, French, Welsh, and German lineage.[28]

The Republican Party, conceived in the maelstrom of sectional politics in the 1850s, opposed the extension of slavery to the vast territories west of the Mississippi. It co-opted not only many former Whigs, Free-Soilers, and abolitionists, but even some nativists, rallying this motley crew around opposition to the unholy triad of "Slavery, Rum, and Romanism." Democrats lost no time in conflating Republican free statism with support of racial equality and "amalgamation." They adopted the derisive—and politically potent—cognomen "black Republicans" to characterize their emerging competitors on the national political scene. When black New Yorkers lobbied to eliminate the property qualifications for voting to which African Americans were subjected, Democrats warned that the eradication of this discriminatory provision would jeopardize white immigrants by strengthening the hands of nativists inclined to exclude European newcomers. Yet, notwithstanding Democratic demagoguery, Republican Free-Soilism shared more than one postulate of the white republic. As noted in the introduction to this study, the Western soil that Republicans wished to keep free of slavery was seized from American Indians in a manner that made the operation of "enforceable property rights" contingent on whiteness.[29] Moreover, the "frontier" against slavery in the trans-Mississippi West frequently translated into apartheid zones against *all* blacks—whether slave or free—so that whiteness itself became a "property interest," a necessary condition for land ownership in free territory. At the same time, back east, New York Republicans, anxious to disprove Democratic allegations that they preferred the "Negro" over white men and supported race mixing, ignored black pleas for equality in voting rights. Thus black suffrage in the state remained hobbled until the adoption of the Fifteenth Amendment to the U.S. Constitution in 1870. Indeed, professions of white supremacy were on full display in New York City on the eve of South Carolina's secession from the Union in December 1861, when two thousand local merchants rallied to the cause of their Southern compatriots, assuring them that in the event of race war, "the people of the city of New York will stand by their brethren, the white race."[30]

From Immigrant Pauper to (White) Citizen Worker: A Reorganized Alms House Department

The political meaning of whiteness unfolded in tandem with important developments in public relief arrangements that furthered the bipolar fabrication of New York society into black and white. Immigrant advocates drew attention to the ruthless exploitation to which transatlantic voyagers were subjected, especially during the age of mass immigration from 1845 to 1855, which brought over 1.5 million Irish and 1.2 million Germans to American shores. The dreadful conditions of overcrowding, low rations, poor sanitation, typhus, and death in steerage, combined with a medley of swindlers, from pickpockets to transportation agents and boardinghouse racketeers on shore, sent the rate of foreign-born pauperism skyrocketing, heightened the threat of epidemics, and imposed a staggering pressure on city hospitals. Under the circumstances, reformers and immigrant-aid societies urged the enactment of protective legislation to prevent the newcomer from "being robbed, to facilitate his passage through the city to the interior, to aid him with good advice, and, in cases of the most urgent necessity, to furnish him with a small amount of money; in short, not to treat him as a pauper with the ultimate view of making him an inmate of the Almshouse, but as *an independent citizen, whose future career would become interwoven with the best interests of the country.*"[31] The iconic "independent citizen" was both white and male, granted the legal right to own property, enter into contracts, and "exercise self-representation before one's peers in court."[32]

Accordingly, in 1847 the New York legislature created a Board of Commissioners of Emigration to both reimburse municipal and county authorities for the relief of needy immigrants and help immigrants make a transition to citizenship by protecting them against hustlers, helping them to migrate to other parts of the state, and providing them with advice, lodgings, and jobs. The 1847 statute, amended by subsequent laws, laid down that the Commissioners' responsibilities would be financed by head taxes and special indemnity bonds imposed on passengers likely to become public charges, including "lunatic, idiot, deaf, dumb, blind or infirm persons" without families, seniors older than sixty years, and single women with children. The Emigration Commissioners were charged with the supervision of the Marine Hospital located on Staten Island for the treatment of sick immigrants. This institution quickly proved inadequate to deal with the scope of immigrant need, prompting the establishment of a new Emigrant Refuge and Hospital as well as a nursery for immigrant children on Ward's Island. Meanwhile, in order to better discharge their mandate of shielding newcomers from would-be con artists, the Commissioners rented and transformed the old fort of Castle Garden at the foot of Manhattan into a central landing depot. Inaugurated in August 1855, Castle Garden continued to serve in this capacity until 1891, when it—together with the emigration board itself—was supplanted by federal control over immigration. Ellis Island opened the following year.[33]

If the Board of Commissioners of Emigration represented one major prong in the public enterprise to acculturate European aliens into the racialized and gendered status of "independent citizenship," the Alms House Department constituted another, more coercive, even punitive, path to the same end. The era of mass immigration in the 1840s and 1850s saw a major reorganization of public relief centered around the principle of "making *labor* the uniform condition of relief to the able-bodied poor." Of course, the idea of work as a cure for the idle, dissolute ways of habitual paupers was an old legacy of welfare reform inherited from the English. The high proportion of immigrant paupers of uncertain whiteness, however, lent the debate over work and relief a significant new context because of the historical connection between an individual's economic sovereignty and fitness for self-government. Universal white manhood suffrage made the willingness to work—whether through persuasion or force—more than a matter of simply reducing the costs of public relief. At stake was nothing less than making out of destitute Europeans true "American" citizens vested with all the racialized opportunities, rights, and responsibilities implied by that status. Faced with declining revenues thanks to the depression, Democratic and Whig administrations alike concurred on the need to wean the sturdy poor away from their alleged habits of dependence.[34]

As early as 1841, Democratic Mayor Robert H. Morris had offered a proposal to reorganize the Alms House Department in order to facilitate the classification, employment, and reform of different categories of relief-seekers. The keystone of this plan was the creation of a Work House to employ and segregate healthy paupers from the "virtuous" aged and infirm, who were to be housed in the Alms House. It called for the removal of the Alms House complex to new premises on Blackwell's Island in the East River, because, as the Commissioners declared in 1843, the organization of a Work House Department and the erection of workshops could not "be effected at Bellevue." Moreover, the island's isolation from the bustle of metropolitan life would offer distinct advantages. The Commissioners recalled that when the Alms House was first moved from Chambers Street to Bellevue, the remoteness of its new location prevented "facility of intercourse between the inmates and friends without." The growth of the city had, however, "surrounded the buildings at Bellevue and destroyed the advantages of position it formerly possessed." The removal of the Alms House establishment to Blackwell's Island would "permanently retain" these advantages and make it difficult for the inmates to vote en bloc in city elections. Moreover, it would promote self-sufficiency, because many inmates "would prefer to select their own branch of industry, and when required to work out their support, will do so without the confinement of the Alms House." The Work House would also discourage outdoor relief, which "made more paupers than it relieved" by fostering dependence on public charity "whenever labor [was] interrupted, either by . . . the weather, by accidents, or even by disease" generated by "dissipated or extravagant" lifestyles. Although the Work House was expected to supply the establishment's consumption needs, the Commissioners hastened to add that surplus labor should not "be put to such use as would interfere with the industrious pursuits of our fellow citizens."[35]

By mid-century, Morris's vision of reorganization had materialized in the creation of a new relief, Work House, and penal complex on Blackwell's Island. An imposing structure of blue stone rubble masonry hacked out of the rock on its new site, New York City's new Alms House occupied the island's center, opposite Seventieth Street. It separated men and women in two separate edifices, in an apparent attempt to address the charge that the promiscuous mixing of inmates bred not only indiscipline, but also new generations of paupers born to the poorhouse. Each edifice boasted a magnificent central structure containing apartments for the staff as well the kitchen and laundry room of the establishment. Rising to eighty-seven feet, it was topped by a cupola and flanked by wings that quartered the poor in tiny rooms opening onto verandas. A chapel with pews affording eight hundred seats stood near the island's western shore. To the east rose a three-storied bakery equipped with five ovens, a warehouse for storing flour and bread, and workrooms for carpenters, coopers, and shoemakers.[36]

Blackwell's Island was also the site of an octagonal-structured Lunatic Asylum, located at its northern end, and the Penitentiary, lying across from Fifty-fifth Street. Four stories high, the physical contours of this prison paralleled those of the Alms House. It too consisted of a middle edifice edged with wings fitted with cells for nearly five hundred inmates. Placed back to back, the cells opened onto iron galleries connected to the central building by stone staircases. Those in the northern wing confined males and those in the southern held female prisoners. The Penitentiary's physical appearance and proximity to the Alms House made it an emblem of the confusion between crime and pauperism in nineteenth-century welfare discourse.

Administrative restructuring accompanied the move of the municipal relief establishment to Blackwell's Island. In 1849 the state legislature established a new, bipartisan Board of ten Alms House Governors to be elected for five-year terms, one every year from the nominees of the two main political parties. This arrangement was designed to insulate the Alms House administration from partisan control centered in the Common Council, reduce costs, redress corruption and inefficiency among officials running the department, and eliminate alleged inmate abuse. The Alms House Department now embraced under its jurisdiction the Department of Outdoor Relief, the city prisons, Bellevue Hospital, the Penitentiary, the Alms House and Lunatic Asylum on Blackwell's Island, and the nurseries on Randall's Island. In order to reduce waste, a newly created storehouse supplied these institutions with provisions requisitioned by the wardens of the various institutions on a weekly basis, with the approval of the Governors. One of the most significant new mandates of the Board was to oversee the construction of a new Work House designed for the employment of able-bodied prison and Alms House inmates, authorized by an act passed in April 1849. In 1850 a legislative appropriation of seventy-five thousand dollars launched the construction of a northern wing, consisting of male quarters. In May 1854 a full-fledged female department went into operation, supported by the completion, several months later, of a women's wing to the south and "shops in the cross T."[37]

Meanwhile, the Alms House administration had, since the early 1840s, contracted with two voluntary associations to care for its African American clients, effectively segregating the black poor from those defined as "white"—whether native-born or immigrant. In 1843 the Society for the Relief of Worthy, Aged, Indigent Colored Persons petitioned the mayor and aldermen, requesting a one-thousand-dollar appropriation to pay a lien on twelve lots of land on Murray Hill, the site of their home for the meritorious black poor. In exchange, the directresses of the Colored Home offered to transfer from the Alms House twelve to fifteen inmates, arguing that their enterprise supported "a class of people whose necessities would generally compel them . . . to become a permanent annual expense to the city."[38] The city approved the petition. By the time that Blackwell's Island opened, the Colored Home had become the chief receptacle of African American relief applicants who would otherwise have been sent to the municipal Alms House. The city entered into a similar arrangement with the Colored Orphan Asylum, whose operators had secured in 1842 a land grant from the city on Fifth Avenue at Forty-third Street, where they built an impressive brick building to minister to destitute black children.[39]

Even as public authorities relegated the care of African Americans to more sympathetic private associations like the Colored Home and the Colored Orphan Asylum, they reduced the proportion of outdoor aid supplied to black New Yorkers (see table 19B, in appendix). One result of the importance of the Irish vote to the Democratic Party was that the Irish came to dominate the ranks of outdoor relief recipients. At mid-century the Outdoor Poor Department's beneficiaries were arranged according to their residence into two regional groups representing the eastern and western sections of the city. Prospective clients applied to the Superintendent of the Outdoor Poor for relief, and their names and addresses were registered in an entry book maintained for that purpose. Visitors, appointed annually for each ward requesting assistance, selected from this book all the names belonging to their route, investigated the merits of each case, and recorded the outcome of their enquiries for future reference. Every Tuesday, candidates judged worthy of relief presented themselves to the check clerk at the Superintendent's office, who, after verifying their "propriety" with the help of a visitor, gave each client a voucher to present for payment at the Superintendent's desk. This system, designed to prevent fraud and "imposition," did nothing of the sort. Pensioners learned very quickly that their applications for aid were less likely to be rejected if made through their ward politicians. In 1848 the Alms House Commissioners complained rather delicately that "within [the council members'] respective wards are many persons . . . not *always* sufficiently [poor] to be entitled to the charity they ask who make their applications to [their representatives] for relief. The annoyance often becomes so intolerable, and the humanity of the act so apparent, that few, if any aldermen can withstand the appeals for relief."[40]

Needless to say, African Americans who qualified for relief were highly unlikely to qualify for the vote, burdened as that right was for black people by the requirement of the $250 freehold. No wonder, then, that their proportion among outdoor aid recipients fell sharply in the decade before the Civil War. Whereas they made up almost a third of those receiving public assistance in their homes in 1813–14, they accounted for only 5 percent of all adults qualifying for such aid during the panic year of 1855. The corresponding proportions for the Irish, non-Irish (overwhelmingly European) immigrants, and native-born whites were 66 percent, 16 percent, and 12 percent, respectively. The black proportion of aid in money—as opposed to fuel—was even lower. They made up only 2 percent of all adults receiving money. The Irish share of cash aid was lower than that for fuel—53 percent and 69 percent, respectively. Conversely, native-born white and non-Irish immigrant adults' share of cash was higher than their share of fuel. Thus, 22 percent of all adults receiving money and 10 percent of those receiving fuel in 1855 were native-born whites. The corresponding figures for non-Irish immigrants were 23 percent and nearly 15 percent. Cash conferred greater flexibility in spending power and called for responsible decision making. Its differential dispensation reflected the political capital of the various groups receiving it.[41]

The pensioners of the Outdoor Poor Department also included impoverished widows hired as "nurses" for the numerous foundlings and infants abandoned to public care. In 1848, for instance, 160 to 200 children were "nursed out" to women judged "careful and competent." This system ostensibly offered the advantage of not only caring for infants in private homes, but also "saving" widows with families from having to enter relief rolls; unfortunately, abuses abounded. One visitor noted in 1848 that a number of nurses had been dismissed owing to their neglect or "positive ill-treatment" of the children in their care. When they reached the age of two, white children who had been "nursed out" were transferred to the Alms House Department's nursery establishment on Randall's Island. Those defined as black were dispatched to the Colored Home, unless adopted by foster parents. The "white" nursery complex included twelve sturdy buildings spread over a plot of land 960,000 square feet in size and enclosed by a picket fence overlooking Flushing Bay. The structures accommodated dormitories for children, a school, a kitchen, a Quarantine Home, an Infant's Home, a hospital, and playhouses, as well as quarters for the superintendent and staff. An administrator noted with pride that Croton water crossed beneath the bed of the river and flowed "like a beautiful streamlet throughout the whole villa." An extensive avenue linked the nursery complex to the western wharf. A farm and dairy worked by paupers supplied the establishment with milk and other provisions. The Alms House Department sought to indenture older children in adjoining states, often to farmers in New Jersey.[42]

The inauguration of Blackwell's Island formalized the separate institutionalization of relief applicants defined as "white." The Irish made up 63 percent of this group of 3,096 indigent New Yorkers in 1855. The 868 African Americans eligible for the Alms House were dispatched to the Colored Home (discussed in the next chapter). Small numbers of blacks were admitted to other institutions on the island, primarily the Penitentiary Hospital, the Lunatic Asylum, and the Work House. However tiny the size of their African American populations, all of these institutions adopted the attribute of color as the overarching paradigm for organizing information about their clients. As an example, consider the facsimiles of statistical information about Penitentiary Hospital inmates incorporated into the 1855 annual report of the Alms House Governors. Table 20 (in Appendix) offers a frequency distribution of admissions arranged by national origin into the categories "natives" and "foreigners." Each of these categories is further broken down by place of birth into groups that the Penitentiary data gatherers clearly defined as "natural," namely color and sex. Thus, we learn, for instance, that New York contributed 168 "white males," 235 "white females," 26 "colored males," and 26 "colored females." The Alms House officials organized an impressive panoply of foreigners into a bipolar color scheme identical to that applied to native-born relief seekers, with the result that particular nationalities—usually European—came overwhelmingly to be defined as "white." In this regard, municipal officials—like other institutions in American society—adopted the "binary logic" of natural history's classification scheme by "filtering out the confusing complexity of nature" and creating simple taxonomies of race based on seemingly stable, readily observable physical criteria.[43] Thus, whatever the nativists might say, table 20 represented the largest contingent of immigrants—the Irish—as "white," while "East Indians" and "West Indians" were depicted as "black." Table 21, which recorded the drinking habits of Penitentiary Hospital inmates, is only one example of the statistical discourse of relief that "naturalized" color as the crucial marker of difference in New York's social order. It merged native-born and immigrant patients into just two unified races—"white" and "colored." Together these tabulations gave a particular meaning to whiteness that transcended nationality and embodied a vision of European (or, conversely, West Indian) acculturation to American racial categories.

Working Poor Uses of Blackwell's Island

As the Penitentiary figures suggest, the Irish dominated the inmate populations of every institution on Blackwell's Island (see table 22, in appendix). At the same time, native-born whites outnumbered other European immigrant groups everywhere but in the Lunatic Asylum. In 1855—a year that began harshly with a severe winter and a recession—the Irish made up 53 percent of the 2,158 patients receiving treatment at the Penitentiary Hospital and 48 percent of the 371 men and women lodged in the Lunatic Asylum. Native-born whites accounted for a quarter of those confined in the Alms House and the Penitentiary Hospital, and nearly a fifth of those in the Lunatic Asylum. The same year, African Americans constituted 4 percent of the population of the Penitentiary Hospital and 2 percent of Lunatic Asylum inmates. The year 1854 was the first for which the Alms House Governors, in their annual report, provided a detailed demographic profile of Work House inmates. Their data suggested that nearly 72 percent of the 4,423 people who passed through the institution that year were foreign-born, four-fifths of them Irish. Indeed, the Irish accounted for about 57 percent of all those confined in the Work House—over double the proportion of their numbers in New York's population in the mid-1850s.[44]

Men constituted 70 percent of the Work House population in 1854, although it is important to keep in mind that because women were not counted until May of that year, their numbers may have been rather underrepresented in the institution's schedule. Some of these women were, as we shall see, syphilitic prostitutes who entered the Penitentiary Hospital voluntarily for treatment. A few were committed by their "lawful protectors"—their husbands—in the "heat of angry passion," thus turning the supposed house of industry into a site for playing out domestic conflict in the neighborhoods of working-class New York.⁴⁵ Women predominated at most of the other institutions on Blackwell's Island, including the Alms House, the Penitentiary Hospital, and the Lunatic Asylum. They accounted for 56 percent of Alms House adults in 1855. Only in the winter months of January and February, when construction work was in short supply, did men outnumber women in this population.

These figures are not surprising in light of the significant presence of single women with or without children among New York's working poor (detailed in the previous chapter), the limited employment options available to them, and possibly the greater sympathy with which Alms House officials regarded them. At the Penitentiary Hospital, the inmate sex ratio was the most imbalanced among the Irish than for any other group, with women outnumbering men by almost three to one. Among famine-era patients, who made up nearly half of all Irish women in the hospital and about 44 percent of the men, the proportion of women was even greater—over three-quarters of all recent Irish immigrant inmates were women. By contrast, the sex ratio among African Americans seeking treatment at the Penitentiary Hospital was more balanced than that for any white group, with women making up only a little over half of the black population. In 1855 the typical hospital inmate—whether black or white, male or female, native-born or immigrant—was likely to be single, twentysomething, a servant (if a woman), a laborer (if a man), Catholic (if white), and Protestant (if black). Between a fifth and a third of these patients claimed to have worked within days of their commitment. The predominance of Irish women over men seeking admission to the Penitentiary Hospital may have had something to do with the fact that, as seen in the previous chapter, younger Irish women who emigrated to America between 1845 and 1855 remained in New York in larger numbers than men, lived independently of kin, and married somewhat late.⁴⁶

The uses to which these women put the hospital are instructive, suggesting the propensity of the "dangerous classes" to see the Alms House Department more as a public service vehicle to minister to their immediate material needs than as a mint for potential citizens. Not only did several commit themselves voluntarily in order to get treatment for sexually transmitted diseases, others used the institution—together with Bellevue Hospital—as a maternity ward and the Alms House as a maternity home. In 1850 the Lying-in Department of Bellevue reported 163 obstetrical cases, resulting in 168 births (including twins), many of them born to unmarried mothers. In 1854 the Alms House reported that the nursery apartments were particularly crowded and had to be expanded in order to accommodate more mothers and their children. Some women placed their offspring in the infant nursery, using the Alms House's mediation to force errant fathers to pay child support. Women availed of public facilities to obtain abortions as well. In 1853 seven women were reported to have died as a result of botched abortions at the Blackwell's Island hospital, while four others were discharged after successful procedures.[47]

Women also outnumbered men, 56 percent to 44 percent overall, at the Lunatic Asylum. Interestingly enough, this particular inmate population was most feminized among its largest demographic: inmates in their twenties, in which group women outnumbered men two to one. The sex composition became progressively more balanced with the advance of age until the number of men actually exceeded that of women in the age groups above fifty years. The dominant presence of young, female, Irish immigrants in the Lunatic Asylum is not surprising, given the resident physician's diagnosis of the trauma of immigration as a major source of "insanity": "the combined moral and physical influences of their leaving the homes of their childhood, coming destitute to a strange land, and often after great suffering." In addition, "recently confined and nursing women," suffering from what we would perhaps regard today as postpartum depression, swelled the tide of admissions to the Asylum. As far as the male inmates were concerned, their presence was explained partly in terms of the "political excitement" of refugees fleeing Europe in the wake of the abortive liberal revolutions of 1848. These men's states of mind were likened to the "effects of Millerism, Mormonism and c. in our own country."[48] There is, however, a great deal of evidence to suggest that many desperate newcomers admitted themselves or their relatives to the institution for board rather than treatment, leading the city to incur much expense in weeding out such cases from "legitimate" victims of insanity.[49] Allegedly insane persons committed to the prisons or reported to the Department of the Outdoor Poor were first dispatched to the city prison to be examined by its resident physician. In 1852 the examining physician deemed only 292 out of a total of 665 applicants "fit subjects" for the Lunatic Asylum. When asked by Asylum authorities what they considered to be the causes of their dependents' insanity, the relatives of inmates offered a bewildering range of responses representing the entire panoply of human experience: from physical ailments (epilepsy, typhus, and puerperal fever) through cultural habits (intemperance), to the use of "concentrated tea," ill treatment, "religious excitement," grief at personal losses, fright, nostalgia, maternal anxiety, domestic trouble, disappointment in love or business, and, most importantly, poverty. "In many cases, poverty and want of employment seem to be the existing causes of insanity," declared an Asylum staff member. In such cases, temporary residence at the asylum was likely to "restore the reason" but not "prevent the recurrence of the cause." He prescribed the provision of work as the major cure for insanity.[50]

The Asylum staffer spoke from experience. Two years previously, one twenty-five-year-old had committed suicide by suffocating herself with a strip of cloth the day after she entered the institution. The reason was her despair at her inability to find employment. In this context, the Asylum's recreational programs offered revealing insights into the self-image of its inmates. Some of these activities consisted in holding "Moot Courts" in which the inmates participated as plaintiffs, defendants, counsel, witness, judge, and jury. An Asylum report in 1855 noted that on one such occasion, the "Judge" of the "Supreme Court of Blackwell's Island" declared that the reason he was committed as "insane" was that he was "just carrying into effect a favorite project of establishing a bank, with a capital of five hundred million dollars, in each of the large cities, to accommodate young men who, wishing to engage in business, were unable to give security for the money or pay the interest." This particular "client" clearly harbored visions of a utopian world where the dispossessed had access to equal opportunity and debt forgiveness.[51]

Nineteenth-century Meanings of "Workfare": Patrons Versus Clients

The transfer of the Alms House enterprise to Blackwell's Island greatly expanded the opportunity to assimilate would-be citizens through the "toil of liberty" while at the same time buoying hopes for reducing relief costs. Able-bodied inmates were put to work in the island's extensive quarries, while the less robust were assigned various domestic, farming, and mechanical chores. Penitentiary inmates organized in gangs reportedly cut stone, graded and blasted rocks, built sewers and walls, and dug trenches for the structures on Blackwell's Island and a potter's field cemetery on Randall's Island. Work House carpenters repaired carts, wheelbarrows, and stoneboats for the quarries and built a gatekeeper's lodge for the Alms House and a two-storied storehouse for the storekeeper. Work House blacksmiths made tools used in the quarry such as drills, hammers, picks, and wedges.[52]

Female convicts sewed garments, bound shoes, and knitted stockings not only for the prison population, but also for the children on Randall's Island and for the aged and infirm in the Alms House. Older relief-seekers served as nurses for poorhouse infants. In 1848 the Alms House Matron's Department reported $1,949.49 in estimated value of pauper work engaged in the sewing of shirts, chemises, dresses, and bed linen. A separate tailor's department, staffed by men, produced nearly six hundred dollars' worth of overcoats, jackets, and trousers. A shoemaker's shop repaired and manufactured shoes at an estimated cost of $4,165.70. In addition, inmates tended a variety of vegetables—cabbage, potatoes, and turnips—that supplied the institution's dinner table. Meanwhile, at Bellevue Hospital female convalescents sewed much of the bedding and clothing used by the institution and performed a great deal of the domestic labor required to keep the hospital running, including washing, cooking, and scrubbing. The use of prison labor in service capacities at the island's various institutions did entail some risks. A Lunatic Asylum patient was discovered on the morning after her admission with her head completely shorn of its remarkable ringlets of hair. A caretaker recruited from the Penitentiary had apparently divested the victim of her tresses, reportedly her source of "self-esteem," for sale to a wig maker.[53]

More than any other institution on Blackwell's Island, the Work House was designed to acclimatize paupers to the regimen of wage labor and economic self-sufficiency through coercion. Its organization was intended to facilitate the systematization and classification of different categories of inmates according to the modes and causes of their commitment, and by their presumed ability and willingness (or, rather, *unwillingness*) to work. In theory, the Work House was set apart from other establishments of municipal relief—like the Alms House itself, the Lunatic Asylum, and the hospital at Bellevue—by the familiar distinction between the "worthy poor" on the one hand, and able-bodied "paupers by choice" on the other. One Work House functionary urged that institutions like the "poorhouse" function as a "refuge from the miseries of life," for "the old and infirm, the sick, indeed, all who are providentially afflicted." The Work House, on the other hand, "should be a place of hardships, of ample, though coarse fare; it should be administered with strictness," because it was primarily a tool "to incite the laboring classes" deterred from finding work "by habits of indolence" to "depend upon themselves." That it proved difficult to maintain these distinctions in practice is evident from the various categories of "causes of commitment" to the Work House constructed by relief officials. These "cause" categories included not simply the traditional vices associated with unworthy paupers, such as "intemperance," "prostitution," "vagrancy," "idleness," and "debauchery," but also the conditions thought to afflict more deserving victims of Providence, such as "old age," "destitution," "blindness, deafness, dumbness and lameness," and "sickness." More often than not, these categories overlapped.[54]

The challenge to neat moral classifications of the poor—not to mention the idea of a unified white fraternity of potential citizens—was shaped by both the spatial and administrative aspects of the relief establishment, as well as by assertions of subaltern agency. As we have seen, reform discourse in New York had historically obfuscated the boundary between charity and correction in many ways. The administration of poor relief and criminal justice overlapped under the jurisdiction of the Alms House Governors. Inmate labor was conscripted for a variety of services without making distinctions between paupers and criminals, so that, for instance, women prisoners served as nurses at Bellevue Hospital. The city prison housed ship personnel whom magistrates deemed "temporarily insane" by virtue of intoxication and incarcerated in order to "avoid new excesses previous to the sailing of their respective ships."[55] Moreover, as Eric Monkkonen has observed, the monumental physical presence of a dense network of public institutions in close proximity—Alms House, prison, Lunatic Asylum, Work House, hospitals—invited the working poor to "read" the functions of these buildings as interchangeable. The result was that needy New Yorkers adopted a range of tactics to adapt these institutions to their own needs, subverting the reform goals of their betters.

The phenomenon of inmate agency surfaced in the categories of "debauchery" and "vagrancy" as causes of Work House commitments. The "debauched" and the "vagrant" were frequently voluntary prisoners who submitted to incarceration in order to secure medical attention at the Penitentiary Hospital. That body reportedly became the "venereal refuge" of the city. In 1848 the resident physician reported that a vast majority of the patients had "consented" to imprisonment in order to secure the medical care offered by the hospital; 106 of 175 patients in the female hospital fell in this category. Men afflicted with syphilis, several of them "good mechanics," were compelled by "their destitution to suffer themselves to be committed (as vagrants) by police magistrates." In 1851, they numbered 91 out of 110 men in the Penitentiary Hospital.[56]

The proposal to commit these "voluntary prisoners" to the Work House stemmed from the practice of many female inmates, upon getting well, of securing early discharges by obtaining writs of habeas corpus with the help of brothel keepers. Thus, "this public charity is made the means of perpetuating and sustaining vice and immorality," observed the warden of the Penitentiary Hospital. In 1849 the Governors recommended that prostitutes who solicited incarceration for medical reasons be committed to the Work House after their cure for three reasons. First, sexually transmitted diseases, they claimed, resulted not from misfortune, but rather were the "direct product of vice." Therefore, justice demanded that "the recipient of this charity, when able to labor, should discharge the debt thus incurred." Second, such a course would discourage brothel keepers, who allegedly procured the commitments, from taking recourse to public charity for the cure of diseases contracted in their service. And last, work house service would allow the women to form "industrious habits" and a chance of "escape from the pollution" of the sex trade. These female subjects were admitted to the Work House as "debauchees."[57]

The Work House sought not simply to remove the "inducements of idleness" and immorality, which had allegedly created a "permanent family of dependents" distinguished by their "natural repugnance" to honest and respectable labor, but also to inculcate thrift and respect for private property. Thus the city opened accounts for each Work House inmate, from which expenses for his or her board, clothing, and medical treatment were debited, and to which wages were credited. The institution established a scale of pay for artisans in accordance with the proportion of time devoted to work per day. The idea was to socialize the inmate to the time discipline of sustained labor rather than to reward skill. "Time" devoted to work was defined rather nebulously. For instance, tailors received wages of 50 cents, 40 cents, or 37.5 cents depending on whether they were capable of performing "a day's work," "a good part of a day's work," or "a more moderate day's work." Shoemakers, carpenters, bakers, masons, blacksmiths, tinsmiths, coopers, painters, and laborers were similarly classified according to these vague standards of productivity.

The official classification of Work House inmates reflected the physical, emotional, and moral disabilities associated with the stigma of pauperism (intemperance, debauchery, lunacy, idiocy, etc.) without making any allusion to the vagaries of the wage market that drew many to Blackwell's Island. Yet Work House reports of client behavior suggest the importance of economic imperatives that, from the inmates' perspective, drove many able-bodied poor to seek public employment. From the beginning, the institution's books recorded a significant presence of artisans who earned monthly wages ranging from $0.73 to $5.88. In 1854 nearly one out of four men committed to the Work House was a craftsman—carpenter, cooper, mason, blacksmith, shoemaker, tailor, tinsmith, or baker. Shoemakers and tailors accounted for nearly 60 percent of this group. The rest of the inmates—three-quarters of the total—described themselves as laborers. Fifty-six percent of the men and 61 percent of the women were under the age of forty. The establishment of a Work House that paid out wages attracted repeat offenders, either during lean employment periods or allegedly as a product of the alumnus's return to intemperate ways. One functionary complained that many former inmates returned—often of their own accord—to fill their old positions, so that the Work House was turning out to encourage "pauperism instead of producing a contrary effect, . . . instead of being looked upon with shame and fear, . . . the Institutions on Blackwell's Island are estimated by a very numerous class of paupers and criminals as a sort of 'Land of Promise' to which they intend to hold and keep in reserve on the slightest provocation." Public employment, by offering a measure of job security, was threatening competition with work in the private sector.[58]

Work House officials thus faced an anomalous situation. The very rationale for a house of industry assumed the reluctance of the "able-bodied paupers" to earn an honest living, yet here the institution was, viewed as a public employment agency by willing workers. To counter the "growing evil" of voluntary inmates, administrators suggested that Work House inmates be informed that if they returned without trying to "gain an honest livelihood" in the wider world of private enterprise, they could not expect to be restored to their old positions and receive "the prices which are paid to the first class laborers and mechanics, but they must fall back into the second class with an increased length of commitment." Even good workers could not expect to be paid the highest wages if they returned time and again. Thus wage reductions substituted the alleged "fear" of work as a disincentive to seek public welfare for clients who showed that they were not afraid to work. The Work House officer did recommend "honorable exceptions" for genuinely needy cases to be granted on special application by the Governors.[59]

The Governors also experimented with reducing Work House wages by fifteen cents per diem on each category of workers as a punitive gesture supposedly against "the desire so eagerly manifested by a majority of them to earn a few dollars over their board and clothing, to spend in a drunken debauch at the expiration of their terms, with the knowledge that they return to the institution at their pleasure." Thus welfare "reform" went beyond the mission of enforcing a work ethic to regulating the way in which the working poor spent the wages they earned, as well as to preventing any interference with the private labor market.[60]

Inmate responses to the wage cut suggested that they regarded their employment under municipal auspices as a *right of citizenship* rather than charity. They were *workers* rather than paupers. No wonder, then that Work House inmates expressed "considerable excitement and dissatisfaction" at the announcement of the wage cut. Their reactions underscored the paradox of nineteenth-century workfare as an instrument of acculturation to whiteness. In theory, it was supposed to turn immigrant paupers into self-sufficient citizens, implicitly colored white. On the other hand, the coercion inherent in the Work House idea violated the principle of a *free* market for labor in which workers traded their labor for remuneration at the existing wage rate. Moreover, the bourgeois concern that pauper labor not undermine "the industrious pursuits of our fellow citizens" translated into steadily reducing Work House wages when the inmates proved only too willing to embrace "workfare" as an alternative to unemployment. Work House pay certainly did not qualify as what labor leaders would have called "white man's wages." In this context, it is useful to remember that, as David Roediger has argued, the development of working-class consciousness among the Irish in antebellum America went hand in hand with their assimilation of a sense of whiteness: "Catholic Irish immigrants were . . . the best consumers of Democratic appeals that equated 'white men' and 'workingmen.'" Irish workers battled nativist charges that they were driving down the wages of American-born artisans by "casting job competition and neighborhood rivalries as racial, rather than ethnic." At the same time, they sought to purge the low-paid occupations identified as "nigger work"; furthermore, they wanted to cut all association with African Americans by driving "all Blacks, and if possible their memories, from the places where the Irish labored."[61] The Work House, on the other hand, tended to erase the distinctions between free (white) labor and "nigger work" in the most immediate and palpable way by its coercive underpinnings and below-market wage rates.

No wonder, then, that Work House inmates reacted to wage reductions by asserting their collective identity as white citizen-workers entitled to public employment in hard times. Their Superintendent noticed that they worked with "more reluctance than formerly"; their supervisors had difficulty extracting from them "the same amount of labor." On the other hand, the provision that any worker who provided satisfactory "evidence" of his intention to make "proper use of his money" could, with the Governors' approval, receive the highest wages on the Work House scale supplied an avenue for exercising their political privileges as white voters by enlisting the help of ward bosses with influence in city government. The Superintendent freely admitted that the Governors were frequently "deceived in the true character of persons so presented . . . for special awards . . . But we must profit from experience."[62] Inmates dissatisfied with the conditions of Work House labor mounted other forms of resistance. They left with the winter clothing supplied to them upon admission well before their labor had paid for the attire, causing the institution an estimated loss of $837.76 in 1854. Above all, they often managed to procure early discharges by obtaining writs of habeas corpus courtesy of helpful local politicians. The "informality in the commitment" of such cases, or the fact of "the commitment not being recorded," made such releases possible, prompting Work House officials to urge the passage of a law requiring magistrates to record and certify commitments in the Court of General Sessions to prevent premature discharges through writs of habeas corpus.[63] A few years after this recommendation was made, the debate over work and relief spilled out of the closed chambers of Alms House administrators and on to the streets and squares of antebellum New York under the pressures of a debilitating economic panic.

White Voters and the Debate over Public Works

The very privilege of whiteness empowered destitute voters to open up chinks in the political armor of the white fraternity by helping shape an important conversation about the relationship between citizens and the state during hard times. During the panics of 1855 and 1857, their perspectives on municipal relief as a right of citizenship won the support of a mayor swept into office in large part by immigrant voters. Their pleas for help elicited calls for public works programs by Democratic politicians and whites-only labor unions that opposed black rights.

The economic downturn of 1855 fizzled out relatively quickly, but a confluence of circumstances located at home and abroad turned the Panic of 1857 into a more serious affair. It was preceded by over a decade of feverish speculations in railroad construction and Western lands, spawned in part by European demand for American grain to replace the flow of Russian wheat, cut off by the Crimean War. A variety of banks—from state-owned enterprises to unchartered private concerns—proliferated to meet the credit needs of an expanding economy, animated by the influx of California gold. Manufacturing boomed, and conspicuous consumption by the wealthy peaked, throwing the U.S. trade account into a deficit. By 1856 merchant magazines and newspaper editors, among them Horace Greeley, nervously apprehended signs of trouble. Sure enough, the end of the Crimean War restored the supply of Russian grain, depriving American farmers of their European market and American shippers a good deal of their business. The *New York Herald* reported, "Our wharves are crowded with ships, most of them without employment."[64] To exacerbate matters, war and imperial adventures drained European treasuries of specie, prompting interest rates in Britain and France to spiral upward. British investors diverted their money from speculative American ventures into domestic securities. This plunged the New York Stock Exchange into a bear market, bringing down with it the banks that its assets had supported. This unraveling was triggered in August 1857 by a shocking revelation by Charles Stetson, the president of the Ohio Life Insurance and Trust Company: its New York branch was suspending payments because, as it turned out, the company had made heavy investments in risky railroad bonds, and its cashier had hatched a massive scheme of embezzlement. The collapse of what used to be a highly respected financial institution set in motion an economic paralysis of devastating proportions, made worse by the news that a ship carrying two million dollars' worth of gold from California had perished in a storm. There followed bank runs and business failures, a stock market crash, shuttered factories, and a land and railroad bust. Although the depression ended sooner than expected, with banks saving themselves from destruction by temporarily suspending specie payments, it took a terrific toll on clerks and factory workers, mechanics and day laborers, and servants and seamstresses, who found themselves jobless and homeless.[65]

Mayor Fernando Wood, a well-to-do-businessman with a reputation for civic reform, had won election to City Hall in 1854, against nativist opposition, with the staunch support of the city's working-class Irish wards, especially the "bloody auld sixth," which registered a few thousand more votes than there were voters. Much to the alarm of conservatives, Wood, up for reelection, delivered an October address to the City Council similar to his inaugural speech at the height of the recession of January 1855.

In flush times, he said, working people labored at subsistence wages while other social classes accumulated wealth. When depressions hit, the poor were "the first to feel the change, without the means to avoid or endure reverses. Truly may it be said that in New York those who produce everything get nothing, and those who produce nothing get everything. They labor without income whilst surrounded by thousands living in affluence and splendor who have income without labor." Estimating that fifty thousand New Yorkers would be unemployed by January, Wood advocated a public works program centered on building and repairing roads, engine houses, police stations, docks, and a new reservoir, as well as the improvement of Central Park. He also proposed that the city purchase vast quantities of flour, cornmeal, and potatoes to distribute as payment to laborers working on public projects; this project was to be funded by the issue of public construction stock redeemable in fifty years. So desperate were the unemployed that failure to act would foment violence, Wood warned. A New York customs officer, arguing for federal expenditures on public assistance, advanced a political reason for alleviating want during hard times: neglect of the destitute "would act most injuriously to the Democratic party in this state."[66]

New Yorkers affiliated with the newborn Republican Party expressed outrage at the "communist" flavor of Wood's proposals. To the antislavery *Washington National Era* and other Republican commentators, public relief smacked of "foreign origin" and violated the fundamental principle of "our government, which supposes every man capable of taking care of himself, and leaves him to do so." The familiar connection between sturdy self-sufficiency and republican government emerged as a vital corollary of the free labor ideology of the Republican Party, which had risen from the ashes of the hapless Whigs, done to death by the slavery extension crisis of the 1850s. The free labor ideology, expressing middle-class values and aspirations in an evolving industrial capitalist order, maintained that slavery violated the dignity of labor, defined broadly to include, besides factory workers, small producers and farmers. It asserted that a free market for labor would give wage earners access to social mobility and economic independence as long as they exhibited the virtues of the Protestant ethic—hard work, thrift, and moral discipline. Labor and capital could therefore work in perfect harmony. Public assistance would erode the quality of rugged individualism that lent free society its dynamism and republican government its integrity. The *Evening Post* articulated this link, thought to exist between free enterprise and free institutions:

"Despotic governments do incur such obligations [of public relief] but our republican system of government . . . incurs no obligation to take care of the vicious and the thriftless and improvident."[67] No organization reflected this thinking better than the Association for the Improvement of the Condition of the Poor, whose Whig-turned-Republican industrial reformers played a crucial role in "creating a Republican presence in the factory districts," as Iver Bernstein has noted. Fernando Wood's proposal of municipal assistance to the unemployed represented the very essence of the indiscriminate "pseudo-philanthropy" against which the AICP had long inveighed. The Association thwarted the establishment of the sort of ward-based citizens' emergency-relief committees and soup kitchens that had sprung up during the economic crises of 1837–42 and 1854–55; in fact, the organization centralized its own regime of means-tested aid, turning away three times as many people as it helped.[68]

The unemployed dissented vigorously from this line of thinking. An assortment of labor leaders—German Forty-eighters, Locofocos, and Irish unionists—rallied in Tompkins Square on November 5 and marched to City Hall Park. Claiming that "every human being has a right to live, not as a mere charity, but as right" and that governments had a duty to find work for their citizens if individual exertions failed, they petitioned Mayor Wood in favor of a wide-ranging public works program guaranteeing a minimum wage, low-income municipal housing, and an injunction against evictions of the unemployed. The following day, a procession of five thousand "disorderly, fierce, and noisy" protesters brought its grievances to Wall Street, where one of the speakers, a blacksmith, warned that workingmen did not intend to starve while millions of dollars in specie lay idle in New York banks. Three days later, another great demonstration took the battle to City Hall itself, inducing a somewhat nervous Wood to summon the police to protect government buildings and flour warehouses while federal troops, under General Winfield Scott of Mexican War fame, stood guard over the Custom House. Wood had decidedly lost his luster as a working people's advocate when another major rally convened in Tompkins Square on November 11. Their patience exhausted, the crowds ransacked bakeshops and grocery stores. Thereafter, however, the protests of workmen lost steam. A new employer promised to materialize: the Board of Councilmen had approved an appropriation of $250,000 for Central Park, asking the park's Commissioners to hire immediately 1,500 to 2,000 workers, ideally those with families, whose wages would be paid by the Common Council.[69] Wood's other proposals, however, were turned down. Moreover, even Central Park failed to provide emergency unemployment relief thanks to delays occasioned by the issue and sale of municipal bonds. As tens of thousands of homeless New Yorkers jammed into police stations through the winter, the Governors of the Alms House returned to outdoor relief, much castigated by reformers as encouraging "pauperism." The aldermen asked the Governors to "purchase and store flour, corn-meal, and other provisions, in anticipation of extreme destitution among the laboring population," as well as to organize "an efficient corps of out-door visitors for the suffering poor." Sure enough, the Alms House Department reported that during 1857, it had received applications from "a class who never before were recipients of the charity of the city." Admissions to Bellevue Hospital, Randall's Island, and the Alms House climbed by 36 percent, 30 percent, and 8 percent, respectively. Most significantly, large numbers of white New Yorkers committed themselves to the Work House in search of employment. The Work House population skyrocketed by 76 percent over the previous year.[70] The newly unemployed flocked to Blackwell's Island in droves to avail themselves of municipal "workfare" in lieu of public works, thus asserting their own construct of the Work House as a relief agency for needy citizens—however limited the scope of that relief or undesirable the terms of its employment—rather than a punitive preserve of idle wasters. Work House statistics during the Panic of 1857 embodied compelling subaltern testimony against arbitrary distinctions between the "worthy" poor and "undeserving" paupers.

But what of African Americans? A comparative statement of the number of inmates in the various institutions of the Alms House Department in 1856 and 1857 contained in the Department's 1857 Annual Report revealed only two exceptions to the overall pattern of increased inmate admissions supported at public expense: the Colored Home and the Colored Orphan Asylum. Indeed the number of admissions charged to the municipality went down by three in the Colored Home compared with the previous year (even though the overall admissions to that refuge increased considerably). The black proportion of outdoor assistance—a crucial source of relief during the Panic of 1857—slipped even further. Even as the Superintendent of Outdoor Poor reported a rise in expenditure of $13,234.15 over the year before, African Americans constituted only 1.8 percent of all impoverished adults receiving money. The Irish accounted for 62 percent of that number, non-Irish European immigrants approximately 20 percent, and native-born whites 16 percent. The season of devastation in 1857 highlighted a fact that black New Yorkers had always known: in desperate moments, without the power of the franchise, impoverished black people must turn to private resources—however slim, and from whichever source—in order to survive.[71]

3

Not White, but Worthy
Maternalists and the "Pious Poor" of the Colored Home

> No one can read these simple annals of the pious poor—the aged, infirm and suffering children of Africa—without being moved to ears. Nothing can be more pathetic than the testimony given by some of those simple-hearted Christians to the truth of our common religious faith.
> —Review of *Broken Gloom* by a "distinguished divine," cited in 11th Annual Report of the CH for 1850–51, 13–14

In the autumn of 1839, ten benevolent women of New York City congregated in the Bond Street home of Maria Bauyer, a daughter of the first chief justice of the United States Supreme Court, John Jay. Mostly Quakers and evangelicals with ties to the New York Manumission Society and its decidedly conservative protégé, the New York Colonization Society, many of these women had participated in the establishment of the Colored Orphan Asylum three years earlier. Now they gathered to devise a strategy of relief for what they considered a particularly deserving constituency of impoverished black New Yorkers—namely, retired servants and ex-slaves who, "having spent their best years in our service," found themselves at the mercy of "public charity or private bounty" for support in their old age.[1] On their periodic visits to the city's Alms House at Bellevue on the East River, the women met several candidates worthy of philanthropy: like Tommy Warner, born free in West Africa, kidnapped and transported to bondage in the West Indies and thence to the American South before he arrived in New York under mysterious circumstances; or Amy Jordan, born a slave in Virginia, who worked herself nearly to death in order to purchase freedom for herself and her children; or the blind and emaciated Sophia, who usually greeted her visitors' offerings with "broken thanks" and tears.[2]

These black "clients" of public relief were living out their days in the most wretched section of the Alms House—a damp filthy cellar, surrounded by prostitutes and thieves. The daughters of some of New York's most celebrated patrician families assembled in Bauyer's parlor in the fall of 1839 to discuss a plan to rescue these ex-slaves from such conditions. One of these benevolent women, Mary Shotwell, proposed her era's characteristic solution to the problem of want: the creation of an institution for freedmen and women. Bauyer's sister Elizabeth Clarkson Jay seconded the proposal with a donation of one thousand dollars. A subsequent meeting gave birth to the Society for the Relief of Worthy, Aged, Indigent Colored Persons, designed especially to support the "sick and respectable" needy. A constitution was framed and a Board of Managers, led by first directress Anna Mott, constituted. The women inaugurated their enterprise by admitting twelve applicants judged "worthy of relief" to temporary quarters on the North River. In 1842 a bequest of two thousand dollars helped the Managers purchase a piece of property on Fortieth Street and Fourth Avenue for the erection of a permanent building to house their "pensioners."[3]

At the same time, it became evident that the problem of poor relief for black New Yorkers was larger than providing for worn-out servants in the last stages of their lives. There were also worthy claimants to charity among younger African Americans of both sexes, exposed by poor nutrition and unsanitary living conditions to a range of life-threatening diseases. The "worthy sick" of color who entered the Alms House for medical care were "thrown indiscriminately with those who justly come under criminal discipline." Such association was thought to have led many a "respectable" African American astray. Thus, in 1842, the architects of the Colored Home sought to enlarge the scope of their benevolent activity by attaching an infirmary to their refuge.[4] The following year they petitioned the mayor and aldermen of New York City for a public subsidy to pay for a thousand-dollar lien on property (twelve lots of land in Murray Hill at Fortieth Street) that they had acquired for building their expanded accommodations. They proposed that in exchange, they would, upon the completion of their asylum, transfer twelve to fifteen "aged indigent colored persons" from the Alms House and "furnish them with permanent means of support."[5] The petition clearly bore fruit, for in 1844 the Colored Home started to receive inmates from the Alms House. The

Managers contracted with the Alms House Commissioners to board and clothe black applicants for public relief for the sum of sixty cents per week, raised in 1853 to seventy cents per week.[6]

In 1845 the New York State Legislature incorporated the Colored Home of the City of New York "to provide for the support and comfort of infirm and destitute colored persons of both sexes."[7] The Home successfully petitioned the legislature to repeal earlier laws appropriating ten thousand dollars for a new state hospital in the city; instead, the money would be transferred to its Managers in order to finance the building of a permanent refuge for black paupers.[8] Empowered by the act of 1845 to "take and hold real estate in the city and county of New York not exceeding in value $50,000 and personal property not exceeding $50,000," the Colored Home was subject to state jurisdiction. The state governor and other officials, as well as the Common Council of New York City, reserved the right to visit and inspect the institution; they also required of it an annual report. In 1848 the Society purchased forty-four lots of ground located on Sixty-fifth Street, between Avenue A and First Avenue, as the site for its permanent quarters. There, within an open square, it proceeded to build an imposing structure, which divided male and female inmates into segregated wings, four stories high, and separated by a plot of land. A generous legacy left by philanthropist Maria Shatzel permitted the Managers to add a Lying-in Department to the Home. Destitute African Americans approached the Superintendent of Outdoor Poor for permits to enter the Colored Home. Within the first ten years of its existence, the CH ministered to seven thousand persons, of which a thousand reportedly ended their days in the institution.[9]

Broken Gloom:
Intersecting Voices of Maternalists and the "Pious Poor"

The Colored Home was now part of New York City's confederation of municipal relief agencies, the private arm of a public entity. Born in an age of gathering conflicts over the destiny of the American nation, the institution addressed, through its philosophy and practice, vital intersecting controversies of its day—those of slavery and race relations, poverty and poor relief, and immigration and reform. The visibility and notoriety of "pauperism" in the bustling metropolises of the free North tied antebellum America's emerging debate over slavery to discussions about the promises and pitfalls of free labor capitalism. Proslavery polemicists like

George Fitzhugh contended that slavery was a positively humane alternative to profit-driven free societies. Slavery, in effect, guaranteed an ostensibly inherently inferior group of people the security of subsistence from the cradle to the grave—a safeguard to which the white "wage slaves" of Northern factories had no access. Self-avowed paternalists of the slaveholding South maintained that Africans Americans' allegedly innate limitations would spell their certain extinction in a competitive, individualistic world that failed to take care of its weakest members.[10]

The Colored Home's project of maternalistic benevolence countered these Southern claims about the superiority of slaveholder paternalism vis-à-vis the moral bankruptcy of Northern institutions. At the same time, by questioning secular measures for assessing human worth, the reformers mounted a challenge to white men of their *own* class and section. The CH upheld a gendered vision of racial comity based on a common spirituality that supposedly bound women with African Americans across lines of race and class. Such a vision may tacitly have offered an inclusive alternative to the idea of a white male fraternity on which republican nationalism rested; yet its potential for achieving true equality was stymied by the CH women's narrow conception of African American abilities and destiny. Indeed the operators of the Colored Home frequently lapsed into familiar racialized and gendered constructions of black folks: black minds were "sluggish" and African Americans were "slow to learn." Yet, "blessed with warm susceptibilities," "capable of deep gratitude and intense affection," they were particularly malleable objects of reform: "Show them that you are their friend, and you win their confidence,–gain their confidence and you can mold their character," claimed the benevolent women. Their pensioners' "firmness of purpose" and "patient perseverance" made them promising pupils.[11] These views of black aptitude, combined with the reformers' sense of the intransigence of white racism, prompted them to advocate colonization as the best means of realizing black faculties for success.

Important elements of the philosophy of the Colored Home were set forth in a book of memorials published in 1851 as part of the institution's campaign to raise money for its new-building fund. Entitled *Broken Gloom: Sketches of the History, Character, and Dying Testimony of the Beneficiaries of the Colored Home in the City of New York*, this work, authored by one of its Managers, Mary W. Thompson, was intended primarily to underscore the respectability and worthiness of the Home's candidates for relief. It sought to avoid alienating wealthy white supporters by offering a conservative perspective on black people's future in the United States. Yet what made the slim pamphlet intriguing was the evidence that it contained of the resourcefulness with which the Home's black clients seized their benefactors' discourse of Christian benevolence—with its emphasis on the perfectibility of all races and the primacy of grace over lucre—to register their own pleas for racial justice. By drawing on the direct testimonies of impoverished freed people, the pamphlet spoke to readers in many overlapping voices, sometimes impossible to pry apart. The language of evangelical religion established a framework within which former slaves—much like their brethren down South—could challenge established racial hierarchies in universalist terms mediated by their elite custodians. At the same time, ex-slave biographies offered reformers an opportunity to couch their own pleas against the most virulent forms of antiblack racism in the always-poignant, sometimes-heroic life stories of their wards, ostensibly rendered in the wards' own words.

Broken Gloom prefaced its inmate character sketches with a brief account of the Colored Home's mission. The Home sought primarily to provide "protection and a peaceful home for the respectable, worn-out colored servants of both sexes of our city by sheltering and sustaining them during the lingering days of declining life"; it also sought to furnish them "in their last moments the consolations of religion."[12] Its clients were thus constructed as the ultimate "worthy" poor, worlds apart from the intemperate idlers who were believed to adulterate the halls of the city Alms House with all manner of vice. Reformers maintained that the inmates of the Colored Home, having devoted a lifetime of loyal service to former masters and mistresses, did not deserve to be thrown to their own devices in the uncertain aftermath of emancipation. *Broken Gloom* did go on to acknowledge the Home's stewardship of another group of "colored persons"—dispatched by the Alms House Department—"who, being sick or diseased, hopeless and helpless, have no means to provide for themselves, and who would necessarily, otherwise, become a burden upon society." Such persons found a refuge in the institution for a season, "or until they [were] healed of their sickness and able to resume employment." During their tenure in the Home, they received training in "habits of industry and propriety."[13] Despite the numerical preponderance of this latter group—younger, usually freeborn laborers, sailors, and single women (including prostitutes)—the fund-raising pamphlet focused on the institution's older, more sympathetic, formerly servile dependents. The six men and seventeen women it featured were overwhelmingly aged, and most had begun their lives in chains, whether in the West Indies, the American South, or the environs of New York.

In *Broken Gloom*, Thompson cast in terms of Christian duty the Colored Home's pledge to fulfill the responsibility of a free society toward its most marginal members. Jesus sought out "the wretched and lost; His mercy extended to all ranks and conditions of men; none were too humble for His eye of kingly love—none too depraved for His compassion." It was the spirit of Jesus Christ that animated the benevolent women's efforts on behalf of the "wretched and impoverished children of Africa." As to the raging debates of their day over racial equality, the architects of the Home deliberately made a gendered distinction between "male" and "female" measures of equality. Thompson acknowledged, but preferred not to confront, the debate over the African's alleged biological inferiority, on the grounds that "scientific" criteria for judging race belonged in the realm of *men*. She preferred to dwell instead on black people's lack of opportunity and their potential for spiritual equality. The women did not question the assumption that Africans constituted a "separate caste." Although they preferred to defer the issue of how "the formation of the head and brain make the man or woman what they are" to "the philosopher and man of science," they conceded that "the providence of God, as also the usages and order of society," had placed black Americans "in a different sphere from those who are made of fairer dust."[14]

Nevertheless, the women drew attention to the role of equal opportunity in shaping the human condition. A great deal depended not simply on "the strength of the physical system," but also its "immediate connection with circumstances and advantages, its occupations, means and disposition for improvement." In this context, Thompson drew explicit comparisons between America's treatment of the lowly European immigrants who flocked to its shores on the one hand, and its oppression of African Americans on the other. Many white newcomers to the United States were "miserable outcastes from their own country," victims of "poverty and woe" who fled to "the land of light, liberty, and enterprise" in order to escape the "burdens that oppressed them." "Here, they are taken by the hand, treated as human beings, placed upon the same level as ourselves, and made fellow citizens," Thompson wrote. Such civic equality eventually elevated the formerly degraded to "exalted place and honor." Africans in America had no such advantages. Although Thompson called into question the alleged innateness of the Africans' shortcomings, she could foresee no progress for the race in America: "Of their *seeming* inferiority . . .

much might be said in vindication and defense, from the position in which they have ever been held, since their introduction among civilized communities; taught from the beginning to view themselves as constituted by nature of an inferior order, subject to the will, and to labor for, their superiors." As long as they remained in the midst of those who were unable or unwilling to admit them to the "constitutional privileges" of equal citizenship, persons of color, indoctrinated in negative self-image, were likely to exist in a state of perpetual "vassalage."[15]

America held a promise for Europeans—however debased—that no African could realistically expect, asserted the Managers. Thompson wrote that blacks were no more "degraded" than the "emigrants that crowd our streets, and swarm in every village, and on every canal and railway route in the land." These fresh arrivals displayed an ignorance and viciousness spawned by "those schools of iniquity, the prisons and alms-houses of the old world." Yet America's free shores inspired in them a sentiment that no black person was allowed to harbor, namely "hope, for their children if not for themselves." For the person of color, on the other hand, "no future dawns with brightening ray, no star gild his horizon; his doom, if he remains in this his native land, is moral, intellectual and civil inferiority."[16] Thus, however sympathetic the reformers may have been to the plight of African Americans, their vision of black future in the United States was ultimately static, profoundly pessimistic. Even as they declared their faith in the African's capacity for progress, they argued that in the face of stubborn white racism, such capacity could flourish only outside America.

Under the circumstances, the women saw colonization as the best option for the development of black potential. Liberia would serve as the black person's America—a land of promise that would unleash the subordinated African's genius, as America freed the oppressed European's. *Broken Gloom* claimed that the "growing success" of the colony of freed New World slaves on the West African coast attested to the wisdom of settling black Americans outside the land of their birth. In the meantime, however, the Colored Home proposed to advance "the moral culture and physical condition of those . . . whom Providence has thrown upon our charities."[17]

Benevolent women's support of colonization had significant implications for welfare discourse as articulated by both white reformers and their black "clients." Behind the cover of their conservative rhetoric, CH's welfare discourse became an arena for criticizing the worst abuses of slavery and championing racial harmony based on Christian communalism.

At the same time, however, the Home's advocacy of colonization exposed the limits of their highly cautious brand of racial concord. Public relief for white paupers—overwhelmingly of immigrant extraction—was premised on the logic that the beneficiaries of relief must be prepared to exercise the privileges of eventual citizenship. The architects of the Colored Home, on the other hand, conveyed the sense that their mission was a temporary expedient, designed to help vulnerable and deserving sections of the black population until they could be resettled in more hospitable climes. In this context, the Home's lessons in "industry" and religion would equip future missionaries to carry the torch of enlightenment to heathen lands rather than smooth the path to civic equality.

Broken Gloom attempted, above all, to underscore the relief-worthiness of the Colored Home's charges and simultaneously defy the specter of race war that proslavery polemicists insisted would follow universal emancipation. Toward these ends, the work depicted the inmates as docile, uncomplaining, and grateful beneficiaries of public largesse, first at the city Alms House, and then at the Colored Home. Almost every pensioner profiled in *Broken Gloom* was either very old or very young, debilitated by disease or old age. Portrait after portrait of the ideal slave—not only industrious, but also imbued with deep affection for a white master or mistress—diffused apprehensions of the interracial antagonism that antislavery activists were accused of fomenting. Thus, Betsey Johnson, described as "a pure native of Africa" who arrived in Virginia by way of the West Indies during the American Revolution, "often spoke of her young mistress, whom she tenderly loved," and who gave Johnson her "first lessons of religious truth."[18] Likewise, "blind Sophia," stolen from Africa at the age of seventeen, spoke of her master "with much affection," despite having spent a "long life of accumulated sufferings," four years of which were spent in the city Alms House.[19] Thompson wrote that Sophia "had previously been accustomed to the best food," presumably while in service; in her old age, her changed diet took a toll on her system, "yet she never complained or asked for anything." While at the Alms House, she received her weekly allowance from benevolent visitors "with broken thanks" and tears.[20]

The very young, no less than the old, emerged in the pages of *Broken Gloom* as submissive, grateful, and patient beyond their years. "Poor Johnny," a thirteen-year-old crippled by scrofulous disease in his right hip, was described as being "of a meek and gentle spirit and grateful for every mark of attention shown him, so that it was a pleasure to do him kindness." He was "a great pet" of his physicians, whose dinner table he visited when he was able to walk to receive "whatever had been set aside for him." In the last, painful year of his life, he bore his suffering "with a submission that astonished the beholder."[21] Tommy Warner, like Sophia, spent a lifetime in bondage in the West Indies and the American South before finding refuge in the city Alms House for sixteen years. From there he was transferred to the Colored Home, where he died in 1847 at the age of one hundred, apparently loved by all who knew him.[22] The pamphlet suggested that several inmates transferred their devotion from former owners to their current benefactors, thus reinforcing the image of African Americans as loyal servants. For instance, Eliza Didymus was reported to harbor a strong attachment for the Managers and "each week longed for the visiting day, that she might once more see them, and thank them for all their kindness."[23]

Unlike able-bodied white paupers, whom reformers often portrayed as lazy idlers, Colored Home characters who populated the pages of *Broken Gloom* needed no introduction to the work ethic. Margaret Simpson, a native of North Hampton on Maryland's eastern shore, moved to New York as a child and joined the household of "widow Townsend." She was reported to have said that she had "worked hard all her life," was "fairly worn out in service," and was "thankful that she had so good a home in her last days." Several others had purchased their freedom through hard labor: not once, but over and over again. Amy Jordan, born in bondage in Virginia, worked and paid for her freedom twice, once to her mistress "who died before making out her free papers," and then again to her new owner—or as she put it, "once to her *old mistress*, and once to her *young master*."[24]

The inmates' life histories laid bare the foremost cruelty of slavery—namely, the destruction of family ties. The tale of Peter Bense's odyssey from the royal courts of Europe to the penury of a New World alms house wove this theme into a critique of both slavery and race prejudice. As noted above in the introduction, few Americans—slave or free—could match the cosmopolitan adventures of "Peter Polite," so nicknamed because of his perfect manners. *Broken Gloom*'s account of Peter's experiences simultaneously underscored the irony of racial slavery and the power of acculturation. Peppered with references to Peter's intimate knowledge not simply of the intricacies of European court conduct, but also of complex questions of war and politics across time and space, the narrative undercut popular stereotypes of black degradation and ignorance. The picture the pamphlet sketched of this aged former slave did not resemble a house servant as much as it did a well-bred aristocrat from overseas. Peter Bense was "remarkable for his fluency of expression,—he spoke with a French accent," wrote Mary Thompson. His most precious possessions included "a large parchment, on which was written his passport in the Russian language." With his hand clamped around a brass-headed cane, he cut a dignified figure on the street. Moreover, "his head was covered with full bushy hair, which, being whitened by age, had much the appearance of a wig." Yet this dandified appearance belied the tragedy of Bense's slave past, best captured by his unfulfilled desire for a reunion with his lost family. Mary Thompson wrote that Peter's "retentive" memory broke down when he tried to estimate the time that had elapsed since he last saw his wife and children. It was only when he was close to death that "his spirits revived, and he spoke cheerfully of the hope of again meeting them; associating always the idea that he should find them as youthful and juvenile as when he parted from them–although nearly half a century had passed away."[25]

Amy Jordan, confined to a Virginia plantation for much of her days, had led a far less eventful life than "Peter Polite." Yet their shared experience of bondage visited on them the common sorrow of separation from family. Jordan's only child, a son, was sold away from her at an early age and never heard from again. Jordan crossed many hurdles to make her home in a free city. She supported herself for several years "by honest industry, until her health and strength failed." She then applied to the Alms House for admission and served as one of the Colored Home's pioneer inmates. During her "lingering days" she spoke frequently of her long lost son "with maternal tenderness." Such reminiscences, however, carried no hint of vengeance. Rather, they displayed "gentle humility, and forgiveness" in the spirit of her "Divine Master." As she lay dying, she refused all medication, declaring that she longed to be *"Home."* Jordan's embrace of a divine resting place prompted the institution's physician James Fitch to remark, "How unlike the dying words of the skeptical, yet intellectual and accomplished Charles Lamb: 'I am unwilling to leave this beautiful spot called earth . . . for that unknown land that men call heaven.' What a contrast with the faith of this humble child of Africa! Her last words were, 'Christ is near me; I want nothing more.'"[26]

Fitch's musings about Jordan's faith illustrated another significant element of the Colored Home's approach to the race question. The Home depicted its elderly pensioners as inherently pious. Piety not only offered the basis for forging a sense of religious solidarity between white reformers and their black pensioners, but also presented a different criterion for judging human worth than worldly success or intellectual prowess. Historians have argued that some women reformers in Jacksonian America—such as those of the Female Moral Reform Society—established interclass gender unity by emphasizing the superiority of feminine morality over material wealth. By the 1850s, when class hierarchies had become firmly established, women continued to exercise moral authority by claiming innate virtue and piety. Indeed the language of virtue became a code of class. Yet the rhetoric of Christian piety could also become a code for subverting the racial hierarchies of antebellum America. The women reformers of the Colored Home essentialized African Americans as innately religious, just as the "cult of true womanhood" essentialized women as inherently faithful. To be sure, the inmates' piety was constructed as a docile piety—one that prompted them to identify not with Moses, the liberator of the Old Testament, but rather with the lowly but good Simeon and the submissive but saintly Mary. *Broken Gloom* presented their faith as defined by a complete surrender to God's will, a total abdication of human agency. At her own deathbed, Abigail Dobson was reported to have told the Home's chaplain that she was "happy in the midst of her afflictions" because "I have no will of my own–my Master's will is mine. The Lord is my shepherd, I shall not want."[27]

Dobson exhibited a common trait among the inmates depicted in *Broken Gloom*—namely, detachment from life on earth and a longing for the world beyond. Subject to all kinds of hardship on earth, they appear to have sought solace in contemplations of a happier afterlife. When a member of the Reading Committee asked an aged inmate the secret behind her spirit of calm contentment, the woman was said to have responded, "I live in hope of a better place when I leave this one; I take comfort in thinking of heaven." Moreover, *Broken Gloom*'s inmates apparently saw secular circumstances as ephemeral and the other world as eternal—a worldview that surely made it easier to bear their earthly burdens. Katy Schenck refused to let the new premises of the Colored Home, under construction while she was still alive, excite her too much: "It will be very nice, but it must not make us forget the home in the heavens, . . . This new Home we are to have built for us here, must crumble and fall to the ground; but that in the heavens will last as long as God himself."[28]

Yet even as they appeared to renounce the material world, several residents of the Colored Home were represented as drawing on the discourse of Christian benevolence to raise their own voices against race prejudice in conjunction with their stewards. As scholars of slave religion have argued, the enslaved found in black Christianity the resources for crafting an alternative universe governed by an omnipotent, egalitarian, and just God—an authority higher than the masters who ruled the secular world. The sacred universe of African Americans in slavery breached boundaries erected by modern industrial society between the mundane and spiritual, present and future; it enabled them to develop intensely intimate and immediate relationships with Biblical figures and to experience euphoric states of transfiguration in which they reported "talking" with Christ. The religious practices of enslaved blacks may have proved a poor weapon of assault against the *system* of slavery as a whole, but these beliefs certainly helped them preserve their psychic integrity against the devastation of chattel bondage.[29]

It is possible that evangelical Christianity served a similar psychological and emotional coping mechanism against white supremacy. The shared piety of white benevolent women and their black beneficiaries established the ground for not only claiming a common humanity, but also for challenging racial and social rankings based on wealth and intellect. It offered African American "clients" a standard by which they could assess their self-worth favorably in relation to those more powerful in the secular world. Katy Schenck's conversion experience and encounter with female believers and male skeptics—narrated in the first person to one of the Home's benevolent visitors, and reproduced in *Broken Gloom* through the visitor's medium—illustrates this point. Schenk was born a slave in the family of Gerrit Vandeveer of Monmouth, New Jersey. She spent the first thirty years of her life in the Gerrit household, located "within three miles where *the great battle was fought*," she reminisced. Schenk reportedly praised her master as a "good and kind man" who gave her "plenty to eat" and treated her well. She then went on to describe her struggles with religion. From the ages of twelve to twenty-eight, she "gave" herself to "loose and wicked company" and resisted the call of "the Lord" with all her might. Then one day, she recalled:

> When my mind was thus dreadfully distressed, I was going a milking, but I felt so wretched, I did not know what to do; it seemed that hell was ready to receive me—it was evening–I fell upon my knees—I prayed, *Lord, have mercy upon me and help me!* All at once, I looked up, and I thought I saw heaven open, and it appeared to me the Lord was stooping down and lifted me up; and these words came to me: "*Thy people shall*

be willing in the day of Thy power." I stood still–I felt such a change! I hardly knew what I was doing—I could not milk, I could do nothing but rejoice–I shouted aloud, and ran home, telling all my folks how happy I was. They did not know what to think; they asked me if I was crazy. I went to bed, but I could not sleep for my happiness. I felt now that the Lord had fast hold of me, and I was safe.[30]

Each of the two voices in Schenck's account—her own and that of her benevolent mediator—drew on Schenck's faith in order to subvert conventional racial roles at separate points in the narrative. The mediator, Mrs. T., recalled that on a visit to the bedside of the aged and ailing Schenck, she started to read the story of "good old Simeon" in the Bible. "You remember his history, do you not?" she reportedly asked Schenck. The old woman responded, "What? Old Simeon and Anna? Yes, indeed!" Mrs. T. went on to describe her own astonishment at the eloquence with which Schenck proceeded to expound on the Bible. "I was silent, and waited to listen to her; I had gone to be her instructor and consoler; but she was my teacher, and I felt I could linger at her side, for it was good to be there," Mrs. T declared. As the visitor remembered the story, Schenck said that she identified with both Simeon, ready to depart the world according to God's will, and Mary: "I lay here upon my bed, and I *think*, and *think*; I don't say nothing, but I feel as Mary did–I don't tell all I feel, but I keep it in my heart; I am an ignorant woman, and cannot express myself very well; but I trust I have been taught in the school of Christ, and have learned of Him."[31] Yet Mrs. T. made clear that Schenck's knowledge and commitment to the Bible belied her profession of ignorance and put her in a position of strength vis-à-vis her more fortunate, and *white*, Christian sister. Mrs. T's observation that Schenck "was my teacher" suggested a level of deference to a humble ex-slave that surely challenged established structures of domination based on race and class.

It was during the same visit that Schenk herself apparently questioned conventional social hierarchies by narrating to Mrs. T. the story of an encounter with white skeptics. The former bondswoman said that while traveling on a vessel on the Ohio River many years before, she had made remarks about religion, provoking scorn from her fellow travelers. The captain of the boat, his wife, as well as a group of young men on board "who were going to some college," joined hands "and tried to make sport of me, taunting me for my complexion, making many foolish speeches, such as they thought would hurt my feelings." Schenck said nothing until they had stopped, whereupon she asked, "Gentlemen, have you got through with your speeches?" When they replied in the affirmative, she declared that it was her turn. "Well, you are on your way to College, ain't you?" "Yes," they responded. "Well, you need schooling, but you'll never complete your education till you get it in the school of Christ; and, if you don't get it there, and die in your sins, you will *perish forever!* You have tried to make sport of me, and you think you are fine gentlemen, but I tell you, you ain't hurt my feelings; I feel sorry for you, *because* I think you . . . are not wise unto salvation." A young Englishman then turned to her and asked, "Mother, where did you get your learning . . . Did you get it from the priest?" Schenck replied that she had learned her wisdom "in the school of Christ, and from His blessed word the *Bible*." She so moved her tormentors with her words that they treated her with politeness and civility the rest of the way.[32] This *Broken Gloom* version, whether true or not, conveyed the sense that Schenck, a lowly servant, thus openly questioned the meaning of all those outward signs of gentility to which her social superiors clung, especially their education. Her complexion would matter little more than the "fine gentlemen's" worldly successes on Judgment Day. Thus Schenck emerged as having asserted, boldly and publicly, what the enslaved on Southern plantations discussed in private—namely, justice in the afterlife. Of course, the narrative's reference to the source of her knowledge—the Bible rather than a "priest"—reflected more than a hint of the anti-Catholicism characteristic of many Protestant benevolent enterprises.

    Like Schenck, other inmates experienced conversion experiences, graphically described in *Broken Gloom*. These accounts of spiritual regeneration among the most marginal members of society encoded multiple messages. From the reformers' perspective, they suggested their charges' excellent potential for missionary work. Such potential was, of course, particularly useful in a class of people ostensibly bound for colonization. For the inmates, on the other hand, the attainment of grace became a source not only of solace, but of empowerment as well, especially when it conferred the authority to preach. The reformers of the Colored Home claimed, over and over again, that their great faith and "retentive memory" made black people natural ministers. "Old Hercules," six feet four inches tall, large and muscular, was a good example. Once a slave, Hercules Schureman purchased his freedom "by industry and good conduct" and became a Methodist minister. He was described as "dignified," with a manner that commanded respect. Although "unschooled in human learning," nature had endowed him with "great mental abilities" and an excellent memory, which served him well for fifty years as he spread the word about "that liberty wherewith Christ maketh his people free."[33]

Betsey Johnson, although illiterate, had so "retentive" a memory that she could quote extensively "from the Scriptures and Dr. Watt's hymns." Women were depicted as aspiring to careers as missionaries. Phillis Douglas, while a slave in New Jersey, prayed for freedom and the opportunity to preach. Emancipated late in life, she was able to fulfill her ministerial ambitions when she entered the Colored Home. She could read, and thus spent many happy hours teaching younger inmates their catechism and how to sing hymns. A sixty-year-old woman, hitherto unlettered, learned under Douglas's tutelage "to read the pages of God's word" with "a stammering but exulting tongue." July Richards, although not a formal preacher, was said to devote her waking hours to reading the Scriptures and engaging the sick and dying in religious conversation. So articulate was she that her impressed benefactors claimed, "Gladly would we have sat at her feet to hear her discourse in simple eloquence of the preciousness of *her* Jesus, as it always pleased her to call Him." This observation was a powerful statement on the role of religious communion in bridging chasms of race and class between the well-placed champions of the Colored Home and their less fortunate charges.[34]

On the basis of its inmate profiles, *Broken Gloom* concluded, "We see that the minds of these sable ones were as susceptible of those feelings which dignify and elevate human nature as those of others; . . . The influence of grace upon the heart is the same in its effects upon all classes." Grace humbled pride, subdued the will, and persuaded a "poor, wretched sinner" to aspire to salvation "on God's terms. And this is the same, whether in the son of a prince, or untutored, unlettered child of obscurity, whatever his complexion or circumstances. He who 'made of one blood all nations of men,' careth alike for all."[35] Thus, in the Colored Home's reformist vision, the "pious poor," by virtue of their faith, established legitimate claims not simply to relief, but also to a color-blind Christian community that posed an alternative to the masculinized imaginary of the white republic. That the reformers' conception of spiritual equality did not translate into an activist commitment to civic equality was a measure of their social conservatism. It may also have been prompted by a pragmatic appraisal of the limits of progressivism that an institution dependent on private funding from wealthy patrons could afford to embrace in that age.

The Advent of the "Low and Vicious"

Broken Gloom profiled aged servants without means, the Colored Home's original target constituency. After 1844, however, the nature of the Home's inmate population changed drastically. The arrangement to receive "all colored paupers" who sought municipal relief brought a flood of applicants similar to white clients in the city Alms House. The Managers did not welcome all aspects of the change: "From having been the quiet retreat of the aged and infirm, [the Home] became at once the refuge of the low and vicious . . . occasioning the managers great solicitude and many trials."[36] Until the Alms House Department moved to Blackwell's Island in 1848, it maintained admissions records of paupers dispatched to the Colored Home. These records contain information about the sex, age, birthplaces, and commitment causes of black relief applicants, as well as their "occupations." The "occupation" category connoted paid work for men, and marital status for women, its gendered construction reflecting, of course, the middle-class ideal of "separate spheres." These records offer a more textured portrait of Colored Home clients than the sparse statistics included in the institution's annual reports to the city. They also afford a basis for comparing the profile of black relief-seekers with that of their Irish counterparts.

A random sample of one hundred African Americans who applied for aid to the Alms House Department and were referred to the Colored Home in 1848 shared broad parallels with a similar sample of Irish men, women, and children sent to Blackwell's Island the same year. Both populations were nearly evenly split between men and women. The largest number in each group were in their twenties, laborers if they were men, single or widowed if they were women. The most common cause for seeking municipal aid across the populations was "sickness," followed by "destitution." At the Colored Home, for instance, the greatest proportion of deaths from a range of diseases—phthisis, consumption, typhus, puerperal fever, and the like—occurred among inmates in their twenties and thirties. Blacks were similar to the Irish even in terms of their migrant status—an overwhelming majority of them (85 percent of the men and 75 percent of the women) were born outside New York City, in places that ranged from Trinidad to New Jersey. The largest group of these black migrants came from the Border South—Virginia, Maryland, and Kentucky—and included a disproportionate share of men, bearing out the conclusions reached in the first chapter about the sex ratio of the Southern-born, working poor African Americans in New York. As seen in chapter 1, black New Yorkers formed communal living arrangements and pooled resources for mutual aid. There is no information about the length of time that migrant clients in the sample under discussion had lived in the city, but it seems reasonable to conclude that they may have been less rooted in local communal or "race" networks than native-born New Yorkers—especially if they were young and alone—and hence more in need of public assistance. In any case, few working poor African Americans or Irish—whether native to New York or not, and whether living communally or alone—had immunity against the most common source of destitution: the pervasive scourge of illness and epidemics (see tables 23, 25, and 26, in appendix).[37]

Within these broad patterns of similarity in black and Irish client profiles, however, there were some differences. Not surprisingly, "paupers" of color exhibited less occupational diversity than their Irish counterparts, reflecting the gradual constriction in the work avenues open to African Americans. Nearly 85 percent of black men in the group were laborers, the rest consisting of a few waiters, a coachman, a sailor, and a blacksmith. The Irish, by contrast, included a larger proportion (29 percent) of artisans and members of the construction trades. Laborers were, of course, particularly prone to industrial accidents, poor health, and seasonal unemployment, so their overrepresentation in "pauper populations" across the races is not unexpected. What seems equally clear, however, is that skilled workers fell prey to the ravages of "metropolitan industrialization" as well, to the point of having to apply for public assistance in emergencies like sickness and unemployment (see table 24, in appendix).

Other differences between blacks and the Irish centered on the proportions of married women and children in each group. Only about one-fifth of African American female clients were married, but over 30 percent of their Irish sisters claimed that status. This discrepancy may have had something to do with the higher marriage rates among Irish women (compared with black women), noted in the discussion of working poor social profiles in chapter 1. Moreover, children constituted 9 percent of the black client sample but only 1 percent of the Irish group. Also noted before, Irish women in New York married relatively late, had children relatively late, and were more likely than African Americans to raise them in families with male earners present; this tendency may have accounted in part for the lower proportion of children in the Irish population sent to the Alms House. On the other hand, migrant black women in domestic service—if they had few kin resources in the city—may have viewed the Alms House or the Colored Home as a temporary refuge for children whom they could not take to work. But perhaps more important than any of these reasons was Irish access to a larger number of better-funded private relief and child care agencies—including those run by the Catholic Church—options not readily available to black mothers.

A more diversified inmate population called for systematic classification at the Colored Home. The variables of age, sex, and medical condition governed a client's assignment to one of four departments, which retained the distinction between the so-called deserving and undeserving poor. Members of the Department for the Aged and Infirm clearly offered a profile of the quintessential "worthy poor." Abandoned children and some of the pregnant women sent to the Lying-in Department were also deemed fitting candidates for charity. The male and female hospitals, on the other hand, received able-bodied paupers alleged to have led "vicious lives" and contracted diseases from "exposure, intemperance, or other evil habits." It was this group that the Home targeted most of all in its enterprise to bring about moral regeneration.[38]

Although the random samples of client populations taken from the Alms House records showed a nearly equal distribution of men and women applying for public aid, the statistical tables compiled by the directresses of the Colored Home reveal that women predominated heavily among those received by the institution from all sources, public and private. The female hospital was the most crowded division of the Home during normal years, accounting for well over one-third of the Home's inmate population during the 1850s. The next most populous department was that of the Aged and Infirm. If the sex ratio of the inmates profiled in *Broken Gloom* is any guide, the Aged department harbored more women than men as well. Moreover, the Lying-in Department admitted pregnant women in addition to children. In 1855, for instance, it provided refuge to nineteen prospective or new mothers in addition to seventy-one children. The significant presence of women in the Colored Home population may be explained by the feminization of New York's working poor black population, observed in the first chapter. Moreover, black men were more likely than women to live in nuclear or communal family arrangements, rather than alone, and may therefore have been less vulnerable to homelessness.

Of course, family support or communal wage economies provided little security against medical emergencies, the most common cause for seeking public assistance among African Americans. Men and women—laborers and sailors, laundresses and seamstresses, servants and prostitutes—were susceptible to a variety of illnesses. The most consistently reported affliction for both black men and women was phthisis, which took the lives of fifteen men and eighteen women in 1849, and killed fourteen men and twenty-four women in 1855.[39] In addition, the periodic outbreak of epidemics created special demands for public relief. The cholera scourge of 1849, for instance, claimed nine men and eighteen women at the CH; in addition, it left so many children orphaned that the Colored Orphan Asylum had to step in to relieve some of the pressure.[40] "Female" ailments, like puerperal fever, also featured among the causes of death at the Colored Home. Given the CH Managers' laments about the "depravity" of their post-1844 clients, it is reasonable to assume that a fair number of prostitutes sought refuge in the female hospital.

The architects of the Colored Home relied on religious instruction and work as their primary means of reform. The residents of the institution evidently wished for a minister of their race, because in 1844 the Home invited Reverend Charles Ray, a black minister of the Presbyterian Church, to lead a Tuesday morning service. In addition, it offered prayer services all week led by Methodist ministers of both races.[41] "Reading visits" by the Managers, as well as the establishment of a library, buttressed these efforts to promote "moral and intellectual" progress among the inmates.[42] Like *Broken Gloom*, successive annual reports of Colored Home recounted the "religious anxiety" and "spirit of inquiry" among patients in the male and female hospitals, as well as the many heartening cases of discovery of "the gospel method of salvation."[43] Seventeen-year-old Lucy Adams, described as "depraved and abandoned" when she entered the Home's Shatzel Lying-in Department, was said to have developed a "Christian deportment" by the time she died.[44]

Work represented a vital component of the Home's regimen of reform, although it carried different meanings for different constituencies of inmates. Retired servants were no strangers to hard work, of course. However extensive their employment histories, their continued relief-worthiness required that they contribute toward their own support as far as possible. Moreover, self-sufficiency was materially and symbolically central to the meaning and experience of freedom for many of the Home's formerly enslaved traditional pensioners. Thus, the Managers insisted that some occupation was necessary in order to relieve the tedium of "idleness," which these "children of affliction" had been "obliged to lead for years, while tenants of our Alms House, merely for want of a friendly hand to aid and encourage them to *help themselves.*" In 1844 they reported that two blind men "[made] themselves useful by turning the handle of a washing machine," and victims of rheumatism and paralysis picked wool and sewed carpet rages, while more able residents cultivated a vegetable garden.[45]

For those in the Aged and Infirm department, labor was voluntary. Inmates received a small weekly wage in accordance with the amount and quality of their work. The only requirement imposed on them was that they pay a fee for clothing (the objective of which was to instill self-respect and interest in private property). The Managers considered this principle particularly important in view of the fact that their clients had historically been denied the opportunity to accumulate private property. The resident physician, James Fitch, explained that such a policy "immediately raises them above the grade of paupers—they feel that they have earned what they possess; and consequently soon become very careful of their own property, having acquired, by habits of industry, some sense of its value, and also become more cleanly in their appearance."[46]

The Home's younger generation of inmates, born in the working poor neighborhoods of urban centers, was assumed to require training in the "habits of industry" well-known to their older Home-mates. It was not the "value of their service" that counted as much as "the establishment in their minds of the great principle that industry and happiness are closely associated,—and that the greatest burden in life is want of employment." Indeed, the Managers maintained that work served as the best remedy for the "evils" of discontentment and intractability. They assured the public that those able but unwilling to work were instantly discharged.[47] The Home aimed to place in service those ready to be discharged. In 1849 the institution claimed to have found work for sixteen adults and children, generating a clamor for employment among its other inmates—especially women. "So great has been their demand for employment, that we have had no ability to satisfy it, from our resources," the Managers reported in 1849. "The shelves of our store-room have groaned under the weight of articles of wearing apparel, and bed clothing, which were all prepared for use by our once listless, indolent pensioners. Still the cry came to our ears, for work,—more work." The Home approached a Female Assistance Society for help and obtained from it an order to make garments. Although the Managers credited the inmates' thirst for occupation to the success of the Home's reform program, it is likely that jobless young black women with few options viewed the institution as an employment agency as much as anything else.

In 1850 the Home inaugurated workshops in willow work. Inmates worked on covering bottles and demijohns. Fitch proposed to set up an establishment for spinning cotton in order to offer the inmates steady employment not excessively vulnerable to fluctuations in the market. "This method of labor seems in many respects peculiarly adapted to the capacity and ability of those committed to our charge," he observed.[48] Although Managers hoped to make a "house of industry" out of the Home, the shortage of capital impeded their attempts to provide the inmates with steady employment. The difficulty of selling the willow baskets produced by the inmates jeopardized even this meager enterprise by depriving the Managers of the funds to buy supplies for the work.[49] Like founders of black voluntary associations, they suffered from a severe deficit of private support and discrimination in municipal funding for their benevolent work.

The Civil War brought to a head herrenvolk Democratic animus against the particular brand of charity that the Colored Home represented: Republican, with roots in manumission politics, and ties to evangelical industrialists supportive of a centralizing state and the reform of Roman Catholic immigrants. This hostility played out in a murderous assault on the Colored Home's sister institution, the Colored Orphan Asylum, on the first of five steamy days of civil insurrection in July 1863 known as the New York City Draft Riots. The Civil War may have begun—as President Abraham Lincoln told Congress in July 1861—as an armed struggle to protect the integrity of the American Union and a people's contest to preserve the legitimacy of democratic government; however, a confluence of factors—military exigencies on the ground, the tenacity of Confederate resistance, evolving political opinion in Congress and among the Northern public, and, most importantly, the actions of the enslaved themselves as they fled to Union lines en masse, offering their services as spies, scouts, and laborers of various descriptions—prompted Lincoln to redefine the goals of war. The Emancipation Proclamation, which he issued in January 1863, transformed the war for union into a social revolution promising the dissolution of slavery in the event of a Union victory—a pledge that the Thirteenth Amendment to the U.S. Constitution was to codify two years later.[50]

Meanwhile, the prospect of Emancipation, coupled with the enactment of a Union draft in March 1863 that allowed wealthy men to buy their way out of military service, quickened the flurry of white identity politics in which antiwar Democrats traded. Democratic leaders warned that hordes of black émigrés would take away "white" jobs. According to Roediger, integrated workplaces raised the specter of the sexual "amalgamation" of labor, just as antislavery activism was tagged "political amalgamation."[51] White workers complained about the cheap price placed by the draft on their heads: they were liable to be "sold" for the draft exemption cost of three hundred dollars—a value far below the price of black slaves in the South. They also took umbrage at the encroachments of a centralizing federal government identified with both the privileges of a local elite and the interests of African Americans.[52]

These streams of resentment culminated in five bloody days of murder and pillage beginning in the early hours of July 13 and led first by traditional artisans, including native-born Protestants, and later by Irish Catholic industrial and construction workers. They attacked various symbols of the emerging order—government and draft buildings, policemen and draft officers, factories, shops, docks, and the mansions of wealthy Republicans on Lexington and Fifth avenues. The Colored Orphan Asylum on Fifth Avenue between Forty-third and Forty-fourth streets became an early casualty of this mob fury, going down in flames in a matter of twenty minutes. Other racist atrocities followed. White rioters destroyed African American tenements, boardinghouses, and dance halls on the waterfront and elsewhere in the city, and they dragged black people off downtown streetcars and from their own homes. They killed eleven black men, hanging, burning, stabbing, or drowning their bodies; they dragged one corpse through the streets by its genitals, as though exorcizing both their work spaces of the stain of "nigger" labor and their psyches of the "savage" sensuality that they, in their racism, may have projected onto blacks.[53]

Ultimately, the Civil War underscored the obsolescence of the Colored Home's conservative, maternalist vision of an interracial, hierarchical community of white patrons and black clients bound by their common disposition to piety. It also put out of fashion its commitment to colonization as a goal of public relief. Even as the Fourteenth Amendment undermined the legal logic of black deportation by tying American citizenship to birth or naturalization, irrespective of race, the fury of white reaction dramatized by the Draft Riot presaged the persistence of the white republic for a long time to come. That persistence shaped ambiguous, complex relationships between race and reform, nowhere more apparent than in benevolent projects to preserve republican institutions by saving women and children before and after the Civil War.

PART II

4

The Color of Juvenile Justice
The New York House of Refuge

> It was painful to observe the studied manner in which white and colored children were separated and distinguished from each other, as if moral improvement could be promoted in either by encouraging pride and inflicting humiliation.
> —E. S. Abdy on the New York House of Refuge,
> *Journal of a Residence and Tour in the United States of North America from April, 1833, to October, 1834*

> William H. Brown, colored, from the Jefferson Market Police, aged 13 years, 31st May, 1850. Born in New York. His parents are dead. His sister Catherine Hamilton, lives in Minetta Lane . . . He says since his parents' death, he has lived with his sister, and worked with her husband, who keeps a fish stand. He acquired a habit of running out and staying away nights. For this, his sister had him sent here as a vagrant.
> —Case history of William H. Brown,
> New York House of Refuge, November 6, 1850

New York City in the 1840s embraced within its frenetic shores the best of worlds and the worst of worlds. Within sight of splendid Broadway lay what sensationalist reporters dramatized as the wretched ambit of poverty, its features most grotesquely magnified in the notorious district of Five Points, "just back of City Hall, towards the East River."[1] It was into this latter world of crooked streets, foul air, slouching beggars, overcrowded cellars, predatory epidemics, crime, and prostitution that a thirteen—year-old cabin boy of African descent named James Hubbard stepped, off a Canadian ship on a frosty December day in 1840. Two months later, this young native of Bermuda joined the inmate population of the first juvenile reformatory in the United States, known as the New York House of Refuge [hereafter NYHR]. Hubbard explained to his case recorder that he had jumped ship because he suspected that the captain intended to sell him into slavery in the American South. "A colored man" brought him to the city Alms House, which in turn dispatched him to the Refuge. Subsequently, the youth was indentured to a farmer in New Jersey, who sent glowing reports of the boy's work and conduct. James Hubbard had found in the Refuge a precarious haven against bondage, in part through the intercession of an informal web of "race kin" forged in the public spaces of New York's meanest streets.[2]

A few months before Hubbard's introduction to New York, another young seafaring African American entered the NYHR under somewhat different circumstances. Fifteen-year-old William Groorsbeck, originally of Newark, New Jersey, was the son of a bootblack and a domestic worker who lived in service in the Bowery. When Groorsbeck lost his job as a clerk on a steamboat—and with it his board and lodging—his parents took him to the police and had him committed to the reformatory for vagrancy. The young man assured his new custodians that he "never stole anything." Evidently, for Groorsbeck and his parents, the Refuge was meaningful less as a vehicle of cultural uplift than as a material resource to buttress a precarious family wage economy.[3]

The cases of James Hubbard and William Groorsbeck illustrate an important aspect of the urban black working poor's relationship with Victorian America's first reformatory for "incipient criminals."[4] They defy contemporary popular impressions about the reticence of working poor African Americans to make use of public resources in their hour of need. As shall be seen, the New York House of Refuge deferred to the assumptions of the white republic—a deference manifested in its segregation of black inmates, and corroborated by the racialized statistical language that it adopted to classify its inmates in annual reports prepared for public authorities and private donors. At its inception, the Refuge aimed to sow the seeds of a unified white citizenry worthy of American national belonging. To that end it sought to remove juvenile delinquents of European descent from the noxious influences of their allegedly unworthy families (as well as from the pernicious reach of hardened criminals in regular prisons) and to socialize them in the virtues of honesty, industry, order, obedience, punctuality, sobriety, and thrift.

Yet the institution's decision to accept (although not integrate) black clients after the first ten years of its existence complicated the racial dynamics of its identity and mission. African Americans acted and argued in ways that forged a common subaltern identity with the white poor, especially the Irish. In an age of assault on outdoor relief, the NYHR, like other institutions designed as laboratories for reconstituting the character of the poor, was itself somewhat refashioned, at least partly, by the volition of its targets—black no less than white—into an agency of relief. The reformers' inclusion of the nebulous category of "vagrants" as appropriate subjects for salvation provided a window of opportunity that African Americans—perhaps even more often than whites—seized to enlarge and tap the charitable potential of the reformatory in innumerable ways. Driven by a dynamic between the reformers' aims of cultural assimilation on the one hand, and the laboring poor's material exigencies on the other, the institution emerged as a multipurpose relief institution—a long-term child care center for single mothers, a maternity home for pregnant teenagers, a hospital and insane asylum for sick children, a refuge for fugitive slaves and freed children, a schoolhouse for reluctant child laborers, an arbitrator in family conflicts, and, of course, an orphanage for destitute minors. By creatively manipulating the doctrine of *parens patri*, which underlay juvenile justice, to shore up their family wage economies, as well as mediate sometimes-thorny familial relationships, black working parents and their children joined their poor white compatriots to blur the lines between charity and punitive discipline. They also managed to shake the coherence of moral distinctions between the categories of "worthy" and "unworthy" poor to which bourgeois reformers clung tenaciously throughout the nineteenth century. In the process, they asserted an interracial "underclass" identity that mediated and muddied the premise of absolute racial difference underlying the Refuge's segregationist policies.[5]

Such an identity did not, of course, translate into interracial solidarity. But it did inject into reform discourse a class-specific challenge to the particular configuration of economic self-sufficiency and moral virtue that benevolent reformers touted as the embodiment of a unified (implicitly white) republican masculinity. Further fractures in this racialized imaginary of civic fraternity stemmed from the very nature of the Refuge's reform strategy, especially in the turbulent years of economic revolution following the Civil War. Such a strategy, by relying on reformation through indefinite commitments and contract labor, clouded the boundary between freedom and coercion that set white privilege apart from black dependence. The contradiction between the Refuge's deference to the rhetoric of whiteness on the one hand, and its imposition of forced labor on black and white inmates alike on the other, prompted its white male inmates to assert the citizenship prerogatives attached to their whiteness in violent ways. An all-male inmate insurgency in 1872 prompted a series of state investigations that allowed "white"—mostly Irish—inmates to publicly assert their claims to the "natural rights" of American citizenship, including those of habeas corpus and religious freedom. The public pressure that ensued led to changes in the organization and reform methods of the institution between 1887 and 1910.[6] By contrast, African Americans, without recourse to the sort of political clout that Euro-American inmates and their relatives were able to muster, adopted more informal, less public forms of negotiation with the Refuge throughout the nineteenth century. Yet NYHR inmates—whether black or Irish, male or female—shared the experience of using elements of the institution's own rhetoric and practices to remonstrate against their received subaltern identities in different ways.

Juvenile Justice and Republican Citizenship in an Emerging Market Society

A direct progeny of the Society for the Prevention of Pauperism (SPP), the New York House of Refuge emerged as part of a holistic, multidimensional movement by prominent New York businessmen, philanthropists, and politicians to secure the future of the republic by raising a productive citizenry and saving public funds. By 1823 SPP founders John Griscom and Thomas Eddy, joined by a younger cohort of reformers like the lawyers James Watson Gerard and Charles G. Haines, and the businessman-turned–Tammany politician and mayor Stephen Allen, had concluded that the path to redeeming the poor lay through their children. Lockean notions of the tabula rasa, buttressed by Protestant revivalist doctrines of perfectionism and individual redemption, provided the cultural framework for crafting the theory and practice of juvenile reform; the British-inspired theory of *parens patri* supplied its legal underpinnings. Jacksonian America's market revolution, together with the social transformations and cultural anxieties it unleashed, served as the immediate context in which such reform took shape. The cultural invention of childhood tied to the cult of domesticity became an integral component of bourgeois identity formation in the nineteenth century and supplied a potent rationale for juvenile justice in an age threatened with social disorder. Children were conceived as entitled to the right to be nurtured and educated by loving, pious, and virtuous mothers who stayed home. Indeed such entitlement had public implications, for it presumably translated into the creation of responsible citizens and workers in an emerging world of democratic capitalism. Working poor parent-child relationships, driven by the realities of an ever-changing and uncertain labor market, deviated from middle-class norms; they seemed abusive and exploitative—a fertile breeding ground for juvenile delinquents. Under the circumstances, the SPP deplored the imprisonment of youthful transgressors alongside hardened criminals in regular prisons and argued that children gone astray should instead be rehabilitated by placing them in a more wholesome environment.[7]

The Society founded the NYHR in order to reclaim petty criminals and vagrants "sliding gradually but certainly into dangerous and evil causes," yet young enough to be reformed by removing them from homes where they were "accustomed to witness . . . nothing but a degenerating example, taught to observe intemperance favorably, and to hear obscene and profane language without disgust, obliged to beg, and even encouraged to acts of dishonesty, to satisfy the wants induced by the indolence of their parents."[8] Instead, the juvenile reformatory, as a model of "that time-honored institution—the Christian family," would supplant the "corrupting" influence of the children's natural families.[9] Thus, it would join a cohort of "moral engines," including free schools and Sunday schools, in the project to "extirpate crime and pauperism" by "fortify[ing] the infant mind with good principles and placing it above the contagion of bad example."[10]

At stake was nothing less than the future of the republican experiment. Stephen Allen expressed a common perspective on the issue when he warned that the "rising generation of the poor" represented a threat to the republic. At a meeting of the SPP on December 19, 1823, Griscom made the case for a juvenile refuge, urging the government to assume the "paternal" role of safeguarding the virtues of the community by bestowing on its youth "the right which every child may demand of its parents, of being well-instructed in the nature of its duties, before it is punished for the breach of their observance."[11] At the same meeting, the SPP dissolved, yielding to the creation of the Society for the Reformation of Juvenile Delinquents. The following year, on March 28, 1824, the state legislature incorporated the Society, empowering it to receive "all such children as shall be taken up or committed as vagrants, or convicted of criminal offenses" in New York City. Two years later, the legislature declared the Refuge the official juvenile reformatory in New York State, the receptacle of any children below the age of sixteen who were deemed improper subjects of the state prison. Intended to represent "the happy union of public and private action," the New York House of Refuge, while privately managed, received its subjects through commitment by such public authorities as the courts, police magistrates, and the Commissioners of the Alms House (reconstituted as the Department of Public Charities and Correction after 1860). The state, moreover, played a significant role in funding the enterprise through legislative appropriations, the proceeds from a head tax on arriving transatlantic immigrants, and license fees from New York City's taverns, theaters, and circuses. The choice of these revenue sources reflected the assumption that juvenile crime stemmed in part from immigration, intemperance, and commercial entertainment. It also highlighted the Refuge's political clout, vested in well-connected supporters, such as mayors Allen and Cadwallader D. Colden, the latter of whom later entered the state senate at Albany.[12]

On January 1, 1825, at an inaugural ceremony graced by the presence of New York Governor DeWitt Clinton, juvenile reform in the United States made its debut in a modest building within the walls of an abandoned federal arsenal situated at the intersection of Bloomingdale and Old Boston Post roads between Twenty-second and Twenty-third streets, on the periphery of the city. Boys and girls received by the Refuge were segregated into two stone buildings separated by a high wooden fence; these children were permitted no communication with each other, except at public worship.[13] With slavery not yet dead, and most free blacks disfranchised by property qualifications, the reformatory, at its inception, and for ten years thereafter, excluded African American children from its project of turning "reprobates" into worthwhile citizens.

The reform program of the Refuge combined a regimen of supervised work with basic education and evangelical Protestant religious training, strictly regulated by the clock and the bell. The children rose at dawn each day, made their own beds, and marched to the washroom in order, following which they paraded in close formation for inspection "as to cleanliness and dress." Then they attended morning prayers, went to school, and partook of a breakfast of bread, molasses, and rye coffee. Labor at their respective workshops took up the rest of the day, punctuated by dinner, where "nutritious soups, meat, potatoes and bread" constituted the most commonly served fare. Evening school and prayers capped their day, which ended when they were locked into their "Sleeping Halls" at 8 p.m.[14]

Work and indenture practices deferred to the middle-class cult of separate spheres. Male inmates produced articles such as brushes, cane chairs, shoes, wallets, and spectacle cases under contract to businessmen, who submitted closed bids for inmate labor. Such labor was, however, to be regarded "principally with reference to the moral benefits, and not merely to the profits to be derived from it," the Managers insisted. The young women, directed by the matron, sewed uniforms, worked in the laundry, and mended and cleaned in order to master the skills of "housewifery." Children judged to have completed the reform program successfully were indentured, preferably in the rural districts of New York and New Jersey, to masters who contracted to provide their apprentices with training in a trade, in addition to board and lodging, clothing, and instruction in religion and the three R's. Upon the expiration of the term of his or her servitude, each child was to receive a new Bible, a suit of new clothes, and some money. While boys were indentured to farmers, mechanics, manufacturers, or masters of vessels engaged in whale fishery or the U.S. Navy until they reached the age of twenty-one, girls were usually placed in domestic service until they turned eighteen. Thus the project of reform was founded on the underlying assumption that the path to individual redemption lay in acculturation to the values of the Protestant ethic and the bourgeois cult of domesticity.[15] During the first ten years of its operation, the Refuge claimed to have rescued 1,148 minors from the jaws of "crime and infamy" and placed them on the course to becoming "from degraded outcastes, useful and reputable citizens of this Republic."[16]

By the beginning of the Civil War, the NYHR had moved to a complex of imposing Italian-style buildings bordering the East River on Randall's Island, directly opposite the area of Manhattan between 115th and 120th streets. The much-vaunted efficiency of its methods had won it praise from esteemed reformers like the jurist Edward Livingston and the penologist Dorothea Dix.

The Color of Juvenile Justice

Two years after the passing of slavery in 1827, the state of black New York seemed to the Managers of the Society for the Reformation of Juvenile Delinquents desperate enough to merit attention. The reformers estimated that only a tenth of the black population had regular employment and that at least 15 percent belonged to families that exposed their children to "dissipation and crime of the grossest kind" or to uncaring guardians.

They expressed small wonder that as many as 219 children of color had been committed to the Penitentiary as criminals or to the Alms House as vagrants. The Managers believed that black children were not only vulnerable to the "same inducements to become criminals, by the vicious examples of their parents" as their white counterparts, but that they had even fewer opportunities to learn "any mechanical occupation, by the difference in their color, and other circumstances incident to their situation in this country." This situation was exacerbated by the alleged "prejudice" of their parents, who, the Managers averred, "having been slaves themselves, feel the utmost repugnance to bind their children as apprentices to any useful employment, under the apprehension, that [the children] may be treated as they themselves have been while slaves." Accordingly, they sought from the Common Council the grant of a piece of land adjoining the site of the Refuge for the erection of separate accommodations for clients of color. The Council obliged, helping the Refuge to open its doors to black children in 1834.[17]

The rationale for admitting black children to the NYHR focused exclusively on fitting them for participation in the labor force, without any reference to preparing them to exercise the rights and responsibilities of citizenship. Admission to the Refuge did not spell a vision of interracial civic equality, which became quite clear from the regimen of separate treatment to which African Americans were subjected upon their arrival. The British visitor E. S. Abdy, a fellow of Jesus College, Cambridge, on a visit to the NYHR, was struck by the prevalence of racial discrimination in an establishment otherwise marked by "comfort, cleanliness, and convenient arrangement." He was pained to observe the "studied manner in which the white and colored children were separated and distinguished from each other, as if moral improvement could be promoted in either by encouraging pride and inflicting humiliation." His remark to a fellow visitor that he failed to understand the rationale for treating "the children of one common parent" so differently was greeted by a "contemptuous smile and a very silly assertion that Nature, by degrading the one race, had placed an insuperable barrier to a closer approximation with the other." Abdy concluded that an "Englishman may wish in vain that this feature in the national character were less frequently and obtrusively thrust forward."[18]

The physical segregation of black children was accompanied by their symbolic exclusion from American national belonging in the statistical snapshots of inmate populations compiled by the Refuge for inclusion in its annual reports. Consider for a moment the facsimiles (table 27, in appendix of this volume) of two important tables that appeared in the appendix to the 1860 annual report.

Table I, entitled "Showing the Sources Whence Were Received 468 Children, During the Year 1860," displayed the frequency distribution of inmates committed by various categories of public authorities—sessions courts, police, and the Department of Public Charities and Corrections—of seventeen counties in New York State. The populations attributed to each source were classified primarily by color, and secondarily by gender. The binary opposites of "white" and "colored" became the chief symbols of difference, subsuming distinctions of nationality, which certainly existed to a great degree, as seen from the figures in table III. The major variable in this latter table, showing the "Parentage" of the children admitted to the Refuge during 1860, is of course national origin, but here it is implicitly conflated with race. The label "American" does not include children of color, who are characterized as having "African" parentage. Rather, the qualifier "American" defined in relation to "African" implies European descent. Whiteness is the normative color quality of "American" as represented in this table. The salience of color as the chief trope of difference becomes clearer when we consider that table I homogenizes all the European nationalities listed in table III (Irish, English, Germans, Scotch, French, and Italian) together with "Americans" into one "white" race, setting them apart from the twenty-seven "Africans"—many, if not most, of whom were likely to have been born in the United States. Thus, however foreign the Irish may have seemed to some native-born Americans in the decade before the Civil War, their European heritage apparently fitted them for acculturation to Americanism—implicitly colored white.

The labels "white" and "colored" also served to organize information about the Refuge's indenture policies, offering a glimpse of black people's place in the larger society. The monolithic occupational profile of African American apprentices mirrored the severely restricted nature of the economic opportunities open to black men in New York City. The institution's statistics on the disposition of children before the Civil War show that while it is true that farmers in New Jersey and on the outskirts of New York claimed the largest proportion of male indentures of both races, a healthy proportion of all white boys apprenticed (45 percent in 1850, 42 percent in 1860) were dispatched to masters in crafts and manufacturing, to bakers and butchers, and to clerks, porters, peddlers, and cartmen. By contrast, African American boys might occasionally be apprenticed to a mariner, but, as a rule, they were almost exclusively confined to farm labor, accounting for 93 percent and 100 percent of all black male apprentices in 1850 and 1860, respectively. The indenture statistics reveal far fewer racial distinctions among the Refuge's female charges. Girls not returned to their families were destined overwhelmingly for domestic service, irrespective of race.

Politics of Subaltern Engagement I: The Antebellum Refuge as "Welfare" Agency

Notwithstanding the racial distinctions evident in the structure of juvenile reform, African Americans and whites in antebellum New York adopted very similar rhetorical strategies and practices in their interactions with the New York House of Refuge. The institution offers especially promising prospects for charting an interracial subaltern politics of engagement with Victorian New York's reform establishment. As an institution that admitted inmates of both African and European descent, it generated case histories for children across a wide spectrum of race and ethnicity, designed, as the Managers put it, "to . . . trace the downward course of guilt and shame" of their subjects.[19] The case histories—brief, handwritten narratives generated before the professionalization of social work in the Progressive era—provide information about each inmate's name, address, age, ethnicity/race, birthplace, parentage, experiences with work and school, the circumstances under which he or she entered the reformatory, and indenture or other mode of disposition. Influenced by the emphasis on more systematic data gathering in the postbellum age of scientific charity, the Refuge added a printed form to each case record after 1878. Titled "Examination of the Home," and filled out by an agent who visited the child's family at the time of the child's admission to the institution, it contained information about the physical condition of the home, the size of the family; the parents' marital status, occupation, and habits of temperance; the child's propensity for truancy; and previous criminal record, if any. Several of the African American case records did not include this form because many working poor black parents who lived in private service or at sea did not maintain independent households. Case histories, as instruments of reform, became, in the hands of subalterns, a medium through which the inmates could present their own versions of working poor experiences.

The present chapter draws on a sample of 135 case histories of black children admitted the New York House of Refuge in the years 1840, 1850,

1860, 1870, 1880, and 1890, in order to explore the seamlessly scrambled private and public worlds of New York's black plebeians. It places their experiences in comparative context by reviewing a sample of two hundred white inmates dispatched to the institution after the start of the Irish exodus to New York in the mid-1840s. The sample of white inmates approximates the ethnic and sexual composition of a total population of 1841 European immigrant and Euro-American children received during the years 1850, 1860, 1870, 1880, and 1890 whose ethnic background the Refuge was able to document. These case histories, together with other evidence—like the NYHR's official reports and minutes, the Superintendent's diary, and the chaplain's accounts of home visits—offer social portraits and self-representations of African Americans and whites most likely to be forced to seek public assistance. They illuminate the myriad ways in which many of these clients apparently embraced the goals of the country's first juvenile reformatory, but quite often in order to serve their own ends. The working poor exhibited a consciousness of the nexus between pauperism and crime that did not necessarily translate into a sense of interracial class cohesion. It did, however, mount a powerful challenge to the genteel discourse on vice and virtue as a code of class and culture and helped define an alternative sense of subaltern identity that divorced poverty from charges of moral degeneracy.

In the decade before the Civil War, the African American population of the Refuge most closely resembled its Irish counterpart. Both were overrepresented among Refuge inmates in relation to their numbers in the general population of New York City (see tables 29 and 30, in appendix). For instance, black New Yorkers, accounting for nearly 3 percent of New York's population in 1850, constituted approximately 7 percent of the reformatory's inmates in the same year. Not surprisingly, the Irish predominated among the Refuge's white inmates in the antebellum period, making up over 60 percent of the European and Euro-American children whose parentage could be ascertained in 1850 and 1860. Native-born whites and non-Irish European immigrants each constituted approximately one-fifth of the white inmate population in these years. The largest number of children, whether of African or European descent, varied in age from thirteen to fifteen years. Moreover, boys consistently outnumbered girls in all groups, although they did so by a greater percentage among whites than they did among African Americans (see table 31, in appendix).

Most significantly, African Americans in antebellum New York were no less likely—indeed perhaps somewhat more likely—than whites to have been committed to the Refuge at the initiative of their own kin rather than that of public authorities. My sample of case histories suggests that at mid-century, half of all black and Irish children reviewed had entered the reformatory on charges of vagrancy or disorderly conduct rather than for larceny or arson. Moreover, in 1850, 36 percent of the commitments in both groups were set in motion by relatives, compared with only about 7 percent of their non-Irish immigrant and native-born white counterparts. These discrepancies among African Americans, the Irish, and other categories of whites varied widely over the course of the nineteenth century (see tables 32–34, in appendix). Yet it seems clear that black kin played a major role in dispatching their charges to the Refuge, raising the question, who were these kin? The cases sampled for the pre–Civil war years of 1850 and 1860 suggest that African Americans were slightly less likely to have two natural surviving parents than any other group—about 30 percent of black children did, compared with a third each of the Irish and native-born whites and 53 percent of non-Irish white immigrants. The most striking difference between black children and whites—whether native-born or immigrant—lay, however, in the prominence of extended family and surrogate kin arrangements among African Americans. Over one-third of the total number of black children surveyed in the years 1850 and 1860 hailed from households governed by nonparent kin, whereas less than 13 percent of the Irish and insignificant proportions of the other groups came from similar homes (see tables 36 and 37, in appendix).

The occupational profile of black parents who were living explains a good deal, both about the prevalence of surrogacy as well as about the appeal of the Refuge as a temporary haven during familial crises of various sorts. Many children were not able to live with parents whose work took them away from home. Seafarers—who constituted approximately 29 percent of male custodians whose occupations were known in 1850 and 1860—could not, more often than not, have children accompany them on voyages. Nor could domestic servants or steamboat chambermaids—accounting for 45 percent of the female guardians in these years—take their charges to work, especially if they boarded with their employers. These working parents saw the New York House of Refuge as a material resource to help defray the expenses of supporting dependents; they transferred their children to the temporary charge of the institution as vagrants (see tables 39 and 41, in appendix).

Even in cases where parents were able to maintain independent households, their precarious economic circumstances occasionally dictated the imperative to seek charity. African American mothers sampled for the antebellum years were clustered in the lowest strata of the economic ladder, barely eking out a living as laundresses, domestic servants, boardinghouse keepers, cooks, waitresses, steamboat chambermaids, peddlers, and, in one case, a "root-doctress." The work of male relatives offered no more economic security against unemployment, sickness, or death than did that of their female counterparts. Indeed, as has been noted before, the greatest proportion of employed fathers worked away from the city, as seafarers and seasonal farm laborers. Skilled workers were rare, represented by an occasional carpenter. The remaining male guardians worked as grooms/coachmen, porters, laborers, waiters, longshoremen, wood sawyers, printing office workers, whitewashers, distillery workers, grain measurers, bootblacks, cart drivers, bell foundry workers, janitors, store employees, lobster-stand keepers, peddlers, fishermen, and sewage cleaners. Even the poorest black neighborhoods had their share of ministers drawn from the ranks of the local population. For example, Joseph Lyons's father, who lived on Elizabeth Street, combined the calling of preaching with wood sawing. Lyons occasionally worked as farm boy and helped his father "when he had nothing else to do."[20]

As the case of Lyons suggests, children's participation in the labor market was essential for sustaining the wage economy of impoverished African American families, whether those of laborers or ministers. While domestic service represented the dominant vocation among the girls I sampled, the boys displayed a far more varied occupational profile (see tables 43 and 45, in appendix). Moreover, young men usually combined several jobs in their short work lives. For example, Theodore Vick helped his uncle make baskets and whitewash buildings, worked at several places as an errand boy, and later assisted a fruit peddler, who accused him of stealing pies from the wagon and had him arrested.[21] Thirteen-year-old James Collins, the son of a seaman and a laundress, spent much of his young life helping his mother with her washing, serving an uncle who ran a sailor's boardinghouse on Richmond Street, and working in a fish market, before he was arrested for stealing a pair of boots from a store.[22] Fourteen-year-old Henry Johnson lived with his "laborer" parents for a brief interlude between his first job as farm help and his second as a butcher boy.[23] A few children worked as mess boys on seafaring vessels.[24]

Work that provided children with accommodations proved particularly useful to single parents who lived in service or were too poor or unwell to maintain independent households. When such working children lost their jobs, forfeiting their board and lodging in the process, their parents entrusted the reformatory with their care. Such was the case with Lany Candy. Candy's mother, who lived in service, placed the child with a family in Buffalo, for whom the child performed errands. When the family dismissed her, she was sent to the Refuge "for a home."[25]

On the other hand, fathers unable to care for motherless children too young to work turned to public relief for help, which often served as a conduit to the Refuge. Mary Ellen Vanness, eight years old in 1860, was placed in the Colored Home by her father at an early age. Her mother had presumably died. The Home sent her to live with a Brooklyn family, who turned her over to the Alms House, which in turn committed her to the NYHR. When the Refuge discharged her to the care of her father, he placed her in the Colored Orphan Asylum.[26] Black children often displayed a rather sophisticated understanding of their parents' material plight. A washerwoman's son, John Patterson, who attended a public school and Sunday school regularly, told his case recorder that he "supposed the cause of his mother getting him committed to us was her poverty."[27]

African American adults' deliberate use of the Refuge as a material resource contradicted the institution's intended focus on the problem of juvenile delinquency. At the same time, black parents' resort to the reformatory to mediate family conflicts of various sorts suggests a dynamic of creative adaption to the NYHR's goal of achieving reform by acculturating the progeny of the "dangerous classes" to bourgeois norms of conduct. It is difficult to say whether African American guardians of the laboring classes consciously embraced, as their middle-class counterparts did, what historian Evelyn Brooks Higginbotham calls the "politics of respectability"—adopting bourgeois moral and social conventions as a way of countering negative stereotypes of the black female character and habits of hygiene.[28] Nevertheless, the deep religious and moral convictions of many black mothers, not to mention their desire to protect their daughters from unwanted pregnancies, prompted them to play an active role in shaping what reformers characterized as an emerging "girl problem"—the specter of female sexuality run amuck.[29] Numerous guardians committed their female wards to the Refuge for "staying out nights," keeping the company of "bad girls," or frequenting houses of "ill fame." The irony of these attempts to seek public assistance in disciplining errant daughters lay in the fact that black parents' seeming acquiescence in middle-class standards of Victorian morality undermined the reformers' indictment of working poor guardians as vicious, intemperate, dishonest, and idle instigators of juvenile crime.

For instance, when Mary Neal's father abandoned his family, her mother Harriet went into domestic service at Oyster Bay, Long Island, leaving Mary in the care of friends in New York. Upon learning that Mary had fallen into the company of "naughty girls," Harriet undertook a trip to New York for the singular purpose of committing her daughter to the Refuge on charges of vagrancy.[30] Likewise, Sarah Bryan, the sixteen-year-old daughter of a sailor and a washerwoman, who lived at home and helped her mother with her laundry, found herself in the reformatory, at her mother's initiative, for "acquiring the habit of disobeying her." When the institution discharged Bryan to the care of her parents, her mother sent her to Haiti to live with family friends, suggesting a serious attempt on the parent's part to remove her from the distractions of New York City.[31]

A few African American women used the reformatory to negotiate a range of other family disputes, including those involving domestic abuse and incest. For instance, Mary Johnson's mother placed her out in service to protect her against an abusive stepfather. That did not work. The stepfather would "come to Johnson's new home under the influence of liquor and get her away and finally by his ugliness and nothing else" forced Mary's mother to send the child to the Refuge.[32] Sarah M. Simmons's aunt shielded the fourteen-year-old from "stay[ing] in the house where [the girl's uncle] was without the presence of a third person."[33] On the other hand, the narrative of Henrietta Davis offered a different twist in family politics, suggesting that warring parents occasionally wielded the Refuge as a tool of vengeance in their internecine struggles. Henrietta's boatman father, when intoxicated, allegedly "beat the whole family who left the house and went to [Henrietta's] aunt until he became sober." The fourteen-year-old claimed that her father "induced" her to leave their home in Jersey City and come to New York, where he secured her commitment to the Refuge for vagrancy to "spite" her mother, who did not know the child's whereabouts. The Refuge indentured her to a Fairfield County farmer, whom the child served satisfactorily for a term of six years, at the end of which she was returned to the care of her mother.[34]

Family strife emanating from the dynamics of the family economy impelled some parents to enlist public assistance in subduing their children. When parental expectations that children would contribute to the family income clashed with the adolescent instinct for independence, generating intergenerational disputes over employment and control of wages, beleaguered parents turned to the Refuge to enforce obedience. Cornelius Jackson's widowed mother tried to place her son successively in domestic service in the city, in farm work in the country, and in a New York public school. When he showed no inclination to work, "the mother had him sent to us by complaining to the police."³⁵ William Wilson on the other hand, clashed with his mother over the "ownership" of his wages. This thirteen-year-old son of an absentee waiter father had always lived with his mother and contributed his earnings as an errand boy to the family kitty. Although his commitment stated that he had stolen fifty cents from his mother, the boy claimed that the "money was his and his mother refused to give it to him, so he took it without her consent."³⁶

The presence of public institutions, on the other hand, occasionally facilitated the attempts of laboring children to elude parental—especially maternal—discipline, as the mother of George Coles discovered, seeking to raise her young son in the absence of her seaman husband. Coles ran away from home at a young age and found refuge at the Flatbush poorhouse. There he was discovered by a Long Island farmer, with whom he lived until his mother found him and "went after him." He returned to her unwillingly, only to prove so "ungovernable" that his mother committed him to the NYHR. He was eventually discharged to the care of his father, who took him to sea on a vessel bound for Liverpool.³⁷ Other varieties of family politics propelled children into the arms of the Refuge. The remarriage of parents, especially fathers, frequently drove traumatized children into the streets and their stepmothers before magistrates to seek their commitment to the reformatory as vagrants. Twelve-year-old John Dumont had always lived at home until his father remarried. He then began to "sleep out nights," prompting his stepmother to take him to court for disorderly conduct. This young man served out his indenture on a New Jersey farm, where he remained for ten years.³⁸

Parents were not the only parties to initiate the commitment of their charges to the Refuge. As we have already noted, a significant proportion of the Refuge's black inmates came from homes headed by nonparent or surrogate kin, including grandparents, aunts and uncles, and siblings and their in-laws (see table 37, in appendix). Scholars have noted the widespread prevalence of fosterage among African Americans and have traced the roots of this tradition to African family structures.³⁹ The function of surrogate kin networks in sustaining slave families torn asunder through sale has, of course, been well documented.⁴⁰ Studies of the twentieth-century urban poor have also emphasized the intimate "domestic cooperation" of inner-city communities, the members of which "swapped" money, food stamps, and goods and services, including child care, with each other on a daily basis in order to survive.[41]

The NYHR case records suggest a similar pattern of mutual aid among Victorian-era African Americans. Migrants to New York from the slave states frequently boarded with relatives already established in the city. Relatives—such as sisters, aunts, and grandmothers—as well as guardians unrelated by blood, frequently assumed charge of children whose parents had died, lived in service or in prison, or had simply relinquished their responsibilities. Surrogate parents drew on public resources for the same reasons that their "natural" counterparts did—to discipline adolescents, secure medical attention for sick children, or simply to find them a "home."[42] Occasionally, social networks that materialized in fosterage were surprisingly extensive in their geographic reach—encompassing distant nations and many seas. When Cuban-born Andrew Mauradev lost both his parents in his native land, his godmother brought him to New York and left him in the custody of an African American woman living on West Seventeenth Street. He earned his keep by running errands for his guardian, until she turned him over to the Refuge as a vagrant in 1866. He was found to be in poor health and was transferred to the Colored Home. This young immigrant's life unfolded in an unusual manner. In 1891 Mauradev, now thirty-five years of age and calling himself A. P. Morris, sought a letter indicating that he had been an inmate of the Refuge. He needed such certification in order to realize his quest for a homestead claim in New Mexico.[43]

The black convention of extended family relationships translated on the streets of impoverished neighborhoods into informal networks of "race kin," which served as clearinghouses of information about public services. Destitute black children could draw on the resources of these webs of race-based surrogate relationships to seek public assistance. For instance, when Boston-born Robert Haley's father, a ship steward, died of smallpox at sea, leaving him a homeless orphan en route from Liverpool to New York, a "colored woman"—evidently not a natural relative—secured lodgings for him in a watch house, which in turn sent him to the Refuge.[44] Casual fosterage among African Americans in public spaces proved to be a particularly useful survival tool for a significant category of refuge inmates: newcomers to the city. Over half the children in my sample who entered the Refuge in the decade before the Civil War were born outside New York City (see table 38, in appendix). Over a fifth hailed from the counties of Albany, Broome, Dutchess, Erie, Green, Kings, Orange, Rensselaer, Suffolk, Ulster, and Westchester in New York State, and another 13 percent hailed from the neighboring regions of New Jersey, New Jersey, Connecticut, and the rest of New England. The cities of the Upper South—Richmond and Baltimore—sent forth a sprinkling of black vagrants, as did Florida and North Carolina in the post–Civil War era. These figures indicate a significant presence of migrants in the reformatory's black population. The flotsam and jetsam of political economies in transition converged in America's greatest metropolis in search of work, adventure, and freedom. The not-insignificant proportion of farm workers among male relatives of NYHR inmates supports the contention that the institution drew migrants from families of casual, seasonal agricultural laborers. Deprived of support networks that sustained local African Americans, these new arrivals constituted ready recruits to reform institutions, which offered board and lodging through the mediation of acquaintances made on city streets.

Of course, not all children migrated to New York of their own free will. Twelve-year-old Isabella Vanderpool told a fascinating tale of a deadly sojourn fraught with sexual abuse and the threat of enslavement that led her from the Caribbean to the New York reformatory. Born on the island of St. Thomas, Isabella was sent by her mother to live with an aunt in St. Martin. There, on a beach, the child came upon a ship, whose captain offered to take her to New York. When she refused, she said that "a large white thing was thrown over her" and she was taken aboard the ship, where the captain "committed improprieties against her." She managed to flee from him when they arrived in New York, and she found refuge, according to her case recorder, with "some colored people of not very good character." From such associations to the reformatory was but a short step.[45]

As the foregoing accounts suggest, children on their own in the city constituted an important constituency among the reformatory's black population. Thus, it is fair to say that it was as an orphanage that the NYHR served one of its most important "welfare" functions. Over a quarter of the children sampled for this study had lost both parents to death or other circumstances. Their case histories offer poignant glimpses of a hardscrabble existence marked by rootlessness and constant mobility. A litany of hardships, borne with evident fortitude, shaped some remarkably self-sufficient youth out of New York's African American orphan population. Buffeted by the vagaries of an uncertain labor market and fragile family lives, these black children of the streets showed extraordinary resilience in their lonesome quest for survival. By the very act of narrating their life stories of hard-fought struggles, they daily challenged the portrait of wanton idleness crafted by some reformers. For example, Guy Brunt of Long Island lost his parents when they drowned while collecting a load of sand on the beach. The boy found work with an employer, who "turned him adrift" in the winter, prompting him to move to New York. After several nights on the streets, he found refuge in a watch house, which in turn dispatched him to the reformatory.[46]

A few young orphans purportedly saw the Refuge as a source of educational opportunities denied them by the larger society. That their aspiration for learning may have been tied to the need for immediate subsistence, and presented an avenue of escape from the brutal and erratic market for child labor, by no means diminishes its significance. Historians of the Reconstruction South have noted the enthusiasm for reading exhibited by freed people of all ages, who had for centuries been barred by law from penetrating the mysteries of the written word. George Francis of Long Island, left to his own devices when his father drowned and his mother entered a county home with an amputated limb, at first sought domestic work in the city. Before long, however, the unlettered thirteen-year-old "took it into his head that he needed some learning," so he approached a police officer and asked to be sent to the New York House of Refuge so that he might attend the institution's school.[47]

As these cases suggest, African Americans were no less resourceful in tapping the welfare potential of Victorian New York's "benevolent empire," as the need arose, than working poor whites, who used public institutions in similar ways. The Irish, clustered in the treacherous niche of casual labor, represented the most materially vulnerable constituency of white New Yorkers in antebellum New York. They too sent their children to the Refuge in an attempt to discipline them or when forced to bolt their tenements in order to avoid persistent rent collectors (see tables 34, 35, 40, 42, 44, and 46, in appendix).[48] What set them apart from their black brethren was the greater assertiveness with which they articulated their sense of entitlement to the Refuge's relief and reform function by demanding jurisdiction over the timing of their wards' commitment to, and discharge from, the institution. This theme will be investigated below, in the context of postbellum conflicts between the Managers and white inmates of the Refuge over the latter's rights to discharge by habeas corpus. Here, suffice it to note the reception the reformatory's chaplain met when he visited the home of Frank Farley's aunt in order to evaluate her application for Frank's discharge. The chaplain found the guardian's apartments to be "dirty and redolent of infamous smells," crowded with squalid children who went barefoot on the cold day of the visit. The visitor recorded, "The aunt very stoutly affirmed without the slightest challenge from your peace loving Chaplain, that she was a *citizen* of New York, and that she intended to have the boy. . . . ' She had placed him here for such a time as she pleased, as she had assured the Court when he was sentenced, 'for fear he would become a thief. She should come to the institution with her counsel and remove the child.'"[49]

The confidence with which Farley's aunt claimed the "white right" of citizenship to control the terms of her ward's relationship with the Refuge no doubt stemmed from the political power that even the laboring Irish, as proprietors of the "property" of whiteness, could command. Disfranchised black guardians had little opportunity to make similar claims and few resources to mount the kind of legal challenges to the Refuge's authority threatened by the Irishwoman. Nevertheless, their children joined the white working poor in narrating life stories that disputed official versions of the sources of juvenile delinquency. The practical uses to which the inmates and their guardians put the Refuge were corroborated by rhetorical approaches that promoted an interracial, class-specific interpretation of poverty and incipient "criminality" at odds with bourgeois constructions of working poor debasement.

Politics of Subaltern Engagement II: "Proto-structural" Perspectives on Crime

In addition to those committed for vagrancy, a significant proportion of children entered the Refuge on charges of stealing items such as a few pounds of butter from a grocer, carpet rags from a neighbor's home, or articles of clothing from storefronts and employers.[50] Inmates remanded to the NYHR's custody for crimes like larceny, arson, or assault mounted their own challenge to middle-class perspectives on the interplay among cultural identity, vice, and crime by interpreting their misdemeanors through the prism of adult working-class and race-conscious sensibilities. Children convicted of petty crime frequently offered explanations for their transgressions that defied official interpretations of working poor frailties. While the reformers attributed crime to working-class traditions of drinking—sustained by a related evil, the pawn shop—and nurtured by the nefarious influence of the theater and the circus, the inmates articulated a "proto-structural" view of poverty's origins and its relationship with crime. Inmate stories linked the alleged delinquents' transgressions to poverty, misfortune, and exploitation by those more powerful than them. Some justified their resort to violence as a measure to defend their mothers' honor, while young women claimed that they were not inherently immoral, but rather victims of sexual abuse.

Twelve-year-old African American William H. Thomas, who helped his father tend a lobster stand, made an explicit connection between destitution and crime. He said that he stole a pair of women's shoes because he needed money to buy bread for his siblings while his parents were at work.[51] William Henry King, the son of an oysterman, displayed on the other hand a race-conscious perspective on chattel slavery as a source of moral bankruptcy. When asked to explain his propensity to steal, he narrated "a curious tale about being taken away from his father and sold for a wagon and then a dog, and then a horse and so went about from place to place says this boy until I am now good for nothing." The significance of this tale lay not so much in the question of its authenticity as in its reflection of the narrator's self-image. King saw himself less as a natural delinquent than as a victim of adverse circumstances grounded in the dominant society's racialized definition of his legal identity as chattel—as something less than human.[52]

A twelve year-old Irish boy of immigrant extraction, Francis Agnew, on the other hand, explained his charge of "assault and battery" by claiming that he had merely been upholding his mother's honor. He had struck a man in the eye with a stick because this man had "called his mother a bad name."[53] Some women presented themselves as victims of sexual abuse, unjustly punished for the transgressions of debauched men. A black teenager, Mary Thomas, professed bewilderment at her commitment to the Refuge. A domestic servant in Troy, New York, she had merely been trying to flee the unwelcome attentions of a male stranger, who intercepted her in a grocery store, when a police officer arrested her for vagrancy.[54] Similarly, Evelina Miller implicated a white man in a theft charge, which landed her in the Refuge. The eldest child born to a carpenter and a homemaker, this fifteen-year-old was arrested for allegedly stealing a shawl. She insisted, however, that "a white man" had presented her with the item. Her case recorder judged her to be a worldly woman who spoke "understandingly" of her foibles.[55] Miller's outlook, however, implicitly faulted her suitor for availing himself of her favors, rather than herself for accepting his payment. However different the stories of the black and Irish children recounted above, a consistent thematic thread bound them: the exoneration of themselves and their parents of middle-class charges of degradation rooted in innate character failings.

The politics of subaltern engagement with the NYHR may well have influenced the evolution of national juvenile reform discourse in the decade before the Civil War, including the establishment of institutions to "save" children not charged with crimes. For instance, the Second Convention of the Managers and Superintendents of Houses of Refuge, Schools of Reform, and Institutions for the Prevention and Correction of Juvenile Destitution, Delinquency, and Crime, held in New York City in May 1859, took up as its very first topic of discussion the proposition that there existed a distinction "between Vagrancy and Destitution on the one hand, and Crime on the other." In this context, John A. Bryan of the New York Juvenile Asylum sketched a trajectory of juvenile institution building that implicitly acknowledged the role of working poor agency in complicating the accepted parameters of incipient criminality. Making distinctions among the New York House of Refuge, the New York Juvenile Asylum, and the Children's Aid Society (CAS), Bryan declared that the Refuge had been founded to "reform incipient criminals," but that "*after many years it was found* that the House of Refuge *was not calculated* to meet a certain want that existed here." That want concerned the imperative to rescue "beggars, petty pilferers, children who take ash-barrels, fuel, sugar out of hogsheads on the wharves, fruit and other trifling things" either "through ignorance . . . or the compulsion of parents," without knowing that they were doing wrong. Significantly, Bryan included in this category not only the offspring of "low gamblers" and "degraded women," but also those of "*poor parents.*" It was to save these children from the danger of ruin that the New York Juvenile Asylum was inaugurated: "It was intended to relieve a class that the House of Refuge could not." Bryan proceeded: "It was discovered, after a short time, the peculiar objects of the Juvenile Asylum did not supply all the requirements" of the young among New York's "vagrant and destitute population."

The subsequent formation of the Children's Aid Society acknowledged that misfortune, rather than misconduct, sometimes drove working poor need for public relief. The CAS, Bryan argued, "confined its efforts to *unfortunate* children, those who had been measurably well-cared for, those who had enjoyed some of the influences of comparatively decent homes, but who, through the *misfortune* of parents, stood in need of assistance from the benevolent. By the terms of its charter, its purpose was to improve the condition of the *poor and destitute* children of the city of New York." In a further acknowledgment of the dynamic between reformers' intentions and the will of their "clients," Bryan testified to the overlap in the categories of children received by all three institutions: "Each receives kids who would have been appropriate subjects for one of the others." Bryan's statement that the NYHR experience awakened reformers to *uncalculated* "wants" existing among poor New Yorkers, and his assertion that such wants led to the formation of more relief-oriented juvenile agencies like the CAS, made clear the fact that needy guardians and children used the Refuge in ways unintended by the institution's architects. Moreover, Bryan's recognition of the role of misfortune in triggering the need for public assistance highlighted the evolving, reciprocal quality of the reformer-client dynamic in shaping the discourse of juvenile justice. Yet the convention at which he expressed these arguably sympathetic views of "underclass" exigencies occurred on the eve of a civil war that would inaugurate a far more combative phase in the Refuge's relations with subaltern New York, especially its white component.[56]

The Civil War Era

In May 1862 J. M., a former inmate of the Refuge, now a Union soldier, reported to Superintendent John W. Ketcham the utter devastation of Pensacola before his unit reclaimed it from the Confederates:

> The rebels burned everything belonging to the Government. . . . They destroyed the Navy Yard, Fort McRae, and had it not been for our shells, they would have destroyed the light-house. . . . Nearly all the inhabitants have left, only a few of the poorest and the darkeys remaining. When we landed, they crowded round us to see if Colonel W— had a horn on his head, as they had been told by the rebels he had. While we were marching through the town, the darkeys followed us, saying, "Dem's de boys we's bin waitin for." "Dat de flag for us"; and they seemed more pleased than the white inhabitants.[57]

If the debate over slavery in the 1850s embroiled many European immigrants in white identity politics, the outbreak of military hostilities in April 1861 offered these newcomers the opportunity to participate in American nationalism through military service to the Union. Until the preliminary and final Emancipation Proclamations authorized the recruitment of black soldiers in 1862–63, such service generally remained a prerogative of whiteness, accentuating the association of citizenship with race maintained by most antebellum American institutions, including those devoted to benevolent reform. J. M.'s use of the derogatory, color-conscious appellation "darkey" to designate the enslaved underscored the sense of racial separateness evidently felt and articulated by white inmates-turned-Union soldiers who encountered African Americans in the South.

J. M. was one of two hundred volunteers dispatched by the Refuge to the Union army and navy during the first two years of the Civil War. In addition, ten of the institution's charges entered the U.S. military as substitutes, receiving three hundred dollars each in bounty, held for them in trust in a savings bank by the Managers.[58] Meanwhile, the black proportion of the inmate population dipped from 7 percent to less than 5 percent during 1864—a decline spurred in part by the opportunities for military service offered by passage of the Emancipation Proclamation in 1863. Overall, these enlistments prompted a temporary increase in the female proportion of the white inmate population, more or less equalizing white and black sex ratios to about one girl for every three boys during the years 1862 and 1863. Yet if the war siphoned off to the battlefield boys fifteen years and older, it also created breeding grounds for fresh recruits. Street urchins swept up in the dragnet of arrests following the New York City Draft Riots swelled the inmate population in 1863. The story of one Irish twelve-year-old was not atypical: an occasional worker in a hoopskirt factory, he claimed that he was passing down Twenty-first Street, where several men were hurling furniture from the window of a house. He picked up several items and made off with them, thus courting arrest.[59] At the same time, the appearance in the Refuge's annual reports of a category labeled "social condition of the children" included entries for fathers enlisted in the army, showing a possible reason for the upsurge in admissions in the last years of the war.

The Civil War also brought a fresh stream of Southern-born migrants—most of them freed slaves—into the Refuge. A few children accompanied Union soldiers to New York; left unemployed after the army disbanded, they were taken up for vagrancy. Fourteen-year-old James Curtiss—born in Virginia, where his parents still lived—found work with the military as a waiter and migrated in that capacity to New York, where he was discharged. A policeman sent him to the Colored Home, which in turn dispatched him to the Refuge under the auspices of the Commissioners of

Public Charities and Correction.⁶⁰ There Curtiss met a fellow freedman, eighteen-year-old Sylvester Johnson of Delaware. Johnson served Union soldiers during the war, carrying their baggage and performing various other chores. At the end of the conflict, he moved to New York, where he lived off the streets during the day and lodged with a "colored woman" at night in exchange for a dollar. He was arrested for stealing a watch.⁶¹

It may be that Union officers, teachers, aspiring planters, and other Northerners who went South during the Civil War occasionally sent orphaned freed-children to live in private homes or public institutions in New York. Mary Cook, raised on a Maryland plantation, was eleven years old when the Civil War ended. Her parents already dead, she was sent to the Colored Orphan Asylum in New York, which in turn dispatched her to the Refuge for committing a petty theft. Her tenure with a Suffolk County family as a maid in training ended when she was charged with an attempt to poison the family.⁶² Another orphaned former slave from Virginia, twelve-year-old Zoe Young, was sent to live with a Brooklyn family in the winter of 1864. Six months later, she confessed that she had tried to poison a washerwoman who worked for the family; subsequently, she was sent to the Refuge.⁶³ For Cook and Young, indentured servitude may have smacked of chattel bondage and prompted forms of resistance forged in slavery.

"Race" After Slavery

The Civil War revolutionized the legal definition of American identity by hastening the advent of the Fourteenth Amendment to the U.S. Constitution, which based American citizenship on birth or naturalization, irrespective or race or nationality. Yet custom trumped the law in the popular national imaginary of what it meant to be "American." The postbellum era brought a number of developments that heightened the contrast between whiteness and "its Others." Popular travel accounts by white explorers of non-Western cultures, especially those of Africa, adopted "race" as the trope of difference—a signifier of nonwhite savagery against which the superiority of America's "white" civilization was defined. "Frontier" skirmishes with Mexicans and Indians on America's own lush prairies cemented the link between whiteness and civilization. Anti-Chinese agitation in the West and its reception in Congress reaffirmed the "1790 principle that republican institutions require a 'white' polity." At the same time, such agitation sought to protect the interests of white workers in the marketplace.⁶⁴

Meanwhile, through the portal of Castle Garden (and after 1890, Ellis Island) there streamed into New York hundreds of thousands of what David Roediger has described as "in-between peoples"—the "new immigrants," drawn from the Jewish shtetls of the Russian Pale and the Roman Catholic peasantry of southern Italy. Derided as "guineas," "dagos," and "niggers," turned inside out to signify their perceived affiliations with Africans, non–English speaking, non-"Nordic" groups (such as the Italians, the Jews, and the Greeks) fell prey to physical attacks by lynch mobs, as well legislative assaults by nativists in Congress. Decades later, in 1924, these attacks culminated in the enactment of immigration quotas designed to restore the Nordic proportion of the American population. Yet European immigrants, however ambiguous their position in popular perceptions of America's racial hierarchy, "gained the powerful symbolic argument that the law declared them white and fit" for naturalized citizenship. Even as the courts ruled Asians decidedly nonwhite in case after case, the U.S. judicial system deemed the "new immigrants" from Europe suited for racialized national belonging, thus empowering these groups as potential voters.[65]

In 1870 Congress allowed African immigrants the privilege of naturalization. Yet the advent of a post-Reconstruction regime of antiblack racism drained this right of all meaning. Tired of fratricidal conflict over black rights, and anxious to get on with the task of economic development, the nation accomplished its reunion with the former Confederacy at the expense of black Southerners, who were now left unceremoniously at the mercy of the post-Reconstruction South's white supremacist "Bourbon Redeemers." By the advent of the twentieth century, white Southerners had devised what Grace Elizabeth Hale calls a "culture of segregation" to reassert their dominance over their slaves-turned-citizens, some of whom presented the alarming specter of black economic and even social mobility. Progressive America's emergent mass consumer market at once perpetuated and muddied Jim Crow's premise of a dichromatic society—one polarized between total whiteness and total blackness. Advertisers used black imagery to sell their wares to consumers constructed as white, even as the spaces of consumption—from railway coaches to grocery stores—presented opportunities to strain the established conventions of race relations. Yet, however fraught with contradictions the practice of Southern segregation, its culture buttressed the racial meaning of American identity, especially as the great migration of African Americans from their Southern homes to Northern cities gained momentum.[66]

Against this background, binary constructions of race continued to guide the organization of information about the children received by the NYHR throughout the nineteenth century. The national origins of Refuge inmates grew progressively more diverse from the 1870s, so that late nineteenth-century "Parentage" tables in the institution's annual reports added new groups—most conspicuously, "Italians." They also conflated nationality, religion, and ethnicity in the formulation of another group— "Jews." Yet color, dichotomized into "white" and "colored," remained the overriding paradigm of difference in most tables containing information about the inmates. Like the antebellum Irish, the Italians and Jews of a later era—however different culturally—were still merged with native-born Protestant Euro-Americans as members of the "white" group. Those identified as "colored" continued to be described as "African" until the year 1900, when, for the very first time, the category "African" disappeared from the "Parentage" table. It was replaced by a new label designated "American, Colored," placed directly under the first nationality listed in that table—namely, "American." The very existence of the linguistic category "Colored," and the order of its placement, symbolically announced the separateness—and subordinate status—of black Americans in the institution's inmate hierarchy (see facsimiles of NYHR tables in appendix, table 28).

Postbellum Black Uses of the Refuge

Despite their experience of discrimination, however, New Yorkers of African descent maintained a remarkably consistent relationship with the Refuge in the latter half of the nineteenth century. Indeed, the most striking demographic change in this period centered on the fact that the African American proportion of the institution's charges remained far steadier than its Irish counterpart, accounting for approximately 6 percent to 8 percent of the reformatory's inmates. There were temporary departures from this norm—a dip to 5 percent in 1864 and a jump to 15 percent in 1890. Yet the absolute numbers of black children accepted by the Refuge did not change significantly between 1850 and 1890—it hovered around an annual average of thirty-seven. The Irish proportion of the inmate population, on the other hand, declined steadily over the course of the nineteenth century, while the non-Irish European immigrant population rose, until each stood at around 41 percent in 1889–90. Meanwhile, the native-born white population remained more or less constant—between 15 percent and 20 percent of the white cohort. Moreover, while girls consistently constituted between 25 percent and 30 percent of African American children admitted to the Refuge in the latter half of the nineteenth century, the female proportion of the white population declined steadily, from nearly one-fifth of the white population in 1850 to less than a tenth of that demographic in 1890. During this period, the commitments of white children were more likely than those of blacks to be initiated by public authorities rather than by their own kin, involve criminal offenses rather than mere destitution, and involve boys far more frequently than girls. On the other hand, the higher—and generally steady—female presence among African American inmates may have had something to do with the fact that indigent black guardians with few options for public assistance continued to play a major role in originating commitments to the Refuge, not discriminating between male and female charges as they did so.

The "welfare" uses to which black parents put the Refuge in the decades following the Civil War closely paralleled those of the antebellum period. Guardians moving out of town in search of work may have viewed the Refuge as a temporary asylum for their children. James Dillard was committed for allegedly "running away from home," yet the circumstances surrounding his case suggested that he had no home to flee from. While his father served as a fireman aboard a steamboat, his mother moved to Florida, from where she sought unsuccessfully to cancel her son's indenture to a Connecticut farmer so that he could join her in her new home. Thereafter, she regularly enquired after Dillard's well-being, calling on her daughter in New York to contact the Refuge when the boy's master failed to answer one of her letters. The lad, meanwhile, apparently completed his indenture successfully and went to work for the same master for wages.[67] A few mothers used the reformatory as an employment agency for their children. One single mother, a cook at a boardinghouse, committed her son George Smith to the Refuge for "truancy" and called soon after to request that the institution find "a good place" for the youth.[68]

Some parents may have committed sick children incapable of earning a living wage, or whom they could not provide with adequate care at home. The case of William Gilmore suggests an attempt on the part of parents to secure long-term care for an ailing child. The thirteen-year-old son of a laborer and a washerwoman of Ulster County—both members of the Baptist Church—Gilmore entered the Refuge "on complaint of his mother for running away from home." A month later, when epileptic fits seized the boy, his sister responded to the reformatory's queries about his health history: "When William was five years old he fell downstairs and ever since that time he has had fits. Any excitement will throw him into one." The family treated these attacks by "putting salt in his mouth and his feet in hot mustard water." Adjudged an unfit subject for the Refuge, Gilmore was discharged to his parents. Two years later, a police officer brought him back with a commitment for "disorderly conduct." A member of the staff recognized him and declined to receive him at the institution. He was once again returned to his family.[69] Yet another inmate admitted on the basis of his stepmother's charge of "disorderly conduct" was found to suffer from "poor eyes."[70]

Friction with stepmothers remained a perennial theme of family conflict through the nineteenth century.[71] Florence Anderson, reared by her grandmother until she turned fourteen, went to live with her coachman father and his new wife thereafter. Quarrels with her stepmother induced her to leave home for domestic service, goading her father into having her arrested for truancy. Three years after her admission to the Refuge, Anderson was discharged to the care of her grandfather.[72] As these cases suggest, when the various conditions of urban life strained the legendary cohesiveness of black families, some African Americans proved willing to seek social intervention to mediate their personal relationships. Other black children continued to see the Refuge as a source of board and education. Fourteen-year-old Jane Hilton, originally of Rome, New York, assured her case recorder that she had "done nothing wrong." Rather, having lost track of her only surviving parent and "having no home she went to [a judge] and asked to be sent here that she might have the benefit of the school"—apparently in preference to the otherwise-inevitable alternative of domestic service. She was indentured "for housewifery" to a family in Bergen County, New Jersey, a year after she had entered the Refuge. Despite favorable initial reports of her conduct, within two months her master wrote to say that she had run away, perhaps in search of that elusive education.[73]

The continuity of black New Yorkers' relationship with the NYHR stood in stark contrast with changes in the institution's equation with a new generation of white inmates—especially Irish and native-born—in the post–Civil War era. Fewer Irish youth entered the Refuge as a proportion of the white population, as already noted. More significantly, however, many that did enter the Refuge reacted to the reform regimen, centered on indefinite sentences and contract labor, with all the fury of indignant and self-consciously *free white* working men of the Gilded Age. As the Irish, now citizens colored white, claimed the rights of fair working conditions, religious worship, and habeas corpus, they cleaved with blood the reformers' imagined white community into hostile camps defined by class and culture.

Justin Dunn Versus Horatio Alger: Gilded Age Fractures Within the White Fraternity

"The opportunities for the young in this country are great; and no matter how humble their condition, all may aspire to the best and highest positions. . . . Some of the wisest and best men and women of this country were poor boys and girls. They struggled hard under great difficulties, but trusting in God, they persevered with determined will, overcoming every obstacle, and were rewarded with complete success."[74] These words of counsel to every child crossing the threshold of the New York House of Refuge were firmly entrenched in the success ethos of Gilded Age America, nurtured by the era's remarkable economic and technological triumphs. Machines and inventions completed the transformation of a largely agrarian society into an industrial behemoth. Railroads and telegraph and telephone lines knit the reunited, transcontinental nation into a gigantic national and international market driven by the managerial strategies of a ruthlessly competitive band of entrepreneurs. Andrew Carnegie and John D. Rockefeller became emblems of a meritocracy that, according to popular mythology, propelled plucky paupers to industrial captaincy in a mobile society rich with opportunity. And the Brooklyn Bridge, the world's longest suspension bridge, completed in 1883, bore the grandest testimony to the technological might of the United States. Yet the economic revolution bred other, less triumphant symbols as well—such as the thirty-four-year old cloak maker who, as the labor reformer Florence Kelley reported, was found after twenty years of sweated labor to be too "old" and weak to work anymore.[75]

Moreover, the Gilded Age was rife with industrial strife. In the last two decades of the nineteenth century, there erupted twenty-three thousand strikes affecting 6.5 million workers. In the course of some of these, workers fought pitched battles with armed militia and federal troops. As David Roediger has shown, working-class formation occurred in tandem with the "systematic development of a sense of whiteness" in the United States. Even as successive waves of European immigrants were pigeonholed into not-quite-white categories, labor unions taught them to uphold "white men's wages," while the allegiance of many to Catholicism won them the favor of Irish employers. The popular arts of minstrelsy and a consumer culture, rife with racialized icons of black service, acculturated them to the racial conventions of their adopted home.[76] Above all, the civic and political privileges attached to European descent not only accustomed many newcomers to think that "American" meant "white," but also fostered the association of "white" identity with European heritage. By the postbellum era, the Irish had, of course, been exposed to racialized constructs of working-class identity and American citizenship longer than their successors from southern and eastern Europe. Unrest at the New York House of Refuge in the early months of 1872 brought to the fore Irish assertions of their civic identity as workers and as *Americans* entitled to civil liberties and religious freedom, reinforced by the political advantage of whiteness.

On Monday, February 26, 1872, eighteen-year-old Peter Donnelly, a former kindling wood factory–worker–turned Refuge inmate, slashed the Principal of schools in the face with the blade of a shoe knife. The Principal had sentenced Donnelly and five of his mates to the "punishment closet" for having "stomped" their feet loudly during Sabbath school sessions the previous day. Donnelly and the rest were disciplined within the framework of the institution. Yet they had unknowingly inaugurated a three-month-long ordeal of turmoil that would engulf the NYHR in a tide of adverse publicity, prompt state investigations into the institution's relationship with its charges, and spur lasting changes in its reform regimen. Murder followed Donnelly's act of insubordination. At about 6:30 p.m. on March 17, 1872, Refuge inmate Justin Dunn plunged a worn shoe knife into the right leg of a shoe shop overseer named Samuel Calvert at the entrance of the boy's cell door. Four hours later, Calvert died of a severed femoral artery, and Dunn was remanded to the custody of the local police.[77]

In the course of the next month, the inmate "insurgency," as Refuge officers described it, gained steam. Teams of boys attempted armed escapes. When recaptured, "their curses and threats were terrible to hear, and of course were communicated to the other boys" with whom they shared sleeping quarters, testified Superintendent Israel Jones later before a committee of the State Commissioners of Public Charities. In April, ten of the worst troublemakers were separated from their mates, dragged into the tailor's shop, and suspended from strings attached to their thumbs, provoking a public outcry and allegations of torture. The institution then sought to rid itself of the group by turning one over to the Penitentiary, another to the state prison, discharging a few others by writs of habeas corpus, and hiring out the rest under indenture agreements. An uneasy calm settled on the establishment for a few weeks. Then, on May 17, at about 10 a.m., seventeen-year-old Thomas McDonald—one of Donnelly's band of foot stompers in church during the February incident—lay down his tools and prepared to storm out of his workshop, knifing the assistant foreman on his right temple. Several of McDonald's fellow inmates, including Donnelly, who had been watching the proceedings with interest, bellowed in solidarity and followed the rebel out into the yard, armed with knives and clubs. After a pitched confrontation with revolver-wielding officers of the institution, later fortified by reinforcements from the local station house, the boys surrendered. Twenty-eight of the rebels, deemed the "ringleaders" of the recent disturbances, were turned over to the police. Two days later, on Sunday, the older inmates—most of them Irish Catholic—refused to participate in the Sabbath services led by the chaplain, and a few "made a noise with their feet as though keeping time" with the minister's sermon.[78]

The inmate riots in the spring of 1872 took such a toll on the NYHR's public reputation that the institution's Managers requested an investigation by the State Board of Charities. The proceedings of this inquiry illuminate assertions of white identity that shaped the violence of 1872 and throw into sharp relief the rather different modes of resistance that African Americans adopted in contrast with many of their Gilded Age Irish counterparts. Blacks were conspicuous by their absence among the twenty-eight lead rioters of 1872, a group dominated by Irish or Irish American youths between the ages of seventeen and twenty. It was an all-male revolt, led by inmates who entered the Refuge in the postbellum era. Over 50 percent of their number had been born of Irish parents in New York, Brooklyn, or Philadelphia, and another fifth—also of Irish extraction—had immigrated from the British Isles. The remaining "culprits" were German, Scottish, or simply "Americans"—that is, native-born white Protestants. Significantly, these boys hailed predominantly from families of artisans or factory workers rather than casual laborers. Of the twenty who had worked for wages when they entered the Refuge, as many as fourteen had been employed in printer's offices, foundries, or factories making boilers, sewing machines, or umbrellas, or were training as tailors, hatters, or painters, frequently under the direction of their fathers. It is very likely that these young men were not indifferent to the appeals of labor radicalism or the rhetoric of "white men's wages."[79]

Testimonies offered at the official investigations of the troubles of 1872 suggested that for many of the rioters involved, the rebellion amounted to an assertion of their claims to the rights of freemen—decent wages and working conditions, the civic protections of habeas corpus, and the freedom of religious worship. These prerogatives set *citizens* apart from de facto *slaves*, and distinguished "whites" from "nonwhite Others." In his testimony before the State Commissioners, Superintendent Israel Jones traced the ferment among the inmates to their ready access to newspapers, in which they read about the famous *Huber* case. The inmates' newspaper privileges were taken away from them in the spring of 1872, but that restriction came too late to prevent a hubbub over expectations of mass discharges from the reformatory arising from a court decision involving a convicted plaintiff. Huber, who had been sentenced to the Penitentiary by New York's Court of Special Sessions, appealed the decision on the grounds that the sentencing court was unconstitutional. A provision, attached by the infamous "Boss" Tweed of Tammany Hall, to a tax levy adopted in 1870 gave the mayor power to "designate" any two police justices for the Special Sessions, stipulating that in their absence, the city judge and recorder could dispense justice in that court. One such mayoral appointee convicted and sentenced Huber. The boy's lawyers appealed the decision on the basis that the provision giving the mayor power to designate justices for the court violated the Constitution, "as no private or local bill passed by the Legislature shall embrace more than one subject, and that shall be expressed by the title." Huber won his case, prompting the State Supreme Court judge to rule, in a case brought on a writ of habeas corpus, that all commitments from the Court of Special Sessions were illegal and that persons held under those commitments must be discharged and be allowed to stand trial under the original charges of which they had been judged guilty. Many cases proved impossible to retry because of a lack of evidence.[80]

The Court of Special Sessions had dispatched a large proportion of NYHR inmates. Those whose relatives—overwhelmingly white—had access to politicians and lawyers were able to secure writs of habeas corpus. It was in this environment of turmoil—when "the friends of these lads were here daily looking for their discharge, and the boys had the idea that they would be very soon out because they were illegally held and the commitments not good for anything and they anticipated a general discharge," testified Superintendent Jones—that he noticed a decided change in their comportment. They had become "very bold and impudent and insubordinate." The atmosphere, in other words, was ripe for revolt.[81]

That revolt, when it came, became a perfect occasion for the inmates to air their grievances against the NYHR's alleged violations of their rights as workers and citizens entitled to constitutional protections of religious freedom. During the public hearings of 1872, the inmates leveled the charge that the "Managers compel the . . . inmates to labor incessantly" to the detriment of the laborers' health and spirits, and that they subordinated reform "to the interests of the contractors and to the purpose of realizing the greatest amount of money from the labor of the inmates."[82] Moreover, the boys alleged that their custodians induced them to take on extra work for profit, only to "defeat their hopes and take away their earnings." The Refuge administrators responded that the boys received wages of three dollars a week after the first three months of work; they forfeited their pay only if they broke the rules of the House or absconded before their terms were up.[83]

An equally serious accusation held that the Managers denied their charges the resources to pursue their own faith; instead, inmate were forced to practice what one witness, Father Renaud of the College of St. Francis Xavier of West Fifteenth Street, called "Practical Protestantism." Those who refused to attend chapel services at the Refuge received corporal punishment. Such persecution, Renaud contended, was less a matter of religion or theology than a question of the *civic rights* of American citizenship, which, according to the Democratic Party, to which most Irish bore allegiance, rested on "natural rights within government 'made by the white men, for the benefit of the white man.'"[84] The importance of religious freedom as a civil right emerged clearly in the course of an exchange between the priest and a Refuge Manager. The institution's administrators claimed in their own defense that they were nonsectarian, giving the children the "truths of the gospel in the simplest and plainest form"; they maintained that complying with "the strict requirements of Roman Catholic priests" would interpose an extraneous authority between the Superintendent and the boys, to the detriment of overall discipline. When Manager Edgar Ketchum asked Renaud, "Are we responsible, do you think, to any party other than to the state?" the clergyman answered, "You are responsible to the Constitution of the United States, which gives to *every American citizen* the free exercise of any religion he chooses to adopt."[85]

Roman Catholic identity and practice, in Father Renaud's formulation, became not a matter of deference to an extra-statist religious authority (such as the pope), but rather a political assertion of American civic identity. One inmate, James Downing, professed to speak for all those who claimed this right of American citizenship when he testified, "The Bible is read, and there is devotion, but I do not follow it up; I merely stand and look on." After the "troubles" of March 1872 surrounding the death of Calvert, his mates formed a "combination" that refused to join in the responses customarily made after the prayers led by the Refuge chaplain: "They wanted the Catholic boys to stand together and not respond." Downing joined in this "combination" because "I looked into it and saw it was not our religion," he explained. The siege of the yards in May stemmed from the determination of the boys not to go to chapel service. Asked what "made the boys get together in this way," he answered that he believed it was "their religion and time." By "time" he meant the fact that "we did not know the time we were to go out—when we were to be discharged."[86]

Downing's testimony encapsulated the triple conception of freedom that lay at the heart of the inmates' sense of citizenship. The Managers of the Refuge reported that during the May 17 insurgency, several boys—even those not directly implicated in the revolt—refused to perform their prescribed tasks at the workshop, demanding instead that they be given new trials together with those who had been discharged on habeas corpus in the wake of the *Huber* decision. They preferred to go to the Penitentiary rather than stay at the Refuge, the Managers stated, because "then they would know when their time would be out, but here they did not."[87] Indefinite commitment—which a Refuge sentence spelled—clearly smacked of a level of unfreedom not worthy of white men. Such unfreedom entailed not only doing unspecified "time," but also *wages* and *working conditions* appropriate to slavery, thus undermining their rights as autonomous white working men. Moreover, the privileges of full citizenship to which the youths laid claim encompassed not simply access to justice and "white men's wages," but also religious independence, even within the framework of a "total" institution. The explicit association that Downing made between the boys' intransigence and their sense of religious persecution, plus Father Renaud's reference to religious freedom as a prerogative of *American citizenship*, rather than deference to the religious authority of the pope, underscored this sense of entitlement on the part of the Refuge's most assertive charges—the majority of whom were Irish.

The inmates' civic assertiveness drew strength from the politico-cultural capital of whiteness to which the Irish were becoming rapidly acculturated. Witness Manager Ketchum's observation that the Refuge had received "recommendations from gentlemen high in authority, . . . from members of the legislature, soliciting the discharge of inmates, on which inmates have been discharged—from Senators, and ex-Senators, and from the Executive Chamber, from Police Justices."[88] Moreover, pressure from white inmates and their allies prompted a series of state investigations even beyond 1872, which led to organizational changes in the operation of the institution between 1887 and 1910. A new regimen of industrial education replaced contract labor, a program of military drill became the primary vehicle to inculcate discipline among the boys, and a parole system sought to review the eligibility of candidates for release and to monitor their progress afterward.[89]

African American Modes of Negotiation: A Study in Contrast with the Irish

As a disempowered minority alienated from the political machines of the city, African Americans had less recourse to the avenues of rebellion embraced by their Irish counterparts. Indeed, as we have already noted, blacks did not number among the rebellious cohort of 1872. Any incident of violent insubordination on the part of black youth was bound to evoke ferocious reprisals unmitigated by public sympathy or political pressure against inmate oppression. Furthermore, the lack of economic opportunity in the face of a rising tide of immigration from Europe left black children with fewer options upon their departure from the Refuge. Under the circumstances, African Americans adopted more gradual and less overt forms of resistance than whites. Outright escapes from the Refuge were conspicuous by their absence in the case studies in my sample of black children received by the institution between 1840 and 1890. About 60 percent of the children were indentured—the girls as domestic servants, and the boys as farm help, usually in rural New York and New Jersey. Another 27 percent were discharged to relatives and 6 percent turned over to other institutions, such as the Colored Home and the Alms House, usually because they were judged too ill or mentally incapacitated to be indentured. A tiny proportion of the children (2 percent) died of such ailments as consumption. The remaining were conscripted in the army, as during the Civil War, or sent away to sea (see table 47A, in appendix).

It is in the children's post-Refuge experiences—particularly those that involved indentures—that clues to some forms of resistance lie. Most children who returned to their relatives or joined the navy were forever lost to history from the moment of their departure from the Refuge. Inmates indentured to farmers and families in the vicinity of New York, on the other hand, left a somewhat longer trail of their lives within entries on their progress added periodically to their case records. If the successful completion of indentures was any index of the effectiveness of the Refuge's reform program, these entries suggest that the reformatory had little reason for satisfaction. About 68 percent of children bound to service left on their own or at the instigation of relatives well before the completion of their indentures. The significant aspect of this mode of rebellion consists in its operation outside the punitive context of the reformatory. Escape from the country was more feasible and carried less of a threat of retaliation than revolt within the premises of the Refuge. William Carter, thought to be particularly amenable to reform by virtue of his "light color," nevertheless forsook his farmer master within three months of joining him.[90] Seemingly contented charges surprised their masters by leaving without notice. William Garnett's mistress reported that although he was "not industrious and [was] self-willed," she had grown attached to him. Subsequently she wrote to say that he had left the previous day, despite the fact that "until recently he had seemed happy and contented."[91] Out-of-wedlock pregnancies cut other indentures short.[92] The children's failure to complete their terms of service may have signified not simply resistance, but also a desire to reunite with their families and communities (see table 47B, in appendix).

On the other hand, indentured charges occasionally sought the institution's mediation in disputes with masters indifferent to the terms of the apprenticeship. Christopher Anderson complained to the reformatory when his master, a New Jersey farmer named A. G. Van Nortwick, failed to provide him with "a new suit, a Bible, and thirty dollars" at the end of his stipulated three-year term. The master justified his violation of the contract on the ground that Christopher was "the worst boy he ever had." The Refuge, however, took Anderson's side, pointing out that "during . . . the apprenticeship [the master] sent no news of the boy"; in fact, the Refuge threatened a lawsuit to bring about a just settlement. The master then relented with the observation that Christopher was "a dangerous boy but smart at work. . . . Would have locked him up for his mis-doings . . . but was afraid he would burn his buildings on getting out." Anderson, meanwhile, had secured another wage-paying position.[93]

Notwithstanding the various forms of defiance displayed by African Americans, their case histories are also sprinkled with success stories, which helped sustain the Refuge's claim as an instrument of reform even in the midst of unfavorable publicity over the Irish revolt of 1872. Approximately one-third of the children in my sample completed their terms of service. There were significant discrepancies in the sex distribution of these satisfactory outcomes. While 48 percent of the girls fulfilled their indentures, only about 28 percent of the boys did as well. Part of the answer to this sexual difference may lie in the greater variety of work, as well opportunities for escape, available to boys. For young women limited to domestic service, on the other hand, the Refuge may well have seemed a useful source of future employment. When Sarah M. Simmons returned after a year's indenture "well-dressed" and in possession of "a good character from her master," the Refuge had no trouble finding her wage work.[94] A few women, including former prostitutes, got married. Of the young men who appeared to have passed the test of reform successfully, Thomas Wright was touted as a prime example. The son of a sewer cleaner, Wright entered the Refuge on a charge of burglary for stealing a bracelet. He was indentured to a Suffolk County farmer, completed his term of service successfully six years later, secured a job with the "Express Business" in Brooklyn, and visited his old "Home," leaving the impression that "he looked very respectable."[95] Yet whatever the significance of these cases as triumphs of the reformatory's acculturative mission, they underscored as well the institution's economic value as a path to paid employment, to its more tractable charges.

The willingness of the most defenseless segments of New York's black community to negotiate with the House of Refuge in less confrontational ways than the Irish stemmed not only from their political disempowerment and small numbers in the postwar era, but also from their lack of access to the multiple relief options available to European immigrants. Yet in different ways, both an Irish James Downing and a black Jane Hilton, together with hundreds of other NYHR clients, exposed hegemony as a terrain of contest in which the working poor used the language and symbols of domination to challenge their prescribed identities. Downing and his comrades applied their lessons in white license to protest their own class and religious subordination, thereby rupturing the Refuge's conception of monolithic whiteness. Jane Hilton, on the other hand, was more broadly representative of Victorian New York's "dangerous classes" who joined hands to wage a canny guerilla movement against what one historian has described as "the core of most welfare reform in America since the early nineteenth-century"—namely, a campaign to "define, locate and purge [the able-bodied poor] from the rolls of relief."[96] As outdoor relief gave way to a movement to remake the poor by institutionalizing them in reformatories, the laboring classes assimilated these acculturative institutions into their subsistence economies in ways that subverted conventional wisdom about the moral differences between the "worthy" and "unworthy" poor. Impoverished parents' use of the reformatory for relief *as well as* discipline implicitly defied the middle-class construction of their subaltern identity as idle wasters and unworthy guardians. The youthful inmates of the Refuge, for their part, contested bourgeois perspectives on crime through the medium of narratives—shaped by the institution's own case records—that advanced a "proto-structural" version of the juveniles' fall from "virtue." Black female adolescents' emphasis on their own sexual abuse at the hands of men—often white men—contradicted the "Jezebel" image in which white racists had historically cast black women. The legacy of working poor agency for the evolution of social welfare policy may be debated. What is more certain, however, is that such agency ensured that the hegemony of the bourgeois reform vision would be a field of negotiation rather than complete domination.

5

Celtic Sisters, Saxon Keepers
Class, Whiteness, and the Women of the Hopper Home

> I have so lively a recollection of the time when we were in the transitive state—when the old well-trained slaves had disappeared—when the few black servants to be hired were shiftless, lazy, and unfaithful, ... that I felt grateful for Irish servants with all their Celtic infirmities on their heads ... they are willing servants—they are sympathetic and progressive.... Providence makes of our homes Irish school-houses!
>
> —Catharine Maria Sedgwick

The prison reformer Catharine Maria Sedgwick—a daughter of the influential Federalist lawyer and congressman Theodore Sedgwick of Stockbridge, Massachusetts—harbored immense affection and regard for a servant of her family by the name of Elizabeth Freeman. Freeman was a former slave who successfully sued for freedom in the courts of Berkshire County in 1781, with Theodore Sedgwick as her counsel, and later joined the Sedgwick household in Stockbridge. Catharine Sedgwick remembered Mumbet—the name by which Freeman was known to the family—as "Mother—my nurse—my faithful friend ... who first received me into her arms." Sedgwick praised her character and sense of duty in terms that invoked the imagery of a Southern "mammy." She wrote in her autobiography that "Mumbet had a clear ... perception of justice, and a stern love of it, an uncompromising honesty in word and deed, and conduct of high intelligence that made her the ... moral teacher of the children she tenderly nursed." Sedgwick asserted that upon entering the hut of her old nurse as she lay dying years later, she "felt awed as if

I had entered the presence of Washington." Such high regard, however, threw into sharp relief Sedgwick's disapproval of black people in general. Mumbet, she claimed, "was a remarkable exception to the general character of her race." Sedgwick deplored especially the strategies of resistance to authority and loyal service that slavery appeared to have nurtured among African Americans, to the alleged detriment of their progress after emancipation: "Injustice and oppression have confounded their moral sense, . . . What wonder that they allow themselves petty reprisals—a sort of predatory warfare in the households of their masters or employers—for, though they now among us be free, they retain the vices of a degraded and subjected people."[1]

By contrast, the Irish made good servants, ultimately integrating into the Anglo-Saxon households that represented the American nation in microcosm, Sedgwick believed. It was the Manifest Destiny of Protestant kitchens to prepare Emerald Isle apprentices to participate in the great American story of unfolding progress. Sedgwick declared in her autobiography:

> I have so lively a recollection of the time when we were in the transitive state—when the old well-trained slaves had disappeared—when the few black servants to be hired were shiftless, lazy, and unfaithful, and our own people scarcely to be obtained, . . . that I felt grateful for Irish *servants* with all their Celtic infirmities on their heads—their half savage ways—their blunders—their imaginativeness–indefiniteness. . . . They desire employment—they are willing servants—they are sympathetic and progressive—and I have at this moment, June 1853, a girl in my service, Margaret Pollock, a pearl of great price. She is a Protestant to be sure, but she was born and bred in Ireland, and I would not exchange her for all the service I could distill in Yankeedom.

There is no question that Sedgwick essentialized the Irish as a "distinct race, with marked characteristics, and a religion of their own." Yet she considered them an *assimilable* race dispatched by Providence to take the place of low-born Yankees who answered the call of fresh pastures to the west. Providence impelled these immigrant "starving hewers of wood and drawers of water" to America, "to be taught in our kitchens," so that they could ride the "mighty wave of progress that is steadily tending onward and upward here . . . Providence makes of our homes Irish school-houses! Of our mothers and daughters involuntary missionaries."[2]

Sedgwick's contrasting perspectives on African Americans and the Irish offer insights into the deeply ambiguous relationship between race and white female reform in Victorian New York. Sedgwick was the first directress of the Women's Prison Association (WPA), which ran a halfway house for the redemption and rehabilitation of female convicts.[3] The refuge was known as the Isaac T. Hopper Home, named after the famed antislavery activist, prison reformer, and father of WPA architect Abby Hopper Gibbons. Several of the WPA's earliest generation of Managers—notably Gibbons herself—could rightfully claim the progressive mantle of abolitionist politics and women's rights activism. Yet the WPA's twin practices of dispatching women of color to segregated institutions like the Colored Home on the one hand, and its explicit emphasis on the redemptive potential of its mostly Irish charges on the other, pointed to the racialized national imaginary that underpinned its reform enterprise. Such practices implicitly drew a distinction between two subordinate groups whom racists and nativists cast similarly as indolent, improvident, and immoral. Sedgwick's unflattering commentaries on African Americans, juxtaposed against her prophecy of Irish absorption into the American narrative of progress, establish a context for making sense of the tacitly exclusionary approach of the institution that she helped run. Her observation that black people resorted to "predatory" warfare against their employers underscored a sense of alienation between mistress and servant, white and black, that militated against a vision of interracial sorority. Her subsequent lament about the unavailability of servants belonging in the ranks of "our own people"—meaning white New England Protestants, defined in relation to "shiftless and lazy" blacks—accentuated the gulf that she cleaved between "them" and "us." The African diaspora in America was, to Sedgwick, a people of the *past*, too immutably stained with the burden of history to achieve the sort of moral uplift of which Irish women were thought capable—an opinion she made clear by her comment that black people, although free in the North, retained "the vices of a degraded and subjected people."

The Irish, by contrast, heralded the dynamism of America's melting pot, for now and for the *future*, smoothly assimilating into their adopted society in order that they might "till and [be] tilled." Sedgwick predicted that despite their peculiarities, the children of the Irish "will melt into our population, in which there must be an amalgamation of various elements, the calculating, cold, intellectual Saxon, the metaphysical, patient German, the vivacious, imaginative, indefinite, changeful, uncertain Celt, . . .

A strange compound will come out of this . . . a perfecting and consummation of the species." Although Sedgwick assigned each ethnic group in this amalgam a body of inherent traits, they shared the common attribute of European descent. Thus, foreign as the Irish seemed to her in the 1850s, she still saw them as an integral element of her imagined nation—a white nation in which people of color were invisible. Prison reformers' portrait of the Irish immigrant as a forlorn fallen sister from a faraway land countered the vicious stereotypes of "simian Paddy" that pervaded antebellum society. Their rhetoric of Christian sisterhood, with its emphasis on the interchangeability of the material circumstances of Celtic servants and their Saxon mistresses, diffused the "Otherness" that defined the allegedly savage Bridget of nativist construction. The WPA's language of gender solidarity and reference to the ephemerality of worldly status, while obscuring real class differences, may have reinforced the sense of color-based inclusiveness conveyed by Sedgwick's thoughts on Irish immigrants. Yet this sense of inclusiveness defined by European lineage projected by prison reformers shut out millions of "nonwhite" American women.[4]

The model of the assimilable "fallen woman" who populated the pages of the WPA's prison reform literature evolved out of a multidimensional, sometimes paradoxical, but always interactive dialogue between bourgeois Saxon reformers and their plebeian Celtic "clients." Inmate narratives recorded in unpublished case histories, as well as in occasional letters written by prison inmates, afford glimpses into this intra-"white," cross-class, gendered exchange. The self-portraits of white female outcasts, as well as the material strategies that they adopted to retool the Hopper Home to serve their own ends, resembled the interracial subaltern worldviews on display at the New York House of Refuge.

At the same time, however, Hopper Home clients helped shape the racialized trajectory of female prison reform in important ways. As the WPA reformers—themselves a heterogeneous group of elite and middle-class Euro-American women, some of whom had experienced the vicissitudes of fickle fortune—wrestled with the credibility of their charges' stories, they were forced to reconfigure some of their own assumptions about female crime and "pauperism." Inmate testimonies persuaded benevolent women to interpret the legal transgressions of their fallen sisters less as the product of inherent character failings than of adversity. In the process, they reinforced the reformers' arguments about both the interchangeability of the worldly circumstances of different classes of women, and Irish women's potential to forsake their alien identity in favor of middle-class

Protestant norms of womanhood. Thus the interactive language of gender solidarity mediated the Hopper Home's participation in the discourse by which impoverished European immigrants "became white"—not simply by their own definition, but also in the perception of the larger society. The WPA's embrace of the Irish as "white" is particularly significant in light of the eugenic tone that the Association's fresh cohort of Managers adopted as waves of "new immigrants" arrived to complicate their mission in the late nineteenth century. The advent of these newcomers from southern and eastern Europe gave rise to new concerns about the supposedly indiscriminate reproductive proclivities of inferior aliens—an anxiety voiced in connection with the "welfare queen" paradigm of our own times. Such concerns helped shape the WPA's campaign to launch a state reformatory to hold female offenders long enough to not simply train them to earn a living, but also to prevent them from having children (who would "inherit" their vices).

The Social Origins of the Hopper Home

The Women's Prison Association grew out of the Female Department of the Prison Association of New York (PANY), established in 1844 with the objectives of reforming prisons, improving prison discipline, and reclaiming discharged convicts. Incorporated in 1854, the WPA campaigned to ameliorate prison conditions for women and rehabilitate those judged "redeemable" by committing them to a halfway house that it operated, known as the Isaac T. Hopper Home.[5] The key architects of the WPA were born in the late-eighteenth and early-nineteenth centuries into a world that straddled the cusp of a fading agrarianism and a rising commercialism. In the bourgeois imagination, the doctrine of "true womanhood" idealized women out of playing any economic role in the emerging market society. The domestic ideology could, however, be interpreted as vesting mothers and sisters with the moral authority to step beyond the private realm of the home to rid society of a host of sins, from intemperance to slavery. Women claimed a special mandate to protect and reform those of their sex who inhabited an alien and frightening world, epitomized by the distinguishable working-class neighborhoods that Christine Stansell portrayed so vividly in *City of Women*. As Lori Ginzberg has argued, "The conflation of the ideologies of morality and gender" played a vital role in the creation of middle-class identity in the nineteenth century "both by adapting revolutionary era rhetoric about virtue to an expanding, industrializing, and urbanizing society and by obscuring the interests and identities that informed benevolent women's work."[6]

The construction of middle-class identity did not proceed without conflict. Carroll Smith-Rosenberg has captured a moment in Jacksonian America when female moral reformers used sexual imagery to articulate a metaphoric discourse of opposition to commercialism; these women offered the vision of a society in which morality rather than wealth determined social status. The wild vagaries of fortune, which tossed nascent entrepreneurial families in and out of the middle class with abandon, reinforced the women's sense of the tenuous material foundations of class identity. By the 1850s, however, the middle class had solidified as an economic and cultural entity, its aspirations manifested best in the ideology of the Republican Party's celebration of social mobility through free labor. With its emphasis on the role of personal responsibility in determining economic success, free labor Republicanism complemented the premise of individual redemption that lay at the heart of Christian benevolence. As noted before, it could be applied to train virtuous domestic servants as well as disciplined factory workers.[7]

The reformers of the WPA represented a transitional generation whose lives spanned the turbulent era of middle-class formation. The Association's president, Abby Hopper Gibbons, and corresponding secretary, Caroline M. Kirkland, both born in 1801, were the daughters or wives of men who moved from the margins to the center of the new economic order. Both women had firsthand experience with the wavering ways of material fortune, so that for each, her genteel education signified her privileged status (rather than her wealth), especially during the early phase of her life. Abby Hopper's father, Isaac T. Hopper, operated a tailor shop in Philadelphia and later a bookstore in New York. Hopper's marriage to the merchant, banker, and business writer James Sloan Gibbons did not bring immediate economic security. Indeed, the Gibbonses lived in rented homes until 1851, when at last they achieved the wealth to purchase a handsome house off Nineteenth Street in New York. More progressive, perhaps, than many of her colleagues in prison reform, Gibbons espoused a variety of causes, including abolitionism, women's rights, an industrial school for German girls, and the Colored Home in Washington.[8]

Caroline Kirkland was the New York–born daughter of Samuel Stansbury, who started his career as a clerk in a dry goods store, failed in his bid to run a bookstore in Connecticut, and returned to an old job in a New York insurance company. Supported by her father and a Quaker school mistress aunt, Kirkland acquired an excellent formal education, "vitally supplemented by daily talks around the dinner table" with her erudite family. She married William Kirkland, scion of an eminent family of New England educators and himself a scholar of the classics. After a sojourn to frontier Michigan, where their attempts at land speculation and town promotion ended in disaster, the Kirklands returned to New York, where Caroline established a distinguished career as a writer and teacher. No stranger to adversity, whether resulting from the manipulation of frontier swindlers or the early death of her beloved husband, she could probably identify with the misfortunes of the fallen women whose cause she upheld so eloquently in *The Helping Hand*, an official history of the Home published in 1853 for fundraising purposes.[9]

Of the WPA's leading founding figures, Catherine Maria Sedgwick, the first directress, was not only the oldest, but also the most patrician in lineage. She was born in Stockbridge, Massachusetts, in 1789, of a statesman father "born too soon to relish the freedoms of democracy," she wrote. Sedgwick attended a series of private schools in New York, Albany, and Boston, but gained her most valuable education informally, through her association with her learned father and brothers. She chose to remain single all her life, building up a successful literary career rather than a family of her own. As a member of the early republic's entrenched elite, Sedgwick's sense of noblesse oblige may have been shaped as much by the vision of a new role for an old aristocracy as by the bourgeois conflation of womanhood with virtue. As the editor of her autobiography has suggested, Sedgwick "envisioned an elite" whose cultural authority "might yet be critical to the success" of democratic society—"those who could no longer expect to dominate at the polls could retain power . . . in the domain of culture." Sedgwick's works, such as *A Tale of Our Own Times* and *Poor Rich Man and Rich Poor Man*, conveyed a disdain for crass materialism and a celebration of moral integrity; this point of view arguably constituted as well an attack against the class pretensions of the emerging bourgeoisie.[10]

By the time the Hopper Home was founded, the middle class had become well established. The reformers of the WPA fused the ideologies of gender and morality with the assumptions of free labor Republicanism in their project to rehabilitate female outcasts. The Hopper Home embodied an optimistic faith in individual redemption that powered evangelical reform and rationalized a free market for labor in the antebellum North. Redemption was a class- and race-specific gendered concept in that it implied the restoration of *feminine* virtue, bourgeois style, defined by the attributes of piety, purity, domesticity, and deference to white men.[11] Such a project was not, of course, inconsistent with the creation of a diligent white working class. The "private" sphere—emanating out of the nuclear family home to encompass the world of female benevolence—was thought to be the appropriate theater for redemption. The Hopper Home sought to recreate the organic ethos and "quiet regularity of a well-ordered family" amid the physical ambience of a middle-class household—replete with appropriate furniture, utensils, and space—in order to promote its inmates' moral uplift, health, and vigor. At the same time, the spartan living and rigid discipline of this feminized "total institution" was designed to supplant the "disorderly idleness" of its wards' upbringing with the "industry, order, self-restraint and docility" necessary for factory work in the country or domestic service in "that best of all moral schools, the humane and religious private family."[12]

For the first twenty years of its existence, the reformatory repeatedly reminded its patrons of the superior efficiency and economy of private benevolence over public charity and punishment. It reported, for instance, that between 1845 and 1863–64, its average annual expenditure for each inmate amounted to $19.38, while that for state prison inmates was $112.62. Moreover, in the absence of the institution's work of rehabilitation, recommitments would render its potential wards "costly pensioners" of the "sober, hardworking citizen, who if he takes the time to look at the matter, will be somewhat startled to find how much he has to pay to the police, the justices, the prison officials of all degrees."[13]

The Hopper Home opened its doors in June 1845 to 107 discharged convicts recommended by prison authorities as showing signs of retaining "a remnant of womanly feeling." Staffed by two matrons and a teacher, the Home occupied an airy three-storied building on the western side of Tenth Avenue, commanding a view of the Hudson River. Upon arrival, each inmate underwent a physical examination followed by a bath. When she emerged decently clothed, the matron read her the rules of the House. She learned that she must avoid tobacco and alcohol as well as "all profane and indecent language"; she must surrender all money in her possession to the matron "for safekeeping"; she must seek the matron's permission if she wished to leave the premises or make purchases. Any violation of these rules spelled dismissal. Thus examined, cleansed, clothed, and interrogated, she was introduced to a regimen of prayer, work, and plain fare regulated by the clock and the bell. The Home sought to find employment either in domestic service or in factories in the country for inmates who satisfactorily completed their terms of residence.[14]

The Home's reliance on "moral trial" as the staple of domestic therapy lent this total institution of reform and rehabilitation its uniquely bourgeois feminine character. Founded in "woman's power over woman," this approach called for molding "sentiments" in addition to outward conduct through "frequent discussion" about past misconduct and the promise of future rectitude. The inmates themselves were encouraged to act as "moral judges" of one another.[15] The fruits of these interactions were set forth in the private case histories of the Hopper Home. WPA case records, generated before the postbellum advent of scientific charity, embodied the substance of what the Association's corresponding secretary, Caroline Kirkland, called "a mode of moral trial . . . kindly questioning . . . advice, reproof and warning" as a tool of reform.

Although conveyed through the perspectives and in the words of their middle-class recorders, the case histories, when juxtaposed against the WPA's public pronouncements, reveal that official portraits of the fallen woman evolved in response to dynamic interchanges among a variety of clashing voices. Cross-class perspectives on sexual politics, pauperism, and crime traversed and colluded all at once in the construction of varied models of white female transgression. There is no better example of subaltern uses of dominant devices to negotiate interclass relations.[16]

Between the lines of WPA case records lurked the less conspicuous discourse of white identity formation in which the prison reformers' redemption project was embedded. Structured invisibly into the dynamic of gender camaraderie between Saxon and Celt, it emerged more clearly in the inmate ethnic profiles brought to life by the neat handwritten pages of the WPA's earliest case histories. These were entered in longhand in notebooks with unlined sheets. They were not numbered, followed a narrative format, and included the inmate's name, reason for commitment to prison, ethnicity, national origin, age, marital status, dates of and occasionally reasons for admission and discharge. The largest cluster of these records belonged to the years 1845 and 1855. The 1855 case histories were entered in large, hard-covered notebooks with lined paper. A sample of seventy-five of the most detailed case records compiled in 1845 yields the collective portrait of an inmate population overwhelmingly immigrant in extraction but marked by the homogeneity of "white" descent—whether European or Euro-American. Only two women in this group were born in the city of New York. Of the forty-eight inmates who had immigrated from Europe (64 percent of the total population), thirty-four were Irish, eight were English, while the rest came from Scotland, Wales, Canada, and France. Of the twenty-seven native-born women, twenty-five had migrated to the metropolis from other parts of New York State, as well as from New Jersey, Connecticut, and Pennsylvania. A few had traveled from Ohio, Virginia, and South Carolina.[17]

Pushed out by famine, caught in the swirl of commercialism, infected by the impulse for adventure, these women came to New York for all sorts of reasons—several in search of work, autonomy, and excitement; a few in the company of employers, parents, or siblings; others to make illusory homes with fickle suitors or peripatetic seasonal laborers. These were young women for the most part, about 43 percent of them still in their twenties, who had never married. About a fifth were separated from their spouses, while approximately 27 percent were widows. The case records of 61 percent of these women mentioned no occupation at all. The remaining number revealed that the group as a whole was rather isolated from the city's manufacturing sector. Only six women described themselves as artisans—weavers, tassel makers, and seamstresses who had fallen on hard times. The rest included prostitutes, domestic servants, children's nurses, and casual workers who performed a miscellany of odd jobs, from cleaning windows to vending ice cream on street corners.

Intemperance constituted the most common failing of immigrant women, as well as the leading offense of the group as a whole, accounting for the arrest of 40 percent of them under nebulously defined vagrancy statutes. Prostitution came second but led the list of "crimes" committed by native-born women. American-born women disdained domestic service, as Sedgwick noted with some irritation. Prostitution may have offered these women a more lucrative alternative to the low-paying work in the fiercely competitive outwork-manufacturing sector. Only four of the women I surveyed were charged with theft—shoplifting and counterfeiting. Others were rounded up for crossing their employers, quarreling with their neighbors, and beating their children in public spaces. Significantly enough, one-fifth of the women were victims of homelessness, sickness, pregnancy, desertion, or sexual abuse, who had either "given themselves up" or were committed to "the Tombs" (a downtown prison complex) by relatives.

Hardly hardened criminals, the entering class of the Hopper Home presented a collective profile that lent credibility to the reformers' pleas for the fallen's eligibility for public sympathy—pleas that these outcasts and their successors through the 1850s would themselves mold in subtle ways (as did their interracial peers at the New York House of Refuge). In the context of the Hopper Home, the term "woman," applied by the reformers to designate their bond with their fallen sisters, had a color-blind, universalist ring. Yet although the Home did not officially exclude African Americans, its practice of referring black applicants to the Colored Home or the city Alms House, and the resultant European orientation of its inmate population's ethnic/national identity, lent the familiar symbol of the redeemable fallen woman a "race"—the discursively invisible but normative color white. This is not to deny the very sincere sympathy that abolitionist prison reformers like Gibbons showed for African Americans. It is to recognize the complex legacy of female benevolence in the vexatious arena of race relations.

White Sisters: The Dialogic Construction of Fallen Women's Identities

Benevolent women's discussion of men's roles in women's falls from virtue offered a significant context in which fallen women could participate in crafting their own public identity; it also fed the dynamic of gender solidarity that helped bring the Irish into an interclass white sorority.[18] An unpublished letter by an applicant to the Home from Sing Sing prison, signed "Your obliged friend," not only appropriated the language of antebellum America's "war between the sexes," but also appealed to the reformers in terms at once deferential and intimate–terms that located the author as a sort of wayward but penitent younger sister pleading for understanding and help. "You wished to know more particulars about my misfortunes," wrote Mary F. "I became acquainted with the man who led me into . . . trouble soon after I came into New York. He promised marriage on the week he took me to his boarding house. But that week never came." What came instead was a child and the author's "ruin":

> I deserve all the punishment I have, and yet it [is] hard for one to bear who has been . . . hoodwinked by vile persons as I have. Had I fallen into the hand of as upright and kind persons as you . . . I [would] have never been here. I never want to see that man again, only to get my child back. Can you help me in this . . . I will do just what you say. . . . Please let me know if you can do anything by way of getting my child back and getting rid of this man . . . I am uneasy about my mother. Can you let me know anything about her? . . . I cannot be sorry that I came to prison. It was God that done it [sic] to save my poor soul and my child.

Mary F's choice of the term "misfortune" to describe her own plight, the suggestion that but for the association of a "vile" man she would have led an upright life, and her view of prison as a source of redemption for herself and her child—leading up to the plea for protection against an abusive former lover and help with information about her child and mother—all tapped into the most elemental sentiments of female prison reform discourse.[19]

By the very act of narrating the material realities of heterosexual confrontations within their emerging working-class neighborhoods, "clients" helped reinforce the reformers' distaste for the alleged savagery of working-class and immigrant men. A tradition of gender segregation in work and family life, and the primacy of economic aspirations over romance, generated sexual conflict among the Irish. Emigration to the United States may have accentuated such tension. As the uncertainties and opportunities of wage labor undermined men's economic authority within the family, while enhancing women's independence, attempts to reassert masculine power took the form of escalated domestic violence.[20] The case histories from 1845 and 1855 reflect these developments and record other instances of betrayal by unworthy males—seduction, desertion, bigamy, abuse, neglect to provide for family, and enticement into prostitution. For instance, an Irish immigrant claimed that "she was very strictly brought up [by a Methodist father], and never drank until her husband abused her and took all her things from her." Eighteen-year-old Mary Fine of Ohio, a tailor by trade, represented a familiar figure in female reform literature: a naive country girl destroyed by an unscrupulous urban sexual predator. Fine married a New York shoemaker who "appeared honest, industrious," but she discovered shortly after the wedding that he had a wife in Brooklyn. Destitute and friendless on the streets of New York, Fine then sought out a police officer at a Sixth Avenue station house to report her situation; subsequently, she was brought to the Home. The litany of vices alleged against husbands included, in one case, impiety. One woman—described as an "American" of respectable parentage—left her husband and took to drinking because, according to her, he locked her out of the house when she attended church.[21]

The inmates also leveled allegations of sexual abuse against their male social superiors that could simultaneously serve as a class protest and an appeal to interclass sisterhood. Addie Irving, an inmate of Sing Sing, wrote a prison visitor that a navy officer, introduced to her by the prison warden, offered her "a ladies life [sic]" in exchange for sexual favors. Drawing strength from God, she claimed to "[gain] the victory and [foil] the villain." She decided against exposing the "authorities . . . lest I should shame Mr. Keen [the warden]'s wife whoes [sic] gentleness won my love."[22] Out of the fabric of such discourse, reformers fashioned the widely publicized portrait of their fallen sister as a hapless victim of male perfidy, the emblem of their twin late–Victorian era campaigns for women's prisons under female management and against the sexual double standard embedded in male critiques of prostitution. By nature or potential, a mirror image of "true woman," this malleable child-woman stood humbled and "trembling under the sense of weakness and degradation" at the crossroads of virtue and vice, crying out for the moral stewardship her more fortunate sisters were sanctioned by God to provide. The metaphors of "poor patient" and "adult-child" conveyed the hopeful vision of her salvageability—an idea crucial to Christian benevolence in the antebellum North.[23]

If the changed terms of gender relations in the working-class neighborhoods of nineteenth-century New York helped flesh out the image of the fallen woman as innocent victim, they also supplied the ammunition for constructing her evil twin—the "unsexed" creature of the streets. Single working women—loosened from the constraints of family supervision through migration from the farm and overseas—breathed a new air of sexual permissiveness and partook of the pleasures of commercial leisure in the working-class sections of town. Their colorful life histories yield a collective portrait of feisty, spirited womanhood marked by adventure and ambition, risk and rebellion, which surely fueled a second incarnation of the female transgressor as the mirror image of "true woman." Catherine Smith was fairly typical of this "woman of the neighborhood," whose private world merged with the marketplace in a seamless web of eroticism, disorder, flamboyance, and excess.[24] Smith had left Ireland in protest against an authoritarian father's attempts to discipline her for sexual transgressions, and now she earned her own livelihood in the Bowery. Likewise, native-born unwed mother Sarah Thorp, who in the absence of a support network took refuge on Blackwell's Island, declared that "she had not done wrong with the exception of having a child."[25]

Competitive and sexually aggressive, or else "deviant" in her mode of dress and sexuality, the "unsexed" version of the female "outcast" became simultaneously a metaphor for the ills of a "male" marketplace and a prime candidate for socialization to the discipline of wage labor through feminization. Josephine, described in a report of the WPA's Committee on Prisons as a "well known prostitute," challenged the cultural norms that defined bourgeois women's identity and proffered a view of class based on the markers of wealth alone. Convicted of shoplifting, the twenty-one-year-old woman apparently "boastingly" told the prison visitor, "I dressed myself like a lady for I have as good clothes and jewelry as any lady . . . I had stowed away three . . . cloaks and was just sending the fourth one down when I was discovered."[26]

If Josephine desexed herself by conflating genteel womanhood with the appearance of material prosperity rather than morality, nineteen-year-old, Canadian-born Margaret L. did so by her masculine pugnacity. Margaret was reared severely by "a father of bad character," rather than nurtured by the gentle piety of an affectionate mother. Her upbringing infused her with the spirit of aggressive competitiveness: "Her parents taught her to fight—would hold a handkerchief between her and another girl and encourage them to beat and bruise each other over it." Her father reportedly took pride in the fact that in the field, his daughter "did as much work as three boys." In time, Margaret "became very strong"—an allusion to her physical defeminization. Margaret owed her stint in jail to a brawl with another woman on the Canadian border, en route to the United States. While in prison, she struck up a friendship with five men confined in an apartment directly below her, with whom she conversed through a stovepipe: "Feeling very sorry for them, she was persuaded to assist them to escape, which she accomplished by dislodging a large stone—a feat requiring more than *masculine* strength." Although she made no attempt to escape herself, she was betrayed by a fellow inmate, tried, and condemned to the state prison for two years. She was reported to persist "in thinking the helping of five poor fellows out of trouble" a praiseworthy deed.[27]

Prison reformer Isaac T. Hopper's encounter with a Lunatic Asylum resident, also reported in *The Helping Hand*, conveyed a similar sense of the "desexing" influence of crime and the feminizing mission of redemption. Jane defied her received gender identity by using "vulgar and profane language" and making pantaloons out of her blanket, declaring, "It is military; I am an officer of state." She agreed to wear a dress only as a price for "a walk in the fresh air" with Hopper, during which exercise she appeared not only contrite, but "more rational" than ever before. Hopper, who eventually secured for Jane a pardon as well as a position in domestic service, ended his vignette with the comforting image of the young penitent in his mind's eye, "sitting clothed and in her right mind."[28] A woman inmate of Framingham, Massachusetts, assumed a male identity under the aliases of "Captain" Jack, Arthur Holmes, and Fred Fiske; worked as a teamster, sailor, and bartender; and made love to many women.[29] Never defined explicitly by her sexuality, the masculinized fallen woman must, nevertheless, have subsumed within her received persona the lesbian and bisexual incarcerated for "disorderly conduct." Bourgeois women's gendered view of crime as "desexing," as unfeminine, implicitly equated virtue and self-worth with the heterosexual feminine attributes of "true womanhood" rather than wealth. While such a view could be read as a critique of the materialism of the male marketplace, it could also be interpreted as a way of acculturating and reconciling working-class women to the discipline of wage labor.

While discussions of men's complicity in women's degradation generated a broad area of consensus between fallen sisters and their keepers, perspectives on the origin of crime represented a more murky terrain of interclass contest. While WPA reports traced crime to immigrant and working-class intemperance and improvidence, private case records demonstrate that Hopper inmates advanced, like the NYHR juveniles, a "proto-structural" view of their lot in life. Inmate stories established a link between poverty and theft, underpinned by a barely concealed hostility toward exploitative or unjust authority figures—whether employers or judges—that was usually missing from the official construction of their degradation. One woman's explanation for her complicity in a theft charge, which landed her in the Tombs, illustrated well this inmate perspective. She had defaulted on her rent payment, because as a tailor she "could hardly make enough . . . to pay her board." When her landlady insisted on immediate payment, she pawned two pairs of pantaloons, expecting to take out a loan from her brother to redeem the items. In the meantime, the owner of the pantaloons arrived to claim his order and the seamstress found herself in the Tombs. Jane Dougherty, a WPA inmate, found herself on Blackwell's Island for speaking "unhandsomely" to a judge who had sentenced her mother to a prison term for intemperance. The judge apparently warned her that "if she said anything more he would send her [to prison]too." She responded that "he had no right to send her [since] she was not in liquor"; she received a two-month sentence for her trouble while her mother received only a one-month sentence. Several inmates pointed to work-related injuries or conflict over wages as the source of their destitution. A forty-year-old Englishwoman exhausted her savings nursing a head injury sustained at work through "being over the fire." Johanna Murphy, a thirty-four-year-old Irish immigrant was imprisoned because she broke her employers' door in when they refused to pay "her due." Murphy no doubt saw herself as stigmatized for daring to defend her right as a worker in the only way she knew how. The case recorder, however, after noting that Murphy had never been to prison before and "[kept] no bad company or anything," concluded that "her temper took her to prison." A fifty-three-year-old washerwoman said that she was accused of theft for "keeping some clothes she had washed as the lady owed her considerable [sic] she was afraid she should not get her money."[30]

Moreover, inmates turned the reformers' diagnosis of crime as a product of intemperance into a challenge of the dominant discourse on vice as a "code of class" and culture.[31] Ex-convicts responded to questions about when they started drinking by representing their fondness for the bottle or "propensity to steal" not as a class or culture-specific vice, but rather as a response to the brutal challenges of urban or immigrant life, sickness, and loss of family and fortune. Some variation of the phrase "Trouble drove her to the first glass" ran like a refrain through the WPA case records. Bereft of support networks of family or friends, single women—whether divorced, widowed, or never married—were especially likely to succumb to the challenges of illness or a precarious job market. A widow claimed to have begun drinking when she broke her leg by falling off a window that she was cleaning. Some women blamed their recourse to alcoholism and crime on tragic twists of fate and the consequent loss of hope and purpose of living. Such was the saga of Philadelphia-born Elisa Arlington, daughter of a minister and widow of a merchant-turned–Mexican War veteran. Arlington established an ice cream saloon in the Bowery and "was doing very well" when an outbreak of cholera disrupted her private world. She lost four children and nearly her own life to the disease. About the same time, a son—on whom she had lavished "a good education" and pinned all her hopes—died at sea: "She felt as if her trouble was more than she could bear—her husband, children, property, all gone." Therefore, she sought solace in the bottle and ended up on Blackwell's Island.[32]

Detailed accounts of industrious lives turned sour by the brutal challenges of immigration to a strange metropolis countered the stereotype of working poor culture as habitually idle. Such narratives also conveyed a sense of disillusionment with the elusive nature of the "American dream." Twenty-five-year-old Irishwoman Sarah Porter decided after a year in America that she "regret[ted] exceedingly ever having come to this country." Another domestic servant sent "all that she could possibly spare of her wages to her poverty stricken mother and sister in the old country." Maria Gilbert insisted that she had done very well as a weaver in her native Ireland until "persuaded to come over [to America] with the hope of doing better." Margaret Gibson claimed to have been incarcerated for intemperance while she was working for her passage home to Ireland. The fallen took particular pains to exonerate their families of origin of any complicity in their downfall. Irish-born Ann Atkinson, imprisoned for stealing, "appears to feel very much for her parents, thinks it would almost break their hearts should they hear of what she has been guilty." The case of Marcella DeLoinge suggested that an upright upbringing was no insurance against the loss of virtue, thus negating the equation between class and morality. A native of France, DeLoinge had been reared in a Canadian convent for ten years at the instance of her sole guardian, an aunt. Upon her release from the convent and the death of her aunt and a lover, she drifted into prostitution. Another prostitute challenged the cultural compartmentalization of "virtue" and "vice" by declaring that she was also a Sunday school scholar.[33] Fallen women's emphases on themes such as a history of steady work, church membership, and duty toward family may have reflected a shrewd appreciation of the kind of appeals that would engage their recorders' sympathies. At the same time, they undermined the genteel diagnosis of the cultural origins of their fall from virtue. A sense of betrayal by society at large pervaded inmate perspectives on the roots of their transgression. Kirkland conceded as much in a revealing passage from *The Helping Hand*: "If we would believe prisoners, no one of them was ever incarcerated justly. They are all innocent victims of society, which they seem to consider as delighting to persecute and oppress them. The world is not their friend, nor the world's law."[34] The inmates' paradigm of collective victimhood to unjust institutions evoked from their benefactors a complex matrix of responses that revealed the possibilities as well as limitations of interclass solidarity based on gender and color. *The Helping Hand* reflects the struggle of middle-class reformers to reconcile their personal experiences of the fallen with the received prejudices and assumptions of their own social class. The outcome was a multilayered argument that, while operating within the gender conventions of reform discourse and the premises of free labor Republicanism, challenged elements of both in favor of a more sympathetic reading of plebeian predicaments.

The Helping Hand anchored its appeal for sympathy on behalf of the female convict in the nineteenth century's traditionally feminine domain of Christian charity, fortified by a tacitly color-coded ethos of gender solidarity. Making a religious case for classifying transgressors of the law with various "natural" categories of relief-seekers, it admonished readers with the observation that "while other classes of sufferers have awakened the tenderest interest . . . , the prisoner alone—always associated by our Lord in his teachings with the destitute, the sick, and the wretched, whom to neglect is to forfeit the disciple's name—has been comparatively forgotten."[35]

Yet empirical evidence about the lived experiences of the "dangerous classes," garnered from their interaction with fallen women, prompted the reformers to move beyond an acceptance of the presence of the poor and the criminal in their midst as divinely ordained; rather, they began to ask, how did these classes come about? Inquiries into the *sources* of degradation led Kirkland to question the division between the "worthy" and "unworthy" poor erected by male reformers, such as those belonging to the Society for the Prevention of Pauperism. She conceded the public's natural instinct to shun those considered the authors of their own degradation:

> No arguments are needed when we would enlist the general sympathy in the condition of sufferers by unmerited misfortune. . . . But far otherwise with the unhappy objects of our care. They are in possession of the bodily senses they have abused. . . . They do not belong to the class of idiots, nor are they incapacitated from many kinds of occupation, by means of which the necessaries . . . of life are obtained. They seem to be what they are, and to stand where they stand, by their own perverse choice, and the first and most natural thought is to let them abide by that choice.

At this point, Kirkland drew on the revelations of the female convict herself to argue that the question of the fallen's worthiness for relief and potential for reform was far more complex than suggested by the assumption of a "perverse choice." "Has there in truth," asked Kirkland, "been any such deliberate choice—any such insane election? Our experience . . . has shown us conclusively that in nine cases out of ten, no choice was ever made, for none was offered." The lens of white Christian sisterhood refracted the subaltern paradigm of victimhood to social and institutional injustice into an individualized view of crime as a product of personal misfortune and lack of opportunity. "How can we be pitiless toward the transgression of the untaught, the unwarned, the neglected?" Kirkland queried. While "hereditary tendencies" and "evil associations" played a part in making women into criminals, forces beyond the outcast's control bore a large share of the blame: "If all the true stories of these women were written down and published, the world would open its eyes with astonishment at the things going on unsuspected under the specious surface of society. Such instances of deception, enticement, sedulous corrupting of inexperience, and dreadful cruelty, no writer of romance ever invented." More significantly, Kirkland suggested that female crime originated also in "the hard trials of poverty, the harder for women than for the stronger and bolder sex." Thus the case for helping the fallen woman moved beyond an abstract, sentimental, feminine appeal in the spirit of Christian benevolence to embrace a secular argument about the adverse workings of the marketplace against individual women, based on empirical evidence supplied by the victims of misfortune themselves. Accordingly, WPA representatives worked tirelessly for the discharge of women whose misdemeanors they believed to have been induced by poverty. The Association's Prison Report for October 6, 1856, for instance, noted that its agent had investigated and achieved the discharge of twenty-six women on trial for petty larceny, because she was convinced the offenses, committed for the first time, were in every case, "tempted . . . by poverty" and that "forgiveness" rather than "further punishment" would better serve "the cause of justice and humanity."[36]

The Helping Hand suggested that inmate testimonies supported the Hopper Home's claim that crime was neither immutable nor a matter of natural predisposition. "We prevent recommitments; we can prove that we have prevented them in numerous cases," Kirkland claimed.[37] It was on this empirical ground, based on their command of evidence, that the reformers nimbly refuted the gendered assumption that the work of female prison reform constituted "feminine" romanticism as distinct from "masculine" rationalism. They conceded that many people thought their enterprise visionary. Romanticism in the disinterested service of society was indeed a peculiarly feminine attribute: "To those who call us romantic, we must first be allowed to say that few benevolent enterprises are begun in this selfish world without a little romance, and it is because women are more liberally endowed with what passes under this name, that they originate so many of the charitable efforts of the day . . . and carry them through triumphantly by no little personal sacrifice," Kirkland wrote. Yet the Hopper Home experiment revealed the optimistic expectations of its architects to be entirely rational: "As to the romance of this special effort, the experience of years enables us to show that it is at least founded upon reality, since we are able to point to scores of cases . . . where success has crowned our endeavors to reform the female convict." The reformers proceeded logically to dispel the notion that empathy for the fallen woman would encourage further irresponsible behavior. Kirkland assured her readers that it was no more likely that "an unworthy person would commit an offence for the sake of obtaining admission to [the Hopper Home] than that another should put out his own eyes in order to secure a comfortable shelter at the Asylum for the Blind." Kirkland's repeated references to *experience* and *evidence* based on inmate depositions underscored the rational empiricism of female prison reform. She defied—however deferentially—the gendered construction of female benevolence as emotional and utopian; or, rather, she suggested that feminine utopianism was actually perfectly rational in its expectations and effects. At the same time, the WPA's acknowledgment that unfortunate circumstances and "the trials of poverty" occasionally produced personal failure called into question the concept of unbridled human agency lying at the heart of free labor Republicanism.[38]

This important recognition of the limits of individual agency shaped female reformers' emphasis on the fluidity of material circumstances. The *Helping Hand* broached the "painful thought" that "under certain imaginable circumstances . . . we might have been no better than the wretch we despise . . . situated so favorably as we, she might have passed through life with as little reproach. Who knows what equality God may discern between us?" WPA reports buttressed this point with case histories that charted the plummeting fortunes of once-secure, middle-class women.[39] The ideal of Christian sisterhood that this kind of thinking fostered could and did veil the very real class differences that had emerged among women by the 1850s. What has eluded systematic scrutiny is the extent to which the argument for the exchangeability of the temporal fates of different classes of Christian sisters may have promoted the "whitening" of European immigrants by de-ethnicizing crime. Although the WPA frequently attributed the wayward practices of their charges to the "social element of the Irish," their construction of Irishness differed from nativist essentialism in its emphasis on the *reversibility* of Irish identity. The notion that fallen women were redeemable embodied the expectation that Irish *habits*—even those that disposed women to vice and crime—could be *unlearned*. The WPA sketched a Celtic portrait that could easily mutate into a Saxon model of true womanhood. "Who are the inmates of our Home? A few young women . . . strangers in the country, wanderers from their natural homes, who, alone and friendless in this great city, have fallen, not from vicious propensities, but through sheer misfortune" declared the reformers in 1859.[40]

Such characterization, by erasing the "racial" distinctiveness of the Irish constructed by nativists, contributed a gendered public language to the process by which the Irish became white. In WPA literature, the peculiarity of the Irish stemmed from their religion; unlike the condition associated with "race," this difference could be altered through proselytization. Regardless of whether such proselytization actually took place (and there is evidence to suggest that it did not), the point is that religion, rather than color, constituted the visible, articulated mark of difference *within* the community of women imagined by the reformers. "The sphere of the Home has no sectarian boundaries . . . no sect or nation has been excluded or favored," declared *The Helping Hand*, suggesting that religious diversity was no obstacle to the creation of a gender-based sorority. "It is time women . . . should consider themselves as a community," the text continued, "having special common needs, and common obligations." This imagined community was thus avowedly inclusive of religious pluralism.[41] What remained undefined and unsaid was its racial exclusiveness, shaped by the practice of segregating black women in institutions such as the Colored Home. The acculturation of Irish fallen women to bourgeois norms of true womanhood implied the whitening of their ambiguous "racial" identities, especially in relation to those who were excluded from the rehabilitative influence of the Home—namely, black women.

The implied identity of "race" between Celtic sisters and their Saxon keepers did not, of course, blunt the interests and privileges of class any more than the explicit rhetoric of gender solidarity did. Indeed, benevolent women's fractured allegiance to the interests of their class and gender fettered the radical potential of their reform discourse. Not all the tales in the world of poverty, deception, and "dreadful cruelty" could persuade genteel reformers to fashion a structural critique of capitalist class relations of which they were, after all, beneficiaries. However potentially subversive their diagnosis of the source of the women's degradation, their prescription of a solution to the problem exposed the limits of their reform impulse. *The Helping Hand* and the Hopper Home ultimately sought to prepare fallen women to lead productive lives as homemakers, factory workers, or domestic servants by encouraging them to develop suitable personal virtues. The "anchors of [the reformers'] hope" consisted of "household influences, . . . industry, order, self-restraint, temperance, kindness and religion." Thus the WPA's approach to reform called not for systemic change, but rather the transformation of its charges' moral character, even as the reformers recognized that the vagaries of the marketplace could pervert the most upright of characters.[42]

The ambiguity inherent in the WPA's reform discourse was matched by the reformers' sense of ambivalence about the credibility of their charges' self-representation. Moreover, expressions of such skepticism were frequently peppered with references to the cultural habits of the "class" to which the inmates belonged. Kirkland cautioned that "not . . . all the stories of the discharged convict are to be received as true, for if there be any vice developed in the course of a life of intemperance and its consequences, it is that of falsehood." Under the circumstances, the Hopper Home's labor and discipline requirements were designed to discourage "the unrepentant" from either entering the reformatory or staying long.[43] Surely, benevolent women's ambivalence about the nature and habits of their charges was shaped not simply by their own class prejudices, but by inmate agency as well. Reformers' renditions of inmate behavior suggest the ways in which fallen women's modes of accommodation and confrontation—dictated by their own needs and the expectations of their benefactors—both facilitated and subverted the function of the Home as an instrument of social order and cultural assimilation. Applicants for relief saw it less as a path to cultural uplift than as an employment agency. A Sing Sing inmate framed her request for a job in deferential language that could undoubtedly be construed as reflecting her redemptive potential. She asked for the "privilege" of placing herself under the Home's "kind care and protection until a place of work [could] be procured." She stated her preference for a sewing job, as opposed to domestic service. Others made good behavior contingent on incentives like early pardons and assistance in reuniting with family members, especially children remanded to the custody of public authorities. Elizabeth E. wrote a WPA prison visitor, Anna Curtis, that she was "striving to obey God as you desired me to." She then proceeded to remind Curtis of a promise she had made on an earlier visit: "I hope I have not made this effort altogether in reference to the indication you were pleased to give that when my time was half out (and now it is more) you would try and aid me in procuring a pardon. Yet this has, I confess, been a great motive for me to try and redeem my character."[44] Elizabeth was thus quite forthright in framing her promise of reformation in terms of a quid pro quo—her exercise of virtue was directly proportional to her expectation that her benevolent sisters would win her a reduced sentence.

Those who got out occasionally used the Home as not only an employment agency, but also as a way station between stints of work. Mary Ashford, a thirty-year-old Englishwoman who returned to the Home from a washing establishment where she had been placed, combined her expression of displeasure at her paltry wages with an argument that her "keepers" were bound to find compelling: she was required to "wash all day Sundays." Some women sought protection against abusive husbands or medical treatment. A few immigrants saw in the Home an emigrant aid society. When a Scotswoman lost thirty-five dollars in the city, she went to the Tombs "for protection." She found in the Home an ally to help her gain a passage to her friends in Cincinnati. Likewise, a young Danish mother deserted by her husband returned to her native country with the aid of the refuge. For others, the institution served variously as a maternity home, lending institution, and buffer against family discord. Beleaguered parents sought its help to discipline or support their kin. Fifteen-year-old Mary G.'s father committed her to the WPA's custody to protect her from a cruel stepmother. Another man brought his motherless child to the Home on the ground that she needed "female friend[s] to watch over her." Others, unwilling to sacrifice their independence by moving in with married relatives, preferred the female camaraderie that the Home offered. Thirty-nine-year-old Lucy Bebe repeatedly refused her brothers' offers of a home with their families, preferring to return to the home during lean periods.[45] One WPA report noted the "kindliness and good feeling" that many of the women appeared to share. When one of them died, her friends at the Home wished to have a portion of their savings applied toward the funeral cost. Former residents frequently remembered their fellow inmates in their letters to the Managers: "Give my best respects to all the girls—to the sewing girls in particular."[46]

The inmates' responses legitimated the function of the "Home" as an instrument of rehabilitation to the extent that their needs converged with the practical programs of their genteel "keepers." Thus Irish women conscious of economic self-sufficiency may not have viewed domestic service as a vehicle of moral education, but rather welcomed it as a superior alternative to labor in the garment trades.[47] For others, the Home offered a passport to marriage in the country or financial autonomy through factory work. When inmates exercised these options, they received wide publicity in the Home's annual reports as living proofs of the WPA's successful domestic therapy.[48]

On the other hand, the inmates mounted a variety of challenges to the Home's rules and redemptive mission during their stay. In stark contrast to the professions of gratitude and docility evident in inmates' letters reproduced in official publications for the benefit of patrons, the case histories record instances of insubordination even on the part of "good" workers. Some women evidently appreciated the Home's role as employment agency but had little patience for its reform goals. Margaret Masterton, forty years of age and a "competent" worker, "was anxious for a place and thought she was doing us a favor instead of herself . . . by staying at the Home." Disruptive behavior represented another challenge to the Home's regimen for redemption. Many a quiet demeanor masked a rebellious spirit. Sarah Wimms, while "quietly at work" one Saturday morning, "all at once jumped up, demanded her bonnet, said if we did not give it to her she would go without it." All attempts to "reason" with this inmate failed. Several left on the pretext of looking for work, running errands, or "collecting their things" before they had been "redeemed." Others departed openly and boldly, declaring that "the work at the home was too hard." Despite its official professions of strictness, the Home proved reluctant to summarily discharge troublesome inmates, especially if they "seemed" mentally challenged or were accompanied by children. Catherine Pinckney, despite a nine-month stay at the Home with her child, persisted in her "idle" ways, brought liquor into the house, and eventually left without a trace. One woman turned down a position on the grounds that the wages it offered were too low, prompting a resolution requiring inmates to accept offers of employment "without regard to the enumeration."[49]

A few women no doubt believed their presence in the institution unnecessary because they had committed no crime. Fourteen-year-old Mary Hickey professed ignorance of "all kinds of work" because she had devoted her short life to taking care of her sister's children so that "she had no time for anything else." She found herself in a city jail for no reason other than the arrest of her sister, with whom she boarded. Within three weeks of her arrival at the Hopper Home in the summer of 1845, Hickey had "dressed herself and left without the knowledge of anyone." Finally, some inmates thwarted a vital tool of reform—the moral inquisition— by refusing to divulge details of their personal lives. One report on the "social relation," "habits of life," and "education" of the inmates included a category designated "unknown" for those who appeared "insane, could not speak English, or refused to answer."[50]

Postbellum Dialectic of Rehabilitation and Repression: Strains within the White Sorority

Inmate resistance elicited heightened concern in the fractious world of postbellum New York. The intransigence of industrialized America's paradox of poverty amid plenty defied the social mobility assumptions of free labor Republicanism. The virulence of industrial conflict, the rise of anarchism, and the mayoral candidacy of radical social critic Henry George all shaped the benevolent empire's drift toward conservatism. Public discourse focused on the failures of old methods of reform. There emerged a new theory and practice of regeneration known as scientific charity, based on the systematic, statistical study of the poor and their habits. One of the aims of its Gotham vehicle, the New York Charity Organization Society (COS), was to coordinate the work of benevolence and investigate all applicants for relief so as to prevent fraud on the part of the unworthy indigent, thereby "inculcating habits of providence and self-dependence."[51] These developments coincided with a partial generational turnover in the WPA's leadership. Kirkland died in 1864, and Sedgwick in 1867, making way for the ascendancy of a new, more conservative cohort of activists well entrenched in the middle class. Abby Hopper Gibbons alone represented the old order, until her death in 1893.

In the new age of scientific charity, the WPA's old ambivalence about inmate character and credibility generated a carrots-and-stick policy toward female prisoners in general and Hopper Home inmates in particular. That the sense of sisterhood did not altogether disappear in the widening chasm of class is evident from the Association's campaign for police matrons and its strictures against men who hired prostitutes. Moreover, critiques of the existing structure of wage labor occasionally made their way into the reformers' official publications and private correspondence. In 1863 the WPA conceded that it did not pay its inmates fair wages for their labor; the organization professed helplessness in the face of structural deficiencies in the labor market: "It is impossible to escape from the competition of other institutions especially in needle-work, and from the grinding extortion of the shopkeepers, who do not, on the average, pay more than one-half of the true value of work," lamented the reformers.[52]

Yet such recognition of the weaknesses in the structure of the wage economy did not translate into radical relief prescriptions. Instead, the rhetoric of gender solidarity came to be wedded, more firmly than ever before, to the cultural project of embourgeoisement, anchored in the doctrine of separate spheres. Gendered strategies of rehabilitation—the use of "feminine" cultural stimuli—like music, flowers, and suitable books—to kindle the women's taste for "elevating pleasures" sought to counteract the emerging youth culture of commercialized leisure, which took working-class women into the arena of public recreation—into promenades, dance halls, amusement parks, and inexpensive theaters. An evening school begun in 1869, and a temperance society sponsored in 1870, sought to provide the inmates with alternative social spaces under controlled conditions. The attempt to keep the women indoors involved renovation of the Home itself. In 1884 the Home acquired parlor furniture of its own, supplemented later by an oilcloth and gas stove for the women's sitting room, and a "selected" library. Later in the century, institutional rituals established a system of hierarchy based on cultural assimilation. Trustworthy inmates were selected to lead outdoor excursions. At the turn of the twentieth century, a new bathroom on the second floor of the Home served inmates who had "been at the Home long enough to be clean and well cared-for," while newcomers were confined to the one on the first floor. In the meantime, a new image of the acculturated fallen woman began to grace the pages of the WPA's official publications as a testimonial to the success of its gendered reform program. She was a loyal and patient servant whose maternal instincts employers admired, who noticed and objected to the removal of flower vases adorning the Home's entrance, carefully tended flower gardens, and expertly executed needlework "of the daintiest sort for brides and new-born children."[53]

Yet, strict new Home rules regulating discipline and labor help to flesh out an increasingly recalcitrant inmate figure lurking in the shadows of success stories celebrated in official publications, eventually propelling prison reform into Progressive era statist channels. Historians have noted that women's organizational activities during the Civil War infused the work of benevolence with "a passion for efficiency" and an "aptitude" for business.[54] The WPA's original mission to establish a self-supporting refuge took on a new urgency in this changed climate of reform activism. By the 1860s, the inmates were formally classified according to their abilities for housework or sewing. Those assigned to the housework department were obliged to serve a month's probation "in order that something may be known of their character." During this period they were sent out to work by the day, with the Home receiving their earnings to help pay for their food, lodging, and clothing. Upon completing their probations successfully, they were placed in domestic service on trial for another month, receiving their wages at the end of that period. Those who left before the end of the month forfeited their earnings, which the Home collected. The WPA justified this regulation with the rationale that "if they are allowed to receive their wages at the end of the week, they too often squander the money in the indulgence of their vicious appetites."[55] The women assigned to the sewing department, on the other hand, were considered permanent members of the Home. They were leased to families by the week or month, returning to the Home every Saturday evening to spend the Sabbath, returning to work Monday morning. They were allowed to keep their earnings after deducting a small fee for their board and washing on Sunday, "that they may secure such independence as relieves them from the charge of being a burden to their friends."[56] The Home's industrial department assumed a new scale with the establishment's move to larger premises on Second Avenue in 1874. Two "spacious and well-ventilated" rooms on the second floor housed the various branches of its sewing department, while the basement became the site of a commercial laundry, where, under the supervision of a matron, the inmates undertook washing and ironing "at a cheaper rate than the ordinary prices."[57]

Yet as the century progressed, the Home found itself combating a losing battle with "the restlessness of modern life," manifested in the women's demands for higher wages and a growing reluctance to commit to long stints of service on the Home's terms. The inmates' acts of rebellion signified both their self-identification as *working women* (rather than as subjects of moral reform through work) and their view of the Home as a source of *paid employment* (as much as a vehicle of cultural uplift). In 1868 the Managers responded by declaring, "We find the absolute necessity of living up to the rule, that a month's service at the Home shall be required from those who leave their places without sufficient reason as is so often the case, some for higher wages, others possessed with a longing for the city and its temptations."[58] Yet the frequent "coming and going" of the women continued, forcing ever increasing investments in the training of "new and unskilled hands" for the laundry. The Managers lamented that the inmates initially "appeared grateful" for the "fresh clothing," medical treatment, and other "Home comforts"; they stayed long enough to build up savings, which they then demanded, and left.[59] The percentage of women discharged for bad behavior or departing on their own accord increased from approximately 10 percent in 1855 to 35 percent in 1895.[60] Meanwhile, the necessity of establishing telegraphic communications between the Home and the nearest police station suggests growing concern over inmate insubordination.[61] Such lack of discipline appeared to reflect the general laxity of rules in the city prisons, where convicts were allegedly free to employ caterers for their meals, walk the corridors, talk as much as they pleased, communicate with their friends, use bathtubs as often as they wished, and purchase food, tobacco, stationary, comfortable beds, and other privileges from matrons under an arrangement known as "the restaurant system."[62]

"New Immigrants," Eugenics, and the Path to Bedford Hills

The escalation of inmate indiscipline at the Hopper Home and the larger prison population from which it drew its recruits coincided with landmark developments in New York's social and cultural landscape in the last half of the nineteenth century. For one thing, the English biologist Charles Darwin's momentous exposition on the processes by which infinite varieties of life came to be—*On the Origin of the Species by Means of Natural Selection*, published in 1859—lent scientific sanction to the idea that "pauperism" and crime were shaped by heredity and environment. At the same time, the arrival of wave upon wave of "new immigrants" from unfamiliar sources transformed New York's prison population, generating anxieties about the genetic mutation of criminal and dependent groups into more virulent, less redeemable strains. Chapter 4 covered the ambiguous status of "in-between" peoples of southern and eastern Europe. Suffice it to say here that their advent altered the tone and strategy of the WPA's reform agenda. The institution's claim in 1900 that "but for foreign immigration, we should have no need of an almshouse in the municipality, and one correctional institution would hold all our criminals"[63] was fairly typical of the nativist tone that came to color the Association's pronouncements in the last quarter of the nineteenth century. In contrast with the founders' embrace of newly arrived Irishwomen as deliverable fallen sisters in the 1840s and 1850s, the new generation of reformers decried the "new immigrants" as an inevitable "burden on the taxpayers, either as paupers or criminals." Somewhat contradictorily, they castigated the newcomers as a degraded class willing to work for wages below subsistence levels, "knowing that they [could] secure assistance from churches and charitable societies." Immigrant women allegedly manipulated public relief agencies into accepting responsibility for their children and forced native-born women into prostitution by the economic competition they posed. "Our prostitute classes are composed largely of foreign-born women, trained to the life from childhood; or of our own young women from the country, who have come to the city to earn a livelihood and been forced into the street through competition with the foreign born," the WPA declared.[64]

The WPA was largely silent about African Americans in the postbellum period, in part because of the plunge in the black proportion of New York's population. At the same time, its leaders' misgivings about the newest waves of Catholics and Jews prompted the reformers to largely exclude those groups from the Hopper Home. This tendency was reflected in the ethnic profile of the halfway house's inmate population in the late nineteenth century. Statistics collected for the Hopper Home's medical report between 1887 and 1900 suggest that the 1,028 "new patients" admitted during these years did not reflect the rapidly changing ethnic diversity of the general prison population. Rather, they were drawn from the WPA's traditional client sources, with the Irish constituting 57 percent of the group. Another 30 percent consisted of native-born women, over half of them New Yorkers. These women were older than their counterparts in the 1840s and 1850s—53 percent of them were over the age of forty. Of the immigrants among them, about 59 percent had lived in the United States for at least twenty years. Newly arrived Italians, Jews, Russians, and Poles were conspicuous by their absence among the women of the Hopper Home.

The growing resistance of the Hopper Home's own inmates, coupled with the presence of undesirable aliens in the world without, prompted the WPA to reevaluate its reform strategy. If years of private benevolence had failed to subdue the English-speaking Irish, by now relatively acculturated to American life, "whitened," and politically active—however informally—the odds of the reformers' success against the cultural aliens swelling New York's prison population seemed rather slim, especially in the face of widening economic disparities among New Yorkers, old and new. The WPA lamented that the average East Side prostitute—brought to the station house "in the garb of a housewife with a shawl over her head, arrested for soliciting at her own door"—spoke no English and objected to incarceration, because she was "neither intoxicated nor a thief" and failed to "understand that soliciting is an offence against decency." Released on bail arranged by "liquor dealers or dive keepers," such women returned to the streets "to earn their fine."[65] The WPA prison visitor Alice Woodbridge seemed convinced that "many have been trained in foreign countries to this life."[66] Moreover, women "lodgers," who reportedly worked enough during the day "to buy beer and a little bread" and sought shelter in station houses during the night, circumvented the work house by "making the rounds" of station houses.[67]

Other working poor women "lost" their children near station houses, compelling the matrons of such institutions to care for them during the day while the mothers worked. The Eldridge Street station house received nearly a hundred children a month. "It is an undoubted fact," the WPA prison visitor declared, "that the parents . . . in this precinct send their children to the Station-house to be cared for by the matrons. . . . Tiny children scarcely able to walk spend the day in the matron's room, while the parents live but one or two blocks away." While Woodbridge interpreted this practice as "utter [parental] indifference to the welfare of the child," working parents no doubt saw station houses as day care centers that provided a better alternative to leaving infants alone at home or on the streets.[68] Such mothers were reputed to feed their children alcohol to pacify them: "One shudders at the thought of what the future generations of drunkards and criminals will be. It does not seem right that these people should continue to reproduce themselves."[69] "Rounders" who alternated between prisons and saloons—and regarded the courts as "a laughing stock" and the prison "a place to rest . . . for a few days preparatory to another prolonged spree"—appeared to mirror the alleged inmate opportunism that kept the Home's own revolving doors in motion.[70] Thus, the Hopper Home inmates' resistance to acculturation heightened the reformers' sense of the scale of the larger problem of the turn-of-the-century fallen woman, who as a "new immigrant" seemed likely to be impervious to the gentle influence of private benevolence.

These circumstances shaped the WPA's campaign to enlist state aid in providing a more structured environment for reform, fortified by the force of law. Asserting that they spoke from "long years of experience," the reformers repeatedly furnished accounts of incorrigible inmates who returned to the Home over and over again. The "unfortunates of the lower classes" shared "the restlessness of modern life," so that the Hopper Home found it "more and more difficult to retain women in the 'Home' and to induce them to go out to service. They stay for a short time and then fall into the whirl of vicious excitement again." The remedy seemed clear: "Close the salons, have sentences long enough to work a reform, and a reformatory where [the 'fallen woman']may be legally held, and the labors and interests of the WPA and the Isaac T. Hopper Home will not prove a vain endeavor."[71] Abby Hopper Gibbons, with her "unerring intuition," had "divined" that "the growth of the city and its altered life" called for "a larger home . . . where a stronger hold could be maintained upon those committed to its care; . . . the new and larger New York needed not only the 'Isaac T. Hopper Home,' but also its natural outgrowth—a State Reformatory for women." The reformers emphasized that they did not seek a prison, "which demoralizes and has no uplifting influences," but rather an institution in which they could legally hold females from fifteen to thirty years "under such restraint as longer sentences impose, giving an opportunity for school instruction and such employment as would enable them, upon release, to earn a livelihood."[72]

The WPA's case for a state reformatory rested in part on the observation that 60 percent of the women sent to Blackwell's Island were "unfortunate persons" under twenty-five years of age. The short sentences they received afforded little opportunity to earn an honest living, encouraging them to alternate "the time in the prison and in the street, finally becoming incapable of supporting themselves, but *reproducing themselves in their children.*" The annual report for 1890 illustrated this point by citing the case of a thirty-year-old woman who had established a career as a "rounder" for ten years. During this time, she had given birth to four children, all of whom were supported by city institutions. "Had it been possible when she had committed her second offence, to have sent her to a reformatory," the Managers declared, "she might have been an honest woman. Certainly she would have had no children to inherit her vices. Considered as a matter of economy, the tax payers would have been called upon to support one person instead of five."[73] Thus, the argument for a state institution combined the plea for the rehabilitation of young transgressors with an appeal to eugenics and economy—a reformatory would not only guarantee prolonged moral and industrial training, but would limit reproduction by the "degenerate," and hence save tax dollars.

This vision materialized in the inauguration of a state-run reformatory for women in Bedford Hills at the turn of the twentieth century, thanks in large part to the tireless lobbying of the politically savvy Abby Hopper Gibbons. Gibbons joined her friend Josephine Shaw Lowell of the New York State Board of Charities in a campaign to establish in New York reformatories for women on the model of existing institutions in Indianapolis and Sherborn, Massachusetts. The result was the establishment of the Hudson House of Refuge in 1887. Hudson did not, however, receive women from New York City or King's County, which were major sources of the state's prison population. Thus, Gibbons persuaded her nephew Wilson Powell to devise a bill for a reformatory to serve the metropolis.[74]

Upon approval by the WPA board in March 1889, Gibbons sent the bill to a valuable ally, Hamilton Fish, for introduction to the legislature. Fish was a veteran Whig-turned-Republican who had served as governor of New York between 1849 and 1851, was subsequently elected to the U.S. Senate, and was later appointed secretary of state by President Ulysses S. Grant. A president of the New-York Historical Society and trustee of Columbia College, and a frequent delegate to the General Convention of the Protestant Episcopal Church, Fish's extensive philanthropic connections had early brought him in touch with Gibbons. It was he who in 1889 introduced Assembly Bill No. 830 to create a state reformatory for women in New York or Brooklyn, with an appropriation of one hundred thousand dollars, which the state assembly passed unanimously. Fish wrote Gibbons urging her to send letters to "all senators possible" in support of the proposed legislation. In addition, Gibbons led a delegation of three to Albany to lobby personally for the passage of the bill. Upon their return to New York, the women evidently rendered a colorful account of their encounter with the legislators at a meeting of the WPA Executive Committee. The minutes of the meeting recorded that the delegates' version of their experiences "seemed to afford amusement. They thought the average intellect of our Representatives in Albany not so high as it might be."[75]

Although the senate passed the bill, Governor Hill vetoed it on the grounds that the project was too expensive and did not make provision for felons. Hill preferred to have the Hudson bill amended to include women from New York and Brooklyn. Gibbons, acting on Fish's recommendation, submitted a brief in favor of the institution to the governor.[76] The minutes of the WPA's Executive Committee meeting on March 4, 1890, reported that Gibbons had written the governor but had received no reply, "showing that [Hill] has not yet experienced grace."[77] Following protracted negotiations and a campaign of public education on the subject over the next two years, a WPA delegation headed by Gibbons once again addressed the Ways and Means Committee in Albany. This time, the presence of a more sympathetic new governor gave reason for optimism. Yet the reformatory bill stalled in the senate as Gibbons lay ill with erysipelas. At this point, her daughter Lucy Morse took up the cudgels in association with Louisa Lee Schuyler, founder of the State Charities Aid Association, while Morse's husband, James, launched a press campaign on behalf of the reformatory. All these efforts bore fruit. Amended to allow the admission of those "convicted of any felony except murder, manslaughter, or arson," the reformatory bill was passed by a vote of ninety to zero and signed into law by the governor in May 1892. It set aside one hundred thousand dollars for the proposed institution, to be established in New York or Westchester County. On Gibbons's recommendation, the governor appointed a former WPA member, Alice Sandford, to Bedford's Board of Managers.[78] Bedford, where women convicted of misdemeanors were committed for indeterminate terms, adopted the cottage system—separate small buildings designed to replicate family life—rather than dormitories. Its resort to recreation and an incentive system of rewards and punishments testified to women reformers' continued cautious optimism about the salvageability of some of their prodigal sisters.[79] On the other hand, the reformatory bill's provision of long sentences, as well as its sanction of the arrest of escapees without a warrant, suggested that the mood of reform had changed substantially since the 1840s.

Although the WPA initially represented Bedford Hills as the Hopper Home's statist extension, there were, of course, important differences between the coercive powers of the two institutions. Significantly, too, the ethnic profiles of their respective client populations diverged. Bedford accepted large numbers of "new immigrants," while the WPA's halfway house continued to minister primarily to native-born white women as well as Irish, English, and Scottish immigrants who had arrived several years before. This difference pointed to the racialist underpinnings of the WPA's particular brand of prison reform discourse in the nineteenth century. In antebellum New York, the WPA made an implicit distinction between the two groups of "Others" dominating working poor ranks—namely, the Irish and African Americans. The rhetoric and practice of its prison reform, by its acts of omission and commission—the exclusion of black women from the Hopper Home on the one hand, and embrace of the Irish as redeemable and assimilable on the other—imbricated its reform project with the public discourse that allowed the Irish into the national imaginary of the white republic.

In the late nineteenth century by contrast, the Association adopted a new nativist language, which accentuated the ingrained "foreignness" of the southern and eastern European immigrants making their homes in the metropolis. The argument for a state reformatory with indeterminate sentences hinged in part on what the changed identity of the late Victorian era's prison population meant. Some reformers contended that in light of the foreigners' intrinsic tendency toward prostitution and pauperism, not to mention their disposition to manipulate charitable institutions, it was prudent to confine them for long terms—in order to not only train them for work, but also to prevent "rounders" from *having children at public expense* to *"inherit"* their vices. The reformers' choice of language—especially the notion that paupers and prostitutes "inherited" their vices from their progenitors—manifested the influence of Darwinian perspectives on the hereditary and environmental roots of social pathologies and imparted a eugenic logic to the rehabilitation of New York's newest "dangerous classes." It anticipated modern-day conservative concerns about the alleged proliferation of "unfit" mothers.

Bedford Hills came into an America awash in a fresh spirit of reform known to historians as Progressivism. A multifaceted "movement of movements," this early twentieth-century wave of activism sought variously to resolve new and unintended consequences of the Gilded Age's economic revolution and to advance well-worn political and social agendas framed by the public concerns of its own time. It embraced heterogeneous and sometimes contradictory causes—from government regulation of business and the reformation of municipal corruption to Prohibition, women's suffrage, the conservation of natural resources, and the assimilation of immigrants into American society. In the South, political "reform" assumed the perverse face of segregation and disfranchisement, which together with economic incentives and rising racial violence, fueled a great migration of black people from the rural South to the urban North. The face of African American New York was about to change. Although that change was not yet visible enough to register in the WPA's late nineteenth-century discourse on dependence, Bedford Hills, unlike the Hopper Home, admitted black transgressors along with the new immigrants under its more structured and stringent terms of rehabilitation. Meanwhile, the swelling tide of African American New Yorkers was in the process of using the new language of Progressive reform to articulate an alternative vision of national community. No institution offered a more meaningful counterpoint to Bedford's reform approach than black voluntary associations like the Howard Orphanage and Industrial School.

PART III

6

Black Voluntarism and American Identities
The Howard Orphanage and Industrial School

> Some day you may have just cause to be proud of us, for I know I don't intend to spend the rest of my days in the kitchen.
> —An alumnus of the Howard Orphanage to Superintendent Mary Gordon, June 23, 1913

Seventeen-year-old Anne Smith harbored aspirations higher than a lifetime in domestic service. Born in New York of Virginian blacks at the turn of the twentieth century, Smith was reared in a predominantly African American community at the Howard Orphanage and Industrial School (HOIS), originally of Brooklyn, later of King's Park, Long Island. In accordance with institutional practice, soon after Smith entered adolescence, she was placed in housework, with the Orphanage's white treasurer in Westfield, New Jersey. Before long her mistress, Marjorie Snevily, reported that the young woman was anxious to withdraw savings from her wages—held in trust for her by the institution—in order to put herself through business school. The reluctant maid reportedly grew "mean" with her mistress's children when every business school in the Westfield area refused to admit her on account of her race.[1] Subsequently, Snevily attributed Smith's discontent to "a lack of money that she could herself spend on clothes. . . . Her friends are all making good money and dressing a little more up-to-the minute than she is."[2] It was no accident that Smith reportedly combined her longing for a business education with a taste for the latest fashion in clothing. For this first-generation New Yorker of African descent, "putting on style" became a means of challenging her received identities of race, class, and gender by testing the promise of America's much-vaunted success ethic; it also allowed her to contest the color construction of American consumer culture.[3] Moreover, it served as the occasion for Smith's performance of the role of a rational economic actor in an ostensibly laissez-faire world. She was demanding control over her own wages as a worker and the autonomy to spend it however she wished as a consumer. Her bid for such independence accorded well with her interracial custodians' emphasis on self-sufficiency in adulthood, even as it defied their agenda to promote thrift and feminine restraint among their charges.

The story of Smith's upbringing at the HOIS reveals much about "multipositional" African American negotiations with the contested narrative of American exceptionalism—the tension between race and civic equality that it embodied—within the framework of child welfare discourse in the Progressive era. The archival remains of the HOIS provide a rich set of windows to study the ways in which the historical actors associated with one benevolent institution—from their overlapping vantage points as patrons, staff, and "clients"; as surrogate parents, children, and lovers; as workers and consumers; as men and women; and as black and white Americans—offered a pluralistic vision of America.[4] Embedded in this history are engaging plots about the internal social relations of black benevolence and the connection with its Progressive white (Protestant) counterpart. Howard developed from a voluntary association managed by African Americans in the nineteenth century into a Northern industrial school staffed by blacks but directed mostly by whites after 1913. As such, its history affords enticing prospects for comparing and contrasting black and white interpretations of national and community identities implicit in their respective approaches to welfare. These emerge in evidence such as state and city inspection reports of the Orphanage's living arrangements, as well as exchanges between its white Managers and black staff. Used in conjunction with the cultural "texts" that the institution produced, like pantomime scripts, fairs, and promotional literature, they unveil a black bourgeois benevolent world engaged in a dialectic of mediation and subversion with the white establishment that oversaw and funded it.

This dialectic of interracial middle-class perspectives provided a prism through which Howard orphans acted out their own confrontations with whiteness. In this context, the institution's records include rare letters written by and about former residents. They illustrate what the historian Earl Lewis calls the "multipositionality" of historical actors ("the interactive construction of identity—as child, lover, spouse") in addition to that conferred by the variables of class, race, and gender.[5] In other words, the letters illuminate the ways in which the inmates' intersecting locations—as surrogate children, working women and men, aspiring professionals, mass culture consumers, and sexual rebels—forged a spectrum of behavior in the pursuit of individual and group empowerment. Their definitions of freedom, independence, and domesticity were contingent on the various contexts of their daily lives in which they enunciated these ideas. The language, themes, and rhetorical appeals of their letters point to the ways in which the structure and texture of everyday life at the institution, as well as the identities constituted within cultural practices like the pantomimes, may have influenced the orphans' self-image and strategies for mobility and autonomy. Taken together, the records of the HOIS illustrate the fashion in which black and white approaches to welfare, and the notions of "American" identity that they embodied, influenced the orphans' self-expressions as individuals, subalterns, and Americans.

Moreover, the Howard saga suggests that middle-class benevolent blacks, their white patrons, and their working poor "clients" used the idiom of a "hegemonic discourse"—that of American exceptionalism—to challenge the exclusionary assumptions of that discourse. As William Roseberry has shown in his study of Chihuahua, "forms and languages of protest or resistance *must* adopt the forms and languages of domination in order to be registered or heard," thus rendering hegemony a "common material and meaningful" framework for negotiation and struggle. Benevolent institutions like orphanages were embedded in the "meaningful" framework of American exceptionalism, within which contests over national belonging unfolded. This hegemonic frame of reference operated not simply through words and symbols like the national anthem or flag, but more importantly through concrete social relations, economic arrangements, and political structures, as explored in previous chapters. Black voluntary associations—partially subsidized by but marginalized within this national system of "meanings and values"—functioned as material and symbolic modes of representation, throwing all manner of prescriptive identities into disarray. In Progressive New York, African Americans turned to the idea of American exceptionalism—its promise of freedom, egalitarianism, and individualism—to erase the premise of whiteness underlying narratives of American belonging. At the same time, however, Howard's black operators devised through their benevolent practices, an alternative communitarian worldview that complicated and pluralized the national narrative on the most local and informal of levels.[6]

The Howard Orphanage became an Industrial School against the backdrop of vigorous debate about the racial meaning of American identity. Two competing nationalisms shaped Progressive America's schizophrenic sense of self. President Theodore Roosevelt imagined a masculinized, racialized nation of various "white" peoples forged in the crucible of war, one that promised the rights of American citizenship to all European men, no matter what their national origin, as long as they acculturated to American norms. Yet Roosevelt's America was shaped not by racial nationalism alone; it also embraced a version of civic nationalism that offered—at least in theory—equality of opportunity and freedom to all its citizens regardless of color or creed.[7] One racialized the promise of American exceptionalism, while the other opened up that promise to all *individuals* regardless of race. Howard orphans entered a world where the forces of racial nationalism held sway over those of civic equality. They were born black in a land imagined as possessing a white soul and a dichromatic population, each member of which was either white or not white, but not both or in between. To be sure, the arrival of successive waves of immigrants from Ireland, and later southern and eastern Europe, spurred a lively debate in the courts of law and the halls of Congress over who qualified as white. Yet it left intact the hegemony of whiteness itself as a category of privilege—a necessary condition for the enjoyment of the full rights of American citizenship. Indeed, as noted in a previous chapter, new contexts for cross-cultural confrontations in local and global settings in the last quarter of the nineteenth century reified the polarization of American society between whites and nonwhites. The high tide of Western imperialism in Africa, the closing of the "frontier" against American Indians, anti-Chinese demonstrations on the Pacific coast, and the advent of de jure "Jim Crow" in the South accentuated perceptions of *white* exceptionalism. Meanwhile, faced with a society divided between undifferentiated whiteness "and its Others," immigrants seeking to acculturate had to "become white," whether by joining labor unions, participating in race riots, wearing ready-made clothing, or supporting America's adventures with empire from the antebellum age of Manifest Destiny to the days of the Spanish American War in 1898.[8] The evolution of racial nationalism, however, never proceeded unchallenged. Progressive America's civil rights activists and suffragists—among others—continued the legacy of the Civil War by championing a version of civic nationalism that, within the structure of democratic capitalism, offered equality of opportunity and freedom to all individuals regardless of color, creed, or gender.

Scholars across a variety of disciplines (and, indeed, in this work) have defined identity as a relation of *difference* (of race, religion, and so on), in which the dominant party depersonalizes or objectifies an allegedly inferior "Other" by attaching to it the "mark of the plural . . . an anonymous collectivity ('They are this'; 'They are all the same')."[9] Howard materials reveal the multiple approaches that Orphanage figures adopted in order to fight the depersonalization of blackness, the objectification of African Americans. In this context, benevolent blacks, their white allies, and African American clients found within Progressive-era controversies over the premises and legitimacy of American exceptionalism the resources to reinvent, however informally, black identities and empower African Americans.

The Institution and Its Managers: From Reconstruction to Progressivism

The Howard Orphanage and Industrial School was conceived in the home of Sarah A. Tillman, the widow of a black pastor, on East Thirteenth Street in Manhattan. In the spring of 1866, Tillman harbored thirteen orphans and half orphans, whose mothers—many of them freedwomen migrants from the South—could not take their wards to work in domestic service. Rejected by institutions like the New York Orphan Asylum, these children grew steadily in number, inducing Tillman to seek help in establishing a refuge for destitute young blacks. She approached the Presbyterian minister and secretary of the Pan-Africanist African Civilization Society (ACS), Henry M. Wilson, who secured for that purpose the Brooklyn premises of the Society at the corner of Dean Street and Troy Avenue. Founded by New York blacks to promote colonization and missionary work in Africa, the ACS joined other black community development organizations during the Civil War in providing services for their brethren emerging from bondage. The home it created in collaboration with Tillman was incorporated in 1868 as the Brooklyn Howard Colored Orphan Asylum—possibly in honor of one of its white supporters, General Oliver A. Howard, head of the Freedmen's Bureau. Through the course of the nineteenth century, the institution retained the hallowed black voluntary association tradition of racial nationalism and self-help from which it had sprung. Until 1902 the BHCA remained almost wholly under the management of local laundresses and other African American women of far less privileged status than their sisters in such national organizations as the National

Association of Colored Women. Its most visible representative was its superintendent of thirty-three years, a blind preacher and indefatigable fund-raiser named William F. Johnson. Appointed in 1870, Johnson was said to "grope" his way about numerous towns and villages, scouring churches and other institutions for aid, spending frigid nights pacing up and down train stations when denied accommodations.[10]

The Orphanage teetered perennially on the verge of financial crisis, as its annual reports to the New York State Board of Charities revealed.[11] Prevailing stereotypes of black financial ineptitude, together with the departure of Johnson after a conflict with the Managers in 1902, prompted a directive from the New York City comptroller under which the Board transformed itself into an all-male, part-white body aided by a Women's Auxiliary.[12] It was this body that reinvented the Orphanage from a community service vehicle run predominantly by black women for black women into a Northern industrial school and farm based on the Tuskegee model.[13] In 1911, with the blessings of the New York State Board of Charities, the HOIS moved to a property in King's Park, Long Island, of nearly six hundred acres. There it adopted the cottage system—separate small buildings within a pastoral setting, designed to foster the individuality thought to be central to family life. The children's first encounter with the country as they walked or rode in wagons to the farm from a Long Island railway station was reportedly a happy one: "Broad waving fields were a new sight to them. . . . When the crowd reached the pretty lake and were told that it was to be theirs, and the house beyond was theirs also, they . . . laughed, jumped, and hurrahed for joy." That afternoon, the matron was startled to find the shirts of several boys protruding, apparently with large-sized tumors. Upon closer inspection, these turned out to be caches of apples, grapes, and nuts, which hung abundantly from the trees on the compound.[14]

The children, who frolicked with joy at the sight of their spacious new accommodations, entered the HOIS under a variety of circumstances. Their nineteenth-century predecessors have, for the most part, disappeared, undocumented, into the shadows of history. All we know from census records is that the proportion of Howard children known to have been born in New York dropped by over half between 1880 and 1910. The greatest change in this thirty-year period consisted in the twentyfold increase in the percentage of those whose birthplaces were unknown. These figures suggest the possibility that the ratio of children admitted voluntarily by living parents to those entering the institution by judicial commitment may have gone down with the passage of time, especially after the Orphanage passed from the exclusive control of black women in 1902. The 1912 HOIS report to the State Board of Charities stated that of the 234 children (132 boys and 102 girls) remaining on September 30, 1912, the largest number (114) was dispatched by poor-law officials, while the second largest group (72) entered under judicial commitment for "improper guardianship" (and 16 for destitution). Relatively few (32) were admitted directly by parents or guardians. Thirty were listed as orphans, 95 as half orphans (that is, those with one parent each), 51 had both parents living, while the parentage of 58 was unknown.[15] Demographic figures for the year 1914 suggest that nearly half of the inmates were between the ages of five and eleven (122 out of 248) and the largest number hailed from New York City (116 out of 224).[16]

While a majority of parents who committed their children to Howard undoubtedly did so for economic reasons, others sought the institution's help to discipline and educate their charges—and, on at least one occasion, to provide them with male role models. One single mother, prompted by concern for her fatherless son's future, was prepared not only to suffer the emotional trauma of sending her child away to school, but to make what would clearly have amounted to a substantial financial sacrifice as well. Her letter suggests the wrenching sense of loss some mothers experienced at the prospect of parting with their offspring. She wrote the Orphanage that she had been trying "for months" to admit her only son to a "suitable training school." She described the child as "silly and childish," as he had "never known a father," and went on to acknowledge, "It will almost break my heart to part with him but I loves him [sic] and want him to become a real man, so I have to leave myself out for a while and think of his future when I will be no more." Nor was she expecting to abdicate her financial responsibility for her son's upbringing to the school: "Last but greatest I'll like to know how much you charges [sic], and whether it is paid in advance, monthly or weekly."[17] A few guardians saw the Orphanage as a potential adoption agency to help ensure a brighter future for their children than they were able to provide. One woman, forced by her husband's sudden death to enter domestic service, placed her mother in a home for the aged and sought Howard's aid in "get[ting] my two little girls into a good home."[18] Another woman wished to admit her twelve-year-old niece, whom she described as "inclined to disobey and very obstinate."[19] One Howard child was born in British Antigua out of wedlock to a destitute black mother and a white father who refused to provide for the child, "owing to it being colored." She found her way to King's Park through the intercession of her mother's network of friends, which extended to New York City and up to the doors of the Society for the Prevention of Cruelty to Children (SPCC).[20]

Howard's move to King's Park entailed a financial crisis, which, amid intra-black friction, prompted a further whitening of the institution's Board in 1913 under the presidency of L. Hollingsworth Wood, a white Quaker lawyer. Secretary of the National League of Urban Conditions Among Colored People, Wood was well connected with the heads of Southern black industrial schools like Booker T. Washington. Wood invited Washington to visit the Long Island farm, solicited his graduates to fill appointments at Howard, and secured his consent to lend his name to the Orphanage's fund-raising efforts. As the HOIS's new leader, Wood sought and received carte blanche in picking his Board of Managers. Its white members included bankers, lawyers, and corporate executives with ties to benevolent and civil rights organizations like the National Association for the Advancement of Colored People, while the black Managers consisted of ministers and physicians well respected in the world of African American philanthropy. Thus in the course of ten years, the social profile of Howard's supervisors changed in favor of those with influence in the charity establishment but less entrenched in the realities of working-class black life.[21]

The Managers' positioning at the crossroads of the sometimes-incompatible worlds of child welfare reform and civil rights shaped a welfare vision informed by civic nationalism and an administrative style committed to efficiency. They were lone stewards of a cause that attracted little public sympathy or financial support. Progressive America's preference for "scientific charity" over voluntarism, coupled with social welfare professionals' lack of confidence in African American managerial skills and financial acumen, impeded the efforts of black voluntary associations to win public support for their projects. The prevailing opinion overwhelmingly favored shifting black dependent children from black-operated institutions to public care.[22]

In this climate, the interracial progressives who ran HOIS couched their mission in the exceptionalist language of mainstream American ideals like equal opportunity and social mobility. The first contingent declared in 1906, "All the colored people ask for is the *opportunity* to fit themselves by industrial, moral and intellectual training for self support and . . . useful citizenship. . . . or as our President Roosevelt puts it, 'a square deal."'²³ The Managers' language of color-blind nationalism was matched by structural changes in the organization of the institution, embodied in its adoption of the cottage system in 1911. In general, reformers believed that the "homelike" quality of the cottage model would help Americanize European immigrant children by personalizing child care. The movement against raising children in institutions was inspired in part by developments in evolutionary biology and child psychology, combined with technological advances and the availability of cheap immigrant labor. These factors led to the cultural invention of childhood as a distinct stage in the life cycle; children were now understood as emotionally valuable persons (rather than economic assets) who deserved to be nurtured in private families by mothers who stayed home. The cottage system was designed to replace the congregate living of institutions with the virtues of private family life, including more individualized child care.[24]

For Howard's black elites and their white allies, however, the cottage ideal's promise of individual regeneration carried a racial connotation. They saw in it a device to counter the "depersonalization" of blacks inherent in racial "Othering." In other words, it facilitated their enterprise to shape African American *subjects* by signifying the capacity of black children to "Americanize" just like white children. It encoded their civic nationalist ideal of what I call *individual sameness* versus the assumption of inherent *racial difference*. Declaring that "what is true of the white race is true of the colored race. Knowledge . . . elevates, while ignorance . . . degrades," Howard's Managers sought to demonstrate the importance of environment by rearing their charges in clean and airy cottages under the "personal supervision" of devout housemothers; by teaching young women "the domestic sciences" and men agriculture, carpentry, and shoemaking; and by requiring them all to go to church.[25]

As black migration to the urban North gathered pace under the pressures of Southern racism and the promise of Northern economic opportunity, the HOIS projected itself forcefully as a vehicle for acculturating, urbanizing, and training the children of destitute Southerners for productive labor and citizenship in their new environment.[26] This endeavor explicitly recalled the Americanization programs of schools and factories directed at European immigrants. The Orphanage's promotional literature had long conveyed the mutability of social identities implied by its project of acculturation. One early flyer, for instance, represented the prospect of black embourgeoisement with the help of a pictorial logo. The picture juxtaposed two images positioned on either side of an inscription that read "Where Does Your Money Go?" The one labeled "undeveloped" depicted a diffident looking sharecropper from the rural South with drooping shoulders, sparse clothing, and bare feet, looking almost as though he was poised to perform a Jim Crow routine. The other figure, labeled "developed," was a portly, obviously urban success story, handsomely attired in a jacket, tie, trousers, breeches, and boots, standing erect with his paunch jutting out—the very picture of confidence. The official identity of the uninitiated Howard Orphan thus took on the character of a malleable, rural, Southern-born black child as capable of transfiguring into urban respectability as one originating in a Russian Pale shtetl or the southern Italian peasantry. The Managers used a similar language of individual sameness, embodying the logic of racial integration, at public gatherings commemorating national heroes. At such events they celebrated the black Booker T. Washington and the white Abraham Lincoln as twin models of the quintessentially "American" traits of initiative and self-reliance, whose humble origins mirrored those of the inmates.[27]

The HOIS campaign of assimilation also contained the implicit promise of defusing a potentially explosive racial situation captured by the *New York Times* report of the institution's 1917 fund-raising campaign under the heading "Negroes Invading North." Claiming that New York City's one hundred thousand blacks made it "the largest center of Negro population in the world," the piece quoted President Wood's observation that the scantily clothed African American migrants from the South, unaccustomed to harsh Northern winters, readily succumbed to pneumonia and other diseases, leaving more orphans than other population groups.[28] The removal of these orphans to the country would serve as an important first step in their orderly absorption into Northern society. The pledge card that accompanied fund-raising letters declared: "We help You give colored orphans a chance" [by taking "colored orphans off the city streets," providing them with "good food, water, air and comfortable clothes," and teaching them "to use their hands and their brains"].[29] A publicity flyer accompanying pledge cards featured glossy photographs of farm buildings and equipment, as well as children at work, study, and play, bearing such captions as "productive exercise," "making use of our farm by-products," "busy and happy," and so forth—all in an attempt to convey the sense of economy, industry, and good cheer that presumably pervaded the farm.[30] By 1917 that farm boasted thirty-one cows, twelve horses, nineteen sheep, and approximately one hundred pigs and three hundred chickens of various breeds. The main building, eight cottages, a school, an infirmary,

The Brooklyn Howard Colored Orphan Asylum
1550 Dean St. — Brooklyn, N.Y.

Where Does Your Money Go?

To feed and clothe the Orphan
To educate and develop them
To instil Christian principles
To train their hands
To make them useful citizens

The Undeveloped

I promise to pay, God helping me, for the support of the Brooklyn Howard Colored Orphan Asylum, $......... per year.

The Developed

Name..

Address..

....

I have promised to pay to the Brooklyn Howard Colored Orphan Asylum $..........per year to support the work.

Signature................................

Date............................

artisan workshops, and barns clustered near the center of the grounds, with the detention house situated about one mile from the rest of the buildings.[31]

The Managers' vision of civic nationalism interacted with their mandate as child welfare reformers to promote a "rational" style of administration. The post-1913 Board sought to combat Progressive pressures against black voluntarism by adopting Progressive measures to advance efficiency and economy in the running of the institution. In an attempt to introduce a spirit of personal responsibility and sensitivity to the profit incentive among the children, Mansfield Snevily, originally vice-president, later treasurer, promised handsome pictures as a reward to the cottage with the best record in discipline, neatness, and lack of breakage.[32] Moreover, he suggested that "free wards"—those admitted by destitute parents and supported at institutional expense—be replaced with "city children" committed by the public authorities so that they would bring in appropriations from the public purse.[33] The Managers also sought to enforce the rules regarding parental support of "half orphans" more vigorously. To ensure regular payment by living parents of Howard children, they devised a standardized form permitting the employers of domestic servants to remit the fee of twelve dollars per child per month directly to the institution from the mother's wages. Those who could not afford that sum were now advised to apply directly to the Department of Charities to admit their children, so as to get that body to defray part of the expenses.[34]

The Staff: A Black Vision of Welfare in Progressive New York

The rules crafted by Howard's white Managers floundered, however, when the mostly white Board—in its role as arbitrator with the officialdom of child welfare—confronted differing perspectives of race, gender, and class within the HOIS. Innovations adopted by the new managerial order to place Howard on a sound financial footing prompted a degree of centralization and bureaucratization in the operation of the institution that may have been necessary to preserve it from extinction. Yet these measures undermined the superintendent's traditional autonomy in such areas as expenditures, the appointment and dismissal of staff, and, significantly, the admission of "free wards." The Managers also frowned on the institution's convention of having the children accompany the superintendent in his rounds of black churches in the city and around the state in an attempt to attract donations, arguing that the practice was an inefficient fund-raising strategy that entailed long absences of key institutional functionaries from King's Park. Besides, Snevily argued, people must give out of "principle rather than emotion." Such moves did not endear the institution's new supervisors to James Gordon, who served as superintendent from 1902 until his death in 1914. Gordon felt that the Managers' clinical penchant for such reform watchwords as "neatness" blinded them to the big picture: the spirit of the home. He invited them to have lunch at the institution and "go all over the place and not look around the barns for a stray bag that is lying around or an old wagon that is being gotten together to be sent to the blacksmith shop."[35] Nor was economy everything, as Gordon made clear in a revealing letter to Wood: "It is not for the dollars and cents we are working . . . but for the uplift of our people. As a black man, I know the needs of the Negro."[36]

Upon his death in 1914, James Gordon was succeeded as superintendent by his wife of twenty-nine years, the fifty-year-old Mary Gordon. Indeed, through much of Howard's brief existence, it was under the fiercely protective maternal wing of this Pennsylvania native that the Orphanage reared its young "clients." Mary Gordon had served as matron of the institution during the long years of her husband's superintendency before stepping into his shoes and remaining there until 1917.[37] Gordon presents a revealing case of the multipositional subaltern whose numerous "locations" shaped her complex approach to race, reform, and American identities. A light-skinned African American married woman, her middle-class sensibilities placed her in sympathy with the Managers' larger mission of broadening the definition of American nationhood to include people of color. Publicly, she fully endorsed the cottage system and its goal of promoting "individuality." Moreover, she shared her white supervisors' attachment to the "politics of respectability"—conformity to Victorian morality as a means of countering negative stereotypes of black women, thereby challenging the color figuration of "true" American womanhood.[38] For instance, Gordon threatened to dismiss a custodian for kissing a teacher within sight of the children; she did the same with a teacher for allegedly borrowing money from men.[39]

On the other hand, Gordon's consciousness of the scope of African American need—combined with her experience as a staff member on the ground forced to grapple with the day-to-day problems of running a large institution with few resources—fostered a management style frequently at odds with the "efficient" approach of Howard's Managers, as well as the standards set by the State Board of Charities. Such friction represented the points at which the civic nationalist discourse of individual sameness dissolved in a clash of different hierarchies rooted in the identities of gender, race, class, and professional experience. For instance, Gordon explicitly invoked both her domestic authority as a *woman*, and her professional credentials as a ground-level *administrator*, in an argument over Wood's proposal to save money by eliminating the offices of housekeeper and matron. She wrote that she was at first surprised but that "when I remember you are a man and have had no experience in running a small house much less an institution of this kind, I can understand. I am sure your sister [Carolena Wood, also a Board member] will understand that it would be utterly impossible for one person to get along here with a farm of this proportion, 11 homes to look after, 350 children and more than forty employees to supervise. It is not even to be thought of."[40] The superintendent boldly chastised Board members for usurping her power to appoint and especially dismiss staff members. She argued that such interference encouraged insubordination on the part of unsatisfactory employees, especially males. These instances suggest the ways in which intra-institutional subaltern hierarchies—that is, the Orphanage's own pecking order—could collide with the tiered power structure of the child welfare establishment.[41]

These collisions emerge even more clearly in reports of inspection conducted under the auspices of New York City's Department of Public Charities and the State Board of Charities between 1913 and 1917. These reports, read *in the context of* evidence of the nature of interpersonal relationships that prevailed at the Orphanage, suggest that under Gordon's direction at King's Park the children were nurtured in a cooperative world that functioned more like an informal and affectionate extended family with its own hierarchies than an institution. The HOIS living arrangements, modes of socialization, and economic system followed a communitarian, black Christian model of organization based on flexible conceptions of time and space, muddying the boundaries between education and work, institution and family, and individual and the community. Several inspection reports juxtaposed complaints about the inadequacy of the institution's frame cottages, hot-water supply, heating and lighting facilities, the poor equipment of its kitchens and workrooms, and its failure to observe the rules of individual property ownership, with observations about the affectionate relations evident between children and staff. One inspector noted disapprovingly that the orphans ate at long dining tables, seating up to fifteen, and recommended cutting them into smaller units.[42]

Government inspectors were also unenthusiastic about the apparent neglect of private property ownership among the children. One lamented the lack of individual ownership of toys as well as the absence of "individual bins and lockers for the children's clothes," which lay unmarked, "jumbled together" in a closet. Another, perhaps as concerned about hygiene as about individual property ownership, observed, "The toothbrushes and combs were not marked but the cottage mothers could identify each child's brush by its appearance." Nor was he pleased to learn that the infirmary and detention houses were used as bedrooms by some of the children and that two young women shared a bed in the superintendent's cottage.[43] Recommendations by the public authorities simultaneously upheld hygiene standards and struck against the communitarian principle of ownership and living: "Number all toilet articles and provide a definite place to keep them; provide a locker or bin for each child's wardrobe; number all the face towels; cut the tables into smaller units, each to seat 6–8 children," and so forth.[44]

The communal features displayed by Howard may have existed in some white institutions, but what gave them a different *meaning* at the black orphanage was the context of the familial nature of relationships existing between the staff and their charges.[45] One city inspector reported: "Conversation is permitted in the dining rooms. . . . One notable feature of the home [is] the spirit of cordial relationship and friendliness evident between staff and children. . . . Nothing resembling military discipline prevails at the institution; the children freely go about their work and play."[46] Along a similar vein, Booker T. Washington wrote Wood after a visit to the farm: "The thing that pleased me perhaps most was to note the natural bearing of the children, they had nothing of the 'institutional' atmosphere. A natural relation seemed to exist between them and their instructors."[47] Self-government—"participatory democracy"—governed the Orphanage's method of discipline. A child accused of a misdemeanor was tried by a jury of his or her peers, drawn from the student body. The chief form of punishment consisted of extra work.[48]

Washington's observations about the "natural relations" existing between Howard staff and their charges are borne out in part by the intimate ways that residents addressed Mary Gordon in their letters—often as "dearest mother." Gordon, on her part, went beyond the bounds of ordinary institutional duty to protect the interests of her charges long after they had left her care. When a Howard alum (I will call him Thomas Marshall), a hall boy employed by the Brooklyn Hospital, was arrested for alleged theft, she pleaded earnestly with Wood to intervene on Marshall's behalf with all the anguish of a concerned mother: "He [Marshall] has fallen into temptation . . . but he is so sorry . . . my poor heart is aching . . . I am his mother in love, trust and purpose . . . I have labored so hard . . . to raise him as a Christian gentleman . . . I will do anything, anything to save him." Marshall was discharged to Wood's care, and Gordon arranged for "her boy" to live with her brother, Reverend George E. Stevens of St. Louis, Missouri. There Marshall prospered, eventually becoming an independent farmer. With her permission, he took Gordon's last name, referring to her as "his mother" in his letters to Wood. It appears that in Marshall's case, at least, the child savers' concern that institutions both stymied the emotional development of dependent children and robbed them of support networks to help them in their careers proved unfounded.[49]

Gordon's relationship with her wards suggests that although other (nonblack) orphanages displayed some of the same group-oriented modes of living as the HOIS, communitarianism carried an entirely different meaning in the context of a black institution.[50] Progressive-era reformers concerned about dependent children opposed all those features (like long dining tables) that they felt made orphanages seem less like a private family and more like an institution.[51] Certainly, there is much evidence to suggest that at predominantly "white" orphanages, congregate living spelled "total institution"–like features that bothered child welfare advocates of all faiths. Even at turn-of-the-century Jewish orphanages—arguably some of the most enlightened of their kind[52]–children were identified by number rather than by name, had their hair cropped short, wore uniforms, and "marched to their various activities in silent rows to the clanging of a bell."[53] These institutions liberalized their policies a great deal in the twentieth century, yet their staff-inmate relations were often marked by a certain degree of formality. For instance, alums of the Jewish Foster Home of Philadelphia remembered their Superintendent Aaron Faber as a "disciplinarian" who expected the children to greet him in a "military-like manner."[54] Hymen Bogen, an alumnus of the Hebrew Orphan Asylum, has written that the institution's early twentieth-century superintendent, Solomon Lowenstein, was reputed to be "kind and gentle"; even so, he did not address the children by their first names.[55] Likewise, a chronicler of the Rochester Jewish Children's Home has recorded that the "best the alumni could say [about the matrons of the institution] is that they told us what was right and wrong . . . encouraged us to be neat and clean. . . .

there was no hugging stuff in the Baby Cottage. Whatever hugs I got came from elsewhere."[56]

The level of intimacy between custodians and their charges distinguished Howard's brand of communitarianism from that of some Catholic orphanages as well. When the Catholic social worker Mary Anne Kennedy visited St. Paul's Roman Catholic Orphan Asylum in Pittsburgh in 1919, she found some of the same *physical* elements of group living that abounded at the HOIS. At St. Paul's, too, children sat at long tables, clothing "was not marked for individual use," and the same hairbrush served several children. Yet what separated the Pittsburgh institution from Howard was Kennedy's finding that "no semblance of homelikeness" prevailed. At dinner, a whistle sounded after grace was said, signaling that it was time to eat. Kennedy was especially critical of the distance between the living standards of the superintendent on the one hand and that of the children on the other: "In his own study, he [the superintendent] shows a commendable appreciation of what a homelike room should be; books, pictures and some fine plants are strongly in evidence. And yet, not in one place throughout the building, has there been any attempt made to provide a homelike atmosphere for the children." Kennedy complained that the Superintendent cared more about his "prize ferns," which he left in the custody of an expert gardener when he went abroad, even as he neglected the broken arm of one of his charges, an Italian boy named Gregory.[57]

The foregoing discussion suggests that based on their observations of a majority of orphanages, Progressives had reason to regard group living as the antithesis of that ostensible bastion of emotional security, the nuclear family. The historical experiences of African Americans, however, made congregate living perfectly compatible with family life. Surrogate kin networks that adapted African consanguineous traditions to New World exigencies were not only common in slavery, but also helped black migrants withstand the harshest challenges of urban living both before and after emancipation. Notwithstanding its adoption of the cottage system, the HOIS retained features that might be considered "institutional" in the context of nonblack orphanages because they undermined "individuality," but in the context of a black establishment merely reified the tradition of group solidarity central to African American family life. Recall that one state inspector noted that although the brushes assigned to Howard children were not labeled, cottage mothers could tell their owners by their appearance. Thus, a black style of benevolence management that obfuscated the lines between (extended) family and "institution"—as evident not primarily in practices such as the communal ownership of toys and the use of long tables, but in the nature of staff-client relationships—was rooted in the historic conditions of black life in America.[58]

The familiar black cultural model of family organization upheld by Gordon was reinforced by the children's frequent interaction with black churches and civic organizations in New York City. Several African American religious institutions in Brooklyn participated in the Orphanage's fund-raising festivals and bazaars, setting up tables for ice cream, lemonade, clothes, toilet articles, and so forth. Because Howard's alums came to these affairs, they assumed significance not so much because they raised a great deal of money, but more as forums for socializing and community organizing.[59] These cultural affairs, combined with the children's labor pressures, interrupted their academic schedules in a way that confounded the lines between school, work, and community, in stark contrast with the much more regimented routines characteristic of most nonblack orphanages. Public inspections suggested that regular cooking classes were suspended in order to manufacture articles for the annual fair or to practice for public concerts. Work schedules sometimes got in the way of punctuality in school attendance because the older children provided much of the labor on the farm and in the cottages. The 1917 report noted, "When girls were found carrying buckets of coal to the kitchen . . . and ironing clothes, and the boys cleaning the stables, carting away manure, and killing chickens during school hours, it was explained by the Superintendent that this was part of their vocational training. Under the guise of vocational or industrial training as it is called at the institution, the work of the home is performed."[60] These practices violated prevailing concepts of childhood, which opposed child labor and emphasized the importance of nurturing and educating children at home and in school in order to prepare them for the responsibilities of family and citizenship. No wonder that state inspectors disapproved of the practices described above as infringements of Board standards intended to safeguard the health and welfare of dependent children.

From the perspective of Howard's staff, however, the institution was reconciling its financial constraints with the needs of a growing community of indigent African Americans in ways that made creative use of scarce resources. Rather than turn needy children away, it accommodated the overflow in the infirmary and detention houses, occasionally allowing more than one person to share a bed (as in the case of two young women in the superintendent's cottage). Given the shortage of clothing and toys, common ownership ensured variety. A flexible definition of time seemed necessary in a situation where, unable to afford outside labor, the Orphanage was forced to let its charges combine study with household and farm chores. Vocational instructors doubled as the mechanics of the institution, while the school Principal also served as the resident minister.[61] From the vantage point of the white Managers, Gordon's supervisory style made Howard vulnerable to stereotypes of black mismanagement. Yet the fact that state inspectors found overcrowding and other violations a few years *after* the HOIS Board had enacted the efficiency-driven reforms mentioned earlier suggests that Howard's black staff may have resisted the letter of the new laws rather frequently.

Through her style of benevolence management, Gordon and her staff devised an oppositional community identity rooted in black historical experiences—a communitarian universe permeating the physical structure of the ostensibly individualistic cottage system. They questioned their white supervisors' commitment to the virtues of "individuality," order, and economic efficiency when the practical needs of working poor African Americans were at stake. This disruption of the HOIS Managers' worldview of color-blind "sameness" injected a race-conscious vision of pluralism into the mix of black American identity formation.

Pantomimes as Cultural Texts of Black Benevolence

Gordon's dialectical approach to benevolence, racial solidarity, and national identity was mirrored in a variety of cultural "texts," the most significant of which was a series of pantomimes. These materials were apparently crafted by Howard's staff—arguably members of an emerging black bourgeoisie, drawn from such Southern institutions as Fisk and Howard universities, Tuskegee and Hampton institutes, and Northeastern normal colleges, such as those at Danbury, Connecticut, Collingswood, New Jersey, and Cheney, Pennsylvania.[62] The pantomime scripts elucidate important processes of subaltern subject formation through the appropriation and subversion of hegemonic narratives. On one level, they were designed to publicize the School's mission and usefulness in the context of a turbulent, protean society's search for order and harmony in the classic Progressive tradition. Yet the plays also destabilized the insignias of racial nationalism to question the place of African Americans in American society. Their simultaneous appeal to white and black patrons stemmed from their multilayered interpretive potential—from their engagement with the tensions within American exceptionalism, and also from their simultaneous acquiescence in, and opposition to, Progressive reform ideology. When used in conjunction with letters written by former inmates of the Orphanage, they offer a basis for analyzing the ways in which the didactic values they conveyed may have shaped the children's aspirations and sense of self.[63]

The story line of the pantomimes revolved around the same moral refrain: the value of equal opportunity in a fluid, ultimately just society that rewarded personal integrity and industry, irrespective of race. Such a conception of the nature of American society and the individual's relationship with it accorded well with the ethos of self-reliance, individualism, and racial harmony upheld by the institution's civic nationalist management. Yet subtexts woven into the scripts' narrative fabric suggested not only an awareness of pervasive institutional racism that thwarted the color-blind promise of civic nationalism, but also a consciousness of racial solidarity as the path to black success. Moreover, in an inversion of the terms of black-white relations, the black adult often emerged as a heroic savior of the very whites who had oppressed his or her race.

The script of one pantomime offers a good example of these themes. It opens with the protagonist, a newsboy named Restus, shooting craps in a crowded street, surrounded by scenes of "drunkenness, street fights and disorder." Arrested presumably for disorderly conduct, he is sent to the Children's Society, where white kids mock his friendly overtures. When he attempts to save a white girl from a white male tormentor, he is severely reprimanded and locked in a room by himself. Whites who visit the Society to adopt kids shrink from him in disgust so that he is "more lonely than ever before." His journey to the Howard Orphanage, and hence salvation, begins when a young white visitor, Elsie Watson, overcome by pity for the lonesome lad of color, persuades her gentleman father to admit him to the Howard Orphanage. Subsequent scenes depict Restus as he matures from a troubled youth into a well-adjusted and productive adult: Restus in elementary school, Restus saying grace, Restus imparting instruction in farming to younger boys who "throw down their farm implements and rush to him," whereupon he "frolics with them and they all run off toward the house together." Eventually the young man becomes a school teacher in the very Southern town where his old benefactor Watson resides. Walking in the woods one day, Restus notices a trinket, which he recognizes as belonging to Elsie. He follows hoof tracks into the woods and discovers Elsie lying at the bottom of a precipice, where her horse has thrown her. He carries her back to her home and rings for a doctor while her family and servants panic. The doctor felicitates Restus with words capitalized in the script, "young man, you saved her life." Restus then reminds Watson of the favor he did the young man of color a long time ago and leaves while the others are preoccupied with Elsie.

This script encoded a number of ideas that reflected Howard's appeal to potential white donors and its staff's conception of racial identity and welfare. The notion that the School would rehabilitate through education and religious influence Southern immigrants led astray by the pernicious influences of New York's mean streets was, of course, in keeping with the institution's official mission. Moreover, the central role of a white child as a mediator between the black boy and the instrument of his salvation—the Howard School—contained an obvious appeal for white patrons. Furthermore, Restus's saving of Elsie may have been interpreted as an act of gratitude reinforcing the loyal black image in the white mind. On the other hand, the contrast between Restus's experiences in the white Children's Society and the black Howard Orphanage underscored the obduracy of structural racism, the wisdom of raising black children among their own kind, and black children's potential for not simply spiritual redemption, but for productive citizenship as well.

Most important, however, the script challenged the myth of the black rapist by portraying the black male as a white woman's savior on two occasions, during one of which the black protector was punished for daring to raise a hand against a white male offender in defense of a white woman's honor. By turning black Restus into white Elsie's protector rather than violator, the pantomime undercut the rationale of that ultimate and very public expression of white racial nationalism—lynching. As Grace Elizabeth Hale has argued, ritualized lynchings of black men accused of dishonoring white women, "conjured whiteness . . . through their spectacle of a violent African American otherness as much as through the narratives of [white communal] unity they generated." As black Southerners used the culture of segregation to carve autonomous spaces for themselves in their own churches, businesses, and homes, lynch mobs inverted the practice of racial separation to consolidate white dominance; they reminded black people that there was *no* space they could call their own, that even their bodies "were subject to invasion by whites." The technology of mass consumer culture commodified the imagery of this very public message by marketing souvenirs, photographs, even human "leather" goods generated by lynchings.[64] Through their own performance of public resistance—however small—the authors and actors of Restus's story implicitly exposed lynching as a link between white supremacy and savagery, thereby draining whiteness of its monopolistic signification of civilization.

Another pantomime "scenario" begins in a one-room colored tenement home, which, although sparsely furnished, manifests "a general air of cleanliness." It is home to Lulu, "a comely modest negro girl in hat and jacket." She works as a maid to support her four-year-old sister, Mary, who sports "well-brushed" curls and a "clean gingham dress." Lulu kisses Mary goodbye and leaves for work. Upon her return, she discovers that Mary has managed to unlock herself out of their home and pilfered ginger cookies and bananas on the streets. Lulu then secures her mistress's permission to take her sister to work. Ellen and Mary become playmates, despite Mary's rueful longing for Ellen's finery; Ellen occasionally lapses into "aristocratic" indifference to Mary's material deprivation. When Ellen, on her birthday, flaunts her beautiful cake and her many costly presents (including a gold locket) before Mary, the black child gives into the temptation to steal a similarly flashy pendant from a pawnbroker's shop. She shows her wealthy playmate her stolen good, her theft is discovered, and Lulu is persuaded by her mistress to dispatch her little sister to the Howard Orphanage. At the Orphanage, Mary thrives, learns to "rub clothes," and iron. More important, the "selfishness and envy of her manner with Ellen has departed." Years later, she serves as a maid at Ellen's wedding, showing "great respect for Lulu's directions" in the kitchen. When one of the other maids steals Ellen's string of pearls, reducing the bride to tears, it is Mary who discovers the culprit; through her impressive powers of persuasion and faith, she is able to induce the transgressor to repent and return the stolen goods to their rightful owner. A grateful Ellen writes to Mary, "My dear dear Mary, we are ten thousand times obliged to you. . . . Walter says that a detective would have cost three or four times as much and would have made lots of talk and trouble in the papers. . . . Your very grateful friend, Ellen."

This pantomime shared certain thematic parallels with the story of Restus: the danger of exposing unattended children to the streets, as well as the black child's potential for salvation realized at Howard through the mediation of a white patron. Yet the script also emphasized the role of white material flamboyance and condescension in Mary's fall from virtue.

In addition, the figure of Lulu, who despite her modest means maintained a clean, wholesome home and a well-groomed sister, suggested that black women conformed to Victorian ideals of domesticity under far more adverse material circumstances than their middle-class white sisters. Yet, in recognition of Lulu's need to work for wages, the script also conveyed the need for adequate day care facilities for black children. In this context, the Howard Orphanage assumed the role of not just a refuge for parentless children or a safeguard against disorder on the streets, but also an essential social service vehicle for working-class women of color. Moreover, while the script did not challenge the traditional racial and gender identities of black women—every black woman played a maid—Mary's part in saving Ellen's jewelry suggested that Howard had empowered this inmate with the virtue and wisdom to protect a white woman's property, if not her person. Even if the terms of black-white social relations had not changed, the roles of white as paternalist/maternalist-civilizer and black as the beneficiary of protection had been reversed.

Other scripts forcefully projected an environmentalist view of crime by contrasting the fate of youth left to their own devices with the success stories of their siblings unfolding under the protective care of the Howard Orphanage. The various themes interlaced in these narratives—racial solidarity, a challenge of racial stereotypes, black children's potential for not just moral uplift also but professional success through education, wage-earning women's day care needs, the sanctity of feminine virtue, and the environmental interpretation of the roots of poverty and crime—informed the welfare vision of Howard's black staff. On one level, this outlook celebrated equal opportunity, asserted the power of environment in molding the personal traits necessary for individual success, and embraced the trimmings of Victorian morality in accord with the white Managers' civic nationalist template of "sameness." It shaped the black subject as individual—a project furthered by the pantomimes' subversion of the icons of white supremacy. As we have seen, the emblems of white racial nationalism—the fiction of the black rapist, the discourse of mobility, the rhetoric of internalized self-discipline, and the "cult of true womanhood"—functioned as hegemonic markers in flux. They were appropriated, recontextualized, robbed of their racial meaning, and fashioned into an argument *against* racial nationalism. On another level however, the pantomimes manifested a consciousness of institutional racism and promoted black solidarity in concord with the communitarian spirit suffusing Howard's cottages and farms.

Subaltern Hierarchies and Black Benevolence

Howard's communitarianism was, however, complicated by subaltern hierarchies of class, color, and professional positioning.[65] For working poor African American guardians, having a voice in their children's lives and labor constituted a vital element of familial self-determination. Any institution's appropriation of a child's custody smacked of slavery's disregard of family ties. For Gordon, on the other hand, the children's access to equal opportunity sometimes entailed the unfortunate but necessary step of separation from their "unrefined" and often destitute kin, an attitude that injected more than a hint of condescension in her dealings with the relatives of her "boys and girls." One formerly homeless mother, Mrs. S., tried repeatedly to discharge her son from the Orphanage when she returned to work. Gordon refused, referring Wood (who tried to intervene on Mrs. S's behalf) to an outdated report by the Commissioners of the Poor: "Father in prison. Mother and child homeless, staying with old neighbors . . . Mother's physical condition does not warrant her caring for more than one child." Gordon wrote Wood, "Some of *these people* make one very weary of them, even when you *try to be kind*."[66] The superintendent's words clearly reflected her sense of alienation from the likes of Mrs. S.—not simply in terms of class, but also as a welfare "bureaucrat"—despite their shared racial identity. Wood, however, took Mrs. S's side, reminding Gordon that the mother's position had changed since the Commissioners had issued their report.[67] A plaintive letter, from another anxious mother whose repeated enquiries about her son's well-being had gone unanswered, chided Gordon for her insensitivity: "Dear Madam: I write you once more asking you about my son. . . . Please let me heare [sic]from you about him so I can fell a little at ease. . . . I think you should have a little more felling for a pearson [sic]. You don't know what I have suffered. He was taken from me, He is my all . . . and I hope he is alright." This final entreaty did elicit a response from the superintendent, who wrote the mother that her son was well and learning the shoemaking trade.[68]

Intra-subaltern social hierarchies hardened during the tenure of Mary Gordon's successor, J. H. N. Waring. Gordon's resignation as superintendent in 1917 severed an important link between Howard's black-run and white-run phases. The new Superintendent Waring was a "nearly white" medical doctor educated at Howard Medical School, Johns Hopkins University, and Hampton Institute who had served as a school principal in Baltimore and belonged to Howard University's Board of Trustees.[69]

It was on Waring's watch that there surfaced reports of color prejudice on Howard's premises. Color consciousness apparently did prevail even under Mary Gordon. Darker-skinned African Americans served in the highest echelons of the home's administrative structure—a dualism reflected in Gordon's statement to Wood that her appointee for custodian/commandant in 1914 was "jet black *but* good natured."[70] During Waring's tenure, however, color allegedly came to determine a staff member's function. William Pickens, dean of Morgan College in Baltimore, sent Wood a letter from George W. Andrews, a professor at the Oberlin Conservatory of Music, regarding the plight of a young Howard instructor, Alice Smith. Smith, an orphan herself, accepted a teaching position at the Orphanage upon her graduation from Washington University—Seattle. When she arrived in King's Park, however, she was "made ill by the treatment . . . received," Andrews reported. "She came to teach—not to cook and wash . . . for 30 boys—she writes that when Dr. Waring met her and saw that she was rather dark—He and his family and the other teachers are nearly white—he at once told her she could not teach—but must be housemother and cook, etc., for 30 boys—She has written us such a depressed and pitiful letter, depressed and alone as she is." Andrews requested Pickens to help Smith find another job: "I am asking if you know of any teaching position where she could earn a living—anywhere—or assistant in any department. . . . She can do light domestic work . . . [but] has fitted herself to teach—loves it and would succeed, I know."[71]

Color may have played a part in Smith's unfortunate experience at Howard. It is possible, however, that her gender contributed to her lack of access to professional status within the institution's hierarchy as well. Interestingly enough, the home's promotional literature dating to the post-Gordon era reflected a shift in attitude toward the sexual division of labor among Howard staff, apparently linked to an attempt to organize cottage life on the farm within the framework of a heterosexual, two-parent model of family life. A printed sheet of information on the home entitled "Workers' Facts," circulated among patrons during the Waring administration, declared that each cottage at King's Park was placed in charge of "a teacher and *his* wife." This arrangement allowed "the re-establishment of family life"—evidently after the nuclear fashion. The "Workers' Facts" went on: "Instructed by the 'House Mother' as the *teacher's wife* is known, the girls become proficient in the care of a kitchen . . . and in the preparation of food for a large family. The knowledge thus obtained becomes of substantial value, when they come to establish homes of their own or desire to take wage-earning positions." This statement of the institution's commitment to train accomplished housewives and maids represented a departure from the Gordon-era reign of single cottage mothers and predominantly female teachers.[72]

Waring also shared a fractious relationship with the institution's black clients. Employers to whom children were indentured frequently reported that their charges were removed by relatives angry with the institution for not informing them that the children had been "placed out."[73] One irate grandmother accused Waring of misleading her as to the whereabouts of her granddaughter, whose discharge she sought, in a tone that both mocked the superintendent's presumed superiority over her and asserted her right to guardianship over the child: "Now your honor, I am pleased to note that [my granddaughter] is and was not at Ocean City, as I am now made wise to the facts, and am glad that I am, for New Brunswick is not Ocean City. Now I wish to hear from you at an early date as to her discharge."[74]

As the children reached working age, control over their labor occasioned conflicts between their relatives and Howard staff. While many Howard adolescents sided with their kin on these occasions, for others such conflict spelled an opportunity to define themselves as autonomous individuals independent of burdensome family obligations. The case of Ruby Brown offers a window to the different meanings Howard's "placing out" system held for a young woman on the one hand, and a woman who claimed to be her aunt on the other. Fanny Brown, the "aunt"—perhaps a surrogate kinswoman—contacted Wood, repeatedly "begging" him to let her "little girl," Ruby, live with her rather than in the Connecticut household where the young woman had been placed. The elder Brown had evidently approached Waring for her niece's address but greatly resented his demand that she produce references first. She wrote Wood, "That proffessor [sic] wanted all kinds of references from me. What reference did you get from Mr. and Mrs. Martin [Ruby's employers]?" In letter after letter, Brown claimed a lifelong relationship with her niece and stressed the young woman's urgent desire to return to her family: "I promised to train [Ruby] when she was only a baby and if life lasts I mean to give it to her . . . My girl has known me ever since she has known herself." Yet Mary Brown also divulged her own desperate need for household and farm help to assist her in the care of a crippled brother and to tend her fruit and vegetable garden. She complained that Superintendent Waring had peremptorily dismissed her application to Howard for domestic help:

"You had such a Grand Proffessor [sic] out there at Indian Head. I asked him for a boy and he refused." Brown expressed confidence that Ruby would rather aid her aunt than an alien household where she was but a mere servant. The aunt saw the terms of her niece's employment, as she understood them, to be exploitative: "I might as well have her with me as have her bond out for a dollar a week. . . . I took great pride in learning [Ruby] to sew and she is not doing anything in the family she is in but learning to be a servant." When she learned that the dollar Ruby received each week was simply her pocket money, the rest of her wages being placed in trust for her by the institution, Brown expressed her suspicion that Ruby was unaware of the arrangement and that the Orphanage was appropriating the funds: "You know as well as I do that that money goes toward that school she gets only a small sum for herself." Brown wished to know whether she "should take charge of the savings." Meanwhile, when her letters to Ruby elicited no response, she wrote Wood, accusing Howard's staff of giving her the wrong address.[75]

In fact, Wood communicated Brown's sentiments to Ruby faithfully.[76] The Howard alum declared unequivocally that she was aware of and satisfied with the terms of her employment and had no wish to live with Brown, who was not, in any case, her aunt. "And," she continued, "[Brown] knows my right address because she wrote to me several times." Ruby Brown clearly enjoyed the independence and perks that accompanied her service to a prosperous family, including trips to the country, timely visits to dentists and doctors, and, importantly for the teenager, fashionable clothes, including one she described enthusiastically to Wood as "not a silk one . . . [but] a blue serge."[77] She saw herself not as a servant (as her aunt did), but rather a working woman with the autonomy to spend her wages as she saw fit, unconstrained by onerous family obligations.

Another case involving friction over a Howard woman's labor, however, pitted the Orphanage staff against a former resident allied with her family. Rosa Johnson fled the home of an unsatisfactory employer and took refuge with an aunt. She then sought the release of her savings held in trust for her by Howard, offering to donate a portion of the money to the institution as an incentive for the transfer. Superintendent Waring not only refused to comply with her request, he threatened legal action against her unless she returned to work: "Your aunt is harboring a runaway from this Institution and is making it possible for us to prosecute her for this violation of the law just as it is possible for us to prosecute you for running away. . . . If you do not [live right and go to work] I shall take you . . .

to the court and ask them to put you where a disobedient runaway girl belongs."[78] Waring proposed transferring another young woman from her employer in order to remove her from the allegedly pernicious influence of "her people" who lived in the vicinity.[79] Intra-black class friction, dramatized most compellingly by Fanny Brown's repeated references to the light-skinned Waring as "a Grand Proffessor" [sic] and the superintendent's professed willingness to mobilize white punitive institutions against errant black clients, illustrates the complex and shifting character of subaltern identities.

The Children:
"Multipositional" Subalterns and American Exceptionalism

The cases of Ruby Brown and Rosa Johnson invite reflection on the ways in which a Howard upbringing—the children's lifestyle and interpersonal relationships at the Orphanage combined with their exposure to ideas encoded in the institution's cultural productions—mediated the orphans' *own* negotiations of personal, racial, and national identities. In other words, how did the children express themselves as surrogate daughters and sons, workers and consumers, aspiring professionals and lovers, and as black and American? And how did these roles interact with one another, as well as with hegemonic structures, to form multidimensional subaltern subjects? Letters addressed to Superintendent Gordon and Board President Wood by and about former inmates, mostly women placed out by the Orphanage in domestic service, provide valuable clues regarding these questions.[80]

These documents show that the Managers' emphasis on "individuality," thrift, order, self-reliance, and feminine virtue supplied a civic nationalist prism through which the children navigated the fractious terrain of American exceptionalism. In this context the letters framed the themes of respectability and decorum, professional aspirations and consumption patterns, and control over work and sex in the language of individual sameness. At the same time, however, the African American welfare vision, informed by a sense of responsibility for the "race" and profound faith in the black youth's potential for success, also textured the children's quest for empowerment. From their various situations, defined by a plethora of social experiences, the orphans manipulated the paradoxes of American identity constructs to write a multi-vocal African American experience into a national narrative premised on a unidimensional construct of black dependence. By disrupting supposedly immutable identities defined by "natural" difference, the alums sought not only to advance their personal autonomy, but also to challenge the racial meaning of Americanism.

The informal, surrogate family ethos that governed staff-inmate relations at Howard may well have vested the children with the emotional confidence to make assertive claims to freedom and equality. Alumni often addressed Mary Gordon as "My darling Mother," "My dearest Mother," and "My own sweet Mother." Many strove to win her approval by describing themselves as efficient workers and devoted Christians, striving for temporal and spiritual self-improvement in ways that validated the institution's plea for equal opportunity. One wrote: "Mrs. Swartz [her employer] broke her arm a few weeks ago and I had to jump right in like a little woman and help . . . all I could. No one can dress her or comb her hair like I can. She says she don't know [sic] what she'd do without me. I had all Dr. H's bills to make out and checks too." She stressed her own observance of public decorum: "P. [a friend from the Orphanage] tickles me at times. She talks so loud on the streets and I am not used to that and remind her often where she is."[81] This missive reveals interlocking identities at work. Its author was both a surrogate daughter seeking a parent's favor by embracing her values *and* a black woman de-racializing the canon of true womanhood by representing "respectability" as an *individual* attribute as likely to be found among African Americans as among whites.

Similarly, the hallowed American ideal of occupational mobility was integral to the alums' sense of personal security as well as their conception of American identity. The avowed faith of HOIS in its charges' potential for success created several ambitious young aspirants for careers loftier than the menial service to which the dominant society bound their identity as a race. For the girls, black women in key positions of authority at Howard in the pre-Waring era–whether as superintendent, matrons, or teachers—must have served as role models of professional achievement. Thus, work became an important motif in their articulation of racially egalitarian sameness. A night watchman for the City and Suburban Homes Company declared that he was "still fighting to become an able man. Even if I am married which stops many a career."[82] One young woman assured her "own sweet matron" that "some day you may have just cause to be proud of us, for I know I don't intend to spend the rest of my days in the kitchen."[83] Young women who had their sights set on careers in nursing or teaching fared badly in the kitchen and parlor, whether by natural ability or design. One employer, complaining about her domestic help Mary Jackson's listlessness, declared, "I was led to believe 'by herself' that she was to be placed in a school in Hampton, Virginia." Jackson's mistress described her as "slow" with "absolutely no initiative." Yet Jackson enthusiastically sought and filled out an application for nurse's training at the Lincoln Hospital and Home, explaining: "My reason to be a nurse is to try and help somebody. There are so many nobodys [sic] that I'm so anxious to do my part it may be very small but its helping just a little. If I am accepted I will try and do my best."[84] Another woman left her employer when the latter refused to give her the music lessons she had been promised.[85] Thus Ann Smith, whose tale of frustrated ambitions opened this chapter, was not unique in her refusal to resign herself to the status of eternal servility prescribed by her location at the intersection of a "triple jeopardy" of race, class, and gender.

As noted before, the link between Smith's professional and sartorial aspirations was not accidental. Fancy clothing was not only a significant element in the emergence of a working-class youth culture in turn-of-the-century New York, but represented for African Americans a conspicuous mode of rejecting the racial premises American consumer culture. New York women strained the "boundaries of immigrant, working class life" by dressing flamboyantly in public spaces. For some New Yorkers, "putting on style" became a way of expressing a variety of sentiments, from aspirations to upward mobility to the drive for romance and autonomy, while others adopted distinctive clothing as a badge of union membership.[86] For the "new immigrants" from Europe, participation in the consumer economy served as a tool of acculturation to "American" values. Ready-made clothing became a visible symbol of national identity.[87]

Yet the culture of mass consumption was by no means color blind. National advertisers purveyed images of blackness to sell a variety of articles to consumers constructed as white. For instance, the smiling face of Aunt Jemima—repository of mammy's culinary expertise and penchant for service—drew self-consciously white consumers of pancakes. At the same time, the caricatures in trade cards of African Americans in ridiculously mismatched clothing or as inept users of durable consumer goods conveyed the sense that no amount of spending would raise blacks above "their place."[88] As Hale has shown in the context of the South, however, the spaces of consumption could also become sites for transgressing traditional racial hierarchies, as stores courted black customers and well-dressed mulattoes jostled lily-whites in railway compartments. In the cities of the North perhaps more than anywhere else, consumer culture became an arena for straining the boundaries between blackness and whiteness, a theater for contesting the national advertisers' invention of *legitimate* consumers, capable of attaining cultural capital through spending, as white. Howard women's penchant for fashion encoded a struggle to assert their dual identities as consumers and Americans—as black consumers and black Americans. It connoted their defiance of the notion that the prerogative to wear the visible symbols of national identity and social mobility—such as ready-made clothing—was the prerogative of "whiteness" alone. This contest for equal opportunity thus symbolically invoked Howard guardians' civic nationalist premise of individual sameness, even as it contravened their strictures against material extravagance.

A similar dynamic is evident in the women's endeavors to flout etiquettes of class and race relations by violating dress and behavioral codes for maids. Fannie Moore's mistress complained that when the family had visitors, Moore refused to leave the room, joined in the conversation, and, moreover, refused to wear an apron or any dress that was not "dressy": "She refuses to wear anything but silk stockings, silk shirt waists and white skirts when she gets up in the morning and when I call she just takes her own good time to dress and comes out of her room after I have the breakfast ready to serve." To her mistress's horror, Moore spent $1.25 for a pair of stockings. "I told her 50 cent stockings were nicer, but she said *no sir not on me*," complained the employer. "She seems to think she must have everything my daughter has, and go with her everywhere we go, so in some way will you please try to influence her not to forget her place and try to dress for her work, as it has been commented on around the Lake about her working in high heeled shoes and silk stockings, and my daughter and I wearing khaki skirts."[89] Some Howard women combined their appeal to the American "ode to upward mobility"—whether through business training or stylish apparel—with gestures of patriotism. Ann Smith, for example, invested in "liberty bonds" when the United States entered World War I.[90] Through her particular configuration of spending, this black New Yorker, like other Howard alums, was testing both the promise of civic nationalism *and* the limits of her keepers' enforcement of the rules of personal economy.

Because it facilitated interracial mingling, commercialized leisure presented opportunities to subvert racial hierarchies and assert individual sameness through consumption even more fundamentally. Yet the infractions it prompted may also be interpreted as the rebellion of youth against all authority. Movies and amusement parks cast their spell on several of

Howard's first-generation black New Yorkers, much to the distress of their guardians, as institutional entries on visits to children "placed out" suggest. One Brooklyn employer, Mrs. Williamson, complained about her charge's propensity to visit Coney Island in violation of her curfew: "Telling [Juliet] to do or not to do is like putting water in a collander [sic] you just put it in but it runs right out." Williamson reported that Juliet, in company with another Howard woman, was "meeting white boys in secluded places"—a transgression that the girls admitted to when told that they were under police surveillance.[91] Their actions bespoke many roles: black women breaching racial norms in accord with the Managers' logic of individualism, as well as teenage girls violating the discipline regimen and gender expectations of their custodians.

As workers and spenders, Howard women articulated an economic self-image that invoked the right to profit and property in order to question their dependent status on the margins of the national narrative. In this instance, their rhetoric of sameness drew on their common claim (with whites) to the mantle of the rational, freely acting individual motivated by enlightened self-interest. Although the Managers embraced the same rhetoric in their calls for equal opportunity, their charges' appropriation of this stance often conflicted with the institution's parallel mission to encourage thrift. The Managers required that the wages of each charge be held in a savings account in trust for the child until she reached the age of eighteen. However well-meaning, the women saw this decree as infringing on their control over their own earnings in what amounted to a violation of the fundamental American right to private property. Rosa Johnson invoked this sense of proprietorship when she wrote Superintendent Waring, "Let me have my money as I am owner of it." When informed that she could not have her money until she reached the age of eighteen years, she angrily retorted to President Wood, "The home has been telling me that [I am not 18 yet] for the past five years. . . . Will you please look my age up. You know I have worked for the money and can take good care of it. . . . I also will be more than satisfied to give the home which took the place of any mother. I would not feel right if I didn't."[92] To Johnson, the power to dispose of her wages as she wished was inalienable from her elemental right as a worker to the "ownership" of the cash proceeds of her labor; this did not conflict with her sense of loyalty to the institution that she called "home" and likened to "any mother." Indeed, she was willing to donate some of her savings to the home, provided that she (rather than a trustee) reserved the right to make that decision.

Other former residents negotiated their appeal for control over their wages within a framework of hallowed American values, such as financial prudence and economic self-sufficiency, to which they knew the Managers to be attached. One woman pleaded, "I am 18 years old now . . . I think I'm old enough to know the value of money . . . *I think I could be responsible for something. What kind of woman do you think I'll make if depended on someone else all the time.* I promise you I won't touch a cent in the bank. I'll try and save all I can."[93] Many others advanced plausible grounds for taking charge of their savings: economic need, the sickness of loved ones, the desire to invest in liberty bonds, to buy Christmas presents for relatives, or replace broken articles belonging to others. Dorothy Benedict declared tersely, "Mr. Wood, I worked very hard for the money and I think I deserve some of it now because I need it. . . . the money I make [in my present place of employment]goes to my Grandmother. She is very sick in bed."[94] In negotiating the terms of her life with her "benefactor," this young woman resorted to an all-American, laissez-faire argument that, while consistent with the ideals of Howard's trustees, also advanced her own search for self-determination.

Finally, from their locations as consensual lovers, Howard women occasionally engaged the dialectics of sexual politics in ways that interrupted conventional configurations of female respectability, race relations, and national identity. For the orphans, interracial dating may have served both as a symbol of personal independence as well as a challenge to the logic of whiteness. On the other hand, preserving and protecting female black sexual purity was pivotal to both the Howard Managers' mission of creating a respectable black citizenry and the staff's attempts to combat the historic traditions of black women's sexual exploitation and alleged licentiousness. For African American leaders and their white sympathizers, it represented a significant tool for undermining the color fabrication of "true" American womanhood. This concern surfaced with new urgency in 1918, when sixteen-year-old Frances Carter conceived a child as a result of an affair with an Italian named Victor Fuccillo. The Society for the Prevention of Cruelty to Children got wind of the situation and had Fuccillo arrested for rape in the second degree. The Italian's lawyers sought Wood's permission for Carter's marriage to Fuccillo. Their client, they argued, was not only a citizen, but a patriot: "[Fuccillo] was lately on his way to camp as a soldier when the armistice was signed . . . he has purchased from his savings one hundred dollars in Liberty Bonds." Wood, in consultation with Carter's mistress, Bertha

Blackman, and the Brooklyn SPCC, refused on the grounds that Fuccillo's offer of marriage was no more than a device to circumvent the law. Fuccillo went to jail, while Carter returned to the Blackman home, where she had her child.

The case of Frances Carter combined a centuries-old theme of seduction with new concerns shaping the consciousness of a wartime America suspicious of alien radicalism. These concerns included the specter of female sexuality gone riot embodied in the formulation of the alleged "girl problem," the emergence of white ethnic males as the new urban sexual predator (against which to protect and preserve female honor), and the role of professional social welfare agencies as arbiters of these new social alignments and conflicts. For Carter's black well-wishers, Fuccillo became a stand-in for Protestant white males who had long engaged in the sexual exploitation of black women. For her white guardians, he not only symbolized the decrepitude of the ethnic white, but also raised the alarming specter of an alliance between marginal groups.

Where did Carter herself stand in this controversy? She allegedly expressed great distaste for Fuccillo in her letters to Wood and the SPCC and showed no inclination to marry him. She expressed support of her guardians' characterization of her former lover as one who displayed "an awful temper . . . when out of sorts . . . and licentious feelings toward young girls." Under the circumstances, all agreed that although marriage offered the advantage of "legitimizing" Carter's child, it would bring the young mother a "life of misery and unhappiness" while depriving her of the chance to marry another. Yet, while Carter's protectors took comfort from her apparent remorse and rejection of an unworthy suitor, she may actually have won a battle for sexual autonomy against them—premarital sex without the compulsion to marry—although within the parameters of moral and social values set by them.[95] Thus, Carter may have balanced her multiple roles as lover, "single girl about town," and obedient ward (imbued with a renewed sense of domesticity) in ways that furthered her pursuit of personal freedom. On a more symbolic level, however, her act of sexual rebellion, of miscegenation, represented the ultimate sameness discourse. It perforated the heart of the whiteness mythology premised on "absolute racial difference" that defined the national culture of segregation. Frances Carter literally infused life into the figure of the tragic mulatto, who traversed the works of black writers and artists as the most powerful signifier of segregation's contradictions—the living embodiment of the "American dilemma."

By the time the Carter-Fuccillo affair reached its final outcome, the HOIS had been forced into an ignominious demise. In January 1918 a severe winter destroyed the plumbing and central heating system at King's Park. Several children suffered frostbite, two so severely that they had to have their feet amputated. This tragic incident prompted an order by the state commissioner of charities to close down the HOIS. The premature demise of the Howard experiment suggested the tremendous odds against which black voluntary associations had to labor. In an age marked by the professionalization of social welfare, prejudice against the management competence, policy preferences, and financial skills of African Americans kept white donors from contributing money to institutions run even partially by blacks. Wood recalled being told that if only he had a "white person in charge," the school would have survived, suggesting that the white directors had themselves been engaged in something of a dialectic of accommodation and opposition with the larger society of which they were a part.[96]

Yet the history of the Howard Orphanage and Industrial School, however brief, sheds light on the relationship among individual identities, racial formation, and imaginings of the nation through the prism of child welfare. From their myriad positions rooted in particular configurations of race, class, gender, age, color, work, and familial and romantic allegiances, HOIS figures seized through image, word, and action the language and institutions of Progressive reform—and the tension-fraught ideology of exceptionalism in which they were embedded—to redefine subalterns as actors and American identity as pluralistic. Howard's middle-class black and white dispensers of social welfare cast the democratic, capitalist tenets of individualism and equal opportunity into a civic nationalist language of individual sameness; this ideology contradicted the assumption of inherent difference on which the discourse of whiteness was based. The institution's black staff devised cultural productions, most notably the pantomimes, that recontextualized the symbols of white supremacy—the metaphor of rape, the imagery of feminine respectability, the notion of internalized self-discipline, the ethos of upward mobility—in order to unmake the racial nationalist premises underlying notions of American civilization and citizenship. At the same time, however, the peculiar experiences of race—manifested in a combination of black-client needs, the institution's scarce resources, and African American historical experiences—interrupted the Managers' civic nationalist discourse of inclusion. They shaped, under Mary Gordon, an alternative community identity grounded in an informal, extended familial, black Christian, participatory democratic style of management that sometimes clashed with the white trustees' campaign to introduce a spirit of individuality, economy, and "efficiency" to Howard's operation.

By no means was this race-based community monolithic in identity or interest. The variables of class, color, gender, and age invested the concepts of "freedom" and "equality" with sharply different tenors and textures in practical, everyday terms. These nuances emerge in the dialectical interplay of the orphans' own aspirations and consciousness as individuals and subaltern group members with the norms and expectations of their interracial caretakers. Howard alumni appropriated elements of their social superiors' commitment to individualism, consumerism, and Victorian womanhood in ways that shook the coherence of established identities of the white "self" and the black "Other." By so doing, they simultaneously defied their personal dependence and racial subordination, as well as the authority of their custodians, in a variety of circumstances. As surrogate daughters, they pleaded allegiance to the "politics of respectability," thus challenging the racial meaning of feminine virtue. As aspiring professionals, they tapped into their black keepers' lessons in economic uplift to strain the racial boundaries of occupational mobility. As shoppers, they foiled the national advertisers' color fabrication of consumer culture as a tool of racialized Americanization. As sexual rebels, they quite literally hybridized a population divided between "whiteness and its Others." As workers and spenders, Howard's young men and women negotiated their pursuit of autonomy in the very language of self-sufficiency central to the liberal creed that their benefactors promoted. They made everyday attempts to inject a rainbow of colors into a national narrative that, while laden with the promise of equal opportunity and individual freedom, was nonetheless premised on whiteness. Their actions turned American exceptionalism—expressed in reform ideology—into a dialectical arena of accommodation and struggle on the most immediate and intimate of levels: an idiom and an opportunity for the negotiation of individual, racial, and national senses of self.

Epilogue

American society has come nearly a full circle since the patrons and clients of benevolence in Victorian and Progressive New York argued over the meaning of race and nation within the framework of poverty policy. A tentative welfare state for the neediest among us has waxed and waned. Welfare politics have, however, remained a supple and polarizing forum for defining and contesting the gist of color and American nationalism.

Quasi-municipal relief and reform agencies in nineteenth-century New York used the paradigms of race, dependence, and relief to articulate the meaning and boundaries of American citizenship. The Alms House Department, the Colored Home, the New York House of Refuge, and the Women's Prison Association overtly discriminated against the black poor by seeking to colonize, segregate, or exclude them altogether, even as they targeted the Irish for rehabilitation and assimilation into a racialized national imaginary. By contrast, the New Deal launched America's welfare state in the 1930s by creating an ostensibly universalistic social insurance system. The Social Security Act of 1935 instituted an old age pension program funded by employer and employee contributions, as well as unemployment insurance. New labor laws established a minimum wage and strengthened the right to unionize.

Yet these policies did not cover an overwhelming majority of black workers, who worked in the agricultural sector or in domestic service. Instead, racial discrimination in the private labor market and public works agencies, abetted by some labor unions, swelled the numbers of African Americans on relief rolls during the Great Depression. Amendments to the Social Security Act in 1939 extended old age insurance to the widows and dependents of eligible workers, thus setting married women apart from unmarried or divorced ones and buttressing two-parent nuclear families as the proper object of social policy. In the 1960s the persistence of racial discrimination in the labor market, combined with black women's exclusion from unemployment insurance, forced many to go on the "dole"—means-tested public relief, especially the Aid to Families with Dependent Children (AFDC) program. Unwed white mothers outnumbered black ones by two to one. Nevertheless, Southern conservatives, who controlled key congressional committees, aligned with elements of antiwelfare Northern business interests to portray black women as the ultimate epitome of the "welfare queen"—allegedly promiscuous wasters who used their children as meal tickets funded by white taxpayers. Such arguments tapped into the economic anxieties of increasingly embattled blue-collar white workers.[1]

As in the nineteenth century, the case for welfare "reform" in the latter half of the twentieth century rested on the assumptions both that the poor owed their condition to individual failure fed by a pathological culture of dependence and that welfare ran counter to the salient American values of individual self-sufficiency, hard work, and commitment to two-parent families. Moreover, as in the past, reformers used relief to redraw the boundaries of citizenship—in effect, and however inadvertently—around color.

Thus, the Personal Responsibility and Work Opportunity Reconciliation Act (PRWORA) of 1996 imposed a five-year ceiling on aid eligibility, required recipients to work, and replaced AFDC with block grants to states. New rules attached to President George W. Bush's budget bill of 2006 limited acceptable work activity to subsidized and unsubsidized employment, community service, on-the-job training, no more than six weeks of job search, and a maximum of a year's vocational education training.[2] Conspicuous by its absence from this list of "legitimate" workfare was college education. Meanwhile, advocates for the poor reported wide racial disparities in the administration of welfare reform both in New York and across the country. Aid recipients of color were less likely to receive information about educational opportunities or help with transportation and child care. As a result, they frequently faced sanctions for failing to keep appointments. Caseworkers were found to mislead them about their eligibility to receive work supports, like Medicaid and food stamps. Welfare offices in New York did not offer translation services to those who understood little English. Employment discrimination also persisted so that black and Latino citizens and residents were less likely to make a smooth transition from welfare to work.[3]

Significantly, welfare reform resuscitated old links between welfare and racialized citizenship. The original version of PRWORA prohibited most legal immigrants—overwhelmingly from Latin America and Asia in the wake of the Immigration and Nationality Act of 1965—from receiving food stamps and Supplemental Security Income (SSI) until they had worked in the United States for at least ten years. Ten years later, President Bush approved regulations that limited the TEFL (teaching English as a foreign language) training of welfare recipients to only a few weeks. Moreover, he signed into law a new Medicaid provision that would require recipients to produce birth certificates, passports, or other evidence of U.S. citizenship in order to qualify for coverage. The bill overtly targeted a significant population of nonwhite "Others," namely undocumented immigrants from Latin America, especially Mexico. Yet under its provisions, the right to public assistance also became the instrument for erasing impoverished African Americans, American Indians, and homeless people—both symbolically and materially—from the membership rolls of America's civic fraternity. Democratic Governor Chris Gregoire of Washington pointed out that many older African Americans never received birth certificates. Anne M. Winter, a health policy advisor in Arizona, maintained that "Native Americans—the first Americans—do not have documents" to prove American citizenship. Others who are too old or poor to travel or drive do not possess passports or driver's licenses.[4] Disabilities of race and class will thus limit access to relief both as a right of citizenship and a symbol of membership in the national community.

If the symbiotic relationship among nationalism, welfare, and race privilege in our society has persisted, so has subaltern perseverance in finding within welfare discourse the linguistic and material resources to articulate alternative meanings of citizenship and American identity. In Progressive America, the operatives and clients of the Howard Orphanage used child welfare language and institutions somewhat discretely to combat racial inequality and offer a pluralistic vision of national identity. In the more assertive climate of protest in the 1960s, black women who spearheaded welfare rights movements in New York and elsewhere offered a more forceful definition of welfare as a measure of social justice, and therefore a vital element of the civil rights, rather than a crutch of the habitually lazy.[5]

Decades later, following the demise of AFDC, a former welfare recipient argued that public relief, far from undermining American values, can play a central role in helping the needy to fulfill the "American dream." She is Maureen Lane, the very antithesis of the welfare queen construct of conservative imagination. While dependent on state aid, Lane, who is white, acquired a college education and went on to become codirector of the Welfare Rights Initiative based in New York City's Hunter College, as well as a fellow of the progressive public policy organization known as the Drum Major Institute. Lane described the 2006 federal welfare regulations that excluded college education from acceptable workfare as translating into "American dreams denied" rather than American ideals restored. The denial of education to needy students hampered the social mobility not simply of individuals, but that of entire communities as well: "Substantial evidence indicates that motivated students can achieve their economic potential and bring their families, neighborhoods and communities with them up the economic ladder."[6]

On a more informal level, the non-activist poor of our times, like their nineteenth-century counterparts in the Work House and the New York House of Refuge, continue to articulate their dependence on public relief not as a function of their inherent character traits, but rather as the product of structural socioeconomic defects. In 2006 a Commission on Economic Opportunities (CEO), appointed by New York mayor Michael Bloomberg, issued its recommendations to alleviate poverty among 1.5 million New Yorkers belonging to three target groups: the working poor, young adults, and children under five years of age. The *Village Voice* reported that while welfare recipients greeted specific CEO proposals—such as the expansion of free kindergarten for all city kids—with approval, they quickly turned to a critique of "the bigger problems in their lives that were mostly beyond the scope of the commission's report: lousy schools that make kids want to drop out, job programs that make you spend all day cold-calling uninterested employers, [welfare] workers who treat you like dirt, and most of all, the lack of jobs that pay a decent wage." The *Voice* noted that one of its interviewees, Shyneetka Soto of Brooklyn, had actually tried to "shut down her own welfare case" but had been hampered by the revelation that if she did, the two nieces in her charge would lose their benefits. "The mayor, the president, the governor, they all messed up," Soto observed. "There are no jobs for no one out here right now. And the jobs that they have, they can't pay nothing. How are we supposed to live?"[7]

Nearly a century and a half separates Maureen Lane and Shyneetka Soto from Lany Candy's mother, a black domestic servant forced to send her daughter to the New York House of Refuge "for a home," the orphaned George Francis of Long Island who sought out the Refuge in order to get "some learning," or the Irish Hopper House inmate who refused to accept a job arranged by her benefactors on the grounds that the pay was too low. Yet these figures—past and present—remain bound by a shared perspective on not only the relationship between public relief and American values, but also on the identity of those forced to seek welfare. As Lane's words suggest, such a perspective imagines welfare as a form of social contract central to realizing the American promise of social mobility. It implicitly denies the dehumanizing racial, ethnic, and class stereotypes associated with relief beneficiaries; instead, it offers multifaceted views of the working poor as mothers in need of childcare, as students in search of education as a path out of poverty, as workers deserving of living wages, and, above all, as human beings worthy of respect and civil rights. In this context, as the national furor over (mostly Latino) immigration reaches a crescendo, the chapter on nonwhites, whiteness, and welfare is likely to remain an open forum for debate.

Appendix

TABLE 1
Frequency Distribution by Sex of Individuals Living in Different African American and Irish/Irish American Household Types in NYC, 1855

Nationality/Color	African American			Irish/Irish American		
Sex	Male	Female	Total	Male	Female	Total
Household Type						
Nuclear Without Boarder[1]	54	51	105	90	94	184
Nuclear with Boarder[2]	7	5	12	22	26	48
Extended/Communal[3]	69	87	156	43	55	98
Single Woman-headed[4]	9	46	55	4	16	20
Boarders	7	12	19	30	22	52
Servants[5]				3	12	15
Total	146	201	347	192	225	417

1. "Nuclear" is defined here as a family consisting of two parents and single children of all ages. Figures include all family members but exclude servants (if any).

2. Figures include all family members and exclude boarders.

3. "Extended/Communal" is defined here as kin-based family groupings, or households consisting of some combination of kin and non-kin roommates, but excluding boarders and servants.

4. With or without children and/or boarders. Some single women were boardinghouse keepers. Figures include family members and exclude boarders and/or servants (if any).

5. Servants in the sixth ward were almost invariably attached to boarding houses rather than to individual families.

Source: Sample of one hundred African American and one hundred Irish/Irish American households taken from Population Census of the Inhabitants of Sixth and Eighth Wards in the County of New York, 1855.

TABLE 2
Close-up of African American Nuclear Families without Boarders*
Frequency Distribution of Individuals Living in Such Families by
Age, Sex, and Length of Residency in NYC, 1855

Years in NYC	Fewer than 5		5–10		More than 10/NYC-born	
Sex	Male	Female	Male	Female	Male	Female
Age in Years						
0–15				1	16	15
16–20					2	1
21–25		2			9	8
26–30	1			1	1	5
31–35				2	4	5
36–40			1		8	5
41–45			1		2	2
46–50			1		3	3
51–55			1		2	
56–60					1	
60 +					1	1
Total	1	2	4	4	49	45

*Includes the presence of two parents with single children of all ages and excludes servants.

Source: Sample of one hundred African American households taken from Population Census of the Inhabitants of Sixth and Eighth Wards in the County of New York, 1855.

TABLE 3
Close-up of African American Nuclear Families with Boarders*
Frequency Distribution of Individuals Living in Such Families by
Age, Sex, and Length of Residency in NYC, 1855

Years in NYC	Fewer than 5		5–10		More than 10/NYC-born	
Sex	Male	Female	Male	Female	Male	Female
Age in Years						
0–15				1	2	
16–20						
21–25						
26–30					2	1
31–35					1	1
36–40						1
41–45						
46–50						1
51–55					1	
56–60						
60 +					1	
Total				1	7	4

*Includes family members and excludes servants.

Source: Sample of one hundred African American households taken from Population Census of the Inhabitants of Sixth and Eighth Wards in the County of New York, 1855.

TABLE 4
Close-up of African American Extended/Communal Families*
Frequency Distribution of Individuals Living in Such Families by
Age, Sex, and Length of Residency in NYC, 1855

Years in NYC	Fewer than 5		5–10		More than 10/NYC-born	
Sex	Male	Female	Male	Female	Male	Female
Age in Years						
0–15	2	1	4	2	19	19
16–20	1	2	1	1	3	5
21–25	1	2	2	2	7	7
26–30			5	5	4	5
31–35		1	1	1	3	5
36–40		1		1	6	5
41–45						3
46–50					7	9
51–55						3
56–60						2
60 +					3	5
Total	4	7	13	12	52	68

*Defined as kin or surrogate/non-kin-based family groupings.

Source: Sample of one hundred African American households taken from Population Census of the Inhabitants of Sixth and Eighth Wards in the County of New York, 1855.

TABLE 5
*Close-up of African American Families Headed
by Single Women with Children and/or Boarders**
Frequency Distribution of Individuals Living in Such Families by
Age, Sex, and Length of Residency in NYC, 1855

Years in NYC	Fewer than 5		5–10		More than 10/NYC-born	
Sex	Male	Female	Male	Female	Male	Female
Age in Years						
0–15	1				3	6
16–20					4	3
21–25						3
26–30					1	4
31–35						1
36–40		1				3
41–45						2
46–50						4
51–55						1
56–60						
60 +						2
Total	1	1			8	29

* Figures include family members in single women-headed households and exclude servants and boarders.

Source: Sample of one hundred African American households taken from Population Census of the Inhabitants of Sixth and Eighth Wards in the County of New York, 1855.

TABLE 6
Close-up of African American Single Women Householders without Children
Frequency Distribution by Age and Length of Residency in NYC, 1855

Years in NYC	Fewer than 5	5–10	More than 10/NYC-born
Age in Years			
0–15			
16–20			
21–25			
26–30			3
31–35			3
36–40			4
41–45			
46–50		1	1
51–55			1
56–60			1
60 +			2
Total		1	15

Source: Sample of one hundred African American households taken from Population Census of the Inhabitants of Sixth and Eighth Wards in the County of New York, 1855.

TABLE 7
Close-up of African American Boarders
Frequency Distribution by Age, Sex, and Length of Residency in NYC, 1855

Years in NYC	Fewer than 5		5–10		More than 10/NYC-born	
Sex	Male	Female	Male	Female	Male	Female
Age in Years						
0–15		1			4	3
16–20	1	2				
21–25	1	1				2
26–30						1
31–35						
36–40					1	
41–45						2
46–50						
51–55						
56–60						
60 +						
Total	2	4			5	8

Source: Sample of one hundred African American households taken from Population Census of the Inhabitants of Sixth and Eighth Wards in the County of New York, 1855.

TABLE 8
Close-up of Irish/Irish American Nuclear Families without Boarders*
Frequency Distribution of Individuals Living in Them by
Age, Sex, and Length of Residency in NYC, 1855

Years in NYC	Fewer than 5		5–10		More than 10/NYC-born	
Sex	Male	Female	Male	Female	Male	Female
Age in Years						
0–15	2	2	6	5	28	31
16–20	1	2		1	2	6
21–25		1	3	4	5	1
26–30	2	1	7	7	3	6
31–35			5	2	5	2
36–40	2	2		4	7	4
41–45			1		2	4
46–50			1	2	5	4
51–55						
56–60			1	2	1	1
60 +			1			
Total	7	8	25	27	58	59

*Defined as presence of two parents with single children of all ages. Figures include family members and exclude servants.

Source: Sample of one hundred Irish/Irish American households from Population Census of the Inhabitants of Sixth and Eighth Wards in the County of New York, 1855.

TABLE 9
Close-up of Irish/Irish American Nuclear Families with Boarders*
Frequency Distribution of Individuals Living in Them by
Age, Sex, and Length of Residency in NYC, 1855

Years in NYC	Fewer than 5		5–10		More than 10/NYC-born	
Sex	Male	Female	Male	Female	Male	Female
Age in Years						
0–15	1	3	2	1	4	6
16–20				2	1	1
21–25		1		2		1
26–30	1	2	3	2	2	1
31–35	1	1			1	
36–40			1	1		1
41–45	1				1	
46–50						
51–55						
56–60	1		2	1		
60 +						
Total	5	7	8	9	9	10

*Figures include family members and exclude boarders and servants.

Source: Sample of one hundred Irish/Irish American households taken from Population Census of the Inhabitants of Sixth and Eighth Wards in the County of New York, 1855.

TABLE 10
Close-up of Irish/Irish American Extended/Communal Families*
*Frequency Distribution of Individuals Living in Them by
Age, Sex, and Length of Residency in NYC, 1855*

Years in NYC	Fewer than 5		5–10		More than 10/NYC-born	
Sex	Male	Female	Male	Female	Male	Female
Age in Years						
0–15	2	2		1	12	11
16–20		2	3		4	5
21–25		1		1	2	3
26–30	5	4	3	5	1	2
31–35			2	1		1
36–40				1	3	3
41–45	2			1		4
46–50			1	1	1	3
51–55						
56–60	1			1		3
60 +						
Total	10	9	10	11	23	35

*Communal families included kin-based extended families as well as households consisting of non-kin/roommates (usually single women living together).

Source: Sample of one hundred Irish/Irish American households taken from Population Census of the Inhabitants of Sixth and Eighth Wards in the County of New York, 1855.

TABLE 11
Close-up of Irish/Irish American Boarders
Frequency Distribution by Age, Sex, and Length of Residency in NYC, 1855

Years in NYC	Fewer than 5		5–10		More than 10/NYC-born	
Sex	Male	Female	Male	Female	Male	Female
Age in Years						
0–15	1			1		
16–20	1	3	1	1		
21–25	11	3	7	4		
26–30	6	4	1	1		
31–35				1		
36–40		1				1
41–45						
46–50					1	1
51–55					1	
56–60						1
60 +						
Total	19	11	9	8	2	3

Source: Sample of one hundred Irish/Irish American households taken from Population Census of the Inhabitants of Sixth and Eighth Wards in the County of New York, 1855.

TABLE 12
Close-up of Irish/Irish American Servants
Frequency Distribution by Age, Sex, and Length of Residency in NYC, 1855

Years in NYC	Fewer than 5		5–10		More than 10/NYC-born	
Sex	Male	Female	Male	Female	Male	Female
Age in Years						
0–15		2		1		
16–20		8				
21–25	1	1				
26–30	2					
31–35						
36–40						
41–45						
46–50						
51–55						
56–60						
60 +						
Total	3	11		1		

Source: Sample of one hundred Irish/Irish American households taken from Population Census of the Inhabitants of Sixth and Eighth Wards in the County of New York, 1855.

TABLE 13
*Close-up of Irish/Irish American Single Women–headed Households**
Frequency Distribution of Individuals Living in Them by
Age, Sex, and Length of Residency in NYC, 1855

Years in NYC	Fewer than 5		5–10		More than 10/NYC-born	
Sex	Male	Female	Male	Female	Male	Female
Age in Years						
0–15		2			3	5
16–20	1	1				1
21–25		1				
26–30						2
31–35						
36–40		1				1
41–45						
46–50						
51–55						2
56–60						
60 +						
Total	1	5			3	11

*Includes boardinghouse keepers. Figures include family members and exclude boarders and servants.

Source: Sample of one hundred Irish/Irish American households taken from Population Census of the Inhabitants of Sixth and Eighth Wards in the County of New York, 1855.

TABLE 14
Frequency Distribution of Married/Widowed African Americans by Age and Sex in NYC, 1855*

Sex	Male			Female		
Marital Status	Married	Widowed	Married, Not Living with Spouse	Married	Widowed	Married, Not Living with Spouse
Age in Years						
18–30	19		1	26	3	2
31–40	22			25	7	1
41–50	9	1	2	5	13	1
51–60	9		1	4	7	1
60+	6			2	6	
Total	65	1	4	62	36	5

*Note that the rate of marriage among African Americans was actually higher than the proportion of black nuclear families suggests. Married women sometimes lived in extended family arrangements or on their own while their husbands were away at sea or doing other work outside the city.

Source: Sample of one hundred African American households taken from Population Census of the Inhabitants of Sixth and Eighth Wards in the County of New York, 1855.

TABLE 15
Frequency Distribution of Married/Widowed Irish/Irish Americans by Age and Sex, 1855

Sex	Male			Female		
Marital Status	Married	Widowed	Married, Not Living with Spouse	Married	Widowed	Married, Not Living with Spouse
Age in Years						
18–30	19	1		31	1	
31–40	30			23	3	
41–50	15			14	11	
51–60	10			8	5	
60+	5			3	1	
Total	79	1		79	21	

Source: Sample of one hundred Irish/Irish American households taken from Population Census of the Inhabitants of Sixth and Eighth Wards in the County of New York, 1855.

TABLE 16
*Birthplaces of Migrant Members of African American Households by Sex, NYC, 1855**

Household Type	Nuclear		Extended		Single Women-headed		Boarders	
	Male	Female	Male	Female	Male	Female	Male	Female
Birthplace								
Kings Co./Upstate NY	2	8	10	4	1	4	1	2
New Jersey/Pennsylvania	6	9	10	15	2	8	1	2
New England								1
Upper South	9	2		1	2	4		
Lower South	2	1		2		1		1
Africa/Caribbean			3	5		2	1	
Other/Unknown			1	1				

*Migrants, at a total number of 124, represented a little over a third of all African American members of 100 households surveyed.

Source: Sample of one hundred African American households taken from Population Census of the Inhabitants of Sixth and Eighth Wards in the County of New York, 1855.

TABLE 17
Occupational Distribution By Sex of Individuals in
One Hundred African American Households in NYC, 1855*

Household Type	Nuclear		Extended		Single Head of Household (Male or Female)		Boarders	
	Male	Female	Male	Female	Male	Female	Male	Female
Occupation								
Laborer	6		6		4			
Crafts/Manufacturing[1]	5	1	3	2		6		1
Seaman	9		5		2			
Waiter	8		7		2		1	
Peddler/Porter	6		8					
Coachman/Cartman	2		2		2			
Chimney Sweep			1					
Butcher/Barber	4				1			
Domestic Service/Cook		1		2		2	1	1
Washing				4		11		
Teacher/Clergyman	1		1			2		

*These figures reflect the occupations of only those who gave the census taker one, omitting the large number who either did not have regular work or—as in the case of women—may have been prostitutes.

1. Includes seamstress.

Source: Sample of one hundred African American households taken from Population Census of the Inhabitants of Sixth and Eighth Wards in the County of New York, 1855.

TABLE 18
Occupational Distribution By Sex of Individuals in
One Hundred Irish/Irish American Households in NYC, 1855*

Household Type	Nuclear		Extended/ Communal		Single Woman headed		Boarders	
	Male	Female	Male	Female	Male	Female	Male	Female
Occupation								
Laborer	25		8		1		5	
Crafts/Manufacturing[1]	20	3	7	4	1	2	7	7
Grocer	2		2					
Seaman	1		2				1	
Waiter/Butler	4		1				6	
Peddler/Porter/ Coach/Cartman	6		1				1	
Clerk	3						4	
Doctor/Teacher/Priest	1		1					
Domestic Service/Cook		1		1			1	22
Washing		1				1		
Boardinghouse Keeper	1	1						
Other[2]	2						2	

*These figures reflect the occupations of only those household members who gave the census taker one, omitting the large number who either did not have regular work or—as in the case of women—may have been prostitutes.

1 Includes seamstress and printer.

2 Includes policeman, plumber, physician, baker, butcher, brewer, barber, lender, and speculator.

Source: Sample of one hundred Irish/Irish American households taken from Population Census of the Inhabitants of Sixth and Eighth Wards in the County of New York, 1855.

TABLE 19A
African American and Irish/Irish American Population of NYC, 1855

Color/Nationality	Numbers in Population
African American	11,840
Irish	175,735
Non-Irish White (Native-born and Immigrant)	442,329
Total	629,904

Source: Ira Rosenswaike, *Population History of New York* (Syracuse, NY: Syracuse University Press, 1972), 36, 42.

TABLE 19B
Frequency Distribution of Adults Receiving Outdoor Assistance by Color/National Origin in NYC, 1855

Received	Money	Fuel	Total
Color/National Origin			
Native-born White	1,226	2,722	3,948
African American	136	1,540	1,676
Irish	2,953	17,923	20,876
Other*	1,308	3,906	5,214

*Includes mostly non-Irish European immigrants.
Source: Seventh Annual Report of the Governors of the Alms House for the Year 1855.

TABLE 20
Statistics and White Identity Creation I: Facsimile of Penitentiary Hospital Table E, 1855

PENITENTIARY HOSPITAL OFFICE,
January 1, 1856.

STATEMENT OF THE PLACE OF NATIVITY OF EACH PATIENT ADMITTED DURING THE YEAR 1855.

Natives.	White Males.	White Females.	Colored Males.	Colored Females.	Total.	Foreigners.	White Males.	White Females.	Colored Males.	Colored Females.	Total.
Alabama	1	1			2	Canada	9	25	1		35
Carolina, North			1		1	China	1				1
" South	2	2			4	Denmark	1				1
Columbia (District)	1			1	2	England	30	79			109
Connecticut	3	11		1	15	France	4	6			10
Delaware			1	1	2	Germany	75	43			118
Georgia		2			2	Indies, East			1		1
Illinois		1			1	" West	1		1	1	3
Louisiana	1			1	2	Ireland	292	856			1148
Maine	2	9			11	Italy	1				1
Maryland	1	1	1	2	5	Poland	3	1			4
Massachusetts	9	20		4	33	Portugal	1				1
N. Hampshire	4	1			5	Prussia	1	2			3
N. Jersey	6	34	1	4	45	Scotland	11	50			61
New York	168	235	26	26	455	Spain	4				4
Ohio	1	7			8	Switzerland	4				4
Pennsylvania	4	9	6	5	24	Wales	7	2			9
Rhode Island		4		1	5	At Sea	1				2
Vermont	1	2			3	Unascertained	4	12			16
Virginia		1		1	2						
Totals	204	340	36	47	627	Totals	449	1078	3	1	1531

Source: Seventh Annual Report of the Govenors of the Alms House, New York for 1855, 45.

TABLE 21
Statistics and White Identity Creation II: Facsimile of Penitentiary Hospital Table K, 1855.
Statement of the Social Habits of Each Patient Admitted During the Year 1855

	White		Colored				
	Males	Females	Males	Females	Total	Natives	Foreigners
Temperate	72	150	7	3	232	89	143
Moderate Drinkers	206	314	19	18	557	201	356
Intemperate	314	762	12	20	1108	273	835
Habitual Drunkards	55	175	1	7	238	64	174
Unascertained	6	17			23		23
Total	653	1418	39	48	2158	627	1531

Source: Seventh Annual Report of the Govenors of the Alms House, New York for 1855, 45.

TABLE 22
Frequency Distribution of New Yorkers Admitted to
Major Municipal Relief Institutions by Color/National Origin in 1855

Color/National Origin	Native-born White	African American	Irish	Others*
Institution				
Alms House	773		1,949	374
Colored Home/Orphan Asylum		1,163		
Bellevue Hospital	856		4,242	657
Penitentiary Hospital	544	87	1,148	379
Lunatic Asylum	72	8	178	113

* Includes mostly non-Irish European immigrants.

Source: Seventh Annual Report of the Governors of the Alms House for the Year 1855.

TABLE 23
Age Distribution of One Hundred African Americans and One Hundred Irish Applicants for Institutional Relief, Alms House Department, 1848

Color/NationalOrigin	African American		Irish	
Sex	Male	Female	Male	Female
Age in Years				
0–5	1			
6–10	2	2		
11–15	3	2		1
16–20	4	10	6	7
21–25	8	6	12	9
26–30	8	10	7	10
31–35	6	3	4	5
36–40	7	3	7	8
41–45	3	2	7	3
46–50	5	3	1	2
51–55	1	2	1	4
56–60		2		1
61–65	1	1	1	
66–70		1	2	1
Over 70	3	1		1
Total	52	48	48	52

Source: Sample of one hundred African Americans and one hundred Irish from manuscript census of African American and Irish relief-seekers admitted to Colored Home and Alms House by Alms House Department, 1848, New York Municipal Archives.

TABLE 24
Occupation/Marital Status of One Hundred African American and One Hundred Irish Applicants for Institutional Relief, Alms House Department, 1848*

Color/NationalOrigin	African American		Irish	
Sex	Male	Female	Male	Female
Occupation/Marital Status				
Married		9		16
Widow		13		16
Single		23		19
Laborer	39		33	
Waiter	3			
Sailor	1			
Coachman	1			
Artisan/Mason	1		14	
Porter			1	
Other/Unknown	1			

*Note that the Alms House Department identified women by their marital status and men by their occupations—a clear statement of their vision of a social order governed by the "cult of separate spheres"—notwithstanding its inapplicability to the working poor.
 Note too that these figures exclude the children in my sample of one hundred African American and one hundred Irish men and women relief-seekers in 1848.

Source: Sample of one hundred African Americans and one hundred Irish from manuscript census of African American and Irish relief-seekers admitted to Colored Home and Alms House by Alms House Department, 1848, New York Municipal Archives.

TABLE 25
*Admission Causes of One Hundred African American and
One Hundred Irish Applicants for Institutional Relief, Alms House Department, 1848*

Color/NationalOrigin	African American		Irish	
Sex	Male	Female	Male	Female
Admission Cause				
Sickness*	37	32	32	33
Destitution	10	11	10	12
Accidents/Injuries	1		3	
Pregnancy		5		1
Old Age	1			1
"Insanity"	2		1	2
Intemperance			1	2
Vagrancy/Other	1		1	1

*Most common illnesses among African Americans included phthisis and smallpox, and, among the Irish, bronchitis, syphilis, rheumatism, ophthalmia, and ulcers.

Source: Sample of one hundred African Americans and one hundred Irish from manuscript census of African American and Irish relief-seekers admitted to Colored Home and Alms House by Alms House Department, 1848, New York Municipal Archives.

TABLE 26
*Birth Places of One Hundred African American
Applicants for Institutional Relief, Alms House Department, 1848*

Sex	Male	Female
Birth Place		
New York City	15	25
Long Island/Upstate New York	6	6
New Jersey/Pennsylvania	11	6
New England	3	3
Virginia/Maryland/DC	13	6
Kentucky		1
West Indies	2	1
At Sea/Unknown	2	

Source: Sample of one hundred African Americans from manuscript census of African American relief-seekers admitted to Colored Home by Alms House Department, 1848, New York Municipal Archives.

TABLE 27
Statistics and White Identity Creation III: Facsimiles of NYHR Tables I and III, 1860

TABLE I.

Showing the Sources whence were received 468 Children, during the year 1860.

	White Boys.	White Girls.	Colored Boys.	Colored Girls.	Total.
From the New York Police	83	58	5	4	150
" " " Special Sessions	120	16	9	0	145
" Kings Co. " "	25	4	3	0	32
" Rensselaer Co. " "	30	7	0	2	39
" N. Y. Pub. Charities & Cor.	2	0	0	1	3
" Westchester Co. Sessions	4	0	1	0	5
" Queens County "	3	1	0	0	4
" Orange County "	2	0	0	0	2
" Albany County "	15	0	0	0	15
" Erie County "	0	7	0	0	7
" Saratoga County "	•0	1	0	0	1
" Cortlandt Co. "	1	0	0	0	1
" Niagara County "	0	2	0	0	2
" Otsego County "	0	0	0	1	1
" Dutchess County "	1	0	0	0	1
" Onondaga County "	0	1	0	0	1
" Schenectady Co. "	0	1	0	0	1
" Oneida County "	0	0	0	1	1
" Columbia County "	1	0	0	0	1
	287	98	18	9	412
Returned after having been given up to friends or indentured	35	15	5	1	56
Total	322	113	23	10	468

TABLE III.

Showing the Parentage of 412 Children received into the House during the year 1860.

Americans	68
Irish	240
English	22
Germans	39
Scotch	10
French	5
Italian	1
African	27
	412

Source: Thirty-sixth Annual Report of the SRJD for the year 1860, 24, 26.

TABLE 28
Statistics and White Identity Creation IV:
Facsimiles of NYHR Tables II (1890) and III (1900)

TABLE II.—Showing the Parentage of 275 New Inmates Received during the year ending September 30, 1890.

American.	43	Irish.	98
African.	38	Italian.	9
English.	3	Jewish.	14
French.	10	Mixed.	1
German.	56	Scotch	1
Hungarian	1	Swede	1

TABLE III.—Showing the Parentage of 433 children received during the year ending September 30, 1900.

American	96	Irish	47
American, Colored.	45	Italian.	30
Austrian	12	Mixed.	36
Bohemian	6	Mexican	1
Canadian	3	Roumanian	2
English	7	Russian	59
French	4	Scotch	5
German	69	Swedish	2
Hungarian	8	South American	1

Source: Sixty-sixth Annual Report of the SRJD for the year ending September 30, 1890, 18.

TABLE 29
*Parentage of New Admissions to NYHR by National Origin/Color and Sex, 1850–1890**

Color/ National Origin	African American	Irish	Native-born White	Non-Irish White Immigrant	Total
Year Admitted					
1850	30	195	65	63	353
1860	27	240	68	77	412
1870	21	225	70	90	406
1880	36	228	79	204	547
1890	38	98	43	96	275
Total	152	986	325	530	1,993

*These figures do not include those remaining in the institution from the previous year or those returned from indentures or other sources.

Source: Twenty-sixth (1850), Thirty-sixth (1860), Forty-sixth (1870), Fifty-sixth (1880), and Sixty-sixth (1890) Annual Reports of the Managers of the Society for the Reformation of Juvenile Delinquents, Records of the New York House of Refuge, New York State Archives, Albany.

TABLE 30
Proportion of African American Population in NYC and in NYHR, 1850–1890

	African American Population in NYC		African American Population in NYHR	
Year	Number	% African American	Number	% African American
1850	13,815	2.68%	35	7.88%
1860	12,574	1.55%	33	7.05%
1870	13,072	1.39%	31	5.94%
1880	19,663	1.63%	41	6.15%
1890	23,601	1.56%	45	14.61%

Source: Ira Rosenwaike, *Population History of New York City* (Syracuse, NY: Syracuse University Press, 1972), 36, 77; and the Twenty-sixth (1850), Thirty-sixth (1860), Forty-sixth (1870), Fifty-sixth (1880), and Sixty-sixth (1890) Annual Reports of the Managers of the Society for the Reformation of Juvenile Delinquents, Records of the New York House of Refuge, New York State Archives, Albany.

TABLE 31
Distribution of Inmate Population by Color and Sex, NYHR, 1850–1890*

Color	White**		Black	
	Male	Female	Male	Female
Year				
1850	587	139	39	17
1860	773	183	50	17
1870	1,024	178	73	20
1880	1,109	227	79	25
1890	746	73	106	43

*Note that these figures include all inmates, including new admissions and those existing from the previous year for each year.

**Includes all those defined by the NYHR as white—i.e., native-born Euro-Americans—and all European immigrants, including the Irish.

Source: Twenty-sixth (1850), Thirty-sixth (1860), Forty-sixth (1870), Fifty-sixth (1880), and Sixty-sixth (1890) Annual Reports of the Managers of the Society for the Reformation of Juvenile Delinquents, Records of the New York House of Refuge, New York State Archives, Albany.

TABLE 32
Parties Committing African American Children to the NYHR, 1840–1890

Year	1840	1850	1860	1870	1880	1890	Total
Party							
Mother	3	4	3	2	3	4	19
Father	4	2		1		3	10
Other Kin	1	4	2	3	4	2	16
Public Authorities	16	16	19	12	11	8	82
Other Private Institutions		2	1	3			6
Other/Unknown	1			1			2

Source: Sample of 135 case histories of African American children received by NYHR, 1840–1890.

TABLE 33
Reasons for Commitment of African American Children to NYHR by Kin and Non-Kin, 1840–1890

Year	1840		1850		1860		1870		1880		1890		Total	
Party	K	NK	K	NK	K	NK	K	NK	K	NK	K	NK	K	NK
Reason														
Vagrancy/Disorderly Conduct	8	9	9	5	4	5	7	7	7	4	8	4	43	34
Arson		1		1										2
Larceny		7	1	12	1	15		8		7	1	4	3	53
Total	8	17	10	18	5	20	7	15	7	11	9	8	46	89

Note: K (kin) includes surrogate kin; NK (non-kin) includes public authorities and private institutions.
Source: Sample of 135 case histories of African American children received by NYHR, 1840–1890.

TABLE 34
Parties Committing White Children to NYHR, 1850–1890

Year	1850		1860		1870		1880		1890	
Sex	B	G	B	G	B	G	B	G	B	G
Party										
Mother	5		3	1	3	3	6	1	1	
Father	1	2	3	3	3		6	4	1	2
Other Kin		2	1	1	2		1	2		
Public Authorities	23	3	20	6	27	4	32	3	20	1
Other Private Institutions				1						
Other/Unknown			3							

Source: Sample of two hundred case histories of European and Euro-American children received by NYHR, 1850–1890.

TABLE 35
Reasons for Commitment of White Children to NYHR, 1850–1890

Year	1850						1860						1870						1880						1890					
National Origin	I		O		A		I		O		A		I		O		A		I		O		A		I		O		A	
Sex	b	g	b	g	b	g	b	g	b	g	b	g	b	g	b	g	b	g	b	g	b	g	b	g	b	g	b	g	b	g
Cause																														
Vagrancy/Disorderly Conduct	8	3	1			1	5	5	3		2	2	6	1	4	2	2	1	9	4	10	3	3	1	2	1	1	1	2	1
Larceny	9	2	5	1	6	1	14		2		2	3	15	3	3		5	1	11	1	8	1	4		7		7		2	2
Assault/Poisoning															1															
Rape								1					1														1	1		
Arson											1																			

Key: I= Irish, O=Other European immigrants, A=Native-born White Americans, b=boy, g=girl.
Source: Sample of two hundred case histories of Euro-American and European immigrant children received by the NYHR, 1850–1890.

TABLE 36
Number and Relationship of Parents of African American Children Received by NYHR, 1840–1890

Year	1840	1850	1860	1870	1880	1890	Total
Family							
Both Natural	10	9	7	7	5	4	42
Father/Stepmother	1	1			2	3	7
Mother/Stepfather	1		2	3	2		8
Mother Only	3	8	6	3	6	4	30
Father Only	1	4	1	2	3	1	12
Parents Dead/Unknown	9	6	9	7	2	3	36
Total	25	28	25	22	18	17	135

Note: The presence of two parents did not mean that they were married or were living together in every case, or that the child lived with them. For instance, seafaring fathers sailed for many months of the year, while mothers in domestic service often boarded with employers.
Source: Sample of 135 case histories of African American children received by NYHR, 1840–1890.

TABLE 37
Proportion of African American Children Living with Non-parent or Surrogate Kin

Year	1840	1850	1860	1870	1880	1890	Total
Total Number	25	28	25	22	18	17	135
Number in Foster Care	6	8	10	6	6	4	40
Percent in Foster Care	24.0%	28.6%	40.0%	27.3%	33.3%	23.5%	29.6%

Source: Sample of 135 case histories of African American children received by NYHR, 1840–1890.

TABLE 38
Birthplaces of African American Children Received by NYHR, 1840–1890

Year	1840	1850	1860	1870	1880	1890	Total
Place							
New York	11	14	13	4	11	2	55
Brooklyn	1		2	2		5	10
New York State[1]	4	7	4	11	1	7	34
New Jersey[2]	3	1	1	1		1	7
Connecticut[3]	2		1				3
Pennsylvania[4]	1	2		2			5
New England[5]			2				2
Upper South[6]	1	1	1		1		4
Lower South[7]				1	1	1	3
West Indies		1			2	1	4
Not Known	2	2	1	1	2		8
Total	25	28	25	22	18	17	135

1. Excludes Manhattan and Brooklyn. Includes the counties of Albany, Broome, Dutchess, Erie, Greene, Orange, Rensselaer, Suffolk, Ulster, and Westchester.
2. Includes towns of Brunswick, Fort Lee, Morristown, Newark, New Bedford.
3. Includes New Haven.
4. Includes Philadelphia and Pittsburgh.
5. Includes Massachusetts and Maine.
6. Includes Maryland and Virginia.
7. Includes North Carolina and Florida.
Source: Sample of 135 case histories of African American children received by NYHR, 1840–1890.

TABLE 39
Occupations of Female Guardians of African American Children at NYHR, 1840-1890

Year / Occupation	1840	1850	1860	1870	1880	1890	Total
Domestic Service	1	2	2	1	3		9
Laundress	3		4	2	2	6	17
Waitress				1			1
Steamboat cook/ Chambermaid		1					1
Boardinghouse Keeper/Cook					1	1	2
Homemaker					1	3	4
Dressmaker					1		1
"Root Doctress"			1				1
Brothel Keeper					1		1
Peddler			1				1
Total							38

Note: These figures reflect the occupations of the female guardians of only about 28 percent of the 135 children constituting the sample for the table, for the reason that several of the children were orphans or had lost touch with their kin. Moreover, this occupational profile is more representative of single and widowed female guardians than of women with male partners. The case studies frequently neglected to mention the occupations of mothers when men were part of the family, reflecting the reformers' assumption that men were the primary breadwinners.

Source: Sample of 135 case histories of African American children received by NYHR, 1840-1890.

TABLE 40
Occupations of Female Guardians of White Children at NYHR, 1850-1890

Year / Occupation	1850	1860	1870	1880	1890
Homemaker		1		12	10
Laundress	2	3	6	5	3
Seamstress	2		2	2	1
Day Laborer		1	1	1	
Domestic Servant		1		1	
Nurse	1	1			
Factory Worker[1]	1	1		2	
Other[2]	2	1		1	2

1. Includes factories making umbrellas, cigars, and shoes.

2. Includes vendor, rag cutter, store help, janitor, grocer, and boardinghouse keeper.

Source: Sample of two hundred case histories of Euro-American and European immigrant children received by the NYHR, 1850-1890.

TABLE 41
Occupations of Male Guardians of African American Children at NYHR, 1840–1890

Year / Occupation	1840	1850	1860	1870	1880	1890	Total
Seafarer	4	1	4	1	2		12
Farm Worker		2	1	2	3		8
Groom/Coachman	1				2	1	4
Gardner				1	1	1	3
Porter				1		2	3
Laborer	1				1	1	3
Carpenter			1		1	1	3
Waiter	1					1	2
Minister	2						2
Longshoreman	1	1					2
Wood Sawyer	1	1					2
Printing Office Laborer				1	1		2
Whitewasher			1	1			2
Other*	5	1	4	2		2	14
Total	16	6	11	8	12	9	62

*Includes one of each of the following: distillery worker, grain measurer, bootblack, factory worker, cart driver, bell foundry worker, truck driver, barber, janitor, store employee, lobster-stand keeper, peddler, fisherman, and sewage cleaner.

Note: The occupations of the remaining male guardians in the sample were unknown. A few fathers were dead, ailing from consumption, unemployed, or imprisoned.

Source: Sample of 135 case histories of African American children received by the NYHR, 1840–1890.

TABLE 42
Occupations of Male Guardians of White Children at NYHR, 1850–1890

Year / Occupation	1850	1860	1870	1880	1890
Crafts	9	4	5	14	4
Factory Worker[1]		1	4	4	5
Laborer	8	6	4	6	3
Porter/Coachman/Cartman	1	1	2	1	1
Longshoreman	2	2	4	2	
Mason/Building Trades	2	4	3	3	2
Peddler[2]	1	1		5	3
Salesman/Auctioneer		2	1	1	2
Butcher/Baker	2		3		
Grocer/Liquor Store		1		1	1
Professional[3]		2			1
Other[4]	1	5	2	5	1
Total	26	29	28	42	23

1. Includes factories making dye, paper, machine goods, tin, sugar, cigar, boxes, and glassblowing, as well as iron and brass foundries.
2. Includes junk dealers, and fruit, vegetable, ice cream, and flower vendors.
3. Includes engineers and priests.
4. Includes printers, waiters, barbers, locksmiths, painters, boardinghouse and bar keepers, soldiers, firemen, customs officers, and farmers.

Source: Sample of two hundred case histories of Euro-American and European immigrant children received by the NYHR, 1850–1890.

TABLE 43
Occupations of African American Female Inmates of NYHR, 1840–1890

Year	1840	1850	1860	1870	1880	1890
Occupation						
Domestic Service	4	2	2	6		2
Tobacco Factory				1		
Other/Unknown	4	6	5	3	2	3

Source: Sample of 135 case histories of African American children received by the NYHR, 1840–1890.

TABLE 44
Occupations of White Female Inmates of NYHR, 1850–1890

Year	1850	1860	1870	1880	1890
Occupation					
Domestic Service	3	5		2	
Seamstress		2			
Factory Worker[1]	1			1	1
Housework at Home		1		1	
Waitress					1

1. Includes factories making tobacco, paper boxes, and artificial flowers.

Source: Sample of two hundred case histories of Euro-American and European immigrant children received by the NYHR, 1850–1890.

TABLE 45
Occupations of African American Male Inmates of NYHR, 1840–1890

Year	1840	1850	1860	1870	1880	1890
Occupation						
Farm Worker	1	3	1	4		1
Domestic Servant	1	5	1	1		
Cabin Boy	2		2	2		
Stable Boy	1		1		1	2
Dock/Canal Worker	1		2			
Butcher Boy	1	1				
Bootblack				1	1	
Whitewasher				2		
Errand Boy	1					1
Other/Unknown*	10	10	8	5	14	8

*Includes one of each: chimney sweep, fish market worker, oyster saloon worker, waiter, sign painter, rope factory laborer, and cement works laborer. The remaining listed no occupation.

Source: Sample of 135 case histories of African American children at NYHR, 1840–1890.

TABLE 46
Occupations of White Male Inmates of NYHR, 1850–1890

Year / Occupation	1850	1860	1870	1880	1890
Craft Apprentice	4	3	3	5	
Factory Worker	3	8	9	3	5
Errand Boy	2	3		1	2
Farm Boy	2	2	2		1
Construction	1	2			
Theater		1			1
Peddler	3		2		1
Dry Goods	2		1	1	3
Newsboy			2	2	1
Butcher/Fish Market	2			1	1
Other*	2	1	5	8	2

*Includes work with cartmen, oyster men, barbers, workers at the docks, brickyards, fish markets, drug stores, bakeries, junk shops, telegraph offices, and billiards rooms.

Source: Sample of two hundred case histories of Euro-American and European immigrant children received by the NYHR, 1850–1890.

TABLE 47A
Disposition of African American Children by NYHR, 1840–1890

Year	1840		1850		1860		1870		1880		1890		Total	
Disposition	G	B	G	B	G	B	G	B	G	B	G	B	G	B
Indentured	7	16	8	19	2	8	5	4	2	7	1	3	25	57
Discharged Relatives					3	4	4	5		9	4	8	11	26
Discharged Institutions			1			4	1	2					2	6
Died					1	1	1						2	1
Other	1	1				1						1	2	1
Total	8	17	9	19	7	18	10	12	2	16	5	12	41	94

TABLE 47B
Success Rate of Indentures of African American Children by Sex

Year	1840		1850		1860		1870		1880		1890		Total	
	G	B	G	B	G	B	G	B	G	B	G	B	G	B
Success	3	3	6	7		1			2	5	1		12	16
Failure	2	5	1	12		7	4	4		1		3	7	32
Unknown	2	8	1		2		1			1			6	9
Total	7	16	8	19	2	8	5	4	2	7	1	3	25	57

Key: G: Girl; B: Boy.
Source: Sample of 135 case histories of African American children received by NYHR, 1840–1890.

Notes

INTRODUCTION

1. Heather Macdonald, "The Real Welfare Problem is Illegitimacy," *City Journal* (Winter 1998), http://city-journal.org.
2. In general, I use the term *welfare* to include white and black benevolent associations as well as public institutions of relief and reform, because (as I explain in greater detail later) work on black voluntarism has muddied the conceptual and chronological boundaries between private benevolence on the one hand, and government-run social welfare (thought to be statist/professionalized/post-1890s) on the other. As historians have pointed out, African Americans, facing racial discrimination in the formulation and distribution of government-sponsored benefits, both before and after the advent of a national welfare state, strove to take care of their own by establishing voluntary associations dating back to colonial times. On the definition and periodization of welfare history, see: Linda Gordon, "Black and White Visions of Welfare: Women's Welfare Activism, 1890–1945," *The Journal of American History* 78 (September 1991), 559–90; Clarke A. Chambers, "Toward a Redefinition of Welfare History," *The Journal of American History* 73 (September 1986), 407–33; Nancy Fraser and Linda Gordon, "A Genealogy of Dependency: Tracing a Keyword of the U.S. Welfare State," *Signs* 19 (1994), 309–36; and the essays in Michael B. Katz, ed., *The "Underclass" Debate: Views from History* (Princeton, NJ: Princeton University Press, 1993).

On the suspicion of welfare in contemporary America, see Martin Gilens, *Why Americans Hate Welfare: Race, Media, and the Politics of Anti-Poverty Policy* (Chicago: University of Chicago Press, 1999). Ann L. Schneider and Helen M. Ingram explore the social construction of "deservedness" in *Deserving and Entitled: Social Constructions and Public Policy* (Albany: State University of New York Press, 2005). On this point, see also Michael B. Katz, *The Undeserving Poor: From the War on Poverty to the War on Welfare* (New York: Pantheon, 1989). Works that focus on the relationship between race and social welfare/welfare reform in the twentieth century include: Deborah E. Ward, *The White Welfare State: The Racialization of United States Welfare Policy* (Ann Arbor: University of Michigan Press, 2005); Robert C. Lieberman, *Shaping Race Policy: The United States in Comparative Perspective* (Princeton, NJ: Princeton University Press, 2005) and

Shifting the Color Line: Race and the American Welfare State (Cambridge, MA: Harvard University Press, 1998); C. Michael Henry, ed., *Race, Poverty, and Domestic Policy* (New Haven, CT: Yale University Press, 2004); Sanford F. Schram, Joe Soss, and Richard C. Fording, *Race and the Politics of Welfare Reform* (Ann Arbor: University of Michigan Press, 2003); Linda Faye Williams, *The Constraint of Race: Legacies of White Skin Privilege in America* (University Park: Penn State University Press, 2003); John P. Bartkowski and Helen A. Regis, *Charitable Choices: Religion, Race, and Poverty in the Post-welfare Era* (New York: New York University Press, 2003); Kenneth J. Neubeck and Noel A. Cazenave, *Welfare Racism: Playing the Race Card Against America's Poor* (New York: Routledge, 2001); Elijah Anderson and Tukufu Zuberi, *The Study of African American Problems: W. E. B. Du Bois's Agenda, Then and Now* (Thousand Oaks, CA: Sage, 2000); Adolph Reed Jr., ed., *Without Justice for All: The New Liberalism and Our Retreat from Racial Equality* (Boulder, CO: Westview, 1999); Michael K. Brown, *Race, Money, and the American Welfare State* (Ithaca, NY: Cornell University Press, 1999); Susan L. Thomas, "Race, Gender, and Welfare Reform: The Antinatalist Response," *Journal of Black Studies* 28 (March 1998), 419–46; Jill Quadagno, *The Color of Welfare: How Racism Undermined the War on Poverty* (New York: Oxford University Press, 1994); Christopher Jencks, *Rethinking Social Policy: Race, Poverty, and the Underclass* (Cambridge, MA: Harvard University Press, 1992); Herbert Gans, *People, Plans, and Policies: Essays on Poverty, Racism, and Other National Problems* (New York: Columbia University Press, 1991).

On single mothers and social welfare, see: Linda Gordon, *Pitied But Not Entitled: Single Mothers and the History of Welfare, 1890–1935* (Cambridge, MA: Harvard University Press, 1994); Regina Kunzel, *Fallen Women, Problem Girls: Unmarried Mothers and the Professionalization of Social Work, 1890–1945* (New Haven, CT: Yale University Press, 1993); Marion J. Morton, *And Sin No More: Social Policy and Unwed Mothers in Cleveland, 1855–1990* (Columbus: Ohio State University Press, 1993).

The literature on poverty and social welfare set at least partly in the nineteenth century is voluminous. What follows is a tiny sample of this work: Lori D. Ginzberg, *Women and the Work of Benevolence: Morality, Politics, and Class in the Nineteenth-century United States* (New Haven, CT: Yale University Press, 1990); Michael B. Katz, *In the Shadow of the Poorhouse: A Social History of Welfare in America* (New York: Basic, 1986) and *Improving Poor People: The Welfare State, the "Underclass," and Urban Schools as History* (Princeton, NJ: Princeton University Press, 1995); Kenneth L. Kusmer, *Down and Out, on the Road: The Homeless in American History* (New York: Oxford University Press, 2003); Jacqueline Jones, *The Dispossessed: America's Underclasses from the Civil War to the Present* (New York: Basic, 1992); Marilyn Wood Hill, *Their Sisters' Keepers: Prostitution in New York City, 1830–1870* (Berkeley and Los Angeles: University of California Press, 1993); David M. Schneider and Albert Deutsch, *The History of Public Welfare* in New York State, 1867–1940 (Chicago: University of Chicago Press, 1941); Paul Boyer, *Urban Masses and Moral Order in America, 1820–1920* (Cambridge, MA: Harvard University Press, 1968); Raymond A. Mohl, *Poverty in New York, 1783–1825* (New York: Oxford University Press, 1971); David J. Rothman, *The Almshouse Experience: Collected Reports* (New York: Arno, 1971); Stephen Thernstrom, *The Other Bostonians: Poverty and Progress in the American Metropolis, 1880–1960* (Cambridge, MA: Harvard University Press, 1973); Walter I. Trattner, *From Poor Law to Welfare State: A History of Social Welfare in America* (New York: Free Press, 1974) and *Social Welfare or Social Control? Some Historical Reflections on Regulating the Poor* (Knoxville: University of Tennessee Press, 1983); Thomas Bender, *Toward an Urban Vision: Ideas and Institutions in Nineteenth-century America* (Lexington: University of Kentucky Press, 1975); Eric Monkkonen, *The Dangerous Class: Crime and Poverty in Columbus, Ohio, 1860–1885* (Cambridge, MA: Harvard University Press, 1975) and *Walking to Work: Tramps in America, 1790–1935* (Lincoln: University of Nebraska Press, 1984); Leroy Ashby, *Saving the Waifs: Reformers and Dependent Children, 1890–1917* (Philadelphia: Temple University Press, 1984); Susan Grigg, *The Dependent Poor of Newburyport: Studies in Social History, 1800–1830* (Ann Arbor: University of Michigan Press, 1984); Frank R. Breul and Steven J. Diner, eds., *Compassion and Responsibility: Readings in the History of Social Welfare Policy in the United States* (Chicago: University of Chicago Press, 1980); Mimi Abramovitz, *Regulating the Lives of Women: Social Welfare Policy from Colonial Times to the Present* (Boston: South End Press, 1988); Kathleen D. McCarthy, ed., *Lady Bountiful Revisited: Women, Philanthropy, and Power* (New Brunswick, NJ: Rutgers University Press, 1990); Joel Handler and Yeheskel Hasenfeld, *The Moral Construction of Poverty: Welfare Reform in America* (Newbury Park, CA: Sage, 1991); Ruth Hutchinson Crocker, *Social Work and Social Order: The Settlement Movement in Two Industrial Cities, 1889–1930* (Urbana: University of Illinois Press, 1992); Timothy A. Hacsi, *Second Home: Orphan Asylums and Poor Families in America* (Cambridge, MA: Harvard University Press, 1997); Ruta J. Wilk, ed., "Annual Bibliography of Scholarship in Social Welfare History," *Social Welfare History Group* 93 (December 1997), 1–82.

Works on poverty, welfare, and welfare reform that focus on the twentieth century include: Jennifer Mittelstadt, *From Welfare to Workfare: The Unintended Consequences of Liberal Reform, 1945–1965* (Chapel Hill: University of North Carolina Press, 2005); Joel Bleu and Mimi Abramovitz, *The Dynamics of Social Welfare* (New York: Oxford University Press, 2004); Stephen Pimpare, *The New Victorians: Poverty, Politics, and Propaganda in the Two Gilded Ages* (New York: New Press, 2004); John Iceland, *Poverty in America: A Handbook* (Berkeley and Los Angeles: University of California Press, 2003); John M. Herrick and Paul H. Stewart, *Encyclopedia of Social Welfare in North America* (Thousand Oaks, CA: Sage, 2005); Emilie Stoltzfus, *Citizen, Mother, Worker: Debating Public Responsibility for Childcare After the Second World War* (Chapel Hill: University of North

Carolina Press, 2003); Randy Albelda and Ann Withorn, eds., *Lost Ground: Welfare Reform, Poverty, and Beyond* (Cambridge, MA: South End Press, 2002); Judith Goode and Jeff Maskovsky, *New Poverty Studies: The Ethnography of Power, Politics, and Impoverished People in the United States* (New York: New York University Press, 2001); James T. Patterson, *America's Struggle Against Poverty in the Twentieth Century* (Cambridge, MA: Harvard University Press, 2000); Madonna Harrington Meyer, ed., *Care Work: Gender, Labor, and Welfare States* (New York: Routledge, 2000); Elizabeth Bussiere, *(Dis)Entitling the Poor: The Warren Court, Welfare Rights, and the American Political Tradition* (University Park: Penn State University Press, 1997); Robert Halpern, *Rebuilding the Inner City: A History of Neighborhood Initiatives to Address Poverty in the United States* (New York: Columbia University Press, 1995); George J. Demko and Michael C. Jackson, *Populations at Risk in America: Vulnerable Groups at the End of the Twentieth Century* (Boulder, CO: Westview, 1995); Nancy E. Rose, *Workfare or Fair Work: Women, Welfare, and Government Work Programs* (New Brunswick, NJ: Rutgers University Press, 1995); Francis Fox Piven and Richard Cloward, *Regulating the Poor: The Functions of Public Welfare* (New York: Pantheon, 1971); Beverly Stadum, *Poor Women and Their Families: Hard Working Charity Cases, 1900–1930* (Albany: State University Press, 1992); Ruth Crocker, *Social Work and Social Order* (Urbana: University of Illinois Press, 1992).

On maternalism and the welfare state, see: papers on the topic "Maternalism as a Paradigm" prepared for the 1992 Social Science History Association meeting and published in *The Journal of Women's History* 5 (Fall 1993), 95–131; Sonya Michel and Seth Kovan, eds., *Mothers of a New World: Maternalist Politics and the Origins of Welfare States* (New York: Routledge, 1993) and "Womanly Duties: Maternalist Politics and the Origins of the Welfare State in France, Great Britain, and the United States, 1880–1920," *American Historical Review* 95 (October 1990), 1076–1108; Theda Skocpol, *Protecting Soldiers and Mothers: The Political Origins of Social Policy in the United States* (Cambridge, MA: Belknap Press of Harvard University Press, 1992); Susan Pedersen, *Family, Dependence, and the Origins of the Welfare State: Britain and France, 1914–1945* (New York: Cambridge University Press, 1993); Linda Gordon, ed., *Women, the State, and Welfare* (Madison: University of Wisconsin Press, 1990); Molly Ladd-Taylor, *Mother-Work: Women, Child Welfare, and the State, 1890–1930* (Urbana: University of Illinois Press, 1994); Gwendolyn Mink, *The Wages of Motherhood: Inequality in the Welfare State, 1917–1942* (Ithaca, NY: Cornell University Press, 1995); Joanne Goodwin, *Gender and the Politics of Welfare Reform: Mothers' Pensions in Chicago, 1911–1929* (Chicago: University of Chicago Press, 1997); Walter W. Powell and Elisabeth S. Clemens, eds., *Private Action and Public Good* (New Haven, CT: Yale University Press, 1998).

On benevolence in the South, see: Christine Jacobson Carter, *Southern Single Blessedness: Unmarried Women in the Urban South, 1800–1865* (Urbana: University of Illinois Press, 2006); Barbara L. Bellows, *Benevolence Among Slaveholders:*

Assisting the Poor in Charleston, 1670–1860 (Baton Rouge: Louisiana State University Press, 1993); Daniel Levine, "A Single Standard of Civilization: Black Private Social Welfare Institutions in the South, 1880s–1920s," *Georgia Historical Quarterly* 81 (Spring 1997), 52–77; Susan L. Smith, "Welfare for Black Mothers and Children: Health and Home in the American South," *Social Politics* 4 (Spring 1997), 49–64.

3. Thelma Wills Foote, *Black and White Manhattan: The History of Racial Formation in Colonial New York City* (New York: Oxford University Press, 2004), 52–158. Edmund S. Morgan made the classic case for the correlation between black slavery and white freedom in the context of colonial Virginia in *American Slavery, American Freedom: The Ordeal of Colonial Virginia* (New York: Norton, 1975). On the origins of slavery in national perspective, see Ira Berlin, *Many Thousands Gone: The First Two Centuries of Slavery in North America* (Cambridge, MA: Belknap Press of Harvard University Press, 1998), and for New York, see Ira Berlin and Leslie Harris, eds., *Slavery in New York* (New York: New Press, 2005).

My thinking on the relationship among slavery, blackness constructs, and nation has been shaped by the different perspectives offered by the following works: Barbara Fields, "Slavery, Race, and Ideology in the United States," *New Left Review* 181 (May–June 1990), 95–118; Nell Irvin Painter, "Of Lily, Linda Brent, and Freud: A Non-Exceptionalist Approach to Race, Class, and Gender in the Slave South," *Georgia Historical Quarterly* 86 (Summer 1992), 241–259; David Brion Davis, "Constructing Race: A Reflection," *William and Mary Quarterly*, 3rd ser., 54, no. 1 (January 1997), 7–18; Evelyn Brooks Higginbotham, "African American Women's History and the Meta-language of Race," *Signs* 17 (Winter 1992), 251–74; George M. Frederickson, *The Black Image in the White Mind: The Debate on the Afro-American Character and Destiny* (New York: Harper and Row, 1971). The following works have also shaped my understanding of blackness constructs and nationhood: Thomas Holt, "Marking: Race, Race-making, and the Writing of History," *American Historical Review* 100 (February 1995), 1–28; Kenan Malik, *The Meaning of Race: Race, History, and Culture in Western Society* (Basingstoke, UK: Macmillan, 1996); Derrick Bell, *Faces at the Bottom of the Well: The Permanence of Racism* (New York: Basic, 1992); Dominick La Capra, ed., *The Bounds of Race: Perspectives of Hegemony and Resistance* (Ithaca, NY: Cornell University Press, 1991); Etienne Balibar and Immanuel Wallerstein, eds., *Race, Nation, and Class: Ambiguous Identities* (London: Verso, 1991); Benedict Anderson, *Imagined Communities: Reflections on the Origin and Spread of Nationalism* (London: Verso, 1983); Pierre L. Van den Berghe, *Race and Ethnicity: Essays in Comparative Sociology* (New York: Basic, 1970); Thomas F. Gossett, ed., *Race: The History of an Idea in America* (New York: Oxford University Press, 1997).

4. On the racial meaning of republicanism, see Matthew Frye Jacobson, *Whiteness of a Different Color: European Immigrants and the Alchemy of Race*

(Cambridge, MA: Harvard University Press, 1998), 25– 26. On republican thought, see also: Sean Wilentz, *Chants Democratic: New York City and the Rise of the American Working Class, 1788–1850* (New York: Oxford University Press, 1984), 14; J. G. A. Pocock, *The Machiavellian Moment: Florentine Political Thought and the Atlantic Republican Tradition* (Princeton, NJ: Princeton University Press, 1975); Gordon S. Wood, *The Creation of the American Republic, 1776–1787* (Chapel Hill: University of North Carolina Press, 1969); Daniel T. Rodgers, "Republicanism: The Career of a Concept," *Journal of American History* 79 (June 1992), 11–38. For the gendered meaning of republicanism, see Stephanie McCurry, "The Two Faces of Republicanism: Gender and Proslavery Politics in Antebellum South Carolina," *Journal of American History* 78 (March 1992), 1245–64. On modern manifestations of the connection between ideas of republicanism and dependency, see Alan F. Zundel, *Declarations of Dependency: The Civic Republican Tradition in U.S. Poverty Policy* (Albany: State University of New York Press, 2000).

5. Dana D. Nelson, *National Manhood: Capitalist Citizenship and the Imagined Fraternity of White Men* (Durham, NC: Duke University Press, 1998), 6. On whiteness's qualities of "normativeness" and "structured invisibility," see Ruth Frankenberg, *White Women, Race Matters: The Social Construction of Whiteness* (Minneapolis: University of Minnesota Press, 1993), 6. I also owe my understanding of whiteness to: David R. Roediger, *The Wages of Whiteness: Race and the Making of the American Working Class* (London: Verso, 1991), *Towards the Abolition of Whiteness* (London: Verso, 1994), and *Colored White: Transcending the Racial Past* (Berkeley and Los Angeles: University of California Press, 2003); Jacobson, *Whiteness of a Different Color*; Noel Ignatiev, *How the Irish Became White* (New York: Routledge, 1995); Grace Elizabeth Hale, *Making Whiteness: The Culture of Segregation in the South, 1890–1940* (New York: Pantheon, 1998); and Ronald Takaki, *Iron Cages: Race and Culture in Nineteenth-century America*, rev. ed. (New York: Oxford University Press, 2000). On the relationship between whiteness and various forms of popular culture, see: Linda Frost, *Never One Nation: Freaks, Savages, and Whiteness in U.S. Popular Culture, 1850–1877* (Minneapolis: University of Minnesota Press, 2005); Eric Lott, *Love and Theft: Blackface Minstrelsy and the American Working Class* (New York: Oxford University Press, 1993); Michael Rogin, *Blackface, White Noise: Jewish Immigrants in the Hollywood Melting Pot* (Berkeley and Los Angeles: University of California Press, 1996); Daniel Bernardi, ed., *The Birth of Whiteness: Race and the Emergence of U.S. Cinema* (New Brunswick, NJ: Rutgers University Press, 1996); Jesse Algeron Rhines, *Black Film/White Money* (New Brunswick, NJ: Rutgers University Press, 1996); Susan Gubar, *Racechanges: White Skin, Black Face in American Culture* (New York: Oxford University Press, 1997). On gender and whiteness, see Michael Moon and Cathy N. Davidson, eds., *Subjects and Citizens: Nation, Race, and Gender from Oroonoko to Anita Hill* (Durham, NC: Duke University Press, 1995);

Angela Woollacott, "'All This Is the Empire, I Told Myself': Australian Women's Voyages 'Home' and the Articulation of Colonial Whiteness," *American Historical Review* 102 (October 1997), 1003–29. See also Mike Hill, ed., *Whiteness: A Critical Reader* (New York: New York University Press, 1997); John Hartigan Jr., *Racial Situations: Class Predicaments of Whiteness in Detroit* (Princeton, NJ: Princeton University Press, 1999); Alexander Saxton, *The Rise and Fall of the White Republic: Class Politics and Mass Culture in Nineteenth-century America* (London: Verso, 1990); Theodore W. Allen, *The Invention of the White Race: Racial Oppression and Social Control*, vol. 1 (London: Verso, 1994); Matt Wray and Annalee Newitz, eds., *White Trash: Race and Class in America* (New York: Routledge, 1997); Saidiya Hartman, *Scenes of Subjection: Terror, Slavery, and Self-making in Nineteenth-century America* (New York: Oxford University Press, 1997); Ian F. Haney-Lopez, *White by Law: The Legal Construction of Race* (New York: New York University Press, 1996). For an evaluation of whiteness studies, see Peter Kolchin, "Whiteness Studies: The New History of Race in America," *Journal of American History* 89 (June 2002), 154–73.

Please note that I do not place the terms *white*, *black*, or *white republic* within quotation marks within the text of this work except in the context of explicit discussions of racial formation. I do, however, assume that these concepts, and the language used to convey them, developed historically.

6. Mary W. Thompson, *Broken Gloom: Sketches of the History, Character, and Dying Testimony of the Beneficiaries of the Colored Home in the City of New York* (New York: John F. Trow, 1851), 68–70. Peter Linebaugh and Marcus Rediker's *The Many-headed Hydra: Sailors, Slaves, Commoners, and the Hidden History of the Revolutionary Atlantic* (Boston: Beacon, 2000) provides an excellent context for understanding Bense's Atlantic world.

7. Immigrant population figures between 1820 and 1860 are taken from Robert Ernst, *Immigrant Life in New York City, 1825–1863* (1949; repr., New York: Octagon, 1979), 187.

8. Descriptions of New York's harbor occur in Charles Dickens, *American Notes*, reproduced in Edward S. Martin, *The Wayfarer in New York* (New York: Macmillan, 1909), 39. See also Edwin Burrows and Mike Wallace, *Gotham: A History of New York City to 1898* (New York: Oxford University Press, 1999). On the literary genre of non-fictional urban sensationalism, see the "Introduction" by Stuart M. Blumin to George C. Foster, *New York by Gas-light and Other Urban Sketches*, ed. Blumin (Berkeley and Los Angeles: University of California Press, 1990) and Blumin, "Explaining the New Metropolis: Perception, Depiction, and Analysis in Mid-nineteenth-century New York City," *Journal of Urban History* 11 (November 1984), 9–38. Works that shed light on New York slavery, slave resistance, and the work and community lives of antebellum black New Yorkers include: Walter C. Rucker, *The River Flows On: Black Resistance, Culture, and Identity Formation in Early America* (Baton Rouge: Louisiana State University

Press, 2006); Berlin and Harris, eds., *Slavery in New York*; Berlin, *Many Thousands Gone*; Leslie Harris, *In the Shadow of Slavery: African Americans in New York City, 1626–1863* (Chicago: University of Chicago Press, 2003); Jill Lepore, *New York Burning: Liberty, Slavery, and Conspiracy in Eighteenth-century Manhattan* (New York: Knopf, 2005); Craig Steven Wilder, *In the Company of Black Men: The African Influence on African American Culture in New York City* (New York: New York University Press, 2001) and *Covenant with Color: Race and Social Power in Brooklyn, 1636–1990* (New York: Columbia University Press, 2000); Tyler Anbinder, *Five Points: The 19th-century Neighborhood That Invented Tap Dance, Stole Elections, and Became the World's Most Notorious Slum* (New York: Free Press, 2001); Shane White and Graham White, *The Sounds of Slavery! Discovering African American History Through Songs, Sermons, and Speech* (Boston: Beacon, 2005); Shane White, "'It Was a Proud Day': African Americans, Festivals, and Parades in the North, 1741–1834," *Journal of American History* 81 (June 1994), 3–50 and *Somewhat More Independent: The End of Slavery in New York City, 1770–1810* (Athens: University of Georgia Press, 1991); Peter Hoffer, *The Great New York Conspiracy of 1741: Slavery, Crime, and Colonial Law* (Lawrence: University Press of Kansas, 2003); Graham Russell Hodges, *Root and Branch: African Americans in New York and East Jersey, 1613–1863* (Chapel Hill: University of North Carolina Press, 1999); James Oliver Horton and Lois E. Horton, *In Hope of Liberty: Culture, Community, and Protest Among Northern Blacks, 1700–1860* (New York: Oxford University Press, 1997); William Jeffrey Bolster, *Black Jacks: African American Seamen in the Age of Sail* (Cambridge, MA: Harvard University Press, 1997); Nell Irvin Painter, *Sojourner Truth: A Life, A Symbol* (New York: Norton, 1996); A. J. Williams-Myers, "The Plight of African Americans in Antebellum New York City," *Afro-Americans in New York Life and History* [hereafter *AANYLH*] 22 (July 1998), 74–75; Rhoda Golden Freeman, *The Free Negro in New York City in the Era Before the Civil War* (New York: Garland, 1994); Paul Gilje, "'Sweep O! Sweep O!': African American Chimney Sweeps and Citizenship in the New Nation," *William and Mary Quarterly*, 3rd ser., 51 (1994), 507–19; George Walker, *The Afro-American in New York City, 1827–1860* (New York: Garland, 1993); Richard Stott, *Workers in the Metropolis: Class, Ethnicity, and Youth in Antebellum New York City* (Ithaca, NY: Cornell University Press, 1990); Thomas J. Davis, *A Rumor of Revolt: The "Great Negro Plot" in Colonial New York* (New York: Free Press, 1985); K. H. Strange, *The Climbing Boys: A Study of Sweeps' Apprentices, 1773–1875* (London: Allison and Busby, 1982); Carlton Mabee, *Black Education in New York State from Colonial to Modern Times* (Syracuse, NY: Syracuse University Press, 1979); Herbert Gutman, *The Black Family in Slavery and Freedom, 1750–1925* (New York: Pantheon, 1976); Edgar J. McManus, *A History of Negro Slavery in New York* (Syracuse, NY: Syracuse University Press, 1966).

On children's uses of the streets, see Christine Stansell, "Women, Children, and the Uses of the Streets: Class and Gender Conflict in New York City,

1850–1860," *Feminist Studies* 8 (Summer 1982), 309–35. For an overview of middle-class formation in urban America, see Stuart M. Blumin, *The Emergence of the Middle Class: Social Experience in the American City, 1760–1900* (New York: Cambridge University Press, 1989).

9. On this point, see Craig Steven Wilder, *Covenant with Color*.

10. On the Colored Home, see Henry J. Camman and Hugh N. Camp, *The Charities of New York, Brooklyn, and Staten Island* (New York: Hurd and Houghton, 1868), 387–88; Petition of the Colored Home [Society for the Relief of Worthy, Aged, Indigent Colored Persons] to the Mayor and Alderman of the City of New York, 1843, in New York Municipal Archives [hereafter Municipal Archives]; Fifth Annual Report of the Colored Home (1853), xii, in New York Public Library [hereafter, NYPL].

11. Thompson, *Broken Gloom*, 71.

12. On the precariousness of black freedom in the North, see Carol Wilson, *Freedom at Risk: The Kidnapping of Free Blacks in America, 1780–1865* (Lexington: University of Kentucky Press, 1994); Stanley Campbell, *The Slave Catchers: Enforcement of the Fugitive Slave Law, 1850–1860* (Chapel Hill: University of North Carolina Press, 1970).

13. David P. Thelen and Leslie H. Fishel, "Reconstruction in the North: The *World* Looks at New York's Negroes, March 16, 1867," *New York History* 49 (October 1968), 434; Robert E. Cray Jr., *Paupers and Poor Relief in New York City and Its Rural Environs, 1700–1830* (Philadelphia: Temple University Press, 1988), 191–92.

14. Figures on Alms House/Colored Home populations in 1855 are taken from the Seventh Annual Report of the Governors of the Alms House, New York, for the Year 1855 (New York, 1856), City Hall Library, New York [hereafter CHL], 1–21, 168–69. Peter Mandler has pointed out that the uses of charity were never quite the same as its purposes. See Mandler, "Poverty and Charity in the Nineteenth-century Metropolis: An Introduction," in *The Uses of Charity: The Poor on Relief in the Nineteenth-century Metropolis*, ed. Mandler (Philadelphia: University of Pennsylvania Press, 1990), 2. The essays in this volume, which focus on the European and Euro-American working poor, buttress this point. See especially the essay by Bruce Bellingham entitled "Waifs and Strays: Child Abandonment, Foster Care, and Families in Mid-nineteenth-century New York," 123–60.

15. J. Victor Koshmann, "The Nationalism of Cultural Uniqueness," review of *American Exceptionalism: A Double-Edged Sword* by Seymour Martin Lipset, *American Historical Review* 102 (June 1997), 762.

16. Nancy Isenberg, *Sex and Citizenship in Antebellum America* (Chapel Hill: University of North Carolina Press, 1998), xiv

17. On the market revolution, see Charles Sellers, *The Market Revolution: Jacksonian America, 1815–1846* (New York: Oxford University Press, 1991). On "republican motherhood," see Mary Beth Norton, *Founding Mothers and Fathers:*

Gendered Power and the Forming of American Society (New York: Knopf, 1996); and Linda Kerber, *Women of the Republic: Intellect and Ideology in Revolutionary America* (Chapel Hill: University of North Carolina Press, 1986). On "true womanhood," see Barbara Welter, "The Cult of True Womanhood, 1820–1860," *American Quarterly* 18 (Summer 1966), 151–74. See also Mary Kelley's perspective on Welter's conception of true womanhood in "Commentary," in *Locating American Studies: The Evolution of a Discipline*, ed. Lucy Maddox (Baltimore: Johns Hopkins University Press, 1999), 43–70. On the "cult of domesticity" and its interplay with white female benevolence, see: Katharine Kish Sklar, *Catharine Beecher: A Study in American Domesticity* (New Haven, CT: Yale University Press, 1973); Nancy F. Cott, *The Bonds of Womanhood: Women's Sphere in New England, 1780–1835* (New Haven, CT: Yale University Press, 1977); Linda Kerber, "Separate Spheres, Female Worlds, Woman's Place: The Rhetoric of Woman's History," *The Journal of American History* 75 (June 1988), 9–39; Ginzberg, *Women and the Work of Benevolence*; Christine Stansell, *City of Women: Sex and Class in New York, 1789–1860* (1986; repr., Urbana: University of Illinois Press, 1987); Carroll Smith-Rosenberg, *Disorderly Conduct: Visions of Gender in Victorian America* (New York: Knopf, 1985); Mary P. Ryan, *Cradle of the Middle Class: The Family in Oneida County, New York, 1790–1865* (New York: Cambridge University Press, 1981) and *Women in Public: Between Banners and Ballots, 1825–1880* (Baltimore: Johns Hopkins University Press, 1990). On the contested nature of the domestic ideal, see Lora Romero, *Home Fronts: Domesticity and Its Critics in the Antebellum United States* (Durham, NC: Duke University Press, 1997).

A penetrating discussion of the ideological and political function of the Jezebel stereotype of enslaved women occurs in Deborah Gray White, *Ar'n't...oman? Female Slaves in the Plantation South* (New York: Norton, 1985). On interracial unions in American history, see Werner Sollors, ed., *Interracialism: Black-white Intermarriage in American History, Literature, and Law* (New York: Oxford University Press, 2000); Martha Hodes, *White Women, Black Men: Illicit Sex in the Nineteenth-century South* (New Haven, CT: Yale University Press, 1997) and Hodes, ed., *Sex, Love, Race: Crossing Boundaries in North American History* (New York: New York University Press, 1999).

18. On debates over the capacity for self-government of different groups of whites in the nineteenth century, see Jacobson, *Whiteness of a Different Color*, 7. On interracial unions and the dread they inspired in antebellum New York, see Harris, *In the Shadow of Slavery*, 247–262. See also Graham Russell Hodges, "'Desirable Companions and Lovers': Irish and African Americans in the Sixth Ward of New York City, 1830–1870," in *Slavery, Freedom, and Culture Among Early American Workers* (Armonk, NY: M. E. Sharpe, 1998), 122–40.

19. See, for instance, Carroll Smith-Rosenberg, *Religion and the Rise of the American City: The New York Mission Movement, 1812–1870* (Ithaca, NY: Cornell University Press, 1971); Iver Bernstein, *The New York City Draft Riots: Their*

Significance for American Society and Politics in the Age of the Civil War (New York: Oxford University Press, 1990), 177–80.

20. On free labor Republicanism, see Eric Foner, *Free Soil, Free Labor, Free Men: The Ideology of the Republican Party Before the Civil War* (New York: Oxford University Press, 1970), 13; Jonathan Glickstein, *Concepts of Free Labor in Antebellum America* (New Haven, CT: Yale University Press, 1991). On race and politics in New York, see Anthony Gronowicz, *Race and Class Politics in New York City Before the Civil War* (Boston: Northeastern University Press, 1998); Phyllis F. Field, *The Politics of Race in New York: The Struggle for Black Suffrage in the Civil War Era* (Ithaca, NY: Cornell University Press, 1982).

21. Cheryl Harris, "Whiteness as Property," *Harvard Law Review* 106 (June 1993), 1709–91. An excellent discussion of Harris's argument about whiteness as property occurs in David R. Roediger, *Transcending the Racial Past*, 123–24

22. On the relationship between representation and "reality" in the context of statistical reports, see Joan Wallach Scott, *Gender and the Politics of History* (New York: Columbia University Press, 1988), 115

23. Ruth Alexander, *The "Girl Problem": Female Sexual Delinquency in New York, 1900–1930* (Ithaca, NY: Cornell University Press, 1995); Bruce Bellingham, "Waifs and Strays: Child Abandonement, Foster Care, and Families in Mid-nineteenth-century New York," in *The Uses of Charity: The Poor on Relief in the Nineteenth-century Metroplois*, ed. Peter Mandler (Philadelphia: University of Pennsylvania Press, 1990), 123–60; Barbara M. Brenzel, *Daughters of the State: A Social Portrait of the First Reform School for Girls in North America, 1856–1905* (Cambridge, MA: MIT Press, 1983); Linda Gordon, *Heroes of Their Own Lives: The Politics and History of Family Violence* (New York: Viking, 1988) and *Pitied But Not Entitled*; Katz, *Improving Poor People, In the Shadow of the Poorhouse*, and *The Undeserving Poor*; Kunzel, *Fallen Women*; David Nasaw, *Children of the City: At Work and Play* (Garden City, NY: Doubleday, 1985); Stansell, *City of Women*; Mary E. Odem, *Delinquent Daughters: Protecting and Policing Adolescent Female Sexuality in the United States, 1885–1920* (Chapel Hill: University of North Carolina Press, 1995).

24. Studies of Northern urban black communities set at least partly in nineteenth-century America include the works on New York cited in note 8 of this chapter. See also: Patrick Rael, *Black Identity and Black Protest in the Antebellum North* (Chapel Hill: University of North Carolina Press, 2002); James Oliver Horton and Lois E. Horton, *Black Bostonians: Family Life and Community Struggle in the Antebellum North* (New York: Holmes and Meier, 1979); Harry Reed, *Platform for Change: The Foundations of the Northern Free Black Community, 1775–1865* (East Lansing: Michigan State University Press, 1994); Kenneth W. Goings and Raymond A. Mohl, eds., *The New African American Urban History* (Thousand Oaks, CA: Sage, 1996); Gary Nash, *Forging Freedom: The Formation of Philadelphia's Black Community, 1720–1840* (Cambridge, MA: Harvard University Press,

1988); Jacqueline Jones, *Labor of Love, Labor of Sorrow: Black Women, Work, and the Family from Slavery to the Present* (New York: Basic, 1985); Dennis C. Dickerson, *Out of the Crucible: Black Steelworkers in Western Pennsylvania, 1875-1980* (Albany: State University of New York Press, 1986); Thomas C. Cox, *Blacks in Topeka, Kansas, 1865-1915: A Social History* (Baton Rouge: Louisiana State University Press, 1982); Leonard P. Curry, *The Free Black in Urban America, 1800-1850* (Chicago: University of Chicago Press, 1981); James Borchert, *Alley Life in Washington: Family, Community, Religion, and Folklore in the City, 1850-1970* (Urbana: University of Illinois Press, 1980); Douglas H. Daniels, *Pioneer Urbanites: A Social and Cultural History of Black San Francisco* (Philadelphia: Temple University Press, 1980); Lawrence W. Levine, *Black Culture and Black Consciousness: Afro-American Folk Thought from Slavery to Freedom* (New York: Oxford University Press, 1977); Kenneth Kusmer, *A Ghetto Takes Shape: Black Cleveland, 1870-1930* (Urbana: University of Illinois Press, 1976); David Gerber, *Black Ohio and the Color Line, 1860-1915* (Urbana: University of Illinois Press, 1976); David M. Katzman, *Before the Ghetto: Black Detroit in the Nineteenth Century* (Urbana: University of Illinois Press, 1973); Leon Litwack, *North of Slavery: The Negro in the Free States, 1790-1860* (Chicago: University of Chicago Press, 1961); Gilbert Osofsky, *Harlem: The Making of a Ghetto* (New York: Harper, 1966); Kenneth B. Clark, *Dark Ghetto: Dilemmas of Social Power* (Middletown, CT: Wesleyan University Press, 1967); Allan H. Spear, *Black Chicago: The Making of a Negro Ghetto, 1880-1920* (Chicago: University of Chicago Press, 1967); Kenneth Kusmer, ed., *Black Communities and Urban Development in America, 1720-1990* (New York: Garland, 1991); Nell Painter, *Exodusters: Black Migration to Kansas After Reconstruction* (New York: Knopf, 1976); Willard B. Gatewood, *Aristocrats of Color: The Black Elite, 1880-1920* (Bloomington: Indiana University Press, 1990).

Works that focus primarily on the twentieth century and/or the great migration include: Steven Hahn, *A Nation Under Our Feet: Black Political Struggles in the Rural South, from Slavery to the Great Migration* (Cambridge, MA: Belknap Press of Harvard University Press, 2003); Kevin Gaines, *Uplifting the Race: Black Leadership, Politics, and Culture in the Twentieth Century* (Chapel Hill: University of North Carolina Press, 1996); Robin D. G. Kelley, *Race Rebels: Culture, Politics, and the Black Working Class* (New York: Free Press, 1994); Earl Lewis, *In Their Own Interests: Blacks in Twentieth-century Norfolk* (Berkeley and Los Angeles: University of California Press, 1990); Joe William Trotter, *Black Milwaukee: The Making of an Industrial Proletariat, 1915-1945* (Urbana: University of Illinois Press, 1985), *Coal, Class, and Color: Blacks in Southern West Virginia, 1915-1932* (Urbana: University of Illinois Press, 1990), and Trotter, ed., *The Great Migration in Historical Perspective: New Dimensions of Race, Class, and Gender* (Bloomington: Indiana University Press, 1991); Peter Gottlieb, *Making Their Own Way: Southern Blacks' Migration to Pittsburgh, 1916-1930* (Urbana: University of Illinois Press, 1987); James R. Grossman, *Land of Hope: Chicago, Black Southerners, and the*

Great Migration (Chicago: University of Chicago Press, 1989); Arnold R. Hirsch, *Making the Second Ghetto: Race and Housing in Chicago, 1940-1960* (New York: Cambridge University Press, 1983); Carole Marks, *We're Good and Gone: The Great Black Migration* (Bloomington: Indiana University Press, 1989); Nicholas Lemann, *The Promised Land: The Great Black Migration and How It Changed America* (New York: Knopf, 1991); Gretchen Lemke Santalgelo, *Abiding Courage: African American Migrant Women and the East Bay Community* (Chapel Hill: University of North Carolina Press, 1996); Kimberley Phillips, *Alabama North: African American Migrants, Community, and Working Class Activism in Cleveland, 1915-1945* (Urbana: University of Illinois Press, 1999); Lillian S. Williams, *Strangers in the Land of Paradise: The Creation of an African American Community, Buffalo, New York, 1900-1940* (Bloomington: Indiana University Press, 1999); Shirley Ann Wilson Moore, *To Place Our Deeds: The African American Community in Richmond, California, 1910-1963* (Berkeley and Los Angeles: University of California Press, 2000); Milton Sernett, *Bound for the Promised Land: African American Religion and the Great Migration* (Durham, NC: Duke University Press, 1997); Pat McKissack, *Color Me Dark: The Diary of Nellie Lee Love, the Great Migration North* (New York: Scholastic, 2000); William W. Griffin, *African Americans and the Color Line in Ohio, 1915-1930* (Columbus: Ohio State University Press, 2005).

25. Gordon, "Black and White Visions of Welfare." On black philanthropy and its underlying ideas, see August Meier, *Negro Thought in America, 1880-1915* (Ann Arbor: University of Michigan Press, 1968); Evelyn Brooks Higginbotham, *Righteous Discontent: The Women's Movement in the Black Baptist Church, 1880-1920* (Cambridge, MA: Harvard University Press, 1993) and "Religion, Politics, and Gender: The Leadership of Nannie Helen Burroughs," *Journal of Religious Thought* 44 (Winter-Spring 1988), 7-22; Craig Steven Wilder, *In the Company of Black Men* and "The Rise and Influence of the New York African Society for Mutual Relief, 1808-1865," *AANYLH* 22 (July 1998), 7-18; Elisabeth Lasch-Quinn, *Black Neighbors: Race and the Limits of Reform in the American Settlement House Movement, 1890-1945* (Chapel Hill: University of North Carolina Press, 1993); David Levering Lewis, *W. E. B. Du Bois: The Biography of a Race* (New York: Henry Holt, 1993); Emmett D. Carson, *A Hand Up: Black Philanthropy and Self-help in America* (Washington, DC: Joint Center for Political and Economic Studies Press, 1993); Linda Gordon, "'Don't Wait for Deliverers': Black Women's Welfare Thought," in *Pitied But Not Entitled*, chapter 5; Guichard Parris and Lester Brooks, *Blacks in the City: A History of the National Urban League* (Boston: Little, Brown, 1971); Nancy Weiss, *The National Urban League, 1910-1940* (New York: Oxford University Press, 1974); Edyth L. Ross, *Black Heritage in Social Welfare, 1860-1930* (Metuchen, NJ: Scarecrow, 1978); Julie Winch, *Philadelphia's Black Elite: Activism, Accommodation, and the Struggle for Autonomy, 1787-1848* (Philadelphia: Temple University Press, 1988); Alfred A. Moss, *The American Negro Academy: Voice of the Talented Tenth* (Baton Rouge: Louisiana State

University Press, 1981); Paula Giddings, *When and Where I Enter: The Impact of Black Women on Race and Sex in America* (New York: Morrow, 1984); Wilson Moses, *Alexander Crummell: A Study of Civilization and Discontent* (New York: Oxford University Press, 1989); Elsa Barkley Brown, "Womanist Consciousness: Maggie Lena Walker and the Independent Order of St. Luke," *Signs* 14 (Spring 1989), 610–33; Cynthia Neverdon-Morton, *Afro-American Women of the South and the Advancement of the Race, 1895–1925* (Knoxville: University of Tennessee Press, 1989); Jacqueline Ann Rouse, *Lugenia Burns Hope: Black Southern Reformer* (Athens: University of Georgia Press, 1989); Anne F. Scott, "Most Invisible of All: Black Women's Voluntary Associations," *The Journal of Southern History* 56 (February 1990), 3–22; Darlene Clark Hine, "'We Specialize in the Wholly Impossible': The Philanthropic Work of Black Women," in *Lady Bountiful Revisited*, ed. McCarthy, 70–93; Beverley Washington Jones, *Quest for Equality: The Life and Writings of Mary Eliza Church Terrell, 1863–1954* (Brooklyn: Carlson, 1990); Adrienne Lash Jones, *Jane Edna Hunter: A Case Study of Black Leadership, 1910–1950* (Brooklyn: Carlson, 1990); Dorothy C. Salem, *To Better Our World: Black Women in Organized Reform, 1890–1920* (Brooklyn: Carlson, 1990); Mildred I. Thompson, *Ida B. Wells-Barnett: An Exploratory Study of an American Black Woman* (Brooklyn: Carlson, 1990); Stephanie J. Shaw, "Black Club Women and the Creation of the National Association of Colored Women," *Journal of Women's History* 3 (Fall 1991), 10–25 and *What a Woman Ought to Be and to Do: Black Professional Women Workers During the Jim Crow Era* (Chicago: University of Chicago Press, 1996); Susan L. Smith, *Sick and Tired of Being Sick and Tired: Black Women's Health Activism in America, 1890–1950* (Philadelphia: University of Pennsylvania Press, 1995); Gaines, *Uplifting the Race*; Darlene Clark Hine and Kathleen Thompson, *A Shining Thread of Hope: The History of Black Women in America* (New York: Broadway, 1998); Floris Barnett Cash, "Radicals or Realists: African American Women and the Settlement House Spirit in New York City," *AANYLH* 15 (January 1991), 7–17; Iris Carlton-La Ney, "The Career of Birdye Henrietta Haynes, a Pioneer Settlement House Worker," *Social Science Review* 68 (June 1994), 254–73; Carol Faulkner, "'A Proper Recognition of Our Manhood': The African Civilization Society and the Freedmen's Aid Movement," *AANYLH* 24 (January 2000), 41–62; Inabel Burns Lindsay, "Some Contributions of Negroes to Welfare Services, 1865–1900," *Journal of Negro Education* 25 (Winter 1956), 15–24; Claude F. Jacobs, "Benevolent Societies of New Orleans Blacks During the Late Nineteenth and Early Twentieth Centuries," *Louisiana History* 29 (Winter 1988), 21–33; Kathleen C. Berkeley, "'Colored Ladies Also Contributed': Black Women's Activities from Benevolence to Social Welfare, 1866–1896," in *The Web of Southern Social Relations: Women, Family, and Education*, ed. Walter J. Fraser Jr., Frank Saunders Jr., and Jon L. Wakelyn (Athens: University of Georgia Press, 1985), 181–203; Earline Rae Ferguson, "The Women's Improvement Club of Indianapolis: Black Women Pioneers in Tuberculosis Work, 1903–1938," *Indiana*

Magazine of History 84 (September 1988), 237–61; Marilyn Dell Brady, "Kansas Federation of Colored Women's Clubs, 1900–1930," *Kansas History* 9 (Spring 1986), 19–30; Cheryl Townsend Gilkes, "Building in Many Places: Multiple Commitments and Ideologies in Black Women's Community Work," in *Work and the Politics of Empowerment*, ed. Ann Bookman and Sandra Morgan (Philadelphia: Temple University Press, 1988), 53–76; Dorothy Sterling, *Black Foremothers: Three Lives* (Old Westbury, NY: Feminist Press, 1979); Sharon Harley, "For the Good of the Family and Race: Gender, Work, and Domestic Roles in the Black Community, 1880–1930," *Signs* 15 (Winter 1990), 336–49; Gail Bederman, "'Civilization' and the Decline of Middle-class Manliness and Ida B. Wells's Antilynching Campaign, 1892–94," *Radical History Review* 52 (Winter 1992), 4–30.

26. See the exchange between Joan W. Scott and Linda Gordon over reviews of Gordon, *Heroes of Their Own Lives* and Scott, *Gender and the Politics of History* in *Signs* 15 (Summer 1990), 851, 853; Regina Kunzel, "Pulp Fictions and Problem Girls: Reading and Rewriting Single Pregnancy in the Post-war United States," *American Historical Review* 100 (December 1995), 1486, 1487.

27. William Roseberry, "Hegemony and the Language of Contention," in *Everyday Forms of State Formation: Revolution and the Negotiation of Rule in Modern Mexico*, ed. Gilbert M. Joseph and Daniel Nugent (Durham, NC: Duke University Press, 1994), 360–61; Florencia E. Mallon, "The Promise and Dilemma of Subaltern Studies: Perspectives from Latin American History," AHR Forum, *American Historical Review* 99 (December 1994), 1511; see also the other essays in the same forum: Gyan Prakash, "Subaltern Studies as Postcolonial Criticism," 1475–90, and Frederick Cooper, "Conflict and Connection: Rethinking Colonial African History," 1516–45. For reflections on the connections between African American history and studies of colonialism, see Kevin Gaines, "Rethinking Race and Class in African American Struggles for Equality, 1885–1941," AHR Forum, *American Historical Review* 102 (April 1997), 378–79. On the materiality of "meaningful" discursive frameworks, see Gilbert M. Joseph and Daniel Nugent, "Popular Culture and State Formation in Revolutionary Mexico," in *Everyday Forms of State Formation*, ed. Joseph and Nugent, 20; and Raymond Williams, *Problems in Materialism and Culture* (London: Verso, 1980), 38. In this context, situational subaltern perspectives on hegemony encourage us to think of "languages" or "modes" of representation more expansively than those of literary texts implied in the all-too-familiar debate over whether "experience" or "epistemology" should be the guiding principle of the historian's enterprise. For a good summary of this debate (with its implications for subaltern agency), see Regina Kunzel, "Pulp Fiction and Problem Girls"; the dialogue between Joan W. Scott and Linda Gordon in *Signs* 15 (Summer 1990), 848–59; Christine Stansell, "A Response to Joan Scott," *International Labor and Working Class History* 31 (Spring 1987), 24–29; Scott, "The Evidence of Experience," *Critical Inquiry* 17 (Summer 1991), 773–97.

28. On the evolution and development of case records in social work, see Karen W. Tice, *Tales of Wayward Girls and Immoral Women: Case Records and the Professionalization of Social Work* (Urbana: University of Illinois Press, 1998). On case records as historical sources, see G. J. Parr, "Case Records as Sources for Social History," *Archivaria* 4 (Summer 1977), 122–36; David Klassen, "The Provenance of Social Work Case Records: Implications for Archival Appraisal and Access," *Provenance* 1 (Spring 1983), 5–30; Clarke A. Chambers, "Toward a Redefinition of Welfare History," *Journal of American History* 73 (September 1986), 407–33. Examples of effective use of case histories and parole records to illuminate the worlds of clients include Gordon, *Heroes of Their Own Lives*; Brenzel, *Daughters of the State*; Michael B. Katz, *Poverty and Policy in American History*; Kunzel, *Fallen Women, Problem Girl*; Alexander, *The "Girl Problem."*

29. Quadagno, *The Color of Welfare*, 10. For works on whiteness studies, see note 5.

30. Roseberry, "Hegemony and the Language of Contention," 363–64.

CHAPTER 1

Epigraph. Cited in Susan Page and Maria Puente, "Poll Shows Racial Divide on Storm Response," *USA Today*, September 13, 2005.

1. Thelma Wills Foote, *Black and White Manhattan: The History of Racial Formation in Colonial New York City* (New York: Oxford University Press, 2004), 6; Matthew Frye Jacobson, *Whiteness of a Different Color: European Immigrants and the Alchemy of Race* (Cambridge, MA: Harvard University Press, 1998), 23. On European constructions of American Indians, see: Kathleen M. Brown, "Native Americans and Early Modern Concepts of Race," in *Empire and Others: British Encounters with Indigenous Peoples, 1600–1850*, ed. Martin Daunton and Rick Halpern (Philadelphia: UCL Press, 1999), 79–100; Patricia Seed, *American Pentimento: The Invention of Indians and the Pursuit of Riches* (Minneapolis: University of Minnesota Press, 2001); Philip J. Deloria, *Playing Indian: Otherness and Authenticity in the Assumption of American Indian Identity* (New Haven, CT: Yale University Press, 1999); Robert E. Berkhofer Jr., *The White Man's Indian: Images of the American Indian from Columbus to the Present* (New York: Vintage, 1978). On the cultural and psychic dimension of racism, see also Winthrop Jordan, *White Over Black: American Attitudes Toward the Negro, 1550–1812* (Chapel Hill: University of North Carolina Press, 1968).

2. Edmund S. Morgan, *American Slavery, American Freedom: The Ordeal of Colonial Virginia* (New York: Norton, 1975).

3. David R. Roediger, *The Wages of Whiteness: Race and the Making of the American Working Class* (New York: Verso, 1991), 25; Jordan, *White Over Black*.

4. Peter H. Wood, "Strange New Land, 1619–1776," in *To Make Our World Anew: A History of African Americans*, ed. Robin D. G. Kelley and Earl Lewis (New York: Oxford University Press, 2000), 72; Ira Berlin, *Many Thousands*

Gone: The First Two Centuries of Slavery in North America (Cambridge, MA: Belknap Press of Harvard University Press, 1998), 123; Craig S. Wilder, *A Covenant with Color: Race and Social Power in Brooklyn* (New York: Columbia University Press, 2000), 14; Leon A. Higginbotham Jr., *In the Matter of Color: Race and the American Legal Process* (New York: Oxford University Press, 1978); Evelyn Brooks Higginbotham, "African-American Women's History and the Metalanguage of Race," *Signs* 17 (Winter 1992), 251–74.

5. Foote, *Black and White Manhattan*, 124–58. On the sources of African slaves, see Leslie Harris, *In the Shadow of Slavery: African Americans in New York City, 1626–1863* (Chicago: University of Chicago Press, 2003), 29–30. On slavery in colonial New York, see also entries in note 8 to the introduction of this book.

6. Graham Russell Hodges, *Root and Branch: African Americans in New York and East Jersey, 1613–1863* (Chapel Hill: University of North Carolina Press, 1999), 33, 107–8; Berlin, *Many Thousands Gone*, 179–81; Shane White, *Somewhat More Independent: The End of Slavery in New York City, 1770–1810* (Athens: University of Georgia Press, 1991), 3–4, 11; Wilder, *Covenant with Color*, 5–20.

7. Michael B. Katz, *In the Shadow of the Poorhouse: A Social History of Welfare in America* (New York: Basic, 1986), 3; Walter I. Trattner, *From Poor Law to Welfare State: A History of Social Welfare in America* (New York: Free Press, 1974), 25

8. On public welfare in colonial New York, see David M. Schneider, *The History of Public Welfare in New York State, 1609–1866* (Chicago: University of Chicago Press, 1938).

9. On African Americans in the American Revolution, see: Mary Louise Clifford, *From Slavery to Freetown: Black Loyalists After the American Revolution* (Jefferson, NC: McFarland, 1999); John W. Pullis, ed., *Moving On: Black Loyalists in the Afro-Atlantic World* (New York: Garland, 1999); Sylvia R. Frey, *Water from the Rock: Black Resistance in a Revolutionary Age* (Princeton, NJ: Princeton University Press, 1991); William H. Wiggins, *O' Freedom! Afro-American Emancipation Celebrations* (Knoxville: University of Tennessee Press, 1987); Gary B. Nash, "Forging Freedom: The Emancipation Experience in Northern Seaport Cities," in *Race, Class, and Politics: Essays in American Colonial and Revolutionary Society*, ed. Nash (1986; repr., Urbana: University of Illinois Press, 1986), 283–321; Edward Countryman, *A People in Revolution: The American Revolution and Political Society in New York, 1760–1790* (Baltimore: Johns Hopkins University Press, 1981); Philip Foner, *Blacks in the American Revolution* (Westport, CT: Greenwood, 1976); Joseph T. Wilson, *The Black Phalanx: A History of the Negro Soldiers of the United States in the Wars of 1775–1812, 1861–65* (Hartford: American Publishing, 1888).

10. White, *Somewhat More Independent*, 6, 18, 27.

11. Hodges, *Root and Branch*, 170; White, *Somewhat More Independent*, 31, 43

12. Jacobson, *Whiteness of a Different Color*, 26, 25; Roediger, *Wages of Whiteness*, 36; Sean Wilentz, *Chants Democratic: New York City and the Rise of the American Working Class, 1788–1850* (New York: Oxford University Press, 1984), 14.

13. Harris, *In the Shadow of Slavery*, 116–19.

14. On New York's early black community, see Harris, *In the Shadow of Slavery*; Hodges, *Root and Branch*; White, *Somewhat More Independent*.

15. Robert E. Cray Jr., *Paupers and Poor Relief in New York City and Its Rural Environs, 1700–1830* (Philadelphia: Temple University Press, 1988), 191–92.

16. Craig Steven Wilder, *In the Company of Black Men: The African Influence on African American Culture in New York City* (New York: New York University Press, 2001).

17. My analysis is based on detailed statistical information on the racial distribution of relief in Seventh Annual Report of the Governors of the Alms House, New York, for the Year 1855 (New York, 1856), City Hall Library, New York [hereafter CHL].

18. An excellent and detailed description of these developments appear in Edwin G. Burrows and Mike Wallace, *Gotham: A History of New York City to 1898* (New York: Oxford University Press, 1999), 333–52, 429–51, 542–62.

19. Wilentz, *Chants Democratic*, 107; Burrows and Wallace, *Gotham*, 563–86, 649–90.

20. Burrows and Wallace, *Gotham*, 735–60; Christine Stansell, *City of Women: Sex and Class in New York, 1789–1860* (1986 Urbana: University of Illinois Press, 1987).

21. Burrows and Wallace, *Gotham*, 371–85, 452–72, 712–34, 774–820.

22. Ibid., 735–36.

23. Hasia Diner, "Overview: 'The Most Irish City in the Union': The Era of the Great Urban Migration, 1844–1877," in *The New York Irish*, ed. Ronald H. Bayor and Timothy J. Meagher (Baltimore: Johns Hopkins University Press, 1996), 87; Burrows and Wallace, *Gotham*, 479. On the Irish, see also Hasia Diner, *Erin's Daughters in America: Irish Immigrant Women in the Nineteenth Century* (Baltimore: Johns Hopkins University Press, 1983); and Kerby Miller, *Emigrants and Exiles: Ireland and the Irish Exodus to North America* (New York: Oxford University Press, 1985).

24. Tyler Anbinder, *Five Points: The 19th-century Neighborhood That Invented Tap Dance, Stole Elections, and Became the World's Most Notorious Slum* (New York: Free Press, 2001), 50, 58–59, 63–65; Burrows and Wallace, *Gotham*, 735, Diner, "Overview," 88–90 and *Erin's Daughters*, 5–6.

25. Diner, "Overview," 90.

26. Burrows and Wallace, *Gotham*, 745–47; Stansell, *City of Women*, 42; Robert Ernst, *Immigrant Life in New York City, 1825–1863* (1949; repr., New York: Octagon, 1979), 40. On housing in nineteenth-century New York, see Elizabeth Blackmar, *Manhattan for Rent, 1785–1850* (Ithaca, NY: Cornell University Press, 1989).

27. Burrows and Wallace, *Gotham*, 387, 392; Anbinder, *Five Points*, 97; Ernst, *Immigrant Life in New York City*, 41.

28. Stansell, *City of Women*.

29. Caroline M. Kirkland, *The Helping Hand: Comprising an Account of the Home for Discharged Female Convicts and an Appeal in Behalf of That Institution* (New York: Scribner, 1853), 32, 40–41, 74.

30. New York State Assembly Document No. 205, March 9, 1857: Report of the Select Committee Appointed to Examine into the Condition of Tenement Houses in New York and Brooklyn [hereafter Assembly Doc No. 205], 11–12; Stansell, *City of Women*, 47, 50; Burrows and Wallace, *Gotham*, 587; Anbinder, *Five Points*, 74–75.

31. Assembly Doc No. 205, 39. On sensationalized portrayals of working poor life in antebellum New York, see "Introduction" by Stuart M. Blumin to George C. Foster, *New York by Gas-light and Other Urban Sketches*, ed. Blumin (Berkeley and Los Angeles: University of California Press, 1990).

32. Population Census of the Inhabitants of the Sixth and Eighth Wards in the County of New York, taken in 1855. On the sixth ward, see Carol Groneman, "'The Bloody Ould Sixth': A Social Analysis of a New York City Working-class Community in Mid-nineteenth Century" (PhD diss., University of Rochester, 1973). On the ways in which census records authorize certain visions of the social order, see Joan Scott, *Gender and the Politics of History* (New York: Columbia University Press, 1988), 115.

33. I identify families by the ward of their residence, followed by their household number, assigned according to the place of the household in the order of visitation. Accordingly the Sparrows family occupied the eighth ward, # 248.

34. Eighth Ward, # 684.

35. Eighth Ward, # 666, 287, 680, 251.

36. Kenneth A. Scherzer, *The Unbounded Community: Neighborhood Life and Social Structure on New York City, 1830–1875* (Durham, NC: Duke University Press, 1992), 98–107.

37. Ward, # 188.

38. On the subject of fosterage among African Americans, see Andrew T. Miller, "Social Science, Social Policy, and the Heritage of African American Families," in *The Underclass Debate: Views from History*, ed. Michael B. Katz (Princeton, NJ: Princeton University Press, 1993), 254–89.

39. Eighth Ward, # 252.

40. Eighth Ward, # 691.

41. Eighth Ward, # 185.

42. Eighth Ward, # 721.

43. On ethnicity and work in antebellum New York, see Richard Stott, *Workers in the Metropolis: Class, Ethnicity, and Youth in Antebellum New York City* (Ithaca, NY: Cornell University Press, 1990).

44. Diner, *Erin's Daughters in America*, 77–78; Stansell, *City of Women*.

45. Hodges, *Root and Branch*, 232; Stansell, *City of Women*, 157; Marilynn Wood Hill, *Their Sisters' Keepers: Prostitution in New York City, 1830–1870* (Berkeley and Los Angeles: University of California Press, 1993), 57. On domestic service, see Faye Dudden, *Serving Women: Household Service in Nineteenth-century America* (Middletown, CT: Wesleyan University Press, 1983).

46. Hill, *Their Sisters' Keepers*, 186, 191. On prostitution in New York City, see also Timothy Gilfoyle, *City of Eros: New York City, Prostitution, and the Commercialization of Sex, 1790–1920* (New York: Norton, 1992).

47. James D. McCabe, *Lights and Shadows of New York Life; Or, The Sights and Sensations of the Great City* (1872; New York: Farrar, Straus and Giroux, 1970), 509–10; Hodges, *Root and Branch*, 232–33.

48. Anbinder, *Five Points*, 120; Deborah Gray White, "Let My People Go," in *To Make Our World Anew*, ed. Kelley and Lewis, 206; Edward K. Spann, *The New Metropolis: New York City, 1840–1857* (New York: Columbia University Press, 1981), 71, Stansell, *City of Women*, 111.

49. William Jeffrey Bolster, *Black Jacks: African American Seamen in the Age of Sail* (Cambridge, MA: Harvard University Press, 1997), 179, 182, 200–201.

50. Ibid., 178, 188.

51. Anbinder, *Five Points*, 119; Hodges, *Root and Branch*, 211.

52. On black chimney sweeps, see Paul Gilje, "'Sweep O! African American Chimney Sweeps and Citizenship in the New Nation," *William and Mary Quarterly* 51 (1994), 507–14. On cartmen, see Graham Russell Hodges, *New York City Cartmen, 1667–1850* (New York: New York University Press, 1986).

53. Wilentz, *Chants Democratic*, 137–39.

54. Diner, *Erin's Daughters*, 32.

55. Ibid., 39.

56. Scherzer, *The Unbounded Community*, 103.

57. Burrows and Wallace, *Gotham*, 437–38.

58. Stansell, *City of Women*, 156–60.

59. Ibid., 203–6; Anbinder, *Five Points*, 129–130, 133.

CHAPTER 2

1. See chapter 7 of Joel Tyler Headley, *The Great Riots of New York, 1712–1873; Including a Full and Complete Account of the Four Days' Draft Riots of 1863* (New York: E. B. Treat, 1873), reprinted with an introduction by Pete Hamill (New York: Thunder's Mouth Press, 2004), 64–74, quotation on 67.

2. Ibid., 68–69.

3. Ibid., 70–74; Edwin G. Burrows and Mike Wallace, *Gotham: A History of New York City to 1898* (New York: Oxford University Press, 1999), 609–11, quotation cited on 611; David Moses Schneider, *The History of Public Welfare in New York State, 1609–1866* (Chicago: University of Chicago Press, 1938), 258–60.

4. Burrows and Wallace, *Gotham*, 611–13; Seth Rockman, *Welfare Reform in the Early Republic: A Brief History With Documents* (Boston: Bedford/St. Martin's Press, 2003), 1.

5. First quotation from George C. Foster, *New York by Gas-light and Other Urban Sketches*, ed. Stuart M. Blumin (Berkeley and Los Angeles: University of

California Press, 1990), 69; Raymond A. Mohl, *Poverty in New York, 1783–1825* (New York: Oxford University Press, 1971), 84–85; "Report of the Secretary of State in 1824 on the Relief and Settlement of the Poor," *Assembly Journal*, February 9, 1824, reprinted in David J. Rothman, ed., *Poverty, U.S.A.: The Historical Record* (New York: Arno, 1971), 944. On the new "culture of conflict" on the streets and in the workplace, see Paul A. Gilje, "Culture of Conflict: The Impact of Commercialization on New York Workingmen, 1787–1829," in *New York and the Rise of American Capitalism: Economic Development and the Social and Political History of an American State, 1780–1870*, ed. William Pencak and Conrad Edick Wright (New York: New-York Historical Society, 1989), 249–70. See also Gilje, *The Road to Mobocracy: Popular Disorder in New York City, 1763–1834* (Chapel Hill: University of North Carolina Press, 1987). On poverty in industrializing America, see Thomas J. Sugrue, "The Structures of Urban Poverty: The Reorganization of Space and Work in Three Periods of American History," in *The Underclass Debate: Views from History*, ed. Michael B. Katz (Princeton, NJ: Princeton University Press, 1993), 85–95.

6. Christine Stansell, *City of Women: Sex and Class in New York, 1789–1860* (1986; Urbana: University of Illinois Press, 1987), 34; Burrows and Wallace, *Gotham*, 493–94; Rockman, *Welfare Reform in the Early Republic*, 8. On the revision of old notions of poverty, see Michael Katz, *In the Shadow of the Poorhouse: A Social History of Welfare in America* (New York: Basic, 1986), 18; Lori Ginzberg, *Women in Antebellum Reform* (Wheeling, IL: Harlan Davidson, 2000), 16; Eric Monkkonen, "Nineteenth-century Institutions," in Katz, *The Underclass Debate*, 343.

7. Jonathan A. Glickstein, "Pressures from Below: Pauperism, Chattel Slavery, and the Ideological Construction of Free Market Labor Incentives in Antebellum America," *Radical History Review* 69 (Fall 1997), 122–23; Schneider, *The History of Public Welfare*, 218–29.

8. For Gerard's observations on "mendacity," see "Reminiscences of James W. Gerard, Esq., of New York of the Establishment of the New York House of Refuge," Proceedings of the First Convention of the Managers and Superintendents of Houses of Refuge and Schools of Reform in the United States of America Held in the City of New York on the 12th, 13th, and 14th days of May 1857 [hereafter Proceedings of First Convention], in *Society For the Reformation of Juvenile Delinquents: Reports*, New York State Archives, Albany [hereafter *Reports*], 3:78. For Yates's comments, see "Report of the Secretary of State in 1824 on the Relief and Settlement of the Poor," in David J. Rothman, ed., *Poverty, U.S.A.*, 956.

9. Edward K. Spann, *The New Metropolis: New York City, 1840–1857* (New York: Columbia University Press, 1981), 86–87; Iver Bernstein, *The New York City Draft Riots: Their Significance for American Society and Politics in the Age of the Civil War* (New York: Oxford University Press, 1990), 179, 182; Burrows and Wallace, *Gotham*, 620; Carroll Smith-Rosenberg, *Religion and the Rise of*

the American City: The New York City Mission Movement, 1812–1870 (Ithaca, NY: Cornell University Press, 1971), 245–73.

10. Matthew Frye Jacobson, *Whiteness of a Different Color: European Immigrants and the Alchemy of Race* (Cambridge, MA: Harvard University Press, 1998), 41, 48.

11. David R. Roediger, *The Wages of Whiteness: Race and the Making of the American Working Class* (New York: Verso, 1991), 133; Jacobson, *Whiteness of a Different Color*, 48, Noel Ignatieff, *How the Irish Became White* (New York: Routledge, 1995), 2; Burrows and Wallace, *Gotham*, 830.

12. "Annual Report of the Secretary of State Relative to Statistics of the Poor," New York State Senate Document No. 72, Albany, March 23, 1855 [hereafter Senate Doc No. 72], 82–83.

13. Cited in Tyler Anbinder, *Five Points: The 19th-century Neighborhood That Invented Tap Dance, Stole Elections, and Became the World's Most Notorious Slum* (New York: Free Press, 2001), 23.

14. Anbinder, *Five Points*, 24.

15. Foster, *New York by Gas-light*, 183.

16. Senate Doc No. 72, 84.

17. Foster, *New York by Gas-light*, 96–97.

18. Ibid., 142; my italics.

19. Schneider, *History of Public Welfare*, 132–39, 295; Edward Spann, *The New Metropolis*, 76.

20. Schneider, *History of Public Welfare*, 295. On race and politics in mid-nineteenth-century New York, see Anthony Gronowicz, *Race and Class Politics in New York City Before the Civil War* (Boston: Northeastern University Press, 1998); and Phyllis F. Field, *The Politics of Race in New York: The Struggle for Black Suffrage in the Civil War Era* (Ithaca, NY: Cornell University Press, 1982).

21. Burrows and Wallace, *Gotham*, 502–3, 636.

22. Second Annual Report of the Prison Association of New York (1846), 25–26. See also "Report of the Penitentiary Hospital for the Year Ending December 31, 1848," Annual Report of the Alms House Commissioner for the Year 1848 (New York, 1849); Seventh Annual Report of the Governors of the Alms House, New York, for the Year 1855 (New York, 1856), 7–8; both in City Hall Library, New York [hereafter CHL].

23. Handwritten manuscript of Report of the Committee on Charity and the Alms House, January 6, 1844, New York Municipal Archives [hereafter Municipal Archives].

24. Handwritten manuscript of Report of the Committee on Charity and the Alms House, approved September 26, 1844, Municipal Archives [hereafter Committee on Charity manuscript].

25. James M. McPherson, *Battle Cry of Freedom: The Civil War Era* (New York: Oxford University Press, 1988), 135; Burrows and Wallace, *Gotham*, 829–30.

26. Senate Doc No. 72, 72–74.

27. Quotation cited in Jacobson, *Whiteness of a Different Color*, 44.
28. Roediger, *Wages of Whiteness*, 140-41.
29. Cheryl Harris, "Whiteness as Property," *Harvard Law Review* 106 (June 1993), 1709-91.
30. Graham Russell Hodges, *Root and Branch: African Americans in New York and East Jersey, 1613-1863* (Chapel Hill: University of North Carolina Press, 1999), 256-57; Burrows and Wallace, *Gotham*, 865.
31. Cited in Schneider, *A History of Public Welfare*, 297, 301-2; quotation on 306, my italics.
32. Nancy Isenberg, *Sex and Citizenship in Antebellum America* (Chapel Hill: University of North Carolina Press, 1998), xiv.
33. Schneider, *History of Public Welfare*, 309-15.
34. Committee on Charity manuscript.
35. Report of the Commissioners of the Almshouse and Bridewell in the City of New York, to Whom Were Referred a Report and Resolutions from the Committee on Charity and Alms House of the Board of Assistants, February 10, 1843, Municipal Archives; Spann, *The New Metropolis*, 79.
36. Annual Report of the Alms House Commissioner for the Year 1848, Document No. 44 (New York, 1849), CHL, 11-12.
37. Spann, *The New Metropolis*, 81; First Annual Report of the Governors of the Alms House, New York, for the Year 1849 (New York, 1850), 1-5, 15; Sixth Annual Report of the Governors of the Alms House, New York, for the Year 1854 (New York, 1855), 164, in NYMR.
38. Petition of the Colored Home [Society For the Relief of Worthy, Aged, Indigent Colored Persons] to the Mayor and Alderman of the City of New York, 1843, Municipal Archives.
39. Carlton Mabee, "Charity in Travail: Two Orphan Asylums for Blacks," *New York History* 55 (January 1974), 58; Leslie Harris, *In the Shadow of Slavery: African Americans in New York City, 1626-1863* (Chicago: University of Chicago Press, 2003), 145-68.
40. Annual Report of the Alms House Commissioner for 1848, Document No. 44, 42, 52.
41. Seventh Annual Report of the Governors of the Alms House, New York, for the Year 1855, 189-92.
42. Annual Report of the Alms House Commissioner for 1848, Document No. 44, 22, 42-43, 181.
43. Thelma Wills Foote, *Black and White Manhattan: The History of Racial Formation in Colonial New York City* (New York: Oxford University Press, 2004), 5-6.
44. Seventh Annual Report of the Governors of the Alms House, New York, for the Year 1855, 20-22, 42-47, 102-3, 129, 163-67.
45. Sixth Annual Report of the Governors of the Alms House for 1854, 172.

46. *Seventh Annual Report of the Governors of the Alms House, New York, for the Year 1855*, 42–59.

47. *Sixth Annual Report of the Governors of the Alms House for 1854*, 30; *First Annual Report of the Governors of the Alms House for 1849*, 194–95, 158–59; *Second Annual Report of the Governors of the Alms House for 1850* (New York, 1851), 39–40; *Fifth Annual Report of the Governors of the Alms House for 1853* (New York, 1854), 13.

48. *First Annual Report of the Governors of the Alms House for 1849*, 130, 119; *Fourth Annual Report of the Governors of the Alms House for 1852* (New York, 1853), 82.

49. *First Annual Report of the Governors of the Alms House for 1849*, 103.

50. *Fourth Annual Report of the Governors of the Alms House for 1852*, 41, 98; *Third Annual Report of the Governors of the Alms House for 1851*, 60; *Third Annual Report of the Governors of the Alms House for 1851* (New York, 1852), 106.

51. *First Annual Report of the Governors of the Alms House for 1849*, 112; *Sixth Annual Report of the Governors of the Alms House for 1855*, 94.

52. *Second Annual Report of the Governors of the Alms House for 1850*, 122, 164–66.

53. *Third Annual Report of the Governors of the Alms House for 1851*, 133; *Annual Report of the Alms House Commissioner for 1848*, Appendix to Document No. 44: Report of Marcellus Eells, Superintendent of the Alms House, 62, 63, 93; *Second Annual Report of the Governors of the Alms House for 1850*, 99–100.

54. *Fourth Annual Report of the Governors of the Alms House for 1852*, 158–59.

55. *Second Annual Report for the Governors of the Alms House for 1850*, 60.

56. *Second Annual Report for the Governors of the Alms House for 1850*, 128–29; *Third Annual Report of the Governors of the Alms House for 1851*, 42.

57. *First Annual Report of the Governors of the Alms House for 1849*, 143, 12–13.

58. *First Annual Report for the Governors of the Alms House for 1849*, 16; *Second Annual Report of the Governors of the Alms House for 1850*, 172.

59. *Second Annual Report for the Governors of the Alms House for 1850*, 172–73.

60. *Third Annual Report of the Governors of the Alms House for 1851*, 178.

61. Roediger, *Wages of Whiteness*, 143, 149–50.

62. *Second Annual Report of the Governors of the Alms House for 1851*, 178

63. *Sixth Annual Report of the Governors of the Alms House for 1854*, 168–69.

64. Cited in Kenneth M. Stampp, *America in 1857: A Nation on the Brink* (New York: Oxford University Press, 1990), 219.

65. McPherson, *Battle Cry*, 189–91; Stampp, *America in 1857*, 213–38; Burrows and Wallace, *Gotham*, 846–47.

66. Cited in Stampp, *America in 1857*, 227–28; Burrows and Wallace, *Gotham*, 831–32, 848.

67. Cited in Stampp, *America in 1857*, 228, Burrows and Wallace, *Gotham*, 848.

68. Iver Bernstein, *The New York City Draft Riots: Their Significance for American Society and Politics in the Age of the Civil War* (New York: Oxford University Press, 1990), 177, 183; Burrows and Wallace, *Gotham*, 848–49; Schneider, *History of Public Welfare*, 277.

69. Burrows and Wallace, *Gotham*, 849–50; Stampp, *America in 1857*, 228–29.

70. Ninth Annual Report of the Governors of the Alms House for the Year 1857 (New York, 1858), xv.

71. Ninth Annual Report of the Governors of the Alms House for the Year 1857, 294.

CHAPTER 3

1. Twelfth Annual Report of the Society for the Support of the Colored Home (Society for the Relief of Worthy, Aged, Indigent Colored Persons) [hereafter Colored Home], for 1851–52, New York Public Library [hereafter NYPL], 7.

2. Mary. W. Thompson, *Broken Gloom: Sketches of the History, Character, and Dying Testimony of the Beneficiaries of the Colored Home in the City of New York* (New York: John F. Trow, 1851), 20–22.

3. Henry J. Camman and Hugh N. Camp, *The Charities of New York, Brooklyn, and Staten Island* (New York: Hurd and Houghton, 1868), 387–88.

4. Fifth Annual Report of the Colored Home for 1844, 8–9.

5. Petition of the Colored Home to the Mayor and Alderman of the City of New York, 1843, New York Municipal Archives [hereafter Municipal Archives].

6. Fifth Annual Report of the Governors of the Alms House for 1853, xii; Twelfth Annual Report of the Colored Home for 1851–52, 9.

7. An Act to Incorporate the Colored Home of the City of New York, May 8, 1845, NYPL.

8. Camman and Camp, *The Charities of New York*, 388.

9. Thompson, *Broken Gloom*, 76; Tenth Annual Report of the Colored Home for 1849–50, 12; Ninth Annual Report of the Colored Home for 1848–49, 20; Sixth Annual Report of Governors of the Alms House for 1854, 77.

10. For George Fitzhugh's proslavery ideas, see *Cannibals All! Or Slaves Without Masters*, ed. C. Vann Woodward (Cambridge, MA: Harvard University Press, 1960); *Sociology for the South: Or the Failure of Free Society* (Richmond, VA: A. Morris, 1854); and *Slavery Justified, by a Southerner* (Fredericksburg, VA: Recorder Printing Office, 1850).

11. Ninth Annual Report of the Colored Home for 1848–49, 8.

12. Thompson, *Broken Gloom*, 5.

13. Ibid., 6.

14. Ibid., 12–14.
15. Ibid., 13–15.
16. Twelfth Annual Report of the Colored Home for 1851–52, 8.
17. Thompson, *Broken Gloom*, 14–15.
18. Ibid., 33.
19. Ibid., 21–22.
20. Ibid., 22.
21. Ibid., 39.
22. Ibid., 21.
23. Ibid., 38.
24. Ibid., 48, 23.
25. Ibid., 72–73.
26. Ibid., 23–24.
27. Ibid., 29.
28. Ibid., 65–66, 47.
29. My interpretation of slave religion draws on Lawrence Levine, *Black Culture, Black Consciousness: Afro-American Folk Thought from Slavery to Freedom* (New York: Oxford University Press, 1977), 30–54; Eugene Genovese, *Roll Jordan Roll: The World the Slaves Made* (New York: Pantheon 1974); John W. Blassingame, *Slave Community: Plantation Life in the Antebellum South* (New York: Oxford University Press, 1972); Clarence L. Mohr, "Slaves and White Churches in Confederate Georgia," in *Masters and Slaves in the House of the Lord: Race and Religion in the American South, 1740–1870*, ed. John B. Boles (Lexington: University of Kentucky Press, 1988), 153–72; Albert J. Raboteau, *Slave Religion: The "Invisible Institution" in the Antebellum South* (New York: Oxford University Press, 1978); Mechal Sobel, *Trabelin' On: The Slave Journey to an Afro-Baptist Faith* (Westport, CT: Greenwood, 1979); Milton C. Sernett, *Black Religion and American Evangelicalism: White Protestants, Plantation Missions, and the Flowering of Negro Christianity, 1787–1865* (Metuchen, NJ: Scarecrow, 1975). See also Jon Butler, *Awash in a Sea of Faith: Christianizing the American People* (Cambridge, MA: Harvard University Press, 1990); Nathan O. Hatch, *The Democratization of American Christianity* (New Haven, CT: Yale University Press, 1989).
30. Thompson, *Broken Gloom*, 42–43.
31. Ibid., 44–45.
32. Ibid., 45–47.
33. Ibid., 18–19.
34. Ibid., 33, 32, 25–26.
35. Ibid., 73–74.
36. Twelfth Annual Report of the Colored Home for 1851–52, 9–10.
37. Census of Alms House Inmates, Admissions for 1848, Municipal Archives.
38. Third Annual Report of the Governors of the Alms House for 1851, 73–75.

39. Tenth Annual Report of the Colored Home for 1849–50, 19; Seventh Annual Report of the Governors of the Alms House for 1855, 169.

40. Tenth Annual Report of the Colored Home for 1849–50, 19, 14; Second Annual Report of the Governors of the Alms House for 1850, 64.

41. Fifth Annual Report of the Colored Home for 1844, 10, 9; Eleventh Annual Report of the Colored Home for 1850–51, 9.

42. Twelfth Annual Report of the Colored Home for 1851–52, 9.

43. See, for instance, Tenth Annual Report of Colored Home for 1849–50, 10, 11, 12.

44. Eleventh Annual Report of the Colored Home for 1850–51, 10–11.

45. Fifth Annual Report of the Colored Home for 1844, 11.

46. Second Annual Report of the Governors of the Alms House for 1850, 66.

47. Ninth Annual Report of the Colored Home for 1848–49, 9.

48. Second Annual Report of the Governors of the Alms House for 1850, 68.

49. Third Annual Report of the Governors of the Alms House for 1851, 76.

50. On the relationship between capitalism and humanitarian reform in shaping the coming of the Civil War, see Thomas Bender, ed., *The Antislavery Debate: Capitalism and Abolitionism as a Problem in Historical Interpretation* (Berkeley and Los Angeles: University of California Press, 1992). For overviews of the Civil War and Emancipation, see: James M. McPherson, *Battle Cry of Freedom: The Civil War Era* (New York: Oxford University Press, 1988); Ira Berlin, Barbara J. Fields, Steven F. Miller, Joseph P. Reidy, and Leslie S. Rowland, eds., *Slaves No More: Three Essays on Emancipation and Civil War* (New York: Cambridge University Press, 1992); John Hope Franklin, *The Emancipation Proclamation* (Garden City, NY: Doubleday, 1963). See also Philip Foner, *Business and Slavery: The New York Merchants and the Irrepressible Conflict* (Chapel Hill: University of North Carolina Press, 1941).

51. David Roediger, *Wages of Whiteness: Race and the Making of the American Working Class* (New York: Verso, 1991), 154.

52. Leslie Harris, *In the Shadow of Slavery: African Americans in New York City, 1626–1863* (Chicago: University of Chicago Press, 2003), 280; Iver Bernstein, *The New York City Draft Riots: Their Significance for American Society and Politics in the Age of the Civil War* (New York: Oxford University Press, 1990), 41.

53. Harris, *In the Shadow of Slavery*, 280–86; Roediger, *Wages of Whiteness*, 150–56.

CHAPTER 4

1. James D. McCabe, *Lights and Shadows of New York Life; Or, the Sights and Sensations of the Great City* (1872; repr., New York: Farrar, Straus and Giroux, 1970); Stuart M. Blumin, "Explaining the New Metropolis: Perception, Depiction, and Analysis in Mid-nineteenth-century New York City," *Journal of Urban History* 11

(November 1984), 9–38; Edwin Burrows and Mike Wallace, *Gotham: A History of New York City to 1898* (New York: Oxford University Press, 1999), 473–1038.

2. Case No. 2649 (February 13, 1841), Inmate Case Histories, 1824–1935, Records of the New York House of Refuge, Department of Correctional Services, New York State Archives, Albany, New York [hereafter NYHR Records]. The dates of the case histories indicate the admission dates of the inmates.

3. Case No. 2516 (June 17, 1840), NYHR Records.

4. Proceedings of the Second Convention of Managers and Superintendents of Houses of Refuge, Schools of Reform and Institutions for the Prevention and Correction of Juvenile Destitution, Delinquency, and Crime (in the U.S.A.) Held at the City of New York on the 10th, 11th, and 12th Days of May, 1859 (New York, 1860), NYHR Records, [hereafter Second Convention], 40.

5. On the New York House of Refuge, see Robert S. Pickett, *House of Refuge: Origins of Juvenile Reform in New York State, 1815–1857* (Syracuse, NY: Syracuse University Press, 1969); Steven L. Schlossman, *Love and the American Delinquent: The Theory and Practice of "Progressive" Juvenile Justice, 1825–1920* (Chicago: University of Chicago Press, 1977), 18–32; Alexander W. Pisciotta, "Treatment on Trial: The Rhetoric and Reality of the New York House of Refuge," *American Journal of Legal History* 29 (April 1985), 151–81. On juvenile justice, see also: Joseph M. Hawes, *Children in Urban Society: Juvenile Delinquency in Nineteenth-century America* (New York: Oxford University Press, 1971); Robert M. Mennel, *Thorns and Thistles: Juvenile Delinquents in the United States, 1825–1940* (Hanover, NH: University Press of New England, 1973); Harold Finestone, *Victims of Change: Juvenile Delinquents in Society* (Westport, CT: Greenwood, 1976); John R. Sutton, *Stubborn Children: Controlling Delinquency in the United States, 1640–1981* (Berkeley and Los Angeles: University of California Press, 1988); Eric C. Schneider, *In the Web of Class: Delinquents and Reformers in Boston, 1810s–1930s* (New York: New York University Press, 1992); Mary E. Odem, *Delinquent Daughters: Protecting and Policing Adolescent Female Sexuality in the United States, 1885–1920* (Chapel Hill: University of North Carolina Press, 1995).

6. Pisciotta, "Treatment on Trial," 160–81.

7. On the origins of juvenile justice in Jacksonian America, see Schlossman, *Love and the American Delinquent*, 7–32.

8. Act of Incorporation and Laws Relative to the New York House of Refuge Passed on March 29, 1824, in *Reports*, 1:4; Nineteenth Annual Report of the Managers of the Society For the Reformation of Juvenile Delinquents [hereafter SRJD] to the Legislature of the State and the Corporation of the City of New York (for the Year 1843), *Reports*, 2:8; Thirty-sixth Annual Report of the SRJD (for the Year 1860), *Reports*, 4:14, all in NYHR Records.

9. Proceedings of First Convention, *Reports*, 3:135, NYHR Records.

10. James W. Gerard, Extracts from the Annual Report of the SPP in the City of New York (for the Year 1822), *Reports*, 3:78, 80, NYHR Records.

11. Cited in Pickett, *House of Refuge*, 15, 47.

12. Pickett, *House of Refuge*, 49–51, 65–66; Act of Incorporation and Laws Relative to the New York House of Refuge (New York, 1849); "Origins of the 'Greatest Reform School in the World,' 1824–1857," *A Guide to the Records of the New York House of Refuge*, New York State Archives, 4.

13. Burrows and Wallace, *Gotham*, 501; Second Annual Report of the SRJD (for 1825), microfilm edition, NYPL, 54.

14. Seventh Annual Report of the SRJD (for 1831), 12–13; Thirty-sixth Annual Report of the SRJD (for 1860), *Reports*, 4:10–12, NYHR Records.

15. Rules and Regulations for the Government of the New York House of Refuge, *Reports*, 1:6–9; Twenty-sixth Annual Report of the SRJD (for 1850), *Reports*, 2:6, 30, NYHR Records. See also Pisciotta, "Treatment on Trial," 155.

16. Tenth Annual Report of the Managers of the SRJD (for 1834), microfilm edition, NYPL, 17.

17. Tenth Annual Report of the Managers of the SRJD (for 1834), 14–15; quotation on 16.

18. E. S. Abdy, *Journal of a Residence and Tour in the United States of North America from April 1833, to October, 1834* (London: John Murray, 1835), 1:5.

19. Thirteenth Annual Report of SRJD (for 1837), microfilm edition, NYPL, 15.

20. Case No. 4776 (April 30, 1850), NYHR Records.

21. Case No. 8383 (January 8, 1861), NYHR Records.

22. Case No. 8325 (November 12, 1860), NYHR Records.

23. Case No. 4775 (April 30, 1850), NYHR Records.

24. Examples include case numbers 8310 (October 26, 1860), 8330 (November 17, 1860), 8364 (December 24, 1860), 13520 (July 27, 1870), NYHR Records.

25. Case No. 10610 (September 2, 1865), NYHR Records.

26. Case No. 8157 (June 20, 1860), NYHR Records.

27. Case No. 2609 (November 25, 1840), NYHR Records.

28. Evelyn Brooks Higginbotham, *Righteous Discontent: The Women's Movement in the Black Baptist Church, 1880–1920* (Cambridge, MA: Harvard University Press,1993), 185–229.

29. See Ruth B. Alexander, *The Girl Problem: Female Sexual Delinquency in New York, 1900–1930* (Ithaca, NY: Cornell University Press, 1995); and Odem, *Delinquent Daughters*.

30. Case No. 4895 (August 16, 1850), NYHR Records.

31. Case No. 8310 (October 26, 1860), NYHR Records.

32. Case No. 2465 (March 13, 1840), NYHR Records.

33. Case No. 2509 (June 8, 1840), NYHR Records.

34. Case No. 4839 (June 20 1850), NYHR Records.

35. Case No. 2663 (March 1841), NYHR Records.

36. Case No. 4880 (August 3, 1850), NYHR Records.

37. Case No. 8321 (November 5, 1860), NYHR Records.

38. Case No. 4939 (October 3, 1850), NYHR Records.

39. On fosterage among African Americans, see Andrew T. Miller, "Social Science, Social Policy, and the Heritage of African American Families," in *The Underclass Debate: Views from History*, ed. Michael B. Katz (Princeton, NJ: Princeton University Press, 1993), 254–89.

40. On the slave family, see: John W. Blassingame, *The Slave Community: Plantation Life in the Antebellum South* (New York: Oxford University Press, 1972); Deborah Gray White, *Ar'n't I a Woman: Female Slaves in the Plantation South* (New York: Norton, 1985); Herbert G. Gutman, *The Black Family in Slavery and Freedom* (New York: Pantheon, 1976); Christine Farnham, "Sapphire? The Issue of Dominance in the Slave Family, 1830–1865," in *"To Toil the Livelong Day": America's Women at Work, 1780–1980*, ed. Carole Groneman and Mary Beth Norton (Ithaca, NY: Cornell University Press, 1987), 68–83; Jacqueline Jones, *Labor of Love, Labor of Sorrow: Black Women, Work, and the Family from Slavery to Freedom* (New York: Basic, 1985); Elizabeth Fox-Genovese, *Within the Plantation Household: Black and White Women of the Old South* (Chapel Hill: University of North Carolina Press, 1988); Eugene D. Genovese, *Roll Jordan Roll: The World the Slaves Made* (New York: Pantheon, 1974).

41. Carol B. Stack, *All Our Kin: Strategies for Survival in a Black Community* (New York: Harper and Row, 1974).

42. Case No. 8384 (January 8, 1861) provides an example of cooperation among relatives. William Pitt was born in Richmond, Virginia, of a free mother and a slave father whom he never knew. His mother migrated north with him when he three years old, and they lived with an uncle in New York. He was committed on the charge of stealing jewelry while serving as houseboy in a Fifth Avenue home. Where natural parents were absent, a variety of circumstances drove foster kin to transfer the care of their charges to the Refuge. Since the death of his parents, thirteen-year-old William Brown had lived with his sister on Mulberry Street and helped his brother-in-law tend a fish stand. His sister took him before a magistrate and had him committed to the Refuge for vagrancy for "staying out nights" (Case No. 4969, November 6, 1850). Marietta Moulton moved from home to home when her mother died because her father in St. Louis was in no position to care for her. Her grandmother took her in, but she too passed away, leaving her in the custody of a Mr. Charles Richards in Troy, New York. This new guardian placed Marietta in domestic service with several families successively, but the young woman ran away repeatedly, providing Richards with the grounds to put her away for vagrancy (Case No. 13426, May 18, 1870). Sixteen-year-old Emily Rosevelt's mother had died and the whereabouts of her father were unknown. She went to live with an aunt, who, according to the case recorder, "sent her for 'Disorderly Conduct' it is said, but probably for a home." When Emily died in the Refuge, she was buried in the grounds of the institution, "her friends not feeling able to remove the body" (Case No. 13727, December 30, 1870). The orphaned

Eliza Williams was reared by an uncle and aunt who sent her to "live at service." She was committed for disobedience to her aunt. Subsequently, however, she was discharged to the care of her uncle, who sent her passage fare to join his family in Ohio, where they had moved (Case No. 13574, September 6 1870).

43. Case No. 11470 (October 19, 1866), NYHR Records.
44. Case No. 2665 (March 24, 1841), NYHR Records.
45. Case No. 4870 (July 20, 1850), NYHR Records.
46. Case No. 2655 (February 22, 1841), NYHR Records.
47. Case No. 2685 (April 13, 1841), NYHR Records.
48. As examples of Irish uses of the NYHR, see case numbers 8070 (March 5, 1860); 8119 (May 31, 1860); 8139 (June 6, 1860); 8173 (July 3, 1860), NYHR Records.
49. Chaplain's report to the indenturing committee, February 11, 1864, NYHR Records.
50. Case numbers 5012 (December 16, 1850); 5000 (November 18, 1850); 19560 (December 20, 1880), NYHR Records, constitute examples.
51. Case No. 8235 (August 11, 1860), NYHR Records.
52. Case No. 2852 (December 14, 1841), NYHR Records.
53. Case No. 7230 (September 23, 1857), NYHR Records.
54. Case No. 8241 (August 21, 1860), NYHR Records.
55. Case No. 23841 (January 13, 1890), NYHR Records.
56. My italics; Second Convention, 40–42. On the Children's Aid Society, see Stephen O'Connor, *Orphan Trains: The Story of Charles Loring Brace and the Children He Saved and Failed* (Boston: Houghton Mifflin, 2001); Marilyn Irvin Holt, *The Orphan Trains: Placing Out in America* (Lincoln: University of Nebraska Press, 1992).
57. J. M to J. W. Ketcham, May 17, 1862, reproduced in Thirty-eighth Annual Report of the SRJD (for 1862), 53.
58. Thirty-ninth Annual Report of the SRJD (for 1863), 10.
59. Case No. 9376 (July 21, 1863), NYHR Records.
60. Case No. 10644 (September 12, 1865), NYHR Records.
61. Case No. 10638 (September 9 1865), NYHR Records.
62. Case No. 10411 (June 17, 1865), NYHR Records. On Northern teachers and aspiring planters who went south, see Jacqueline Jones, *Soldiers of Light and Love: Northern Teachers and Georgia Blacks, 1865–1873* (Chapel Hill: University of North Carolina Press, 1980); Clara Merritt DeBoer, *Be Jubilant My Feet: African American Abolitionists in the American Missionary Association, 1839–1861* (New York: Garland, 1994); Lawrence N. Powell, *New Masters: Northern Planters During the Civil War and Reconstruction* (New Haven, CT: Yale University Press, 1980).
63. Case No. 10339 (May 19, 1865), NYHR Records.
64. Matthew Frye Jacobson, *Whiteness of a Different Color: European Immigrants and the Alchemy of Race* (Cambridge, MA: Harvard University Press,

1998), 139–70; quotations occur on 161 and 158, respectively; David Roediger, *Colored White: Transcending the Racial Past* (Berkeley and Los Angeles: University of California Press, 2003), 138–68.

65. Roediger, *Colored White*, 138–68.

66. Grace Elizabeth Hale, *Making Whiteness: The Culture of Segregation in the South, 1890–1940* (New York: Pantheon, 1998).

67. Case No. 19515 (November 18, 1880), NYHR Records.

68. Case No. 19403 (August 27, 1880), NYHR Records.

69. Case No. 23994 (July 21, 1890), NYHR Records.

70. Case No. 23861 (February 8, 1890), NYHR Records.

71. Case No. 19365 (August 9, 1880), NYHR Records.

72. Case No. 23938 (May 16, 1890), NYHR Records.

73. Case No. 13397 (April 7, 1870), NYHR Records.

74. Sixty-sixth Annual Report of the SRDJ (for 1890), 40.

75. Thomas Kessner, *Capital City: New York City and the Men Behind America's Rise to Economic Dominance, 1860–1900* (New York: Simon and Schuster, 2003); Carl N. Degler, *The Age of Economic Revolution, 1876–1900* (Glenview, IL: Scott, Foresman, 1967).

76. David Roediger, *Wages of Whiteness: Race and the Making of the American Working Class* (New York: Verso, 1991), 8; and "Inbetween Peoples," in *Colored White*, 141.

77. Superintendent's Daily Journal, Monday, February 26, 1872, NYHR Records. Full details of the 1872 unrest may also be found in Report of Special Committee to the Managers of the House of Refuge, on the Investigation by the State Commissioners of Public Charities, of Charges Made Through the Public Press, Against the Officers and Managers of the House of Refuge, Adopted by the Board, with Memorial to the Commissioners, and Their Report (New York, 1872) [hereafter Report on Investigation (1872)].

78. Superintendent's Daily Journal, Friday, May 17, 1872, NYHR Records.

79. Information about the background of the insurgents are contained in case histories numbered 11195 (June 25, 1866); 11794 (April 10, 1867); 12261 (1867); 11836 (May 7, 1867); 11907 (June 3, 1867); 12102 (September 9, 1867); 12331 (February 11, 1868); 12260 (December 24, 1867); 12009 (July 23, 1867); 13523 (July 27, 1870); 13590 (September 17, 1870); 13616 (October 8, 1870); 13747 (January 18, 1871); 13793 (February 28, 1871); 13882 (May 4, 1871); 13931 (May 29, 1871); 14159 (October 12, 1871); 14168 (October 14, 1871); 14188 (October 31, 1871); 14264 (December 27, 1871); 14286 (January 13, 1871); 14318 (January 30, 1872); 14321 (February 1, 1872); 14337 (February 14, 1872); 14369 (March 5, 1872); 12321 (February 5, 1868); 12500 (June 1868); 14027 (July 25, 1870), NYHR Records.

80. *New York Times*, March 2, 1872.

81. Report on Investigation (1872), 86.

82. Ibid., 117.

83. Ibid., 202-21.
84. Quotation from Roediger, *Wages of Whiteness*, 144.
85. My italics; quotation from Report on Investigation (1872), 168.
86. Report on Investigation (1872), 182, 185-93.
87. Ibid., 8-9.
88. Ibid., 223-24.
89. Pisciotta, "Treatment on Trial," 160-81.
90. Case numbers 2481 (May 1840); 4782 (May 8, 1850); 4923 (September 18, 1850), NYHR Records.
91. Case No. 19213 (May, 1885), NYHR Records.
92. Case No. 8170 (July 3, 1860), NYHR Records.
93. Case No. 19492 (October 27, 1880), NYHR Records.
94. Case No. 2509 (June 8, 1840), NYHR Records.
95. Case No. 8364 (December 24, 1860), NYHR Records.
96. Michael B. Katz, *In the Shadow of the Poorhouse: A Social History of Welfare in America* (New York: Basic, 1986), 18.

CHAPTER 5

1. Mary Kelley, ed., with an introduction, *The Power of Her Sympathy: The Autobiography and Journal of Catharine Maria Sedgwick* (Boston: Massachusetts Historical Society, 1993), 125, 170.
2. Kelley, *The Power of Her Sympathy*, 51-52.
3. On female benevolence and class identity, see: Lori D. Ginzberg, *Women and the Work of Benevolence: Morality, Politics, and Class in the Nineteenth-century United States* (New Haven, CT: Yale University Press, 1990); Christine Stansell, *City of Women: Sex and Class in New York, 1789-1860* (1986; repr., Urbana: University of Illinois Press, 1987); Carroll Smith-Rosenberg, "Writing History: Language, Class, and Gender," in *Feminist Studies/Critical Studies*, ed. Teresa de Lauretis (Bloomington: Indiana University Press, 1986), 31-54, and *Disorderly Conduct: Visions of Gender in Victorian America* (New York: Knopf, 1985); Mary P. Ryan, *Cradle of the Middle Class: The Family in Oneida County, New York, 1790-1865* (New York: Cambridge University Press, 1981); Nancy A. Hewitt, *Women's Activism and Social Change: Rochester, New York, 1822-1872* (Ithaca, NY: Cornell University Press, 1984); Kathleen D. McCarthy, *Noblesse Oblige: Charity and Cultural Philanthropy in Chicago, 1849-1929* (Chicago: University of Chicago Press, 1982).

On prisons and prison reform, see: Estelle Freedman, *Their Sisters' Keepers: Women's Prison Reform in America, 1830-1930* (Ann Arbor: University of Michigan Press, 1981), "Sentiment and Discipline: Women's Prison Experiences in Nineteenth-century America," *Prologue: Journal of the National Archives* 16 (Winter 1984), 249-59, and *Maternal Justice: Miriam Van Waters and the Female Reform*

Tradition (Chicago: University of Chicago Press, 1996); David J. Rothman, *The Discovery of the Asylum: Social Order and Disorder in the New Republic* (Boston: Little, Brown, 1971); Michel Foucault, *Discipline and Punish: The Birth of the Prison*, trans. Alan Sheridan (New York: Vintage, 1977); Michel Ignatieff, *A Just Measure of Pain: The Penitentiary in the Industrial Revolution, 1750–1850* (New York: Pantheon, 1978); Allen Steinberg, *The Transformation of Criminal Justice: Philadelphia, 1800–1860* (Chapel Hill: University of North Carolina Press, 1989); Alexander W. Pisciotta, *Benevolent Repression: Social Control and the American Prison-reformatory Movement* (New York: New York University Press, 1994); Norval Morris and David J. Rothman, eds., *The Oxford History of the Prison: The Practice of Punishment in Western Society* (New York: Oxford University Press, 1995); Anne M. Butler, *Gendered Justice in the American West: Women Prisoners in Men's Penitentiaries* (Urbana: University of Illinois Press, 1997); Mark Colvin, *Penitentiaries, Reformatories, and Chain Gangs: Social Theory and the History of Punishment in Nineteenth-century America* (New York: St. Martin's Press, 1997).

On mostly white women in moral reform and charity work in the nineteenth century, see also: Nancy Cott, *The Bonds of Womanhood: "Woman's Sphere" in New England, 1780–1835* (New Haven, CT: Yale University Press, 1977); Kathryn Kish Sklar, *Catharine Beecher: A Study in American Domesticity* (New Haven, CT: Yale University Press, 1973), and *Florence Kelley and the Nation's Work: The Rise of Women's Political Culture, 1830–1900* (New Haven, CT: Yale University Press, 1995); Ruth Bordin, *Women and Temperance: The Quest for Power and Liberty, 1873–1900* (Philadelphia: Temple University Press, 1981); Barbara Leslie Epstein, *The Politics of Domesticity: Women, Evangelism, and Temperance in Nineteenth-century America* (Middletown, CT: Wesleyan University Press, 1981); Anne M. Boylan, "Women in Groups: An Analysis of Women's Benevolent Organizations in New York and Boston, 1797–1840," *Journal of American History* 71 (December 1984), 497–523; Mary P. Ryan, *Women in Public: Between Banners and Ballots, 1825–1880* (Baltimore: Johns Hopkins University Press, 1990); Peggy Pascoe, *Relations of Rescue: The Search for Female Moral Authority in the American West, 1874–1939* (New York: Oxford University Press, 1990); Robyn Muncy, *Creating a Female Dominion in American Reform, 1890–1935* (New York: Oxford University Press, 1991); Anne F. Scott, *Natural Allies: Women's Associations in American History* (Urbana: University of Illinois Press, 1991); David Gollaher, *Voice for the Mad: The Life of Dorothea Dix* (New York: Free Press, 1995).

4. Kelley, *The Power of Her Sympathy*, 53; Ginsberg, *Women and the Work of Benevolence*, 214.

5. On the objectives of the PANY, see the Second Report of the Prison Association of New York, Including the Constitution and By-laws and a List of Officers and Members (1846), microfilm edition, NYPL, 21. The Female Department separated from the parent body in 1854. In 1858 the WPA Home was named after Isaac T. Hopper, an inspector of prisons in Philadelphia, founder of the Female

Department, and an antislavery activist. For a biographical sketch of Hopper, see Caroline M. Kirkland, *The Helping Hand: Comprising an Account of the Home, for Discharged Female Convicts, and Appeal in Behalf of That Institution* (New York: Scribner, 1853), 133–34.

6. Ginzberg, *Women and the Work of Benevolence*, 214; see also Stansell, *City of Women*, 41–101.

7. Smith-Rosenberg, "Writing History."

8. For a biography of Gibbons, see Margaret Hope Bacon, *Abby Hopper Gibbons: Prison Reformer and Social Activist* (Albany: State University of New York Press, 2000).

9. William S. Osborne, *Caroline M. Kirkland* (New York: Twayne, 1972), 18.

10. Kelley, *The Power of Her Sympathy*, 8, 32, 38–39.

11. Barbara Welter, "The Cult of True Womanhood, 1820–1860," *American Quarterly* 18 (Summer 1966), 151–74. See also Mary Kelley, "Commentary," in *Locating American Studies: The Evolution of a Discipline*, ed. Lucy Maddox (Baltimore: John Hopkins University Press, 1999), 43–70.

12. Kirkland, *The Helping Hand*, 32, 40–41, 74.

13. Fourteenth Annual Report of the Women's Prison Association and Home (1859), Special Collections, NYPL [hereafter WPA&H], 5–6; Twentieth Annual Report of the WPA&H (1863–64), 8. Funded by private donations and regular subscriptions supplemented after 1858 by grants from the Board of the Corporation of New York, the Hopper Home hoped to achieve economic self-sufficiency through inmate labor before long.

14. Kirkland, *The Helping Hand*, 33, 56, 58, 61–63.

15. Ibid., 57, 62, 84–85; Fourth Annual Report of the Female Department of the Prison Association of New York (1848), microfilm edition, New York Public Library [hereafter FDP], 3–4.

16. Kirkland, *The Helping Hand*, 84–85.

17. Case Descriptions and Rolls, 1845–55, Women's Prison Association Records, Special Collections, NYPL [hereafter WPA Case Records].

18. On female prison reformers' emphasis on men's roles in women's falls from virtue, see Freedman, *Their Sisters' Keepers*, 43.

19. Mary Flynn to Anna Curtis, April 9, 1856, WPA Records.

20. Hasia R. Diner, *Erin's Daughters in America: Irish Immigrant Women in the Nineteenth Century* (Baltimore: Johns Hopkins University Press, 1983), 20, 23, 24, 27, 46; Stansell, *City of Women*, 77–78.

21. Cases of Elizabeth Martin, Rebecca Green, Mary Fine, and Mary/Hester Wyman, WPA Case Records.

22. Cited in Cynthia Owen Philip, ed., *Imprisoned in America: Prison Communications, 1776 to Attica* (New York: Harper and Row, 1973), 82.

23. Eighth Annual Report of the FDP (1852), 3–4; Fifth Annual Report of the FDP (1849), 5; Tenth Annual Report of the WPA&H (1855), 3. On campaigns

for separate women's prisons and against the sexual exploitation of women, see Freedman, *Their Sisters' Keepers*, 28–29, 46–64, 157; Ginzberg, *Women and the Work of Benevolence*, 182.

24. On the "women in the neighborhoods," see Stansell, *City of Women*, 41–75.

25. Cases of Catharine Smith and Sarah Thorp, WPA Case Records.

26. Report of the Committee on Prisons, December 4, 1855, WPA Records.

27. Kirkland, *The Helping Hand*, 104–5.

28. Ibid., 107–9.

29. Cited in Freedman, *Their Sisters' Keepers*, 86.

30. Cases of Jane Dougherty, Maria Warren, Joanna Murphy, and Mary Bantam, WPA Case Records.

31. As Stansell has argued, for evangelical reformers, "the language of virtue and vice" became "code of class." See *City of Women*, 66.

32. Cases of Mary Smith and Elisa Arlington, WPA Case Records.

33. Cases of Ann Jones, Maria Gilbert, Sarah Porter, Margaret Gibson, Ann Atkinson, and Marcella DeLoinge, WPA Case Records; Report of the Committee to Visit Penitentiary on Blackwell's Island, Annual Report of the PANY (1845), 11.

34. Kirkland, *The Helping Hand*, 60.

35. Ibid., 17–18.

36. Ibid., 70–72; Prison Report, October 6, 1856, WPA Records.

37. My italics.

38. Kirkland, *The Helping Hand*, 76–77, 83–84. Estelle Freedman has explained female prison reformers' rejection of hereditarian notions of crime in terms of the professionalization of benevolence, which in the postwar era was accompanied by the eclipse of the doctrine of separate spheres (*Their Sisters' Keepers*, 125, 131). I argue that inmate perspectives also contributed to the reformers' embrace of environmentalist analyses of crime.

39. Kirkland, *The Helping Hand*, 86.

40. Fourteenth Annual Report of the WPA&H (1859), 6.

41. Kirkland, *The Helping Hand*, 14–15, 51.

42. Ibid., 74.

43. Ibid., 60, 81.

44. Margaret Ann Mumpton to Anna Curtis, September 1, 1857; Elizabeth Hamilton to Curtis, April 1, 1858, WPA Records.

45. Cases of Ann Ashford, Ann Drummond, Mary G., Elizabeth Williamson, and Lucy Bebe, WPA Case Records; Seventh Annual Report of the FDP (1851), 11.

46. Twenty-first Annual Report of the WPA (1865), 11.

47. On Irish women's preference for domestic service, see Diner, *Erin's Daughters in America*, 74.

48. Salutations such as "Respected Madams" and "My Noble Benefactor" suggested deference and gratitude. One letter read, "Respected Madams, . . . I can now attend my church, and read my Bible in my leisure hours undisturbed." A

factory worker wrote, "My Dear Mrs. G., we do not know how . . . to show our gratitude to you for sending us to such a respectable place." See Fifth Annual Report of the FDP (1849), 13; the Fifteenth Annual Report of the WPA&H (1860), 9.

49. Cases of Margaret Masterton, Sarah Wims, Catharine Pinckney, Ann Hamilton, Margaret Linar, Bridget King, Ann Garvey, Elizabeth Grey, Elizabeth Hammond, Jane Bradley, Ann McGowen, Mary Carpenter, WPA Case Records; Minutes of the Visiting Committee, July 8, no year, Correspondence and Reports, 1845–1890, WPA Records.

50. Sixth Annual Report of the FDP (1850), 112.

51. "Objects," First Annual Report of the Central Council of the Charity Organization Society of the City of New York, April 1, 1883, Charity Organization Society of the City of New York, Annual Reports and Miscellaneous Papers, microfilm edition, NYPL [hereafter COS Papers]. On the Charity Organization movement, see Michael B. Katz, *In the Shadow of the Poorhouse: A Social History of Welfare in America* (New York: Basic, 1986), 58–84; Frank Dekker Watson, *The Charity Organization Movement of the United States: A Study of American Philanthropy* (New York: Macmillan, 1922). On a founder of the movement, see Joan Waugh, *Unsentimental Reformer: The Life of Josephine Shaw Lowell* (Cambridge, MA: Harvard University Press, 1997).

52. Eighteenth Annual Report of the WPA&H (1862), 6.

53. Sixteenth Annual Report of the WPA&H (1860), 6; Twenty-fifth Annual Report of the WPA&H (1869), 10; Twenty-sixth Annual Report of the WPA&H (1870), 10; Fortieth Annual Report of the WPA&H (1884), 9; Forty-fourth Annual Report of the WPA&H (1888), 9; Forty-seventh Annual Report of the WPA&H (1891), 7; Fifty-first Annual Report of the WPA&H (1895), 5.

54. Ginzberg, *Women and the Work of Benevolence*, 133–73, 190.

55. Twenty-seventh Annual Report of the WPA&H (1871), 10.

56. Quotation from Twenty-sixth Annual Report of the WPA&H (1870), 10; see also Twenty-fourth Annual Report of the WPA&H (1868), 10.

57. Forty-first Annual Report of the WPA&H (1885), 6.

58. Twenty-fourth Annual Report of the WPA&H (1868), 9.

59. Forty-seventh Annual Report of the WPA&H (1891), 5–6.

60. Reports of the Home Department, Eleventh Annual Report of the WPA&H (1855), 11, and the Fifty-first Annual Report of the WPA&H (1895), 10. The proportion of women listed as "discharged," "left to provide for themselves," and "went to work, did not return" increased steadily in the years in between, reaching well above 35 percent in certain years.

61. Fifty-first Annual Report of the WPA&H (1895), 6.

62. Report of the Prison Visitor for 1888, Forty-fourth Annual Report of the WPA&H (1888), 21–24; Fifty-fifth Annual Report of the WPA&H (1899), 21.

63. Fifty-seventh Annual Report of the WPA&H (1901), 40.

64. Ibid., 40–41.

65. Fifty-fourth Annual Report of the WPA&H (1897–98), 23; Fifty-sixth Annual Report of the WPA&H (1900), 29.
66. Fifty-fifth Annual Report of the WPA&H (1899), 22.
67. Forty-third Annual Report of the WPA&H (1887), 23; Fiftieth Annual Report of the WPA&H (1894), 23.
68. Quotations from Fifty-second Annual Report of the WPA&H (1896), 24; see also Report of the Prison Visitor, January 2, 1896, 28, WPA Records; Fifty-fourth Annual Report of the WPA&H (1898), 24.
69. Forty-sixth Annual Report of the WPA&H (1890), 18.
70. Fifty-sixth Annual Report of the WPA&H (1900), 20–21.
71. Forty-seventh Annual Report of the WPA&H (1891), 6.
72. Forty-fifth Annual Report of the WPA&H (1889), 5.
73. Forty-sixth Annual Report of the WPA&H (1890), 25–26; Forty-seventh Annual Report of the WPA&H (1891), 5.
74. Bacon, *Abby Hopper Gibbons*, 164–65.
75. Hamilton Fish to Gibbons, April 6, 1889; Minutes of Executive Committee Meetings, May 14, 1889, WPA Records. On Fish's background, see Proceedings of the Legislature of the State of New York in Memory of Hon. Hamilton Fish Held at the Capitol, Thursday Evening, April 5, 1894 (Albany: J. B. Lyon, 1894).
76. Fish to Gibbons, May 22, 1889, WPA Records.
77. Minutes of the Executive Committee Meeting, March 4, 1890, WPA Records.
78. Bacon, *Abby Hopper Gibbons*, 165; Forty-eighth Annual Report of the WPA&H (1892), 6.
79. Freedman, *Their Sisters' Keepers*, 131. Ruth M. Alexander's *The "Girl Problem": Female Sexual Delinquency in New York, 1900–1930* (Ithaca, NY: Cornell University Press, 1995) is a splendid study of Bedford's inmates.

CHAPTER 6

1. Marjorie C. Snevily to H. Hollingsworth Wood, September 5, 1915, and October 17, 1918, Howard Orphanage and Industrial School Records, Manuscripts, Archives, and Rare Books Division, Schomburg Center for Research in Black Culture, New York [hereafter HOIS]. Wood, a white Quaker lawyer, became president of the Orphanage in 1913. In order to protect the privacy of Howard alumni, I have used pseudonyms for all alums and their families mentioned in the text. In the notes, I have identified letters written to and by them by citing their initials rather than their full names. Anne Smith's true initials were M. J. Her demographic details may be found in the Thirteenth Census of the United States (1910) for the Borough of Brooklyn, under entries for the Brooklyn Howard Colored Orphan Asylum. Before entering the Snevily home, M. J. was placed with the family of a Brooklyn real estate broker named D. S. Willis, who

promised to send her to school. When the Willises reneged on their promise on the grounds that M. J. was "so backward in her work that it required every minute of her time . . . to do her lessons . . . she of course could never become a teacher"; the Orphanage superintendent, Mary Gordon, removed her from the Willis home. See letter by D. S. Willis to Wood, n.d., HOIS. For an institutional history of the Howard Orphanage and Industrial School, see Carlton Mabee, "Charity in Travail: Two Orphan Asylums for Blacks," *New York History* 55 (January 1974), 55–77.

2. Marjorie Snevily to Wood, November 1918 (no day), HOIS.

3. See chapter 3, "Putting on Style," in Kathy Peiss, *Cheap Amusements: Working Women and Leisure in Turn-of-the-century New York* (Philadelphia: Temple University Press, 1986).

4. On America's competing nationalisms of race and civic equality, see Gary Gerstle, *American Crucible: Race and Nation in the Twentieth Century* (Princeton, NJ: Princeton University Press, 2001). My understanding and use of the term "multipositional"—based on Earl Lewis's discussion of that concept in "To Turn as on a Pivot: Writing African Americans into a History of Overlapping Diasporas," *American Historical Review* 100 (June 1995), 783—is developed in greater detail later in the chapter.

5. Lewis, "To Turn as on a Pivot," 783. Lewis has noted that historians have often separated black people's workplace experiences from the worlds of their community and home, treating the class and race aspects of African American identity as "simply additive or subtractive." Instead, he proposes that we scrutinize the "interactive construction of identity—as child, lover, spouse" in conjunction with the more familiar categories of race, class, color, and gender. Historian Evelyn Brooks Higginbotham has also pointed out that the "apparent overdeterminancy" of race in the United States has eclipsed not only other categories of social relations like gender, but also the interrelationships among these categories. See Evelyn Brooks Higginbotham, "African American Women's History and the Meta-language of Race," *Signs* 17 (Winter 1992), 251–74.

6. William Roseberry, "Hegemony and the Language of Contention," in *Everyday Forms of State Formation: Revolution and the Negotiation of Rule in Modern Mexico*, ed. Gilbert M. Joseph and Daniel Nugent (Durham, NC: Duke University Press, 1994), 363–64. In *Nationalist Thought and the Colonial World: A Derivative Discourse?* (London: Zed, 1986), Partha Chatterjee argues that Indian nationalists attacked imperialism at least partly in terms of the very premises of reason and modernity that were used to legitimize colonial rule.

On black orphanages, see Sandra M. O'Donnell, "The Care of Dependent African American Children in Chicago: The Struggle Between Black Self-help and Professionalism," *Journal of Social History* 27 (Summer 1994), 763–76. Timothy A. Hacsi, *Second Home: Orphan Asylums and Poor Families in America* (Cambridge, MA: Harvard University Press, 1997) is a sweeping institutional study of orphanages in general. See also Kenneth Cmiel, *A Home of Another Kind: One Chicago Orphanage and the Tangle of Child Welfare* (Chicago: University of Chicago Press, 1995); Nurith Zmora, *Orphanages Reconsidered: Child Care Institutions in Progressive Era Baltimore* (Philadelphia: Temple University Press, 1994); David R. Contosta, *Philadelphia's Progressive Orphanage: The Carson Valley School* (University Park: Penn State University Press, 1997). On the more recent history of race and child welfare, see Dorothy Roberts, *Shattered Bonds: The Color of Child Welfare* (New York: Basic, 2002); Sondra Jackson and Sheryl Brissett-Chapman, *Serving African American Children: Child Welfare Perspectives* (New Brunswick, NJ: Transaction, 1999). The literature on black philanthropy is vast. See note 25 to the introduction of this work.

7. Gerstle, *American Crucible*.

8. Matthew Frye Jacobson, *Whiteness of a Different Color: European Immigrants and the Alchemy of Race* (Cambridge, MA: Harvard University Press, 1998), 139–70; David R. Roediger, *Colored White: Transcending the Racial Past* (Berkeley and Los Angeles: University of California Press, 2003); Grace Elizabeth Hale, *Making Whiteness: The Culture of Segregation in the South, 1890–1940* (New York: Pantheon, 1998)

9. Ania Loomba, *Colonialism/Postcolonialism* (London: Routledge, 1998), 137; Akhil Gupta and James Ferguson, eds., *Culture, Power, Place: Explorations in Critical Anthropology* (Durham, NC: Duke University Press, 1997), 15.

10. Mabee, "Charity in Travail"; *Review Covering Forty-five Years of Work of the Brooklyn Howard Colored Orphan Asylum*, HOIS, (hereafter cited as *Review*), 8–15; *Brooklyn Eagle*, March 20, 1913. Sarah Tillman's profession is, curiously enough, listed as "Intelligence" in H. Wilson's compiled *Trow's New York City Directory, Volume LXXIX for the Year Ending May 1, 1866* (New York, 1866), NYPL. Tillman left New York in October 1870. The names of the pre-1902 officers and Managers occur in the Seventeenth Annual Report of the Howard Colored Orphan Asylum of the City of Brooklyn, Dean Street, near Troy Avenue, for the Year Ending September 30, 1885, NYPL. Information on three of the officers' professions is available in *Trow's New York City Directory Volume XCVIII for the Year Ending May 1, 1885* (New York, 1885), NYPL. In 1885 the organization's first directress, Mrs. L. A. Cooper, was listed in a New York City directory simply as "widow," while both its second directress, H. E. Thompson, a single woman, and its treasurer and corresponding secretary, Augusta Johnson, a married women, were classified as laundresses.

11. One white minister complained that Howard's policy of keeping its Board of Managers all black alienated white donors. In 1896, for instance, the white-run Colored Orphan Asylum reported total receipts of over $47,000, while the HOIS could claim only $17,666. See Annual Report of the Howard Colored Orphan Asylum—Brooklyn to the State Board of Charities, Albany, New York, for the fiscal year ending September 30, 1896; Annual Report of the Colored Orphan

Asylum and Association for Benefit of Colored Children, New York to the State Board, for the same year, both in *Annual Reports of Orphan Asylums and Homes for the Friendless, 1873–1896*, State Board of Charities, in New York State Archives.

12. On stereotypes of black incompetence in benevolence management, see O'Donnell, "The Care of Dependent African American Children in Chicago," 769.

13. The new Board of Managers that took over in 1902 consisted of eleven gentlemen representing six black churches and five white ones. The Women's Auxiliary, established in 1904, visited, sewed for, and provisioned the children in various ways. Josephine W. Whitlatch, a sixty-year-old white widow and member of the Dutch Reformed Church, led the Auxiliary. See *Review*, 7–13, 19.

14. Ibid., 43–44.

15. Summary and Verification of Schedule D. of the Homes for Children Report filled out by the Howard Orphanage and Industrial School for the New York State Board of Charities, 1912, HOIS.

16. Report of General Inspection of HOIS by New York State Board of Charities, September 1914, HOIS, 4–5.

17. A. G. to Wood, September 10, 1920, HOIS.

18. G. B. to the superintendent, November 21, 1913; Joseph Handy to Wood, January 29, 1914, both in HOIS.

19. A. R. to Wood, October 5, 1918, HOIS.

20. Thomas F. Moore, assistant superintendent, New York SPCC, to Wood, June 4, 1914, HOIS.

21. For evidence about Wood's relationship with Booker T. Washington, see Washington to Wood, August 5, October 1 and 20, 1913, November 13 and 18, 1913, May 17, 1915; Wood to Washington, November 18, 1913; Wood to C. M. Pratt, December 31, 1913, all in HOIS. Ida Tarbell refused to let the Orphanage use her name as one of its patrons at its 1915 annual benefit on the grounds that she had "found it necessary to make the rule not to give my name to any cause which I have not personally investigated." See Tarbell to Wood, March 19, 1915. On the role of the State Board of Charities in prompting the switch to a "cottage system" at King's Park, see "Workers' Facts," a one-page printed sheet in HOIS. *The Amsterdam News*, March 28, 1913, contained information on the following members of Howard's new Board of Managers: whites included Wood; Clinton Rossiter, vice-president of the Brooklyn Trust Company, banker, and philanthropist; Alfred Whitman of the banking firm of Knauth, Nachod, and Kuhne, a trustee of Manassas School for Colored Youth, and member of the NAACP; Willard Bayliss, lawyer and real estate expert; Mansfield B. Snevily, manager of the Oil Seed Company; Edgar McDonald, president of the Nassau Bank; and Carolena M. Wood, the president's sister and first directress of the New York Colored Orphan Asylum at Riverdale-on-Hudson. The black managers included W. H. Brooks,

pastor of St. Marks Methodist Episcopal Church; W. M. Moss, pastor of Concord Baptist Church; E. P. Roberts, a physician and examining doctor for the Board of Education; S. W. Simms, pastor of Holy Trinity Church; and O. M. Waller, physician.

The HOIS records contain stray references to the friction among the institution's African American trustees on the eve of as well as on the occasion of the change in management in 1913, yet they are silent on the details of the dispute. A letter written by Mary Gordon, who became Howard's matron in 1902 and its superintendent in 1914, to Wood is an example: "I tried to treat Mr. Trotman [a black real estate broker and later Howard Manager] with courtesy even when he spoke as he did concerning the past efforts of the Institution. I knew he did not know what he was talking about . . . I do know that many of the best people of both races have worked for the institution. In both races there are jealousies and disgruntled factions who pull apart. There is no such thing as perfect union and harmony among all of the people—we can only hope to blend certain ones as certain notes in a chord" (April 16, 1914, HOIS).

22. O'Donnell, "The Care of Dependent African American Children in Chicago," 763.

23. Annual Report of the Board of Managers and Trustees of the Brooklyn Howard Colored Orphan Asylum, October 1905 to October 1906, NYPL, 19.

24. Michael Katz, *In the Shadow of the Poorhouse: A Social History of Welfare in America* (New York: Basic, 1986), 118–19.

25. *Review*, 51–52.

26. On the black migration and/or urban experience in the North, see note 24 to the introduction of this work. Most African American women secured work in domestic service. On this point, see Elizabeth Clark-Lewis, *Living In, Living Out: African American Domestics in Washington DC, 1900–1940* (Washington, DC: Smithsonian Institution Press, 1994); Sharon Harley, "For the Good of the Race: Gender, Work, and Domestic Roles in the Black Community, 1880–1930," *Signs* 15 (Winter 1990), 336–49; Mary Romero, *Made in the USA* (New York: Routledge, 1992); Bonnie Thornton Dill, *Across the Boundaries of Race and Class: An Exploration of Work and Family Among Black Female Domestic Servants* (New York: Garland, 1994).

27. The pictorial logo juxtaposing "the undeveloped" with "the developed" adorned pledge cards of the Brooklyn Howard Colored Orphan Asylum in HOIS. Information on public events such as concerts and fairs may be found in flyers announcing programs on November 19 (no year), April 27, 1913, the Yule-Tide Bazaar on December 15–19, 1913, Spring Bazaar on April 22–25, 1913; see also Mary Gordon to Wood, February 23, 1915, and *New York Age*, January 6, 1916, all in HOIS.

28. *New York Times*, March 29, 1917.

29. Pledge card accompanying letter written by Wood to Dr. Schieffelin, July 3, 1914, HOIS.

30. Flyer accompanying publicity literature entitled "The Situation Which Faces the New Managers," January 1, 1914, HOIS.

31. The Report of the Bureau of Institutional Inspection, Department of Public Charities, submitted to the New York State Board of Charities [hereafter Inspection Report], February 1917, 16–17.

32. Report of the Superintendent to the Board of Managers, April 23, 1914, HOIS.

33. Snevily to Wood, December 29, 1913, HOIS.

34. Wood to E. C., March 31 and May 10, 1917, HOIS.

35. James Gordon to Wood, July 3, 1913; Snevily to Wood, December 29, 1913. The Orphanage's pre-1913 constitution and bylaws had conferred sweeping powers on the superintendent. Article 7 of that document gave the superintendent under "the advice and direction of the several standing committees . . . full direction and control of the asylum," including the power to appoint staff, edit the Annual Report, and keep all books and records "required by law or the Board of Managers and Trustees." Snevily urged that the superintendent's duties "be changed in such a way that [he] shall perform such duties as he may be instructed in . . . by the Board of Managers. . . . That he shall have no power to purchase or sell property of the Society" without the direction of a relevant standing committee; Snevily also maintained "that he may employ such persons only as may be authorized by the Board of Managers" (Snevily to Wood, April 2, 1913). See also "Suggestions, Change, By-Laws, etc., March 31, 1913," typed manuscript, HOIS.

36. James H. Gordon to Wood, n.d., HOIS. Snevily was especially critical of what he considered James Gordon's lack of efficiency, attention to detail, and economy in the running of the farm, the upkeep of the equipment, and the low standard of technical instruction to the young men. Gordon in return resented attempts to micromanage the farm and institution by men not fully conversant with the exigencies of its operation; she also resented the Managers' seeming lack of sensitivity to the range of tasks that the superintendent had to accomplish on any given day. As he wrote Wood, "There has been no disposition, either on the part of Mrs. Gordon or myself to disregard anything that has been advised but as you know there are a hundred and one things here to look after and it takes a little time for us as well as you gentlemen to get on to the system that you have in mind. . . . I received a letter from Mr. Henry Underhill regarding the silage. I am well aware of the fact that this is not the time to cut the main crop of corn for the silo . . . but the fodder corn was getting dry and it would be very much better to cut the corn and put it in the silo rather than to allow it to dry up and lose its substance" (Gordon to Wood, July 26, 1913, HOIS).

On the Gordon-Snevily standoff, see also Snevily to Gordon, March 21, November 7, and December 5, 1913; Snevily to Wood, July 3 and 29, and September 8, 1913; Wood to Gordon, September 18, 1913, all in HOIS.

37. *Review*, 17; Inspection Report, 1917, 50, both in HOIS. Mary Gordon and both her parents were born in Pennsylvania. James Gordon hailed from Virginia. Their demographic details are available in the Thirteenth Census of the United States (1910) for the Borough of Brooklyn.

38. Evelyn Brooks Higginbotham, *Righteous Discontent: The Women's Movement in the Black Baptist Church* (Cambridge, MA: Harvard University Press, 1993), 185–229.

39. Gordon to Wood, October 16, 1914, HOIS. Howard's promotional literature stressed the centrality of propriety to the children's training. The institution tried to avoid placing its young women in families with young men because, as Gordon's husband and predecessor explained, "the Negro girl is exposed to all kinds of indignities and frequently destroyed by her employer." See James Gordon to Reverend Olin B. Coit, May 7, 1912, HOIS.

40. Gordon to Wood, September 26, 1914, HOIS.

41. Mary Gordon smarted at the appropriation of her authority to hire and fire Orphanage staff: "I would much prefer engaging the bookkeeper and other employees simply upon the authority of superintendent . . . since they are to be directed by me and under my supervision, they must feel they are amenable to me and that I have power to employ and *discharge*, otherwise my authority is weakened. . . . I will add that I feel perfectly competent to judge the competency of help I may have to have" (Gordon to Wood, April 2, 1914, HOIS). She dismissed a custodian for what she deemed promiscuous behavior but reinstated him at the request of his fiancé, a teacher at the institution. She explained her action to Wood thusly: "I think the main thing Mr. Taylor [the custodian] had to learn was that I am not a figurehead here—Miss Campbell [the teacher] said in talking to me last Monday, 'Oh! Mrs. Gordon, Mr. Taylor did not understand you had such authority . . . , he thought . . . you can't discharge him, he is Mr. Snevily's man.'" Thus, Gordon added, her action had demonstrated that employees could not flout institutional standards in disregard of her authority (Gordon to Wood, October 16, 1914, HOIS).

42. City Inspection Report, 1917, 10—48; State Inspection Report, 1914, both in HOIS.

43. City Inspection Report, 1917, 40–41, 48, 54, HOIS.

44. Ibid., 10.

45. See, for instance, Rudolph R. Reeder, *How Two Hundred Children Live and Learn* (New York: Charities Publications Committee, 1909); Dorothy M. Brown and Elizabeth McKeown, *The Poor Belong to Us: Catholic Charities and American Welfare* (Cambridge, MA: Harvard University Press, 1997); Reena Sigman Friedman, *These Are Our Children: Jewish Orphanages in the United States, 1880–1925* (Hanover, NH: University Press of New England, 1994); W. J. Doherty, *A Study of the Results of Institutional Care* (New York: Russell Sage Foundation, 1915).

46. City Inspection Report, 1917, 48, 50–51, HOIS.

47. Washington to Wood, November 18, 1913, HOIS. Washington's words were especially high praise coming from a man who disapproved of orphanages, as is quite evident from his remarks before the 1909 White House conference on dependent children. Of course, such disapproval must be evaluated in the context of Washington's view that black dependence was a peculiar pathology of migration to the urban North. In his White House remarks, he urged whites to help African Americans remain in their Southern homes.

48. State Inspection Report, January 1916, 22; and December 1916, 25, both in HOIS.

49. Thomas Marshall's real initials were W. C. His case may be pieced together from the following pieces of correspondence: Amos Peaslee to Wood, May 1, 1915; George E. Stevens to Wood, May 13 and June 30, 1915; Wood to George E. Stevens, May 22, 1915; Wood to Gordon, May 25, 1915; Gordon to Wood, May 28 and June 3, 1915; Wood to Thomas J. Cuff, assistant U.S. attorney general, Brooklyn, February 7, 1916; Wood to W. C., March 10, 1917; W. C. to Wood, July 13 and October 17, 1915, April 1, 1917; Wood to W. G. Nealy, April 4, 1917, all in HOIS. On the child savers' reservations about institutions, see Katz, *In the Shadow of the Poorhouse*, 118.

50. Orphanages run by religious minorities like Catholics and Jews were similar to black orphanages in terms of their internal class relations, their commitment to a combination of uplift, cultural preservation and Americanization, and their relationship with a sometimes-hostile world. See, for example, Friedman, *These Are Our Children*. On Jewish orphanages, see also Hyman Bogen, *The Luckiest Orphans: A History of the Hebrew Orphan Asylum of New York* (Urbana: University of Illinois Press, 1992); Jules Doneson, *Deeds of Love: A History of the Jewish Foster Home and Orphan Asylum of Philadelphia* (New York: Vantage, 1996); Howard Goldstein, *The Home on Gorham Street and the Voices of its Children* (Tuscaloosa: University of Alabama Press, 1996); Ira A. Greenberg, Richard G. Safran, and Sam George Arcus, eds., *The Hebrew National Orphan Home: Memories of Orphanage Life* (Westport, CT: Greenwood, 2001). Yet, there were also significant differences. For example, Dorothy M. Brown and Elizabeth McKeown, in *The Poor Belong to Us*, have shown that some Catholic charities regarded the practice of benevolence as a sort of meritorious service that would lead to the salvation of their own souls. I would also point out that the rigid construction of supposedly inalienable racial differences in American society, the acute financial challenges faced by black voluntary associations, and the unique historical experiences of African Americans lent the internal and external negotiations of black orphanages a very distinctive meaning on political, cultural, and personal levels. These issues emerge throughout my discussion of the implications of "whiteness" discourse for black subaltern identity formation, as well as my argument about the intimate familial (but hierarchical) character of the Howard Orphanage.

51. On reformers views on orphanages, see "Letter to the President of the United States Embodying the Conclusions of the Conference on the Care of Dependent Children, 1909," reprinted in Robert H. Bremner, *Children and Youth in America: A Documentary History*, 3 vols. (Cambridge, MA: Harvard University Press 1971), 2:365.

52. For instance, as Friedman has reported, as early as 1869 a *New York Times* observer commented on the "homelike" character of the Hebrew Orphan Asylum when compared with other orphanages. See Friedman, *These Are Our Children*, 51. Bogen suggests that Jewish institutions were superior to their Gentile counterparts because they were built later and thus benefitted for from the mistakes of those who had gone before them, and also because they enjoyed the united support of their communities (and thus were better funded). See Bogen, *Luckiest Orphans*, 170.

53. Friedman, *These Are Our Children*, 43, 38.

54. Ibid., 71–72.

55. Bogen, *Luckiest Orphans*, 161–62.

56. Goldstein, *House on Gorham Street*, 128.

57. Brown and McKeown, *Poor Belong to Us*, 100–101.

58. The literature on the African American family in slavery and freedom is rich and voluminous. On the adaptation of the African tradition of consanguineous families to New World exigencies, see Christine Farnham, "Sapphire? The Issue of Dominance in the Slave Family, 1830–1865," in *"To Toil the Livelong Day": America's Women at Work, 1780–1980*, ed. Carol Groneman and Mary Beth Norton (Ithaca, NY: Cornell University Press, 1987), 68–83. On the slave family, see also: Deborah Gray White, *Ar'n't . . . oman? Female Slaves in the Plantation South* (New York: Norton, 1985); Elizabeth Fox-Genovese, *Within the Plantation Household Black and White Women of the Old South* (Chapel Hill: University of North Carolina Press, 1988); Tera Hunter, *To Joy My Freedom: Southern Black Women's Lives and Labors After the Civil War* (Cambridge, MA: Harvard University Press, 1997); John W. Blassingame, *The Slave Community: Plantation Life in the Antebellum South* (New York: Oxford University Press, 1972); Eugene D. Genovese, *Roll Jordan Roll: The World The Slaves Made* (New York: Pantheon, 1974); Herbert G. Gutman. *The Black Family in Slavery and Freedom, 1750–1925* (New York: Pantheon, 1976); Jacqueline Jones, *Labor of Love, Labor of Sorrow: Black Women, Work, and the Family from Slavery to the Present* (New York: Basic, 1985). The inmate case histories of the nation's first juvenile reformatory, the New York House of Refuge, are filled with examples of extended surrogate families among African Americans in nineteenth-century New York. See chapter 4 of this work, and Gunja SenGupta, "Black and 'Dangerous'? African American Working Poor Perspectives on Juvenile Reform and Welfare in Victorian New York, 1840–1890," *Journal of Negro History* 86 (Spring 2001), 99–131.

59. State Inspection Report, 1915, 26, 28–29; Gordon to Wood, December 14,

1915; Superintendent's Report to the Board of Managers, March 1915, 2; flyers advertising Easter Bazaar, March 22–26, 1915; Yuletide Bazaar, December 15–19, 1913; and Spring Bazaar, April 22–25, 1913, all in HOIS.

60. City Inspection Report, 1917, 60; and State Inspection Report, 1915, 23–24, HOIS.

61. City Inspection Report, 1917, 1–8, HOIS.

62. On the background of Howard's teachers, see Superintendent's Report to the Board of Managers for the Year Ending October 31, 1914, 2–3; and State Inspection Report, 1915, 22–25, both in HOIS.

63. Typewritten pantomime scripts, n.d., HOIS. The scripts are untitled, simply labeled "Scenario I," "Scenario II," and so forth.

64. Hale, *Making Whiteness*, 228, 229.

65. For recent examples of work on social inequalities within the black community, see essays by Elizabeth Dale, Beth Tompkins Bates, and Kevin Gaines in *AHA Forum, American Historical Review* 102 (April 1997), 311–87.

66. My italics.

67. Wood to Gordon, July 30, 1915, August 5, 1915; Gordon to Wood, August 4, 1915, HOIS.

68. F. P. to Gordon, April 16, 1914; Gordon to F. P., April 26, 1914, both in HOIS.

69. *Amsterdam News*, March 28, 1917; "Workers' Facts," HOIS.

70. Gordon to Wood, October 9, 1914, HOIS.

71. George W. Andrews to William Pickens, September 15, 1917, HOIS.

72. Quotations taken from "Workers' Facts." The contents of this single printed sheet, including references to Gordon's resignation and Waring's succession, suggest that it was issued during the Waring superintendency. Contrast the "Workers' Facts" with the profile of the employees, including teachers, in a typed manuscript entitled "Employees of the Howard Orphanage and Industrial School," March 24, 1913. This list (compiled while Gordon was still matron) suggests that the institution's employees were predominantly women (including all its teachers, clerks, and agents). The Inspection Report of March 16–18, 1915, listed the teachers as follows: Mrs. F. A. Taylor, graduate of Teacher's Training School at Cheney, PA; Miss W. Smith, graduate of Public School No. 2 of Washington DC; Miss H. Sturgis, graduate of Training School at Collingwood, NJ; Miss G. Frank, graduate of Fisk University, Nashville; Miss V. Saunders, graduate of kindergarten course of Boston Normal School; Miss E. Adair, graduate of Normal College at Danbury, CT; and Miss. C. Berguin, enrollee in a summer school for teachers at Columbia University, New York. It seems likely that the principal listed in this report, A. W. Reason, a graduate of Oberlin Academy and Howard University, was male. In her November 1915 report to the Managers, however, Gordon identified the principal as Miss Francis Gunner of Howard University. See Superintendent's Annual Report to the Society of the Howard Orphanage and Industrial School, November 1915, 1, HOIS.

73. See, for instance, K. H. Gladstone to Wood, April 23, 1919, HOIS.

74. M. E. B. to Waring, August 23, 1918, HOIS.

75. Ruby Brown is a pseudonym for F. B., and Fanny Brown one for M. B. See M. B. to Wood, July 25, 1918, February 6 and 12, 1919; Wood to M. B., April 3, 1919, HOIS.

76. Wood to F. B., July 31, 1918; April 3, 1919, HOIS.

77. F. B. to Wood, November 8, 1918, April 1, 1919; Margaret Martin to Wood, August 4, 1918, all in HOIS.

78. Rosa Johnson's real initials were G. O. Waring to G. O., November 20, 1917, HOIS.

79. Waring to Marks, November 8, 1917, HOIS.

80. In this context, it is important to note that the Waring era proved very brief. The State Commissioner of Charities closed down the institution in 1918. Thus, Gordon left a far more enduring influence than Waring on the young lives she touched. See Wood to Chester A. Allen, vice-president, King's County Trust Company, May 13, 1947, HOIS; Mabee, "Charity in Travail," 55.

81. L. to Gordon, October 3, 1913, HOIS.

82. R. C. D. to Gordon, n.d., HOIS.

83. R. to Gordon, June 23, 1913, HOIS.

84. Mary Jackson's real initials were W. H. See W. H. to Wood, October 1919, HOIS. On African American women in the professions, see Darlene Clark Hine, *Black Women in White: Racial Conflict and Cooperation in the Nursing Profession, 1890–1950* (Bloomington: Indiana University Press, 1989); Stephanie J. Shaw, *What a Woman Ought to Be and to Do: Black Professional Women Workers During the Jim Crow Era* (Chicago: University of Chicago Press, 1996); Gloria Moldow, *Women Doctors in Gilded Age Washington: Gender, Race, and Professionalization* (Urbana: University of Illinois Press, 1987).

85. Mrs. John Meitar to Waring, n.d., HOIS.

86. See chapter 3 in Peiss, *Cheap Amusements*.

87. Peiss, *Cheap Amusements*; Elizabeth Ewen, *Immigrant Women in the Land of Dollars: Life and Culture on the Lower East Side, 1890–1925* (New York: Monthly Review Press, 1985), 15, 25–26. Examples of works that explore the image and role of consumption as an instrument of assimilation include Jenna Weissman Joselit, *The Wonders of America: Reinventing Jewish Culture, 1880–1950* (New York: Hill and Wang, 1994); and Stuart Ewen and Elizabeth Ewen, *Channels of Desire: Mass Images and the Shaping of American Consciousness* (Minneapolis: University of Minnesota Press, 1992).

88. Hale, *Making Whiteness*, 121–97.

89. Florence Caruthers to Ms. Marks, August 7, 1917, HOIS. Fannie Moore is a pseudonym for E.

90. M. J. to Wood, April 28, 1918. The HOIS launched a conference on the movement to increase food supply during the war and apparently conceived of a

plan "whereby each child will have a garden of his own, in order to learn practical truck gardening" (unidentified news clipping; Wood to Francis L. Holmes, April 11, 1917, both in HOIS). In response to reports "emanating from the South that Germans were plotting Negro insurrection," Wood declared that African Americans were "a splendid example of devotion to a country which has done them both good and ill" (*New York Evening Post*, April 5, 1917).

91. Mrs. C. M. Williamson to Mrs. Marks, May 6, 1917. Juliet is a pseudonym for E. See also entries in lined notebook containing information on children "placed out," such as that for R. B. dated November 27, 1916. On attempts to regulate working-class adolescent female sexuality, see Mary E. Odem, *Delinquent Daughters: Protecting and Policing Adolescent Female Sexuality in the United States, 1885–1920* (Chapel Hill: University of North Carolina Press, 1995); Ruth M. Alexander, *The Girl Problem: Female Sexual Delinquency in New York, 1900–1930* (Ithaca, NY: Cornell University Press, 1995).

92. G. O. to Waring, May 9, 1918; G. O. to Wood, May 17, 1918, HOIS.

93. My italics; W. H. to Wood, November 23, 1919, HOIS.

94. Dorothy Benedict's real initials were F. G. See F. G. to Wood, May 8, 20, 1918. See also E. R. to Wood, July 23, 1920, and A. S. to Wood, n.d., HOIS.

95. Carter's real initials were F. M., and Fuccillo's were F. B. See Bertha Blackman to Wood, September 3, 6, November 1, 5, and December 18, 1918; January 7 and March 25, 1919; Wood to Arthur W. Towne, November 4, 1918; Wood to Elizabeth Lawrence, November 4, 1918; Wood to W. B. Codling, November 6, 1918; Nathan O. Petty to Wood, November 23, 1918; Wood to Petty, December 2, 1918; Towne to Wood, December 17, 1918; Wood to Towne, December 18, 1918; Benjamin Blackman to Wood, November 1, 1918; Wood to Bertha Blackman, March 31, November 11, December 18, 1918, all in HOIS. On the "girl problem," see Alexander, *The Girl Problem*.

96. When the institution closed, the mortgage on the King's Park property was foreclosed and the children distributed among various asylums, the majority being sent to the New York Colored Orphan Asylum at Riverdale. Thereafter the trustees of the school devoted all donations to the higher education of young African Americans from Brooklyn. On the demise of the HOIS, see Mabee, "Charity in Travail," 74–75. On black self-help as a casualty of social welfare professionalism, see O'Donnell, "The Care of Dependent African American Children in Chicago."

EPILOGUE

1. Michael K. Brown, "Race in the American Welfare State: The Ambiguities of 'Universalistic' Social Policy," in *Without Justice for All: The New Liberalism and Our Retreat from Racial Equality*, ed. Adolph Reed Jr. (Boulder, CO: Westview, 1999), 93–122; Mimi Abramovitz and Ann Withorn, "Playing by the Rules:

Welfare Reform and the New Authoritarian State," in *Without Justice for All*, ed. Reed, 151–173; Jill Quadagno, *The Color of Welfare: How Racism Undermined the War on Poverty* (New York: Oxford University Press, 1994); Nancy MacLean, "From the War on Poverty to 'the New Equality': The Fight for a Living Wage," *American Quarterly* 59 (March 2007), 219–31.

2. Robert Pear, "New Rules Will Require States to Remove Welfare Recipients to Work," *New York Times*, June 28, 2006.

3. Melanie R. Hallums, Esq., and Maureen Lewis, Esq., Davis Polk, and Wardwell, "Welfare, Poverty, and Racism: The Impact of Race on Welfare Reform," Lawyers Committee for Civil Rights Under Law, June 2003, 1–19, http://www.lawyerscomm.org/2005website/features/40thfeatures/PDF/40thpapers/welfare.pdf; The American Civil Liberty Union's Written Statement for a Hearing on "Welfare Reform Reauthorization Proposals," Submitted to the Subcommittee on Human Resources of the Home Committee on Ways and Means, Thursday, February 24, 2005, by Laura W. Murphy, director, ACLU Washington Legislative Office, and Lenora M. Lapidus, director, ACLU Woman Rights Project, www.aclu.org/womensrights/povertywelfare/13206leg20050222.html.

4. Michael E. Fix and Karen C. Tumlin, "Welfare Reform and the Devolution of Immigrant Policy," A-15 in New Federalism: Issues and Options for States series, Urban Institute, October 1, 1997, www.urban.org/url.cfm?ID=307045&renderforprint=1; Robert Pear, "Medicaid Rule For Immigrants May Bar Others," *New York Times*, April 16, 2006.

5. Premilla Nadasen, *Welfare Warriors: The Welfare Rights Movement in the United States* (Routledge: New York, 2005); Annelise Orleck, *Storming Caesar's Palace: How Black Mothers Fought Their Own War on Poverty* (Boston: Beacon, 2005).

6. Maureen Lane, "Welfare Deformed," http://www.tompaine.com/articles/2006/07/18/welfare_deformed.php.

7. Neil deMause, "Actual Poor People Rate Bloomy's Poverty Plan," *Village Voice*, http://blogs.villagevoice.com/runninscared/archives/2006/09/actual_poor_peo.php.

Index

Abdy, E. S., 131, 138
African Americans, 3, 4, 7, 8, 76, 259, 281; Alms House and, 9, 10, 12, 16, 37–38, 89, 107–108, 114–115, 261–262 (*see also* Colored Home); Blackwell Island's taxonomies of race and, 89–92, 259, 260; changing relationship with municipal relief of, 37–38; "communal" households of, 50–51, 251, 304n42; compared with white poor, 17, 21, 23, 46, 61, 62, 63, 64, 65, 66, 67, 105, 122–124, 133–134, 140–142, 149–150, 159–160, 162, 261, 262; demographic profile of, 46–61; and engagement with racial nationalism (*see* Howard Orphanage and Industrial School(HOIS); female-oriented households of, 51–52, 251–252; and feminization of poverty, 124; and fosterage, 21, 52–54, 57, 142, 146–148, 268; household economies of, 49–61, 142–149, 249–252; images of, 11; in interracial unions, 7, 12, 54–55, 77, 78, 79; in Lunatic Asylum, 92, 260; marriage patterns of, 49–50, 256; migration to New York City of, 36, 48–49, 54–55, 122–123, 203, 215, 216, 257; multipositional identities of, 24–25, 313n5 (*see also* HOIS); neighborhoods of, 43–46; and New York House of Refuge, 131–134, 136, 140–152, 153–160, 162, 263–266; 268–271; 273; nuclear families of, 21, 49–50, 250; and outdoor relief, 9, 10, 21, 37–38, 89–90, 259; and Panic of 1857, 105–106; in Penitentiary Hospital, 92, 93, 259, 260; and public relief in pre-1827 New York, 20, 32–36; and racial construct of dependence, 8, 14, 16, 21, 29–36, 76–85; and racial politics of female benevolence, 170–174, 178–179, 180, 189–191, 197–203 (*see also* Colored Home); and racial politics of welfare, 5–14, 20, 83–85, 243–245; sex ratio of, 47–48; and subculture of boarding, 21, 52–54, 252; surrogate kin of (*see* fosterage, *this entry*); voluntarism of, 9, 15–17, 24, 37–38, 207–242; and work, 36–37, 55–61, 258; as "worthy poor," 12, 107–108, 110–121. *See also* Agency, subaltern; Colored Home; Howard Orphanage and Industrial School; Race; Slavery; Slaves; "Welfare queen"; Whiteness; White republic
African Civilization Society (ACS), 211
Agency, subaltern, 3, 4, 10, 12, 16, 20–21, 23, 25–26, 77; and assertions of identity, 10, 25–26, 95; defined, 10, 17–19, 211; and gender, 110;

Agency, subaltern (*continued*), of HOIS actors, 207–242; impact on female benevolence of, 187–191; impact on juvenile reform of, 152–153; of interracial New York House of Refuge (NYHR) inmates, 131–134, 140–153, 168–169; and self-image of ex-slaves in Colored Home, 111, 117–121; and self-image of Hopper Home women, 178, 180–186; in twenty-first century welfare rights campaign, 245–247; and uses of Blackwell's Island, 92–95; and whiteness, 100–105, 161–166. *See also* Identity

Aid to Families with Dependent Children (AFDC), 1, 245

Allen, Stephen, 134, 135, 136

Alms House, 3, 8, 21, 47, 73, 75, 80, 85, 93, 101, 108, 111, 138, 166, 243, 260; and African Americans, 9, 10, 12, 37, 260; and children, 90–91; Commissioners of, 136; and Panic of 1857, 105; and reorganization of department, 86–92. *See also* Blackwell's Island; Colored Home; Lunatic Asylum; Penitentiary; Work House

American Party, 80. *See also* Immigrants, European

Association for the Improvement of the Condition of the Poor (AICP), 72, 75, 104

Bauyer, Maria, 107

Bedford Hills reformatory, 24; campaign for, 197–202

Bellevue, Almshouse at, 73, 81, 87, 107; Hospital, 88, 96, 105, 260

Benevolent Empire, 8, 23, 73–76; and race, 12, 14, 23; and subaltern agency, 10. *See also* Alms House; Colored Home; Hopper Home; New York House of Refuge; "Pauperism"; Poverty

Bense, Peter, 5, 6, 7, 8

Blacks. *See* African Americans

Blackwell's Island, 21, 25, 76, 89, 105, 122; and administrative restructuring, 88–89; African American and white admissions compared, 122–124, 260; and Hopper Home, 184, 185, 200; as "land of promise," 99; move to, 87; physical layout of, 87–88; and race, 89–92. *See also* Alms House; Lunatic Asylum; Penitentiary; Work House

Board of Commissioners of Emigration, 86

Brace, Charles Loring, 5

Brooklyn Howard Colored Orphan Asylum, 24, 211, 218, 312n1. *See also* Howard Orphanage and Industrial School

Caribbean, as source of immigrants, 5, 6. *See also* African Americans

Case histories, and subaltern perspectives, 19, 140–153, 168–169, 173, 178, 181, 184–186

Castle Garden, 86, 156

Charity Organization Society (COS), 194. *See also* Scientific charity

Children, 23, 68, 79; as African American boarders, 53; and African American orphanages (*see* HOIS); and Catholic orphanages, 223; as clients of relief and juvenile reform (*see* New York House of Refuge); and Jewish orphanages, 222–223; "nursed out," 90–91; and middle class identity, 41; on Randall's Island, 91; on Ward's Island, 86; and work, 67–68

Children's Aid Society, 152
Christian benevolence, 73, 182; and race and gender, 8, 18, 22, 25. *See also* Colored Home; Hopper Home
Civil War, 15, 22, 38, 85, 133, 139, 141; and Fourteenth Amendment, 22, 128, 155; and Hopper Home, 195; and New York City Draft Riots, 22, 127–128, 154; and New York House of Refuge, 153–155, 166; and HOIS, 211
Clark, Aaron, 80
Clarkson, Elizabeth, 108
Clinton, DeWitt, 136
Colden, Cadwallader D., 136
Colonization, and Colored Home, 13, 15, 22, 107, 110, 113–14
Colored Home (CH), 3, 5, 6, 7, 8, 10, 12, 22, 25, 38, 47, 89, 91, 154, 166, 190, 243, 260; and *Broken Gloom*, 22, 107, 109–121; and colonization, 13, 15, 22, 107, 110, 113–114; creation and incorporation of, 107–109; critique of slavery by, 109–116; decline of, 127–128; inmate demography compared with Irish poor, 122–124, 260, 261, 262; and intersections of Christian benevolence, gender and race, 109–121; and maternalism, 22, 109–110; mission of, 111; and Panic of 1857, 105; and profiles of ex-slave-imates as "worthy poor," 114–121; reform strategies of, 124–127; self-image of inmates, 109–121
Colored Orphan Asylum, 89, 107, 260; as conduit to New York House of Refuge, 155; destroyed, 127, 128; and Panic of 1857, 105
Commission on Economic Opportunities (CEO), 246.

"Dangerous classes," 73, 79, 93, 187. *See also* "Pauperism"; Paupers; Poverty
Democratic Party, 14, 21, 69, 80, 83, 84, 87, 89, 101, 164; and Locofocos, 70, 72, 104. *See also* Tammany

Economy: and flour riot (1837), 69–72; and panics, 22, 72, 73, 75, 80, 101–102; progress of, 38–46, 160. *See also* Household economies; Poverty
Eddy, Thomas, 74, 134
Ellis Island, 86, 156

Family: African American varieties of, 49–61, 142–149, 249–252; Irish varieties of, 61–67, 249, 253–255; in reform discourse (*see* "Pauperism"); and "welfare queen" construct, 1–2. *See also* Children; Gender; White republic; Women
Fish, Hamilton, 201
Five Points, 43, 77, 131. *See also* Irish; "Pauperism"; Tenements
Foster, George, 78, 79
Freeman, Elizabeth (Mumbet), 170

Gender: and African Americans, 11–12, 219–220; and Alms House admission records, 122; and 1855 census, 46; and the Irish, 43; and juvenile reform philosophy, 134–135, 137; and middle-class identity, 11–12, 41–42, 174–177; multiple-positioning of, 26; and NYHR, 140; and subaltern identity, 25; and white republic, 4, 11, 12, 13, 23, 85. *See also* Colored Home; Hopper Home; Howard Orphanage and Industrial School; Welfare queen; Women

Gerard, James W., 74, 134
Gibbons, Abby Hopper, 172, 175, 194; and campaign for Bedford Hills reformatory, 199–202. *See also* Hopper Home; Women's Prison Association
Gordon, James, 219, 317n35, 317n36
Gordon, Mary, 207, 219–220, 230, 231, 318n41
Griscom, John, 74, 134, 135; and son John H., 75–76

Haines, Charles, G., 134
Hartley, Robert H., 76
Headley, Joel Tyler, and *Great Riots of New York*, 69–72
Hopper Home, 3, 23, 25, 47, 246; and campaign for Bedford Hills reformatory, 199–203; and Christian sisterhood, 173; and comparisons between African American and Irish women, 170–174; and eugenics, 174, 197, 199, 200; "fallen" woman shaped by subaltern agency at, 173, 178, 180–191; and gender solidarity as interactive language, 174, 178, 180–182, 186–189; inmate profiles of, 178–180, 198, 202–203; inmate resistance to, 193–194, 195–197, 198; inmate uses of, 191–192; and "new immigrants," 174, 197–203; post-bellum generational turnover of, 194; and "proto-structural" inmate perspectives on crime and poverty, 184–186; and race, 23–24; 170–174, 178–179, 180, 189–191, 197–203; reform program of, 176–178, 194–196; sexually deviant as "fallen" woman at, 182–184; and social origins of reformers, 174–177.
Hopper, Isaac T., 172, 175, 183

Household economies: of African American, 49–61, 142–149, 249–252; of Irish, 61–67, 249, 253–255
Howard, Oliver A., 211
Howard Orphanage and Industrial School (HOIS), 3, 15, 19, 24–25, 203; adoption of "cottage system" by, 212, 215; and African American engagement with American exceptionalism, 208, 209–211, 215–218, 225–229, 234–242; and African American vision of (child) welfare, 208, 217–229; client-staff relationships at, 230–234; color consciousness at, 231; compared with white orphanages, 221–225, 319n50; compared with white welfare vision, 208, 218, 219–221, 241–242, 317n35, 317n36; demise of, 241, 323n96; familial nature of, 220–225, 235; gender roles at, 231- 232, 234–242, 321n72; inmate profiles of, 212–214, 230–242; intra-staff hierarchies at, 220, 318n41; managers of, 211, 212, 214–217, 238, 315–316n21; move to Long Island, 212, 216–217; and "multipositional" identities, 208–209, 219–220, 225–229, 234–242, 313n5; origins and incorporation of, 211–212; pantomimes as cultural texts on, 225–229; sources on, 208–209, 225–229, 234; and stereotypes of black mismanagement, 212, 241, 314n11; superintendent as mother figure, 221–222, 234, 235; and Waring, J. H. N., 230–234; and Wood, L. Hollingsworth, 214, 231, 233, 238, 239, 240, 241. *See also* Brooklyn Howard Colored Orphan Asylum; Gordon, James; Gordon, Mary; Johnson, William E.

Identity, 4, 211; in African American visions of nation and self, 10, 207–242; assertions of "white," 134, 149–150, 160–166; constructs of American, 10–11, 24–25, 209–210; epistemology of, 14; interracial subaltern, 131–134, 140–153, 168–169; at intersection of class and gender, 11, 12, 40–42, 183, 194–195; and multiple-positioning of historical actors, 12, 14–15, 18, 22–26, 160–166, 207–242, 313n5; mutability of, 215–218; pantomimes and reinvention of, 225–229; and race, 10–12, 16, 207–242; and social geography, 40–46; welfare discourse as a crucible of, 2, 3–5, 8, 16, 25–26, 44–46, 207–242. *See also* Agency, subaltern; "Pauperism"; Welfare; Welfare queen; Whiteness; White republic

Immigrants, European, 5, 6, 8, 9, 10, 80; and acculturation to white citizenship, 36, 75, 83–92 (*see also* Hopper Home); compared with African Americans, 5–14, 23, 72, 133–134, 140–142, 157–158, 159, 160–166; and Emigration Commissioners, 75; and fate of the republic, 81–83; and female "pauper" reproduction discourse, 80, 174, 197, 199, 200; multipositional identities of, 14–15, 22, 25, 160–166; and naturalization law of 1790, 4, 12, 36, 83; neighborhoods of, 43–44; "New," 24, 156, 197–203, 236, 239–240; and New York House of Refuge, 140–142, 149–150, 157, 162, 166–169, 264, 266, 267, 269, 270, 271, 272; and outdoor relief, 89–90; and pauperism, 80–82; and racial politics of welfare, 83–92; and whiteness, 13, 14, 20, 91–92, 139, 153, 157, 178–179. *See also,* Irish

Immigration, 71, 185. *See also* Bense, Peter; Immigrants, European; Irish

Irish, 42, 259; in Blackwell's Island, 92–95, 259–261; compared with African Americans, 17, 21, 23, 46, 61–67, 122–124, 133–134, 140–142, 149–150, 159–160, 162, 261, 262; exodus to U.S., 42–44; and female benevolence, 23–24, 25 (*see also* Hopper Home); household economies of, 61–67, 249, 253–255; marriage patterns of, 43, 63, 256; neighborhoods, 43–44; and NYHR, 141, 142, 149–150, 160–166, 263, 264, 266, 267, 269, 270, 271, 272; and outdoor relief, 89–90, 259; and party politics of welfare, 21; and white republic, 13, 14, 42, 46, 76–92; and work, 56, 57, 65–68, 258. *See also* Immigrants, Europeans; Whiteness; White republic

Johnson, William E., 212

Kirkland, Caroline M., 175, 178; death of, 194; *the Helping Hand*, 176, 183, 186–190

Lowell, Josephine Shaw, 200
Lunatic Asylum (Blackwell's Island), 21, 88, 91, 92, 96, 260

Maternalism: and African American benevolence, 208, 217–229, 234, 235; and white reformers, 22. *See also* Colored Home
Morris, Robert H., 87
Morse, Lucy, 201
Mott, Anna, 108

National Association for the Advancement of Colored People (NAACP), 214

National Association of Colored Woman, 212
National League of Urban Conditions Among Colored People, 214
New Deal, 3, 20, 243
New York House of Refuge (NYHR), 3, 23, 243, 246; African American inmates' work and family lives, 142–149, 265, 266, 268, 269, 270, 271; African American modes of resistance to, 166–169, 273; African American uses of, 131–134, 140–149, 157–160; and Civil War, 153–155; indenture practices of, 137, 139, 166–168, 273; and inmate insurgency of 1872, 161–166; inmate perspectives on poverty and crime, 150–153, 173, 184; and interracial subaltern identity, 133–134, 140–153; and philosophy of juvenile reform, 134- 137; and race, 132–134, 136, 137–140, 155–157, 263, 264; and white inmates, 140–142, 149–150, 157, 161–169, 264, 266, 267, 269, 270, 271, 272
New York Juvenile Asylum, 152

Orphanages. See Children; Howard Orphanage and Industrial School
Outdoor Poor, Superintendent of, and Colored Home, 109. See also Outdoor Relief
Outdoor Relief, 21, 73, 74, 81, 87, 88, 133; and African Americans, 9, 10, 89–90, 259; and European immigrants, 89–90, 259; and Panic of 1857, 105–106

Panics: of 1819, 73; of 1837, 72, 75, 80; of 1857, 22, 101–102

"Pauperism," 2, 4, 8, 21, 38, 59, 72–74, 76, 81, 99, 109; interracial unions as source of, 12; and juvenile reform, 135; racial typology of, 8, 21, 76–85; and the republic, 68, 81–83, 85; social geography of, 41–46; subaltern perspectives on, 173, 178. See also Paupers; Poverty
Paupers, 66, 76, 79, 100, 115; black, 12, 126. See also "Pauperism"; Poverty
Penitentiary, 138, 161; at Blackwell's Island, 88, 95, 96; Hospital, 21, 91, 92, 97–98, 260
Personal Responsibility and Work Opportunity Reconciliation Act (PRWORA), 1, 244–245
Police, 131. See also Hopper Home; New York House of Refuge; Penitentiary; Women's Prison Association
Poverty, 20, 55, 71, 74; amid economic progress, 38–46, 72, 160; as cause for insanity, 95; connected with crime, 188; and metropolitan industrialization, 40, 123; as motive for committing children to NYHR, 144; and poor relief thought, 21, 72–76; subaltern "proto-structural" perspectives on, 10, 25–26, 151- 152, 184–186; See also "Pauperism"; Welfare
Powell, Wilson, 200
Prison Association of New York, 81, 174
Progressive movement, 203, 208; and child welfare, 214–215, 223, 241. See also Howard Orphanage and Industrial School
Prostitutes, 81, 92, 97–98, 108, 111, 124, 125, 179, 194; and "new immigrants," 197–198; and Work House, 92, 97–98. See also Hopper House; Prostitution

Prostitution, 73, 131, 182, 197; and African Americans, 57–58; and pauperism, 78; and Work House, 97–98. *See also* Hopper House; Prostitutes

Public Charities and Correction, Department of, 136, 139; and state commissioners, 161; and HOIS, 220–221. *See also* Alms House

Race, 3, 9,10; and epistemology of relief, 14, 21, 91–92; and female benevolence, 24, 110, 112–114, 170–174; and language of welfare, 29; and "pauperism," 8, 21, 76–85; and politics of welfare, 5–14; and relationship with dependence, 30–36; statistical representations of, 14, 91–92, 132, 138–140, 157. *See also* African Americans; Identity; Welfare queen; Whiteness; White republic

Randall's Island: cemetery, 95; nursery at, 96; and Panic of 1857, 105

Republicanism, 8, 9, 71; and Colored Home, 110; and "pauperism," 81–83; and republican citizenship, 75, 77, 103. *See also* White republic

Republican Party: and debate over public works, 103; evangelical industrial reformers and, 21, 175, 176, 186, 194; and free labor ideology, 13; and whiteness, 13, 84–85

Riots: Draft (1863), 22, 127–128, 154; flour (1837), 69–72

Roosevelt, Theodore, 210, 214

Sandford, Alice, 202
Schuyler, Louisa Lee, 201
Scientific charity, 75, 178, 194. *See also* Charity Organization Society

Sedgwick, Catharine Maria: African Americans and Irish compared by, 170–174; death of, 194; social origins of, 176

Sedgwick, Theodore, 170
Shatzell, Maria, 109
Shotwell, Mary, 108
Sing Sing (prison), 180
Slavery, 4, 5, 7, 8, 20, 22, 38, 55, 76, 84, 136, 137, 151, 153, 171, 174, 223, 230; and American identity, 10–11, 12, 54; and emancipation, 34–36; and legacy of poverty, 9, 37; maternalist critique of, 109–116; and public relief, before 1827, 31–35, 37–38; and racial construct of dependence, 30–36. *See also* Slaves

Slaves, 6, 12, 37, 49, 83, 156; Hopper Home reformer on, 170–171; as inmates of Colored Home, 107–108, 111, 114–121; and NYHR, 131–132, 133, 138, 148, 154–155. *See also* New York House of Refuge; Slavery

Social Security Act (1935), 243
Society for the Prevention of Cruelty to Children, 214, 239
Society for the Prevention of Pauperism, 73–74; 75, 80, 134, 135, 187
Society for the Reformation of Juvenile Delinquents, 135, 137. *See also* New York House of Refuge
Society for the Relief of Worthy, Aged, Indigent Colored Persons, 89, 108. *See also* Colored Home
State Board of Charities (New York), 162, 200, 212, 213; and criticism of HOIS, 219–221
State Charities Aid Association, 201
Subaltern/s. *See* Agency, subaltern; Identity

Tammany, 61, 70, 80, 163. *See also* Democratic Party

Tenements, as symbols of "pauperism," 44–46, 77–78, 79

Thompson, Mary W., 110. *See also* Colored Home

Tillman, Sarah A., 211

Tombs, 81, 192

"Underclass," 16, 19, 21, 45, 77, 79, 133. *See also* Agency, subaltern; Identity; "Pauperism"

Vagrants, 97, 133, 135. *See also* New York House of Refuge

Waring, J. H. N., 230–234

Washington, Booker T., 214, 221

Welfare, 3, 15, 16, 275n1; African American vision of (*see* Howard Orphanage and Industrial School); and American nationalism, 243; as antebellum public relief (*see* Alms House; Blackwell's Island; Lunatic Asylum; Penitentiary; Work House); and citizenship, 5, 8, 21–22, 243–245; and material foundations of black households, 49–61, 142–149, 249–252; and material foundations of Irish households, 61–67, 249, 253–255; as female benevolence (*see* Colored Home; Hopper Home); and hegemony, 18, 26; hybrid public-private nature of, 8, 109; and juvenile justice (*see* New York House of Refuge); opposition to, 1–2, 275n2; and race, 5–15, 20–21, 29–36, 76–92, 243–244 (*see also* Whiteness; White republic); and subaltern agency and identity, 17–19, 92–101, 245–247. *See also* Poverty

"Welfare queen," 1–2, 16, 245; and American values, 2, 245; and eugenics, 174, 197, 199, 200; nineteenth-century roots of, 2, 24, 81, 97–98, 174; and racial construct of dependence, 8, 21, 29–36, 76–85; and sexual construct of pauperism, 77–80, 97–98. *See also* Welfare

Welfare "reform," 100, 168; and Medicaid, 245; past and present compared, 244; and race and nation, 244–245. *See also* Alms House; Blackwell's Island; Work House

Welfare rights movement, 245; and Maureen Lane, 245–246. *See also* Agency, subaltern

Welfare state, 3, 20, 25, 243

Whig Party, 21, 80, 87, 103

Whiteness, 5, 8, 12, 13, 20, 46–47, 79, 80; and African Americans, 25, 207–242; and American exceptionalism, 210–211; and Civil War, 127–128, 153–154; and debate over public works, 101–106; and Democratic party, 14, 21, 83–84; and gender, 11–12, 13, 23–24, 110, 170–174, 180 (*see also* Hopper Home); and fractures rooted in immigrant multipositionality, 14–15, 21–22, 23, 25, 97, 100–101, 133–134, 160–166, 184–186, 194–203; and free labor Republicanism, 13–14, 84–85; in Hopper Home case histories, 178–179; and immigrants, 13, 76–92; in postbellum America, 15, 155–156; statistical representation of, 14, 91–92, 132, 138–140, 157, 259, 260, 263, 265; subaltern assertions of, 14–15, 25–26, 100–101, 145–146, 160–166; and welfare, 5–15, 20, 29, 83–87, 91–92, 101–106; and Work House, 97, 100. *See also* White republic

White republic, 2–5, 7, 10–12, 42, 82, 281; acculturation of European immigrants to, 83–92; and census of 1855, 46–47; and Colored Home, 121; and NYHR, 132, 133, 135; origins of, 29–36; and pauperism, 46, 68, 74, 78. *See also* Whiteness

Women: and African American benevolence, 207–242; in African American household economies, 46–61, 249–252, 256, 257, 258; as African American NYHR clients, 131–134, 142–149, 151, 154–155, 157–159, 265, 266, 268, 269, 271, 273; as Alms House inmates, 92–101; and antebellum "workfare," 95–96; and Bellevue Hospital, 93–94; as Colored Home reformers, 3, 6, 7, 8, 22; "fallen" as racialized objects of reform, 23–24, 25 (*see also* Hopper Home); Irish, 23–24, 149–150; in Irish/Irish American household economies, 61–67, 253–255, 256, 258; and Lunatic Asylum, 94; and maternalism (*see* Maternalism); predominant among Blackwell's Island clients, 93; predominant among Colored Home clients, 124; sex ratio at NYHR, 141, 154, 158, 265; uses of Penitentiary Hospital, 93, 260; as white NYHR clients, 265, 266, 267, 269, 271; and work (*see* African Americans; Irish, household economies of); and Work House, 97–98; in working poor neighborhoods, 44. *See also* Gender; Welfare queen

Women's Prison Association (WPA), 3, 23, 172. *See also* Hopper Home

Wood, Fernando, 22, 61, 102, 104

Wood, L. Hollingsworth, 214, 231, 233, 238, 239, 240, 241

"Workfare": antebellum, 86, 87, 88–89, 95–101; in twenty-first century, 21, 244, 246. *See also* Work House

Work House, 246; in Blackwell's Island, 22, 91, 92, 95; and challenge to moral classifications of the poor, 96–97; composition of, 92–93; creation of, 88–89; and inmate occupations, 99; and Panic of 1857, 105; in poor relief thought, 75, 86–87, 96; and subaltern agency/identity, 25, 100–101; and whiteness, 100–101; white republic, 97; and working poor uses of, 97–101. *See also* Workfare

Wright, Fanny, 75

Yates, John V. N., 74, 75

About the Author

GUNJA SENGUPTA is Associate Professor of History and Director of the William E. Macaulay CUNY Honors College at Brooklyn College, City University of New York.

www.ingramcontent.com/pod-product-compliance
Lightning Source LLC
Chambersburg PA
CBHW032026290426
44110CB00012B/686